CAPTIVE AUDIENCE

SUSAN CRAWFORD

Captive
Audience

THE TELECOM INDUSTRY AND
MONOPOLY POWER IN THE
NEW GILDED AGE

Yale UNIVERSITY PRESS

NEW HAVEN & LONDON

Yale University Press books may be purchased in quantity for educational, business, or promotional use. For information, please e-mail sales. press@yale.edu (U.S. office) or sales@yaleup.co.uk (U.K. office).

Set in Scala type by IDS Infotech, Ltd.
Printed in the United States of America.

Library of Congress Cataloging-in-Publication Data
Crawford, Susan P., 1963–
Captive audience: the telecom industry and monopoly power in the new gilded age / Susan Crawford.
p. cm.
Includes bibliographical references and index.
ISBN 978-0-300-15313-2
1. Telecommunication—Law and legislation—United States.
2. Antitrust law—United States. I. Title.
KF2765.C73 2013
384.0973—dc23
2012024367

A catalogue record for this book is available from the British Library.

This paper meets the requirements of ANSI/NISO Z39.48–1992 (Permanence of Paper).

10 9 8 7 6 5 4 3 2

To the next generation

CONTENTS

Introduction

ON A GRAY DAY IN FEBRUARY 2010, Brian Roberts sat facing the Senate
Judiciary Committee's Antitrust Subcommittee. The subcommittee was
holding its first hearing on a proposed merger between two of the country's
most powerful media companies, the cable distribution giant Comcast and
the entertainment conglomerate NBC Universal (NBCU). Roberts, the chief
executive officer of Comcast, was a calm and friendly witness that day, as he
testified before the branch of government that had created the antitrust laws
in the first place. If the merger were approved by the Justice Department's
Antitrust Division and the Federal Communications Commission, Comcast's future as the largest vertically integrated distributor of information in
the country would be assured.[1]

Big mergers happen all the time in America. The importance of this one
lay in the fact that Comcast was gaining strength as a monopoly provider of
wired high-speed Internet access in the areas it served, while America was
lagging far behind other countries when it came to the prices charged for
and the speed and capability of this basic communications tool. At the same
time, the Internet was becoming the common global medium, with a
unique capacity to empower individuals, groups, businesses, and governments around the world collectively to change their economic, political,
and social fates. With high-speed Internet access, a farmer in Missouri
can instantly access weather conditions and crop prices while his high
school children get a world-class education; Native Americans on a remote

reservation can have their eyes checked by a distant doctor and avoid the blindness associated with diabetes; entrepreneurs and small businesses in California, New York, and all the states in between can find inexpensive entry points into global markets. Communities can plan their own destinies.

A decade earlier, the United States had led the world in adoption of Internet access. By the time of the hearing, America had fallen behind most other industrialized nations:[2] customers in rural and poorer areas were getting spotty service, while those in wealthier areas were paying much more for high-speed access than their counterparts in other countries. In most of Comcast's market territories, it was the only high-speed access provider selling services at speeds that would be sufficient to satisfy Americans' requirements in the near future. But the access Comcast sold was less useful than it could have been because the network had been designed to be contested among users in the same neighborhood (making speeds unreliable) and favored passive consuming uses (downloads) far more than active uploads. Meanwhile, the service that all Americans would need within five years (truly high-speed Internet access ranging from 100 Mbps, or megabits per second, to gigabit speeds over fiber-optic lines), the service that would allow symmetrical (same-speed) uploads and downloads and extensive use of online streaming video for a host of educational, medical, and economic purposes, was routinely available in other countries but could not be purchased at all in most parts of the United States.[3] Through the merger, Comcast would become even more entrenched and powerful, with unconstrained ability to set prices and conditions for wired Internet access in the areas of the country it served. America would never catch up to the rest of the world if Comcast and its fellow cable distributors controlled truly high-speed wired Internet access.

Because the merger would allow Comcast to more effectively control key sports and other content that many Americans prized, Comcast's new amplified role as a programmer—taken together with its ability to coordinate with its programming brethren—would probably make content too expensive for any potential competing data distributor. Any new high-speed Internet access provider in Comcast territory would have to enter the market for content at the same time it incurred the heavy up-front costs needed to provide wired Internet access. Entering two markets at once is extremely difficult. Competition would be unlikely, leaving Americans in Comcast's territories reliant on Comcast alone for truly high-speed wired Internet access. Indeed, by the time the Comcast-NBCU merger was announced at the end of 2009,[4] Verizon, the only nationwide company installing globally competitive truly high-speed access across fiber-optic lines in America, had already signaled that it was planning to stop doing so.[5] It was just too hard to compete with Comcast.

In turn, Comcast had no incentive to make the Internet access it did sell affordable, globally competitive in terms of its capabilities, or available to everyone within its territories. Nor did it have any incentive to upgrade the networks it had built to fiber optics; the company was ready to reap the rewards of dominance.[6] Truly high-speed wired Internet access is as basic to innovation, economic growth, social communication, and the country's competitiveness as electricity was a century ago, but a limited number of Americans have access to it, many can't afford it, and the country has handed control of it over to Comcast and a few other companies.

It gets worse. Think of Comcast as an operator of a giant waterworks, with a connection to each home in the communities it serves. Some of the "water" it delivers is made up of traditional digital cable channels, and some of it is Internet access. But all of it is data flowing down a single conduit: Comcast's business is carrying digital communications through a wire. A water carrier does not own the water itself. In this merger, however, Comcast was seeking to own the content it provided. This set up a huge conflict of interest: even as the Internet was becoming the world's general-purpose network, the merger would put Comcast in a prime position to be the unchallenged provider of everything—all data, all information, all entertainment—flowing over the wires in its market areas. The company would have every incentive to squeeze online services that were unwilling to pay the freight to Comcast. The future of the Internet itself in America as well as the terms on which Americans would be able to buy wired Internet access would be radically affected by the merger decision.

Although approval of the merger was technically up to the Justice Department's Antitrust Division and the Federal Communications Commission (FCC), the Senate subcommittee was hardly irrelevant. It represented the branch of government that oversees the budgets of the agencies charged with implementing the antitrust laws. But there were other reasons the subcommittee's role was important: the political questions inherent in any major merger—Will it create or destroy jobs? Is the merging company viewed as a good corporate citizen with a friendly relationship with unions? Does the company have a diverse workforce? Is the merger too big to bear?—always come to Congress as a flurry of private meetings and one-page lists of factoids and talking points. Congressional political pressure (or lack of it) is relevant to the Justice Department and the FCC, even if both organizations deny that politics has anything to do with their expert administrative merger review. The hearing was relevant to the optics of the deal.

As Comcast's chief executive officer, chair, and president, Roberts was the first witness. He began his testimony by talking about Comcast's founding nearly fifty years earlier by his father, Ralph Roberts, who sat in the front row directly behind his son, looking on with a mild smile, decked out in a perky bow tie. With his earnest, calm demeanor, pleasant mid-Atlantic accent, and neatly combed appearance, Brian Roberts was a soothing presence. He wasn't flashy, loud, colorful, or arrogant—exactly the kind of respectful, moderate CEO a company would want to put in front of a Senate subcommittee when seeking approval for a world-changing merger. Formal approval of the deal was still eleven months in the future, but Brian Roberts exuded quiet confidence.[7]

He had told investors in a conference call in late 2009, a few months before the Senate hearing, that "with this transaction" Comcast was "strategically complete."[8] In other words, the merger would put Comcast in a position to reap the rewards of operating on a giant scale—keeping its costs of operation as low as possible—as well as allow it to control desirable content so as to make it nearly impossible for a competitor to threaten Comcast's position as the dominant U.S. data-distribution company. After more than forty years of steady acquisitions, including some of the largest deals in the industry, Comcast was done.

So many deals are announced in the media industry and so many shiny new devices are regularly introduced that most Americans probably believe that the communications sector of the economy has room for innumerable competitors. But they might be surprised at how concentrated the market for the modern-day equivalent of the standard phone line is. These days what that basic transmission service is facilitating is high-speed access to the Internet. In that market, there are two enormous monopoly submarkets—one for wireless and one for wired transmission. Both are dominated by two or three large companies.

On the wired side, Comcast is the communications equivalent of Standard Oil. It is a mammoth enterprise: even before its merger with NBC Universal, it was the country's largest cable operator, its largest residential high-speed Internet access company, its third-largest phone company, the owner of many key cable content properties—including eleven regional sports networks—and the manager of a robust Video on Demand platform. Comcast's high-speed Internet access services, bought by nearly 16 million Americans, were flourishing, throwing off more than $2 billion a quarter. (In contrast, the second-largest high-speed Internet access services provider via cable, Time Warner, had about 9 million customers.) Comcast dominated many local markets in major U.S. cities, including Philadelphia, Chicago, San Francisco, Seattle, and Boston.

Now it was seeking to buy NBC Universal, a content conglomerate that owned some of the most popular cable networks in the country and one of the largest broadcast networks, with twenty-five television stations, seven production studios, and several key Internet properties, including iVillage and a one-third interest in Hulu.com. NBC Sports had broadcast more Olympics than any other network and had televised sixteen Super Bowls. Wimbledon, the French Open, the Stanley Cup final, Sunday Night Football, the U.S. Open, and the Kentucky Derby were all NBC Sports properties. Two giant entities, one devoted to distribution of content and the other to programming, were joining forces. Together they would be a media and entertainment colossus with sweeping power to decide what Americans watched and read. The merged company would control one in five hours of all television viewing in the United States, would own more than 125 media outlets (cable channels, television stations, film studios, Web sites), and, most important, could use that control over content to dominate the market for high-speed wired Internet access in most of the country's major cities.[9]

Other players had taken their places that day in that hearing room or were represented by their proxies. The senators on the committee sat on raised platforms behind microphone stands, their staffers pressed against the wall behind them ready to hand a note or listen to a whispered question. Witnesses were arrayed facing the senators behind a plain wooden table: Jeff Zucker, the head of NBC Universal, who had come under harsh criticism for his management of the NBC TV broadcast network, was seated to Brian Roberts's left.

NBC-the-network was almost lost in the rounding when it came to NBC Universal's overall success as a media conglomerate; even as the network continued to lose money, Comcast could leverage NBCU's powerful cable channels—like USA and Bravo—as a means of keeping competition from rival distributors at bay. Comcast had used the enormous profits from its pay-TV services to subsidize the construction of the nation's most subscribed-to wired high-speed Internet access service, but without reasonably priced access to key programming no one would be able to follow suit.

On Zucker's left, the other cable companies were represented by a token competitor, Colleen Abdoulah, president and CEO of WOW! (WideOpen-West Networks). A midsized cable system struggling to compete for subscribers in Comcast's territory in the Midwest, WOW! was trying to win over consumers by providing better customer service, but it was forced to pay high prices for take-it-or-leave-it bundles of programming owned by NBC Universal and other media conglomerates. The big cable-distribution companies like Comcast can get those bundles for far less than the smaller companies. Abdoulah would testify that if Comcast controlled NBC Universal, negotiations for the programming WOW! needed to retain subscribers were likely to become even more one-sided. Two public-interest advocates, Mark Cooper (instantly recognizable with his thick glasses and emphatic delivery) and Andy Schwartzman (white bushy eyebrows and a thick moustache), both veterans of decades-long tussles with the cable industry, were seated to her left.

Behind the witness table, several rows of professional Washington sat quietly facing the senators. In the first row, visible behind Brian Roberts from the senators' perspective, and next to nearly ninety-year-old Ralph Roberts, was David Cohen, the political genius pulling the strings on behalf of Comcast. Long before this hearing, Cohen had used his energetic mastery of national politics and his formidable Democratic credentials to shape the all-important narrative of the merger, the simple political story that would be patiently, ceaselessly repeated until no other story seemed credible: Comcast, a true-blue American success story of a family company, was merging with NBC Universal in order to save the NBC broadcast network and bring order as well as technical innovation to the cable-TV industry. Cohen's strategic genius had molded the narrative in response to his assessment of the political situation in Washington, and he had probably already planned the next several steps following the proceedings.

Cohen was no slouch as an antitrust lawyer either. For anyone willing to engage them on the substance of the deal, Cohen and his team were ready with smooth responses. From their perspective, the deal was a vertical combination of a distributor and a programming company, not a horizontal combination that would result in fewer competing distributors, and thus it was not the kind of transaction with which antitrust law should be concerned. In a year-long process of ticking boxes and being respectful of various political offices and regulatory niche inhabitants, Cohen and his team would meet with all individuals, companies, and agencies that seemed relevant and explain why the Comcast merger aligned precisely with their interests. The Comcast team would show interest and professional engagement with the various conditions that the regulators required in order to clear the merger, as long as those conditions did not interfere with the company's business plans.[10]

Behind the witnesses sat representatives of other media and telecommunications companies, well-groomed, mostly male, and placidly enjoying this rare public ritual. (Major hearings don't happen every week in the telecommunications field.) There is a constant, easy, friendly flow between government and industry in the communications world bounded by the suburbs of Arlington, Virginia, and Bethesda, Maryland. Regulators switch jobs and become the regulated; the regulated leave their posts and take leadership roles in trade associations; everyone stays in touch. This crowd was easy to like; they were well-intentioned, engaging, and undogmatic, with a light touch and a smattering of technical know-how.

Despite the bonhomie of the hearing room, the merger represented a new, frightening moment in U.S. regulatory history. If a few large companies were to get control over electricity or clean water in America in particular geographic regions and could decide without oversight who would have access to it and what kinds of uses they could make of it, at what cost, there would be a public uproar. Instead of electrical utilities or water companies, the entities involved were media conglomerates: Comcast, the dominant distributor of communications in twenty-two of America's twenty-five largest cities,[11] was seeking to buy one of the five media powerhouses that furnished more than 80 percent of America's primetime entertainment and news.[12] Instead of electricity or water, Comcast was gaining dominion over the country's latest utility infrastructure: high-speed Internet access. Simultaneously, rather than install twenty-first-century fiber-optic lines to replace the metal wires that had brought all Americans telephone service, AT&T and Verizon, the giant private telephone companies that had ceded the market for wired high-speed Internet access to the cable companies, were working hard to persuade states that they should be released from any obligation to provide all Americans with telephone service where it was not in line with their business plans. By mid-2012, four states had already removed this requirement, and six others were poised to do so.[13] Americans would be left with a grotesquely skewed communications-utility picture: the rich would pay whatever the cable companies chose to charge for wired Internet access while poor and rural Americans would be relegated to expensive, second-best wireless connections. At the same time, much of the rest of the developed world was racing to install first-best standard fiber connections to their citizens.

Seen from the outside, the Comcast-NBCU deal seemed like a typical big-box media merger. And in some ways it was: the consolidation of market power, deregulation, and tearing of the social fabric in the communications-utility sector had been going on for decades. Opponents of the deal were shooting at a subtarget, in a sense. They argued that media consolidation had reached a saturation point and that the Comcast-NBCU merger would lead to homogenized entertainment sold for high prices by extraordinarily profitable giant companies. Americans would have almost unlimited freedom to watch a dazzling variety of football games, cooking shows, and other forms of entertainment coming from a very small number of sources. Although that was all true, the overarching problem came from control over pipes: with this acquisition Comcast would have even more power in its market areas to dictate the terms on which access to all kinds of information—entertainment, news, sports, data, phone conversations—could be had.

The deal's supporters (chiefly Comcast itself) had only to respond that the merger would not make the situation for consumers worse than it already was. If opponents could not decisively prove "merger-specific harms," the phrase Comcast employees repeated endlessly to staffers across Washington, the deal could not be blocked. If there were problems of concentration in the cable-distribution marketplace, they had existed before the merger was announced and could be taken up at a later date. Whether that date would ever arrive was unclear.

By February 2010, the accepted wisdom in Washington was that the deal would go through. No major company had opposed it publicly, and without an influential corporate entity on the other side to give politicians cover, there was little advantage to fighting the merger. No one wanted to appear unfriendly to business during the dark days of the U.S. recession. Besides, there was some appeal to the vertical argument. If the Department of Justice in a Democratic administration tried to block the merger, it might be pummeled by a conservative reviewing court—there are more Republicans than Democrats on the circuit appeals courts and on the federal bench as a whole—after a protracted litigation battle against one of the deepest-pocketed businesses in America.

But the deal showed Americans their Internet future. Even though there are several large cable companies nationwide, each dominates its own region. The major cable companies never compete with one another because each wants to reap the advantages of scale that come with control over entire markets. Because no other widely available privately provided wired Internet access product is fast enough or can be installed cheaply enough to compete with cable, each of the country's large cable distributors can raise prices in its region for high-speed Internet access without fear of being undercut.

Wireless access, dominated by AT&T and Verizon, is too slow to compete with the cable industry's offerings; mobile wireless services are complementary to the wired access Comcast sells. Verizon Wireless's joint marketing agreement with Comcast, announced in December 2011,[14] made that truth visible: fierce competitors don't offer to sell each other's products. In a nutshell, the giant companies that dominate high-speed Internet access in America have tacitly divided up the marketplace. AT&T and Verizon are devoting themselves to wireless access, where they are by far the two largest players, rather than competing head to head with Comcast for truly high-speed wired Internet access, and they would do almost anything to shed themselves of their traditional obligation to provide wired access to all Americans. Comcast and Time Warner Cable are concentrating on wired access and reaping profit margins of about 95 percent for the service.[15] And consumers are paying more in the United States than people in other countries do—for less speedy service—as inequality between the haves and have-nots is amplified by the digital divide.

It doesn't have to be this way. Other developed countries have a watchdog to ensure that all their citizens are connected at cheap rates to the fastest possible open-access ramps (that is, fiber-optic access) to the Internet. In South Korea, more than half the households are already connected to fiber lines that allow for blazing-fast uploads and downloads, and households in Japan and Hong Kong are close behind.[16] In America, only around 7 percent of households have access to fiber, and the service costs six times as much as it does in Hong Kong (and five times as much as it does in Stockholm).[17] Vertically integrated cable companies, whose Internet access product is not provided over fiber and crimps uploads, are well on the way to controlling America's Internet access destiny, having spent millions of dollars over almost fifteen years lobbying against any rules that might have constrained them.

Instead of ensuring that everyone in America can compete in a global economy, instead of narrowing the divide between rich and poor, instead of supporting competitive free markets for American inventions that use information—instead, that is, of ensuring that America will lead the world in the information age—U.S. politicians have chosen to keep Comcast and its fellow giants happy. The government removed all rules from high-speed Internet access and allowed steep market consolidation in the hope that competition among providers would protect consumers. But that competition has not materialized; the cable industry, whose collusive practices have been largely ignored by regulators, has decisively dominated the wired marketplace and has done its best to foil municipal efforts to provide publicly owned fiber Internet access.[18] As a result, the United States now has neither a competitive market for high-speed wired Internet access nor government oversight.

The giant communications companies unite in claiming that the situation is under control. In response to an op-ed of mine published by the *New York Times* in December 2011, Ivan Seidenberg, CEO of Verizon, wrote, "America has a very good broadband story; someone just has to be willing to tell it." These companies claim that regulation will stifle investment and innovation. This kind of argument is not new. When Brooksley Born, chair of the Commodity Futures Trading Commission (the federal agency which oversees the futures and commodity options markets), suggested during the Clinton administration that derivative financial products should be overseen by regulators, she was immediately met by a firm, flattening political response: interfere with the financial sector, and you will destroy innovation and investment.[19] Several years ago, many people made fun of Al Gore for saying that climate change was endangering our future; his critics insisted that the data he was pointing to represented no more than normal fluctuations magnified by over-anxious minds. To regulate carbon emissions would destroy innovation and investment.

As a policy issue, the crisis in American communications bears some similarity to the banking crisis and global warming: it has taken decades to arrive; it has happened through incremental policy decisions, mergers, and changes in society; it involves technical terms that enable easy obfuscation; large entities have an interest in maintaining the status quo; and there is a great deal of political bluster about the possible effect of regulation on innovation and investment. In the communications industry no signal crisis—no equivalent of the banking collapse—has erupted to trigger public outrage. Reporters usually don't cover regulatory proceedings because they are slow moving and impenetrable. As a result, the players involved, who know exactly what's going on and why it's important, can get away with dazzling political sleight-of-hand. "Look, there, a new gizmo!" they say to their customers, believing (accurately enough) that few of them will put the pieces together and figure out the truth about the grinding monopolistic power and lack of social contract that underlies the American communications industry today.

This issue hits consumers' pocketbooks at the same time that it implicates national industrial policies. When the telephone was the dominant medium of exchange, U.S. law required that every American have access to a phone along with other utility services such as water and electricity. Although the Internet has become the common medium of our era, and no one can get a job or apply for benefits or keep up with the rest of the world without high-speed access, this service is framed as an expensive luxury reserved for the rich; fully a third of Americans don't subscribe to high-speed Internet access, and nonsubscription is highly correlated with low socioeconomic status.[20] This situation has arisen because Americans have allowed the companies involved to cherry-pick wealthy neighborhoods for service and charge whatever they like. Now states, heavily lobbied by telecommunications companies, are seeking to get rid of any obligation to provide communications services to all their citizens. None of this was inevitable; all of it is bad for individual consumers.

Americans are suffering as a result; it is already clear that unless something is done the next disruptive Internet innovation, the new breakthrough invention that depends on the existence of an experimental sandbox of millions of users with fiber high-speed Internet access, will not come from America. The country does not have the critical mass of people connected to fiber that other countries do; instead, those American consumers who can are (over)paying for privately provided, pinched-upload cable services. Symmetrical and highly reliable connections are especially important for businesses, which typically make even heavier use of upstream paths than households. So the much-needed economic boost that comes from creating and marketing the next big thing will go elsewhere. But few people with the power to change the situation seem to understand this.

This book tells the story of the forces that made the Comcast-NBCU merger possible. Three paradigm shifts happened between 1996 and 2010 that shaped the narrative. First, the big new idea behind the Internet was that its language—and language is all the Internet is, a couple of simple agreements that allow computers to "speak Internet"—facilitated a general-purpose global open network of networks that has changed two billion lives around the world while becoming the single common digital platform for communication. Second, the cable and telephone companies across whose wires Internet talk was flowing made a successful concerted effort to persuade the FCC to completely deregulate provision of the two-way, general-purpose communication on which the country's economic, cultural, political, and social life depends: high-speed Internet access. This meant that the success of the cheerfully disruptive activities happening online became entirely contingent on the generosity of the few large companies selling access. And third, newly elected president Barack Obama seemed to understand that high-speed access to the Internet was essential for anyone wanting to participate effectively in the twenty-first-century global economy. He suggested that nondiscriminatory, ubiquitous connections were essential—or he seemed to. It looked as if government intervention to ensure world-leading, reasonably priced, wired open Internet access for everyone would be an important priority for the new administration.

Things did not turn out that way, for a range of reasons that I hope to make clear in this book, and the consequences of this failure in policy are likely to be a drag on America's success for generations.

The February 2010 Senate Antitrust Subcommittee hearing turned out to be a well-produced piece of political theater. It provided a public opportunity for selected opponents of the merger to warn about the risks to communication and culture posed by the merger of Comcast and NBC Universal. But David Cohen had done his work well. All the senators had been visited by well-primed representatives of the merging companies, all the facts had been shaped by messaging experts—this merger is about saving the NBC Peacock!—and nothing would change as a result of any word spoken that morning. Roberts himself was appropriately deferential and polite.

As the hearing wound on, Roberts's calm bearing contrasted sharply with that of consumer advocates Schwartzman and Cooper, who looked comparatively unkempt and sounded far from calm, their voices strained with angry passion as they spoke against the merger. Schwartzman and Cooper understood what was at stake and did their best to explain the threat the merger represented. But they were up against a well-funded, decades-long campaign by the companies involved to free themselves from government review. The two men were there to speak their part on a stage that had been set long before they arrived.

Roberts never faltered during the hearing, and his performance was judged a success by the trade press articles that appeared the following day. The *Wall Street Journal* reported just a few months later that he was already shopping for a multimillion-dollar apartment in New York City within walking distance of the home of the future joint venture, even though the deal would not be formally approved for another eight months.[21] (The head of the merger effort within Comcast, Stephen Burke, later paid almost $17 million for his new New York City home.)[22] Comcast's wealth was no secret: according to Bernstein Research, a media analysis firm, the company was soaking up "torrents of cash" in 2010.[23] Its profits were up in the middle of a recession, its dividends and buybacks were soaring, and its executives were some of the highest paid in the country. But Roberts usually took care to keep a low personal profile and present an air of earnest engagement with the regulatory approval process; having the news come out about his new apartment was a slip.

Still, he had a lot to brag about: Comcast already dominated the market in many American cities as a physical distributor of digital information. Even before the merger, Comcast was in many ways the nation's all-purpose communications wired network provider; post-merger it would have a multibillion-dollar reason to prefer its own digital interests—the water it owned, rather than the water that simply passed through its conduit—over those of its now vulnerable competitors. The hearing, held to provide oversight, masked a profound, little-understood American problem: the lack of supervision over the mammoth companies that sell Americans access to all information, all communications, all entertainment—all the things that make today's economy, politics, and society function.

A hundred years ago, the big basic-infrastructure story—the story of a network that makes other businesses possible—was the power of the railroad, a new technology that tied the country together for the first time and spurred decades of economic growth. After the completion of the first transcontinental railroad in 1869, the railroad system had mushroomed rapidly, and consolidation of independent systems by the railroad barons, chiefly J. P. Morgan, Cornelius Vanderbilt, and James J. Hill, had intro-duced complex new questions involving American competition and con-sumer protection.

Soon enough, barons in different industries began colluding: John D. Rockefeller's Standard Oil worked with the railroad barons (particularly Morgan) to control up to 90 percent of the oil refining business. Morgan-controlled consolidated railroads, operating under collusive trust arrange-ments, granted secret rebates to Standard Oil and undertook corporate espionage, giving Standard Oil information about competing oil shipments, which allowed it to underprice potential rivals.[24] The growing power of the super-rich oil and railroad capitalists created widespread fear that funda-mental American values and public interests were being destroyed in favor of private profits; populists, Progressives, farmers, working-class activists, public leaders, and journalists joined together to call for strict regulation to constrain the power of these giant infrastructure industries.

The railroads were essential scale businesses, and everyone wanted cheap and clean oil. But the cooperation between the two industries (their own "vertical integration"), their abusive practices, and their clear disdain for oversight angered Americans across the political spectrum. The country emerged from the ensuing regulatory battle as a nation with the idea that big essential infrastructure requires vigilant oversight and intervention to ensure that all Americans are served, all Americans are protected, and a level playing field is kept in place for innovation and fair competition. The government passed the Sherman Antitrust Act, launched the first infra-structure oversight agency, the Interstate Commerce Commission (ICC), and sued the railroads for antitrust violations.

It took years of attempts at legislation, public uproar, and litigation to achieve the dismantling of Standard Oil and the creation of a system of over-sight for the railroads. The ICC, understaffed and inexpert, was swiftly overwhelmed by the lobbying efforts of the railway lawyers, and railroad su-pervision is now largely in the hands of the railway industry. Special-purpose agencies, which depend on the particular industry they regulate for informa-tion, for future jobs for underpaid agency employees, and for their institu-tional sense of self-esteem, have not proven effective. And the government has not always shown good stewardship in implementing or enforcing disinterested industrial policy that depends on words that govern behavior. But during the same era, the federal government brought into being the Antitrust Division of the Department of Justice and increased its own capacity to protect the public from the depredations of an unconstrained market system. The Antitrust Division, unlike niche-expert agencies, has been able to act structurally by requiring divestitures and structural separation in monopolistic infrastructure industries so that competition will flourish.

Consider the AT&T divestiture of 1984, which forced long-distance prices down and led to innovations in long-distance service. That divestiture has now been completely undone by litigation and lobbying; instead of the twentieth century's Ma Bell, we now have Ma Cell. Part of the story of communications in America is the fact that in the separate market for wireless access, two giant companies, AT&T and Verizon, have the power that Comcast and Time Warner have in wired access.

In the twenty-first century, America is bound together and connected to the rest of the world not by skinny iron rails but by big communications pipes, an all-purpose digital infrastructure. Where once there was a separation of different media—television, voice, and text—now, thanks to the rise of digital technology and the advent of the Internet, they have become lightly differentiated uses of the same physical connections. The question of who controls the wires is thus about who controls the connections that unite the economy, politics, and society.

Yet the country's regulatory structure, as much because of politics as of reasoned policy making, has not kept up with the consolidation in carriers, the sweeping effects of convergence of all media, and the increasing control over information flows possessed by the giant carriers in this country. The regulators themselves are outmaneuvered, under-resourced, constantly under threat of attack, and short of information.

For more than a hundred years, U.S. policy has been to support regulatory conditions that will foster competition. The notion is that competition will protect consumers; the assumption is that the free market will flourish as long as ground rules for competition are put in place.

When it comes to natural monopoly industries, however, up-front capital costs are high and the marginal cost of serving one additional customer is low—but the presence of that one additional customer will not only mean more revenue for the provider, it will also reduce the company's average cost of serving its entire customer base. Those lower average costs mean huge advantages to the incumbent, particularly if it has managed to control the entire local geographic market where it operates. So it may not make sense for another competitor to enter the market.

Utilities like water and electricity are natural monopoly services. So is telecommunications. It costs a great deal to set up a telecommunications system (and the U.S. government has helped immensely along the way by handing out franchises and access to rights-of-way to the corporate ancestors of today's giants) but very little to add one more revenue-producing customer, and at this point competitors to incumbent cable providers survive only by sufferance of the local monopolist. But Americans persist in hoping for competition to emerge. When it comes to telecommunications the government has a long history of setting up market-enforcing regulatory structures—the state as umpire rather than intervener—that have failed to constrain the naturally monopolistic behavior of incumbents. Who loses? Consumers and innovators.

When it comes to the distribution of information, the situation becomes even more serious. Self-interested agents in a market-driven economy will, naturally, invest only in what they can make a profit from. Access to the Internet can create public benefits—spillovers—in the form of new jobs and new ways of making a living. But a market-dominating private-access provider will want, unless constrained by regulation, to find ways to drive its own profits up through exacting fees and tolls based on differential treatment of information in an atmosphere of continuing scarcity of truly high-speed access. This can't be good for American society as a whole.

That Brian Roberts and his team were brilliant businessmen was apparent. Whether the looming cable monopoly made sense for America was not as clear. The communications landscape was undergoing great change; Comcast was smoothing out all the difficulties and creating one vast, efficient machine. The railroad and oil barons of the early twentieth century had done much the same thing. The difference was that Comcast's machine extruded communications capacity rather than oil or steel.

As the 1990s cable industry mogul John Malone said of Comcast's merger plan at the time it was announced, "If they can't rape and pillage, it's probably not a good investment."[25] In the end, the Antitrust Division chose to allow the Comcast-NBCU merger, subject only to behavioral constraints—obligations framed in words that Comcast will for the most part be able to evade—and the FCC followed suit. Other media and telecommunications businesses stayed quiet; they knew they would have to do business with Comcast later on. In the end, the showing of "merger-specific harms" was not enough to persuade the government to act to block this merger.

Comcast is smart enough to avoid visible rape and pillage now that the merger has been approved. But perhaps Americans will start to care when they realize that, compared to other countries, they are paying more for less and leaving behind many of their fellow citizens. As things are, the United States will be unable to compete with nations whose industrial policy has been more forward-thinking.

This is not the first time that a form of regulation has been out of sync with the characteristics of the industry it purports to regulate. This story starts with railroad regulation. Railroads, a classic natural monopoly, consolidated steadily in the face of ineffective efforts to constrain their behavior by encouraging competition. As J. P. Morgan once said, "The American public seems to be unwilling to admit . . . that it has a choice between regulated legal agreements and unregulated extralegal agreements. We should have cast away more than 50 years ago the impossible doctrine of protection of the public by railway competition."[26]

A gigantic company providing essential infrastructure for every American, a shifting media landscape, a deregulated environment, and a smoothly operating political campaign built on decades of steady effort that made it impossible for federal officials to reject the merger out of hand: the Comcast-NBCU narrative offers a cautionary tale about what has happened to communications in America.

1

From Railroad to Telephone

AT THE BEGINNING OF THE TWENTIETH century, Theodore Roosevelt received complaints from all parts of the country about the depredations of the railroad moguls, a problem that had been decades in the making. Beginning in the 1820s, states and local communities had provided extensive direct aid to railway entrepreneurs in the form of land grants, loans, and outright cash donations hoping to attract routes that would serve their citizens and boost economic growth.[1] By the 1860s, states and localities had provided at least half the capital for the early railways.[2] But all this boosterism was unaccompanied by oversight. Many of the railroad operators of the time were actually groups of companies that had combined in order to get access to land grants whose value they hoped to increase by opening a railway. The general sentiment in the country was for states to provide inducements but no regulation that would intrude into the private affairs of firms—carrots but no sticks. The result: rampant fraud and scandals, as railway executives from the 1830s through the 1850s watered their stock, absconded with public funds, built lines that had no chance of financial success, and freely handed out bribes to short-term state and local public officials.[3] State and local aid to privately held railroads in several states came to an abrupt end in the 1860s with the passage of laws and constitutional provisions outlawing the practice.

But the nation still needed railroad lines crossing the country, and no single state could support rail development across sparsely settled western territories. In the 1850s, the idea of a federally funded national railroad was briefly discussed, but the nation's lack of an expert and disinterested civil service that could carry out such a project scuttled the notion.[4] In the end, Congress followed much the same path the states had, authorizing land grants and federal loan guarantees to the Union Pacific and Central Pacific Railroads to build a line between Sacramento and Omaha. The Pacific Railway Act of 1862 hewed to the line the states had established by providing incentives accompanied by little regulatory authority. Just sixteen federal-level administrators were tasked with administering the grants under the act, and ten of these were part-time and unpaid.[5]

Predictably, scandal followed. The Union Pacific bribed federal officials to ensure that the line would receive massively favorable public assistance—twice the original land grants under the act and guaranteed bonds—and the line's directors (including federal employees) paid themselves generously. In what became known as the Crédit Mobilier scandal, government appointees to the board of the organization formed to allocate profits from the Union Pacific transcontinental construction project took bribes during the early 1860s in the form of stock. Other board members enjoyed cash distributions before the line was completed.[6]

All this turmoil gave a bad name to government promotion of private infrastructure investment by way of land grants and loan guarantees. The entire idea of industrial policy became tainted for Americans; the exercise of state power seemed to engender corruption. As the sociologist Frank Dobbin puts it in *Forging Industrial Policy*, "Americans were certain that their governments had overstepped their bounds in offering aid to railroads, and forswore future government aid to enterprise."[7]

Meanwhile, bolstered by the massive loans and government assistance needed to build new lines, railroad construction grew fivefold between 1860 and 1890.[8] A financial crisis for the railways followed in the 1870s amid the scandalous revelations of fraud and corruption; as much as a third of the trackage in the country at the time was controlled by companies that went bankrupt under their debt burdens.[9] Following these upheavals, the railways went through a period of astonishing consolidation during the 1870s and 1880s, as bankers and bondholders worked to rein in the railroads with "voting trusts" that would run the lines and avoid ruinous competition among systems.[10] By 1905 most of the country's 164,000 railway miles were held by six huge communities of interest—sets of corporations linked by common ownership—allowing entities controlled by J. P. Morgan, Vanderbilt, Harriman-Kuhn-Loeb, Gould, and Rockefeller to wield enormous power.[11] The voting trusts were often groups of Morgan friends who were determined that the railroads be carefully run.[12]

These large regional monopolies flagrantly favored large shippers—manufacturers and middlemen—over small. Farmers were charged exorbitant rates for shipping their agricultural wares, but favored customers like Standard Oil and Andrew Carnegie's steel operations received secret rebates and drawbacks. Drawbacks were particularly alarming to small shippers because they required the railroad to pay a favored customer if the railroad shipped a competitor's products. Small farmers were angry as well at collusion between different regional systems aimed at keeping prices uniform; during the 1860s and 1870s, agreements among systems setting prices and providing shared resources (trains and track) were common. Big shippers routinely paid less for sending goods long distances between major transit hubs than small shippers paid to send their products shorter distances to smaller destinations.[13] As a result of these economic disparities and other factors, independent farmers had a difficult time staying in business at the end of the nineteenth century: millions became tenant farmers or moved to cities as the farmers' share of the country's gross domestic product plummeted from 38 percent in the 1870s to 24 percent in the 1890s.[14]

Irritation mounted among the smaller shippers about the restraints on trade enforced by the giant regional railroad combinations, as well as about the railroads' common practice of giving free tickets to influential people, including officials and newspaper editors, to avoid any suggestions of oversight. Protests erupted; fear of monopolistic and unfair behavior by the railroads grew; legislatures began to work.

The first regulatory response to the regional railroad cartels took place in New England in the 1860s. States set up commissions that could adjudicate disputes between shippers and railroads but could not set prices or punish misbehaving railroads. Massachusetts, for example, passed a law in 1871 making short haul–long haul discrimination illegal and requiring that railroads be subject to an adjudicative procedure before the commission if shippers complained.[15] In the Midwest and the South, the long haul–short haul problem was met with a sterner response: farmer-led "Granger" efforts triggered the establishment of state commissions in the 1870s and 1880s that regulated rates.

But the Granger commissions, as popular as they were, were ineffective. The railroads simply ignored their mandates.[16] Weaker state commissions in the East had little authority to enforce their proclamations; stronger commissions in the Midwest, West, and South had rate-setting ability but no power to carry out structural reforms that would have addressed rate-cutting by carriers in favor of favored customers.[17] Perceiving that these state-level regulatory attempts were not working, small businesses and other interested parties applied mounting pressure in the 1870s and 1880s for a federal solution to the abusive behavior of the railroads. In 1876 federal legislation designed to avoid the domination of transport was introduced, but it failed to pass. So did more than a hundred other railway-constraining efforts debated by Congress during the 1870s and early 1880s.[18] The railroad lawyers—forty thousand strong at the height of their powers—testified before commissions and legislators and used every trick they could find to undermine the effect of any potentially destructive legislation. Railroad lawyers were some of America's first lobbyists, and they argued strenuously that state intervention in the private workings of businesses would be a threat to the American way of life; government power would lead to tyranny and corruption, as the land-grant experience had shown, and was unconstitutional to boot because it would exceed the grant of authority to regulate "commerce." The railroaders maintained that railways were common carriers, not commerce itself.[19]

Despite these arguments, public outrage over the concentrated economic power of the railroads—and the huge companies that controlled them—continued to build. The Supreme Court ruled in the *Wabash* cases that only the federal government—and not the states—could regulate interstate commerce. This put the state commissions out of business and prompted the first successful concrete reaction by the federal government to the widespread anguish of small farmers and others: the Interstate Commerce Act of 1887. The act created the first regulatory commission in America, the Interstate Commerce Commission (ICC). Officially, the act prohibited the railroads from charging unreasonable rates, discriminating between persons, or charging less for a long haul than for a short one included within it where the two trips operated "under substantially similar circumstances."[20]

But the tension between fear of concentration of power in the trusts and of concentration of power in government was managed by limiting the power of the Interstate Commerce Commission to intervene in the railroads' private affairs. The ICC itself was the product of a long list of compromises. And so the short haul–long haul antidiscrimination provision of the act was weak, the "unreasonable rates" provision said nothing about how to define *reasonable*, and the Commission would have to resort to courts to enforce its decisions if a railroad refused to comply. The constitutional claims made by the railroads did not prevail, but concerns over the scope of government entanglement curbed the power of the ICC.

Enforcement, as a result, became nearly impossible. Virtually all the ICC's decisions were referred to the courts and the Commission kept losing; between 1887 and 1905 the Supreme Court ruled against the ICC in fifteen of the sixteen rate-setting cases that came before it.[21] In effect, conservative courts were persuaded by lawyers representing the combinations that the language of the new statute gave power to the government to set aside rates that were unreasonable (a negative power) but no affirmative power to fix rates. The power to set rates was special, the Supreme Court found, and not one that Congress should be considered to have granted absent express language saying so. Canny litigation over the meaning of "substantially similar" went on for years; the railroad lawyers convinced judges that their clients faced competition at the distant points of their lines that made the statute inapplicable to short-haul routes. If no long haul could ever be compared to any short-haul route on an apples-to-apples basis, there could never be a successful claim that an operator had unfairly hiked the price for the short-haul section. Conservative judicial interpretation of the Interstate Commerce Act, coupled with a lack of clarity as to the Commission's powers, impeded the efforts of the nation's first regulatory agency. The attempt to regulate railroads by the ICC had collapsed by 1900, but public demands for reform continued.[22]

Enter Theodore Roosevelt. Consolidation by the railway owners (even after the nation slid into the severe depression of 1893) made their operations more efficient, but these benefits were not being passed along in the form of lower prices for farmers and intermediary merchants forced to deal with the single railway operator in their territory. As the Omaha platform adopted by the Populist Party had put it in 1892: "We believe that the time has come when the railroad corporations will either own the people or the people must own the railroads."[23] By the time Roosevelt became president in 1901, farmers had been agitating for twenty years for a regulator and even for public ownership of the railroads. Rapid consolidation had made these pleas sharper.

Roosevelt had no interest in nationalizing the railroads, but he was convinced that the interests of the railways needed to be balanced with those of the public: "The railway," he said in 1901, "is a public servant. Its rates should be just to and open to all shippers alike. The government should see to it that within its jurisdiction this is so and should provide a speedy, inexpensive, and effective remedy to that end." He recognized the benefits the railroads were bringing to America: "At the same time it must not be forgotten that our railways are the arteries through which the commercial life-blood of this Nation flows. Nothing could be more foolish than the enactment of legislation which would unnecessarily interfere with the development of these commercial agencies."[24] Roosevelt's aim was to establish stronger oversight in the form of explicit rate-setting rules that would ensure that railroads served the public interest. And in a series of bills passed between 1903 and 1910, legislative language that appeared to create this power was put into place.[25]

The problem was that enforcing market competition did not, in the end, constrain the power of the railroads. Without a strategic, positive effort by the federal government aimed at addressing the fundamental questions posed by a privately run transportation system—how should service best be extended to all Americans?—the railroad companies were able to evade the weak legislation by overwhelming the agency that was supposed to regulate them and litigating over niceties in its language for years.

And because they were natural monopoly businesses, railroads were not constrained by the operation of antitrust law either. The Sherman Antitrust Act of 1890, passed in response to populist concern about the role of titans in business, outlawed "every contract, combination or conspiracy in restraint of trade" and treated violations as crimes.[26] But the act represented a compromise written in ambiguous language that provided no guidance as to how it should be applied, and it was little used during the first decade of its existence, despite the tremendous wave of mergers that took place at about that time. Collaboration that squashed rivalry was clearly different from cooperation that promoted growth and advantages of scale and scope. Many courts and economists took the view during the early years of the Sherman Act that unconstrained competition might actually endanger industries with high fixed costs and low marginal costs, like railroads and other utilities.

Even when the Roosevelt administration wielded the Sherman Act in attempts to enforce railway competition it had little effect. A referee enforcing the rules of competition is very different from a manager, and it is difficult to imagine a railway that is not a consolidated, collaborating entity. Policing and facilitating the choices made by private natural monopoly entities operating physical infrastructure used for transportation and communications will not address deep-rooted structural shortcomings in the market economy. Besides, because the Sherman Act is and was interpreted one step at a time by courts, large natural monopoly entities aiming to retain their economies of scale and price-setting power could always keep the fight running for another day.

With his enormous red nose and his shy, imperious demeanor, J. P. Morgan effectively ran U.S. economic policy for decades. Lonely, anxious to please his dead father, and possessed of a strong sense that what was good for his bank was good for America, he advised presidents, wrestled down entire industries, and mastered the art of the holding company. He fervently believed in order and found great satisfaction in the rituals of the Episcopal Church. He believed that unfettered competition in industries (such as railroads) characterized by high initial investment costs was destructive and unnecessary, because the industries' attempts to underprice one another so as to grab a greater share of a given regional market would systematically destroy any hope of lower average costs for their fixed-price operations and eventually drive all the competitors out of business.[27]

Morgan knew that his businesses' monopolistic practices caused great public anger. But to him, as to most of the Gilded Age barons, such a response was naive: the railroads, the web that linked America's great cities together, could function only with the substantial support for investment that protection from price wars provided. Without collaboration and organization of transportation resources, the country would remain a preindustrial backwater.

From Morgan's perspective, pure competition was impossible. True competitors would have to cut workers' wages in order to service debt, making their businesses unsustainable. At the same time, giant shippers were forcing the railroads to grant rebates and give preference to their distribution needs. In Morgan's view, the railroads had no choice but to operate under unregulated extralegal arrangements supporting both cooperation and rebates.

Under his strong guidance, the railroad barons formed trusts—corporate forms that allowed one entity to serve as an umbrella for formerly competing companies through an arrangement by which stockholders in several companies transferred their shares to a single set of trustees. The first true trust had been created in the 1870s by John D. Rockefeller's Standard Oil in an effort to combine companies acquired by Standard under the same management. As Standard Oil had done, the railroad trust company trustees—usually a handful of Morgan's cronies—handed stockholders holding company certificates.[28]

Trust arrangements permitted railroad lines to avoid competition by harmonizing their operations, agreeing not to invade one another's territories, and desisting from mutually destructive behavior. The barons argued that the public benefited from the economies of scale produced by eliminating duplicative facilities and by the increased investment in research and development made possible by the huge volume of activities.

Orderliness was, indeed, the way of business at the time: almost 75 percent of the trusts for which the Gilded Age is famous were created between 1898 and 1904.[29] Great names like U.S. Steel, Consolidated Tobacco, and Amalgamated Copper came into being at this point. Not just Morgans and Rockefellers but also Vanderbilts, Harrimans, Goulds, and Carnegies suddenly gained extraordinary power over the lives of ordinary Americans. The

accumulation of trusts also brought consolidation in utility services: telephone, telegraph, gas, and electric power and light companies joined hands
and ceased competing—while simultaneously avoiding government oversight.[30] The concentration of ownership also brought a tremendous concentration of affluence; in the mid-1890s, about 9 percent of the families in
America owned 71 percent of the wealth.[31]

Roosevelt viewed this process with dismay. In particular, he was irritated
by a trust that had been formed by Morgan, James J. Hill, and E. H.
Harriman to bring the Northern Pacific and Great Northern Railways into
cooperation. Under Morgan's plan, stockholders of the Northern Pacific
and Great Northern companies, railways that together controlled traffic
from Chicago to Seattle, were invited to exchange their stock for shares in
the Northern Securities Company—the largest business entity in the world
next to U.S. Steel.[32] Most accepted the deal, and the holding company eventually held about 90 percent of the Northern Pacific stock and more than
75 percent of Great Northern—and controlled almost all railroads west of
the Mississippi.[33]

In 1902, Roosevelt ordered his attorney general, Philander Knox, to
bring suit against the Northern Securities Company under the Sherman
Act,[34] which prohibited any combination "in the form of trust or otherwise,
or conspiracy, in restraint of trade or commerce."[35] The suit was a surprise
to Morgan and his co-owners. Morgan, peeved, went to visit the president.
Roosevelt reported later that Morgan had seemed puzzled. According
to Edmund Morris, Roosevelt's biographer, the following conversation
ensued:

> MORGAN: If we have done anything wrong, send your man to my man and
> they can fix it up.
> ROOSEVELT: That can't be done.
> KNOX: We don't want to fix it up, we want to stop it.

Theodore Roosevelt found the exchange illuminating. J. Pierpont Morgan
thought of government as just another combination owner—someone
with whom a deal could be done, an equal, a peer. Roosevelt believed
that moguls should not be the government's equal, and stubbornly
moved ahead with a multiyear effort to ensure that the privately operated

railroads were subject to constraints that would serve the public interest.[36]

In 1903, a court in Minnesota backed Roosevelt's use of the Sherman Act.[37] This had not been a self-evident outcome; in 1895 the Supreme Court had rejected use of the act against a sugar trust in *United States v. E. C. Knight Company*. The statute was said to deal with restraint of trade in *interstate commerce* and not restraint of competition through consolidation of *intrastate manufacturing* facilities. Because the *Knight* trust had concerned manufacturing and not interstate commerce, the Court held that it was beyond the reach of the statute.[38] Roosevelt's action against the railway trust was the first case under the Sherman Act that involved a merger between competing firms engaged in interstate commerce. But in March 1904, over a strong dissent by Roosevelt's previously loyal appointee Oliver Wendell Holmes, the Supreme Court in *Northern Securities v. United States* attached "restraint of competition" to the Sherman Act, finding by a bare majority that by combining the shares of the Great Northern and Northern Pacific railroads into a single entity, and thus aligning the interests of their stockholders, the Northern Securities Company had suppressed competition and violated the law. Justice Harlan wrote for a plurality of the Court, joined by Justices Brown, McKenna, and Day; his opinion prevailed because Justice Brewer wrote a separate concurring opinion agreeing with its holding but not its reasoning. Justice Brewer set the stage for future antitrust law, rejecting the idea that all mergers that directly restrain interstate commerce were illegal and instead adopting a "rule of reason" approach; reasonable restraints might be legal, and each challenge would have to be determined on a case-by-case basis.

Wall Street was pleased; as the *New York Times* reported, share prices for both Northern Securities and the Union Pacific rose sharply the day after the decision was announced. Roosevelt's win was perceived by many Americans as a victory for the cause of competition and the role of the national government; the *New York Evening Post*, less tied to Wall Street than the *Times*, pronounced it a sharp limit on consolidation: "Surely the most far-reaching benefit of the decision is the vindication of national control."[39]

Roosevelt had it both ways; business was relieved and the public was proud. The government would be, at most, a neutral rule maker in the economic realm. After 1909 and until the 1940s, attempts at large regional mergers within the railway industry were blocked by the Department of Justice.

But as the railroads began experiencing economic difficulties, the Transportation Act of 1920 was passed, directing the ICC to create a plan for consolidation of the railway properties of the United States into a limited number of systems.[40] Although this mandate was withdrawn by Congress in the 1940s, in the end the Northern Pacific, Great Northern, and Chicago, Burlington and Quincy finally all merged in 1970 to form the Burlington Northern, effectively undoing the 1904 decision of the Supreme Court.[41] Warren Buffett now owns the consolidated Burlington Northern Santa Fe enterprise, the second-largest railroad in the country.

Roosevelt's efforts in this area were vitally interesting to the American public. Edmund Morris reports that "Washington resounded with praise, and predictions of four more Rooseveltian years" following the *Northern Securities* decision.[42] As a 1910 essay about Roosevelt by Ernest Hamlin Abbott (in Roosevelt's *The New Nationalism*) put it, the president had brought about enormous change in public opinion, moving it from a "hard, rather sordid, decidedly materialistic, very complacent," selfish point of view to a lively, aroused debate about "the whole problem of the control of public utilities," focused on the "welfare of the farmer" as well as the "welfare of the manufacturers." This great popular movement was made up of both public feeling and personal leadership "preeminently supplied" by Roosevelt. The president, with his deep affection for the American frontier, had often pointed out that a key characteristic of the frontiersman was his "freedom from provincialism, his feeling that every part of the United States is of concern to him, his desire to uphold the interests of all other Americans." The American people had cheered Roosevelt on.[43]

Roosevelt's answer to the lack of enforcement authority and gap in price-fixing capability given to the Interstate Commerce Commission was administrative oversight. As he said to Congress in his State of the Union Address of 1904, "The Government must in increasing degree supervise and regulate the workings of the railways engaged in interstate commerce; and such increased supervision is the only alternative to an increase of the present evils on one hand or a still more radical policy on the other."[44] The legislation he championed, the Hepburn Act of 1906, gave the ICC the power to set maximum rates and to forbid rebating. Because some rail-roads gave preferential rates to commodities in which they had a financial interest, the Hepburn Act also included a clause prohibiting railroads from hauling commodities they produced or owned, or in which they had a financial interest. Later, the Mann-Elkins Act of 1910 added to the ICC's arsenal the power to block proposed changes in shipping rates.[45]

The ICC was supposed to be an independent entity, operating separately from the legislature, administering technical matters in rates and facilities with a high degree of autonomy. The idea was that such an agency could better respond to changes in the relevant conditions with flexibility, preci-sion, and expertise; no broad legislative wording could accomplish this same goal as well. In the end, the regulation of railroads accomplished less than many had hoped. As the first regulatory agency, the ICC also became the first victim of regulatory capture: it was completely overrun by the industry it purported to regulate.

According to an article by Samuel Huntington ("The Marasmus of the ICC") published in the *Yale Law Journal* in 1952, the decade after the passage of the 1906 act was a golden era for the ICC; by the start of World War I, the Commission had eliminated the worst of the railroads' discriminatory prac-tices. But the railroads were nationalized during the war, and afterward they decided that "the path of wisdom was to accept regulation and to learn to live with the Commission." The shippers (the traditional enemies of the carri-ers) grew lax, less interested, less politically active. Farms were being wiped out by urbanization. And neither President Harding nor President Coolidge was interested in restrictive regulations. So the Commission looked for support in the only place it could find it: from the railroad industry itself. The railroad management group had all the information the Commission needed; it supported the growth of the Commission's agenda and defended the Commission against executive intrusions. As Huntington put it, "The attitude of the railroads towards the Commission since 1935 can only be described as one of satisfaction, approbation, and confidence. At times the railroads have been almost effusive in their praise of the Commission." Huntington charged that to shore up the railroad industry's support for its operations the ICC had permitted the railroads to raise rates, refused to investigate railroads, facilitated the reduction of competition, favored railroads over motor carriers, and generally acted in a passive, dilatory manner. Huntington recommended flatly that "the Interstate Commerce Commission . . . be abolished as an independent agency."[46] Coziness, mutual dependence, and stark asymmetry of information—the railways had all the data—had caused the ICC to deteriorate, and by the 1970s, it was on the way out: Congress passed several laws aimed at deregulating the shipping industry, which diminished the Commission's authority. In 1995, the ICC was abolished and its functions were transferred to the Surface Transportation Board within the Department of Transportation—not itself a model of disinterested civil oversight.[47]

Nonetheless, the idea of regulation by expert commission provided the rationale for the Federal Communications Commission (FCC), created in 1934 on the model of the ICC.[48] The ICC also established a central organizing principle for constraining the power of a private company serving public interests in basic transport and communications: common carriage.

"Common carriage" is an old idea. It is a label attached to private basic transportation and communication businesses that are "affected with the public interest." For hundreds of years, operators of ports, bridges, ferries, and the like operating through a license with the sovereign have historically had a duty to serve all comers and serve them equally. As long as companies in the business of providing basic transport and communications—such as taxi and telephone companies—portrayed themselves as serving the public, and as long as they were clearly in the business of taking parcels or conversations from Point A to Point B, they were obliged to serve all comers fairly and equally. By the 1870s, state legislatures making rules about railroad carriers had picked up on the traditional principle that industries "clothed with public interest"—companies that provided basic, essential transport and communications facilities—were subject to government oversight. The Interstate Commerce Act of 1887 gave the Interstate Commerce Commission explicit jurisdiction over "common carriers": if a shipping line or a railroad was ceded a natural monopoly, it had to offer to all comers equal service and submit its rates to the Commission for approval.[49]

Such nondiscrimination rules were applied to American telegraphy providers from the mid-nineteenth century on, and to telephony providers when they started business in the late nineteenth century. Regardless of whether the telegraph or telephone system was too small to have any chance of dominating a market, it was still obliged to serve every customer on equal, reasonable terms. It was a private business with public effects. It was conduit, not content. Common-carriage regimes give us confidence that we can trust private providers of essential communication services not to discriminate or censor; this framework facilitates competition (the free market has a field on which to operate), forwards personal and commercial freedoms—and lowers barriers to businesses by eliminating one-off negotiations for each transaction. The tradeoff for the carrier is that it avoids liability for the content of the packages (or messages) that it carries.

So when Congress (spurred primarily by the secret rebates, predatory pricing, and collusive activities of the railroads) added telephone systems to the Interstate Commerce Commission's responsibilities in 1910, it simply treated telephone and telegraph companies like railroads, declaring them all to be common carriers. Both railroads and telephones had been given access to extensive public lands and had benefited from the power of the state to condemn property for their use; in exchange, they had to offer their services without discrimination to all comers, and their rates would be set by the ICC.[50]

Congress knew that, in the telephone system, it was dealing with an essential basic business; by 1910, millions of Americans had already installed telephones.[51] And it was also dealing, indirectly, with J. P. Morgan, who had gained financial control of the Bell System by 1907 and was buying up independent phone companies by the dozens; the Bell System's corporate goal under Morgan became to obtain control of all profitable lines.[52] (Morgan knew a good natural monopoly when he saw one.)

Classifications like "common carriage" and legal obligations not to discriminate against particular uses of the phone network have historically been difficult to enforce. The company providing the conduit always wants to find ways to make more profit and drive out competition and will seek to collaborate with other service and content providers to do so. Morgan lost no time in ignoring the Mann-Elkins Act. A year earlier, in 1909, American Telephone & Telegraph had bought thirty thousand shares of Western Union stock, effectively gaining working control of the company that itself controlled 90 percent of the telegraph services market.[53] In 1911 and 1912, Western Union's tiny competitor, the Postal Telegraph Company (with a 10 percent market share) complained that Western Union was charging unreasonable and discriminatory prices to carry Postal-originated messages to their final destination.[54] But AT&T was doing even more than that.

On April 1, 1912, a *New York Times* reporter confirmed Postal's complaints that callers to the Bell Telephone Companies asking for Postal services were instead referred to Western Union. Across the United States, patrons trying to reach Postal experienced long delays and, in some cases, outright blocking by Bell operators. Operators routinely told patrons that the company they really wanted was Western Union, and that "Western Union would give faster service and the toll would be charged on the monthly telephone bill." Postal asserted that this was illegal discrimination: "The law requires a telephone company to treat both telegraph companies impartially and give equal service to both. . . . What, then, is to be said of a telephone monopoly that is using its monopolistic power to divert the legitimate business of the Postal Company to the monopoly's ally, the Western Union?" Postal demanded that Western Union be separated from Bell Telephone.[55] By 1914, following public uproar and additional complaints, AT&T had disposed of Western Union in order to avoid monopoly charges.[56]

Fast-forward to the present day: all the stages of the railroad story are repeated today in the context of Internet access: rebates are being offered by the carriers to giant "shippers" of content in the form of preferential fast lanes; the carriers have thoroughly consolidated and vertically integrated (just as the railroads had interests in commodities prior to the Hepburn Act and AT&T controlled Western Union); the efficiencies of consolidation have not led to lower prices for consumers; the lobbyists for Comcast and AT&T (our era's railroad lawyers) are making generous contributions to legislators; and inequality between the access of the rich and the access of the poor is growing.

Where it is not sufficiently profitable from a carrier's perspective to provide service, it won't. The rich are paying more for services, the poor can't afford the services at all, and the government is left trying to pick up the tab so that all Americans have access—which is more expensive for everyone.

Like the ICC in the early years of the twentieth century, the FCC is now subject to the concentrated influence of a determined industry and is laboring under enormous information asymmetries; like J. P. Morgan, the carriers treat government as (at most) a peer and will litigate unceasingly in support of their claim that any form of regulation will destroy their incentive to invest in infrastructure and innovation.

2

Regulatory Pendulum

THE LONG TWILIGHT STRUGGLE

In the rise of any new medium, a key factor is its relationship to the dominant technology of the day. Since organizations with a large stake in an
existing technology are likely to try to preserve their investment—in today's
idiom, they are reluctant to "cannibalize" their current business—any
policies or legal decisions that give them influence over the new medium
may retard its introduction.

—Paul Starr, *The Creation of the Media*

CABLE STARTED OUT AS A DISRUPTIVE BUSINESS. The first cable systems were
mom-and-pop operations consisting of wire strung from antennas on hill-
sides providing three or four channels of broadcast television to towns that
were too remote to pick up a signal. In the 1950s, these so-called community antenna television systems, or CATVs, were springing up everywhere.[1]
None of them was being regulated by the Federal Communications
Commission, which had virtually no information about CATV. But in the
summer of 1951 a lawyer running the Telephone Service System Facilities
Branch of the Common Carrier Bureau of the FCC, E. Stratford Smith,
was sent out to Pottsville, Pennsylvania, to interview a man named
Martin Malarkey about how CATV worked and how it should be treated as
a regulatory matter.[2] Was this new thing Malarkey was running, a service
called the Trans-Video Corporation, a common-carriage system like a telephone or a broadcast service receiving signals and delivering them to
homes?

In *Blue Skies: A History of Cable Television*, the communications professor Patrick R. Parsons reports that when Smith got back to Washington, he wrote a memo saying that Trans-Video could be treated as a common carrier, but the FCC deferred any action on the recommendation.[3] Smith eventually left the FCC to become counsel to the National Community Television Association (the ancestor of today's National Cable & Telecommunications Association), formerly the National Cable Television Association, which Malarkey had founded in the wake of Smith's visit. In the process of moving from regulator to member of a regulated industry, Smith also changed his opinion: no cable operator has ever wanted to be classified as a regulated common carrier.[4]

At first, over-the-air broadcasters ignored CATV, considering it a niche market that helped spread their signals farther. But as cable distributors began to sell their own ads, the broadcasters began to realize that cable's growth could undermine their profits. Cable-system technology had improved by the mid-1960s, making twelve-channel systems standard.[5] Cable owners used the additional channel territory to rebroadcast signals from distant markets and began exploring non-network, cable-only channels. Television-station owners argued that the cable operators' importation of distant signals reduced their audiences, while the owners whose signals were being imported complained that those signals had not been paid for.[6]

Broadcasters mounted an aggressive legal campaign against the cable industry at the FCC by way of complaints and lawsuits. In 1967, when Southwestern Cable was found to be transmitting Los Angeles broadcasting stations into San Diego, a local San Diego station complained to the FCC. The FCC decided the dispute in favor of the local station: even though its governing statute at the time said nothing about cable, the FCC reasoned that its authority to regulate and protect the nation's broadcasting system carried with it the power to regulate cable. Authority over cable's scope of business was "reasonably ancillary" to its existing powers. This interpretation of the FCC's powers had precedent: in 1965, in an effort to ensure that free over-the-air television was not destroyed by the advent of cable, the FCC had issued "must carry" rules requiring cable systems to carry the signals of local television stations. The Supreme Court upheld the

FCC's broad view of its statutory powers in 1968.[7] Thus, it appeared that the FCC had ancillary jurisdiction to regulate cable, too.

By the late 1960s, the broadcasting companies' view of cable had changed yet again. Now the cable providers were not simply pirating broadcast programming; under the right ownership, cable might provide additional outlets for network programming by reaching otherwise unreachable audiences. Adding to this impression, the Supreme Court in 1974 held that cable systems were not liable for copyright infringement when they retransmitted broadcast signals as long as they paid standardized license fees. This "compulsory license" helped the cable systems: it brought them access to programming without having to negotiate thousands of individual agreements with powerful, centralized broadcasters. The government intervention helped the insurgent cable business grow. It also ensured that the incumbent broadcasters would remain locked in a relationship with the cable operators.[8]

At about the same time, President Richard Nixon's Cabinet-level Committee on Cable Communications submitted a stern recommendation to the president. While the nascent cable industry had much to offer and the programming it transmitted should largely remain unregulated by the FCC, the risk of abuse by local monopoly cable providers was too great to be ignored. As the committee warned: "We recommend adoption of a policy that would separate the ownership and control of cable distribution facilities, or the means of communications, from the ownership and control of the programming or other information services carried on the cable channels."[9] The mainstream conservatives at the heart of the Nixon administration felt strongly that cable's "natural monopoly" of distribution facilities—it was so expensive to install that it made sense to have just one in each town—created a risk of the cable operators' becoming gate-keepers of information. Without a definitive separation between transport and programming, continuous oversight would be needed to ensure that the cable operators' physical monopoly power was not leveraged into editorial power over the availability of speech and information. A clear separation requirement between content and delivery would impose far less regulatory burden than the constant jockeying and influence peddling that would be involved in assessing whether programming was being fairly treated. Separation, in short, was the lesser of two regulatory evils.[10]

But the recommendation that a national policy be adopted that would affirmatively separate conduit from content—effectively turning cable into a common carrier—did not prevail. It was too difficult to get a bill through Congress that would do the job; no one involved had enough will to be clear. As the telecommunications scholar Monroe Price put it at the time, the implicit message back from Congress in response to the White House's draft bill was "to continue to allow the economic bargaining [between the cable industry and the FCC] to take place at the agency level, with Congress available as a last resort, not to be utilized except as an ultimate check on the performance of the Commission."[11]

Broadcasters have thus had a love-hate relationship with cable distributors since television became widespread. When broadcasters were powerful, they used their sway with the FCC to constrain the markets into which cable could bring distant broadcast programming and ensured that cable always carried their signals. The failure to separate conduit from content made it inevitable that broadcasters and cable companies would always be in conflict. Ultimately, both industries would later discover that there was more money to be made through cooperation than opposition.

Consumers, meanwhile, made little fuss about paying for television over a cable wire. As John Malone, the foremost U.S. cable executive of the 1990s, described the situation to the *Wall Street Journal* in 2009, "The way it was successful was blending together the transport service with the charge for the content. When you were a cable subscriber, you weren't sure whether you were paying for connectivity or whether you were paying for the content that was embodied in the connectivity."[12] The cable industry from the beginning had blended connectivity with content and did not allow subscribers to buy access to individual channels. But people loved the service, and over the years cable-designed bundles have served the industry well.

Another industry was afraid that cable companies might soon muscle into its business: the telephone companies. In the 1970s, the issue was not whether cable would replace telephone's voice service; that was decades away. It was something more mundane: whether cable could have access to the millions of telephone poles that phone companies had erected around the country. By the 1970s, 4.5 million Americans had subscribed to cable services. But AT&T was charging the cable companies a hefty fee for the right to use its telephone poles to string cable. At the time there was no particular economic reason for AT&T to refuse the cable companies access to its poles on reasonable terms. But no phone company wanted the cable broadcasters showing up in its neighborhood before it had had a chance to roll out its own video service, even though that service was years in the future.[13]

Representative Ed Markey of Massachusetts, who began his career in the House in 1976 just as the pole-attachment wars began, remembers being mystified by AT&T's attitude. "The phone companies were using their leverage over the poles to jack up prices. Sure, having twenty companies attach their lines to your poles might be a problem. But this wasn't about twenty companies. This was about one or two cable companies. I was amazed that it took invoking the machinery of government to get these guys [the cable companies] in the game." After three decades in the House, Markey is silver-haired but bright-eyed, his strong Boston accent undimmed by years of commuting to Washington, his shining tie descending expertly from a well-turned collar, his hands relaxed and expressive. He has been at the middle of telecom tussles for years—serving as either the chairman or the ranking member of the House Energy and Commerce Committee's Subcommittee on Telecommunications from 1987 to 2008. There he was the principal author of many of the laws now governing the nation's telephone, broadcasting, cable television, wireless, and broadband communications systems—all the while exuberantly holding hearings and handing out pungent quotes. In Markey's mind, pole attachments are a good example of the ongoing struggles between incumbents and new, disruptive actors who want to provide services to the public. As he put it, "The government is the midwife in helping technology get to the marketplace."[14]

Pole attachments had been an issue for cable companies from the beginning. Cable operators can reach houses and offices only by running wires along streets so that lines can be "dropped" to individual subscribers. Wires can be threaded through existing conduits or hung on poles, and in many places early cable-systems operators depended on access to poles that had been built by the local telephone utility. But the phone companies used their control over poles to gouge cable systems, often by doubling or tripling the rates they charged electrical utilities and other phone companies.[15] The FCC took up the issue in 1967 and was asked to expedite the inquiry by the NCTA in 1970.[16] But six years later the FCC decided that it did not have clear jurisdiction over the issue and tossed it over to Congress.[17]

After a great deal of wrangling, in 1978 Congress passed a law requiring that where phone companies gave the cable industry access to their poles they would have to do it on reasonable terms to be set by the FCC. These pole-attachment rules are a good example of government intervention enabling a new market. The law gave cable a subsidy—in the form of a preferential rate on access to telephone poles—that is still in place today.[18]

In the ensuing decades, cable ceased to be a mute pipe for distributing existing content to places with poor reception and became a source of programming. There was a great deal of investment in cable infrastructure to tie together cities and towns, and many new networks cropped up that were delivered solely over cable. But cable operators often overextended themselves and lacked the money to maintain or enhance their networks; they had to raise their prices, and customers complained. Companies began to consolidate, and throughout the 1970s and 1980s, cable distributors fought for control over exclusive municipal franchises. Dozens went out of business.[19]

Meanwhile, the rules that were supposed to govern the relationships between cable and broadcast, and between cable and telephone, were not altogether clear—and regulators began to worry this could be a problem as the market expanded and the technology progressed. There was a patchwork of authority drawn from federal and state sources, and municipalities and city councils were finding creative ways to be persuaded by cable operators to grant exclusive franchises. As Paul Baran, the father of packet-based communications, described the situation in a 1999 speech, "When the economics of cable allowed extending cable to the cities, there was a bidding war for the franchises. All sorts of games were played at the time, including rent-a-citizen, giving out cheap stock to bribe local political figures, etc."[20] Cities made exorbitant demands for "sweetened" bids, and

city officials sometimes used their power to have part of the local cable
company's profits assigned personally to them; in return, cable-system
operators sought affiliations with well-known locals ("rent-a-citizen") to
bolster their bids and promised cities whatever they asked for—services to
libraries and schools, community channels, and interactive systems that
often were never built.[21]

In an attempt to bring order to a complex system of federal and state
requirements and to make the franchising process more certain for the
cable operators—and in response to concerns expressed by state officials
and federal representatives about the discretion and opportunity for corruption inherent in the patchwork of cable-franchising rules—Congress passed
the Cable Communications Policy Act of 1984. The FCC had been concerned throughout the 1970s about local franchising decisions but felt that
it could not impose uniformity without legislative authorization.

The centerpiece of the law was a provision that only locations without
"effective competition" for cable—which the FCC determined to mean
locations that did not have at least three over-the-air broadcast channels—
would be subject to rate regulation. For everywhere else (about 97 percent
of the country) the act lifted price controls at the end of 1986, freeing
the cable industry to charge whatever the market could bear for its local
monopoly services. The only rates that remained regulated were those for
"basic packages," but cable operators were free to remove from "basic" tiers
any channels that were not subject to the "must carry" rules. In effect, this
meant almost anything other than the broadcast networks. In short, the
FCC's definition of competition meant that cable systems were deregulated
by the end of the decade.[22]

The Cable Communications Policy Act was a triumph for the cable
companies, for in addition to deregulating rates it also prohibited phone
companies from competing in the cable business. (Even with the breakup
of AT&T at about the same time, people believed that the local incumbent
Baby Bells could act anticompetitively toward the emerging cable industry
if they were given a chance to offer programming.) Monopoly without
oversight made the cable companies attractive to Wall Street. Almost every
municipality in America had already given a cable company an exclusive
franchise, and those companies were poised to make enormous profits.

As things turned out, the broadcast networks did not provide the "effective competition" that was supposed to constrain cable rates, even if there were many municipalities that had enough over-the-air signals to meet the FCC's requirements. Indeed, no business was in a position to constrain these rates; today's satellite pay-TV services that market directly to consumers had not yet been launched. The cable industry did invest in upgrades that improved the country's overall data infrastructure, but this did not improve day-to-day service for many smaller customers. Although in later years the cable industry began providing new services or other inducements to retain customers when rates went up, in the heady days of 1980s deregulation cable companies simply raised their prices.[23]

By 1990, John Malone's giant Tele-Communications, Inc. (TCI), a Denver business he took over in 1972, was the largest cable distributor in the country, with 8.5 million subscribers, about a fifth of the market.[24] TCI had grown through Malone's tough, shrewd management as well as acquisitions and partnerships; as Ken Auletta reported in a 1994 *New Yorker* profile of Malone, a dollar invested in TCI in 1975 was worth eight hundred dollars in 1989.[25] Believing that cable would grow by offering content that was unavailable from free over-the-air carriers, Malone had cut deals with networks like CNN, ESPN, HBO, and MTV that gave TCI the best discounts for programming in exchange for guaranteed distribution to TCI subscribers. Meanwhile, TCI's rates soared, even as customer service plummeted.[26]

Malone's maneuverings made it clear that it was time to rein in the cable industry. Regulators began to notice that competition from broadcasting services was not keeping cable prices down. TCI's power to obtain programming at the lowest rates going and to control the fate of new programming services was apparent. According to Mark Robichaux's excellent biography of Malone, in 1986 TCI paid ninety cents a subscriber a month for HBO, the largest pay channel of the time, while small cable operators had to pay more than five times that rate.[27] Malone had programmers over a barrel: without access to TCI's portion of the market, cable-network programmers could not be certain of getting enough distribution to attract the national advertising that would make the network viable. Then-senator Al Gore called Malone "a monopolist bent on dominating the television marketplace"; "he called me Darth Vader and the leader of the cable Cosa Nostra," Malone later recalled.[28]

In self-defense, Malone pointed to cable's investment in infrastructure, its wide variety of programming, and consumers' affection for their cable service. He insisted that he wanted to plow his profits back into growth and investment that would bring communications into the twenty-first century—if only Washington would stay out of the way. Big wasn't bad, he reminded Congress in the early 1990s. On the contrary, to have a world-class cable industry, big was necessary; this was a business that depended on scale and scope. But suspecting that government regulators wanted to break TCI into separate content and distribution businesses, Malone preempted them: he spun off most of his content interests into a new company, Liberty Media.[29]

The core issue of rate hikes for cable services remained. The General Accounting Office (now the Government Accountability Office) sent a report in 1991 to Representative Markey, then chairman of the Subcommittee on Telecommunications and Finance of the House Committee on Energy and Commerce, showing that the cable industry had taken advantage of price deregulation by raising rates for the most popular basic-service package by more than 37 percent in real terms since 1986. During a single fifteen-month period alone—from the beginning of 1990 until April 1991—the monthly rates for that package had risen by 15 percent while the average number of channels per package had decreased. Consumers were paying more for less.[30]

In response to public anger over the cable operators' abusive pricing and practices, the FCC suggested that six over-the-air stations (rather than three) would now be needed to show effective competition in markets where cable penetration was less than 50 percent before cable operators would be exempt from price regulation. But Congress objected to the FCC's attempts to regulate without its own explicit authority; the Cable Communications Policy Act had firmly reinserted Congress into the equation, and the legislature acted again to ensure that the FCC would exert no more "ancillary" authority without the go-ahead from Capitol Hill. Markey and Senator John Danforth, in particular, believed that cable operators were running a scandalously abusive business: rates were skyrocketing, customer service was poor, and the growing vertical integration between cable programming and cable distribution was suppressing competition from satellite-based systems. Markey and Danforth doubted that regulators could rein it in alone, and they hoped that consumers' anger over cable rates would be powerful enough to support a large-scale legislative effort. After prolonged wrangling, the two struck a remarkable deal.[31]

The 1992 Cable Television Consumer Protection and Competition Act

Even as cable rates for consumers rose in the late 1980s, the cable industry argued that it needed continued protection from competition from AT&T to enable it to grow large enough to reach all Americans. At the same time, access to programming controlled by the cable distributors was an increasingly contentious issue: satellite-service providers, who were just getting started, would have a hard time surviving unless cable distributors were required to give them access to their programming on reasonable terms. Meanwhile, the broadcasters, who were looking for new revenue streams to supplement their traditional advertising-supported model, wanted to be able to charge cable for the privilege of redistributing their very popular content.[32]

With all these factors to consider, Senator Danforth and Representative Markey envisioned a deal that would finally bring real reform to the industry. The phone companies were looking to get into cable someday (by entering what they then called the "video dialtone" market), and their competition might force the cable industry to ensure that cable programming was made available to satellite companies (and presumably, someday, to phone companies too). Consumer advocates, while not eager to see telephone companies using their monopoly status to sell video, did want to see an end to exclusive cable franchises and a firm reregulation of cable prices, and they were willing to cooperate with the phone companies to achieve this. They could also find common cause with broadcasters who wanted to ensure that cable paid more than a standard license fee for their network programming.[33]

Here was a unique chance to do something big: Congress could tackle cable exclusivity, help satellite services, give broadcasters a chance to make some deals, and impose price regulation on cable, all in one legislative swoop. Senator Danforth introduced the bill, called the Cable Television Consumer Protection and Competition Act, on January 14, 1991; Representative Markey launched the same bill in the House, calling it "a pro-consumer, pro-competition bill designed to rein in the renegades in the cable industry who are gouging consumers with repeated rate increases."[34] What made the deal work was adding the broadcasters into the mix—the phone and satellite providers could make the argument that their competition benefited consumers and the still-powerful broadcasters, acting in their own interest, could push the bill through.

The only problem was that the first Bush administration was pushing a deregulatory agenda, and taking shots at cable did not fit in with that goal. In mid-September 1992 the cable industry launched a full-out campaign to defeat the bill, including ads in the *New York Times* and the *Washington Post* claiming that broadcasters were trying to "add a 20 percent tax to your basic cable bill" and that any money raised in this manner would "go right into the broadcaster's pockets."[35] Nearly four hundred cable executives traveled to Washington to appeal to their representatives to vote against the bill and sustain the expected presidential veto if it passed. *Broadcasting and Cable,* an industry magazine, reported that "congressmen were being bombarded by calls and letters stirred up by the industry's massive media campaign against the bill."[36] After the bill passed, President Bush dutifully vetoed it in October 1992, but the Democratic Congress overrode him—for the first and last time during the Bush presidency.[37]

The resulting legislation, the 1992 Cable Television Consumer Protection and Competition Act, reregulated cable rates, brought competition from the telephone companies into local cable service, helped the fledgling satellite industry gain access to cable programming, and gave the broadcast industry "retransmission consent": the right to ask the cable companies to pay it for broadcasters' programming. The central thing that *did not* happen—the thing that John Malone had feared regulators *would* do, that Nixon's appointees had urged, and that FCC lawyers had considered appropriate in the 1950s—was to separate content from distribution, forcing companies with de facto municipal monopolies over distribution to act as common carriers. In the end, the act created a thicket of rules that the cable industry has been able to sidestep through relentless litigation and creative interpretation. And cable companies have consolidated through a long series of trades, acquisitions, and deals: where once there were thousands of cable operators with a few systems each, now there are just a few serving millions and staying out of one another's territory. By far the biggest of these is Comcast.

Meanwhile, the telephone industry was pursuing its own video market. The pole-attachment wars of the 1970s demonstrated the leverage AT&T could use to protect its existing market power. AT&T was not pressured by competition at that point; it controlled the U.S. telephone system through its equipment-manufacturing arm (Western Electric), its long-distance arm (Long Lines), and its twenty-two local Bell Operating Companies.

In the late 1970s and early 1980s, AT&T was making it difficult for new competitors to get a toehold in a variety of markets by using its power over local and long-distance service as well as its control of the telephone poles. John DeButts, then the president of AT&T, testified at a 1976 hearing before the House Subcommittee on Communications that if someone were to plug non-AT&T equipment into the AT&T network, the entire system might collapse.[38] AT&T also made it difficult for long-distance competitors: MCI tried to connect its microwave-based system (which used the airwaves instead of wired phone connections) to AT&T's local monopoly networks, but AT&T refused; its Long Lines division had a lock on this business.[39]

MCI first filed suit in 1974, to be joined by the Department of Justice later that year. It was not until the beginning of 1981, with the support of William Baxter, President Reagan's first antitrust chief, that the case finally went to trial. Even then, AT&T did its best to stop the case during the summer of 1981 through both pressure from its allies in the White House (Commerce Secretary Malcolm Baldrige and Defense Secretary Casper Weinberger were widely reported to be in favor of dropping the lawsuit— Weinberger's argument was that an integrated AT&T was good for national security)[40] and through legislation: HR 5158 would have forced the Antitrust Division to drop the case by legislating a less onerous solution to AT&T's monopoly power than divestiture. Markey was unable to prevent HR 5158 from leaving the Energy and Commerce Committee in the House, and the bill was subsequently referred to the Judiciary Committee. There Chairman Peter Rodino sat on it, a brave decision, given that his home state of New Jersey was also AT&T's home state. Markey mounted the House of Representatives equivalent of a filibuster in 1980 to stop AT&T's efforts to pass HR 5158. As he told me in an interview, "I came to see that AT&T's resistance to innovation was at their heart." His delaying tactics included demanding a reading of the complete bill (a formality that is usually waived) and the introduction of more than fifty amendments on which he forced debate. "We dragged it out so long that time eventually ran out."[41]

The Reagan Justice Department's antitrust suit continued despite staunch opposition from within the administration. Finally, in 1982, Baxter persuaded AT&T to spin off its local companies and re-form them into seven independent regional Bell Operating Companies (RBOCs, pronounced "ARE-box"), a long-distance company (which retained the AT&T name), and Western Electric. The court document setting forth the terms of the breakup, the Modified Final Judgment (MFJ), was finally implemented in 1984 under the jurisdiction of Judge Harold Greene of the Federal District Court for the District of Columbia.[42]

The breakup of AT&T worked, mostly. It allowed MCI and new competitor GTE Sprint to offer long-distance phone service, creating a more competitive marketplace. Meanwhile, however, the RBOCs were prevented under the MFJ from providing long-distance or computer-processing services and from manufacturing telephone equipment.[43]

The MFJ limitations did not last long. Just three years after the corporate reorganization called for by the MFJ was finished, the RBOCs arranged for the introduction of legislation, the Swift-Tauke bill, that would let them back into these markets. Markey did his best to keep the bill from being voted on; he repeatedly introduced discussion drafts that kept the clock ticking, in an attempt to run out the clock. "I wanted those Baby Bells to develop their own independent lives," he said. He remained focused on the importance of competition: "I thought that innovation would spring out of the best regulatory environment, one that honored competition. The longer we could avoid the mother-and-child reunion, the more innovation we'd be able to bring into the marketplace." He managed to stave off the mother-and-child reunion in 1987, but in 1993 the Baby Bells succeeded in getting the MFJ's limitation on their ability to perform computer-processing tasks lifted through a successful appeal at the D.C. Circuit Court of Appeals. Judge Greene issued a fifty-three-page opinion following a remand from the Appeals Court, forcefully expressing his view that the Baby Bells were anticompetitive and should not be permitted to generate the content of information services. As Judge Greene put it, "Were the Court free to exercise its own judgment, it would conclude without hesitation that removal of the information services restriction is incompatible with the [MFJ] and the public interest." But the Department of Justice had recommended elimination of the restriction and the Court of Appeals had mandated that Judge Greene lift it. With the passage of time the Baby Bells had amassed the political capital they had wanted: they were ready to rid themselves of Judge Greene's control through legislation.[44]

In response, Markey offered a bill in which the telephone companies could be allowed into video services and long-distance services but would have to open their networks up to competition. Markey's bill, which passed the House in June 1994 by a vote of 423 to 5, required the phone companies to open up the "local loop" (the lines between a central switching station and individual houses) to competitors. It preempted state laws against competition with local phone companies and also included a provision to unbundle equipment with cable service. And it let the phone industry into the cable business. Phone would do cable; cable would do phone; manufacturers would be allowed into a new area of competition. All parties—cable as well as phone—would get what they wanted, but in exchange they would have to submit to the marketplace.[45]

When the Republicans took control of both houses of Congress in the 1994 election, however, the bill had to be reintroduced on a bipartisan basis. Many Republicans had already voted for it, so it became the first section of another bill. The other sections of the new bill were not quite what Markey had wanted: Title 2 once more deregulated cable pricing, and Title 3 deregulated other media. Now in the minority, Markey and his team battled on, getting amendments added and changes made, eventually reaching the point at which the bill, though not as strong as the 1994 draft, nonetheless would launch greater competition. It is now known as the 1996 Telecommunications Act.[46]

The 1996 Telecommunications Act

Here are the conditions that shaped the 1996 act: the Baby Bells were demanding permission to compete with the cable companies and to offer long-distance services. The cable companies were finding ways to continue to overcharge consumers. Consumers wanted competition for local phone service. And congressional power now belonged to the Republicans.

The 1996 act set up a grand bargain: it tried to force competition into all telecommunications markets while also deregulating them. The Bells had to give smaller companies access to their circuits, and the cable companies had to allow the Bells to compete with them for cable service. Local telephone companies could now offer long-distance service outside their own service areas, but in order to offer long distance inside their service areas, they had to prove that they had opened their local phone markets to competition. Rate regulation for cable systems was ended other than for the "basic tier" of programs; the theory was that stiffer competition from telephone companies (now in the video business) would constrain rates.[47]

Congress did leave in place an FCC requirement that limited the percentage of the market that one cable provider could control up to 30 percent of all pay-TV subscribers. The FCC argued that the 30-percent-ownership limit was "generally appropriate to prevent the nation's largest MSOs [multiple systems operators—that is, the cable companies] from gaining enhanced leverage from increased horizontal concentration," while ensuring that "the majority of MSOs continue[d] to expand and benefit from the economies of scale necessary to encourage investment in new video programming services and the deployment of advanced cable technologies."[48]

What the act did not do was keep the cable companies from clustering their operations ("you take Minnesota, I'll take Sacramento") or the telephone companies from consolidating. Even before it passed, two of the Baby Bells, NYNEX and Bell Atlantic, were rumored by the *Wall Street Journal* to be considering a merger. Within a few years, the Baby Bells were merging rapidly: SBC bought Pacific Telesis, then Bell Atlantic and NYNEX merged. There was activity in long-distance markets as well: AT&T bought Teleport, and MCI bought a metropolitan fiber network called MFS. Bell Atlantic merged with GTE and renamed itself Verizon.

SBC bought Ameritech. By 2005 America was effectively left with two wired companies—Verizon and SBC.[49]

At the same time, MCI and the old AT&T (still in long distance) kept trying to enter local markets and were having a hard time. They faced a firestorm of litigation over the regulations the FCC had created to force incumbents to share their facilities with their competitors. Essentially, the Baby Bells used the courts to avoid the act's requirement that they open up their local networks to competition. The ensuing litigation went on for ten years. When it was over, the 1996 effort to open up phone lines to competition was widely considered a failure. In the end, the D.C. Circuit and the FCC so softened SBC's obligation to lease its facilities that AT&T had effectively no chance to get into local competition with the Baby Bells. The regulators had been thoroughly out-lawyered.[50]

AT&T gave up and announced in January 2005 that it would be bought by SBC—and bringing everything full circle, SBC renamed the new entity AT&T. Verizon acquired MCI at the same time. Both Verizon and SBC claimed that they could increase efficiency by combining long-distance with local phone services, but whether those cost savings would be passed along to consumers was not clear. The new AT&T, as an integrated company, saw "positive indications of pricing stability" after the merger. In other words, competition would not be a problem.[51]

What had happened to the competition that the 1996 law was supposed to foster? The act's fundamental assumption, that open platforms and alternative technologies would undermine the market power of the incumbent carriers over basic communications platforms—and that behavioral regulations on these actors would make structural limitations unnecessary—has proven overly optimistic. Although the phone companies were supposed to allow competing carriers to share their facilities, and the cable companies were supposed to compete with the phone companies to provide distribution of video content, data, and phone services, the opposite happened. On the phone side, without limits on mergers, consolidation and litigation foiled the act's open-access mandates. At the same time, cross-technology competition between phone and cable turned out to be weak: when it came to wired access, the incumbent cable operators had unbeatable economic advantages over the phone companies.

Internet access, a service provided by both phone and cable companies, could have disrupted all these giant companies' efforts to block competition, if only the open-access mandates of the act had held firm. But the mergers were not what undermined the power of Internet access to eliminate the gatekeeping role that the carriers enjoyed. It was the FCC itself.

Michael Powell, chairman of the FCC from 2001 to 2005 and now the leader of the cable industry's trade association, has an easy speaking style. He is clearly aware of the overstated rhetoric that often characterizes titanic battles over telecommunications policy and is happy to follow suit in his tone and choice of words. He raises his eyebrows, speaks blazingly fast, makes his points lightly, and, having made them, moves on. He often told reporters that he was enjoying being the FCC chairman, and he seemed to mean it.

Powell was born in 1963 in Birmingham, Alabama, and as the only son of General Colin Powell, he heard the call to public duty at a young age. Scholarly by temperament but convinced of the importance of the armed forces, he enlisted in the army after college and suffered a broken back when the jeep he was in crashed in a rainstorm and rolled over on him; he was flown back to Washington and spent more than a year recuperating. Law school, an appellate clerkship, private practice, and a stint as chief of staff at the Antitrust Division of the Department of Justice launched his public career. During the Clinton administration he was named an FCC commissioner, and he became chairman when his party came to power in January 2001.

Powell is a genuine student of technology who was convinced early on of the transformative power of the Internet. He downloaded Skype as soon as it was released. On his arrival at the FCC, he was shocked to find that 40 percent of the staff engineers were close to retirement. Powell brought an intellectual, inquiring joy to his role at the Commission, setting up "FCC University" to ensure that all staff members understood the technologies and economic questions they were dealing with. As he explained in 2002, "I wanted the FCC University to be the very best employee development program that anyone can find in the US government."[52] Robert

Pepper, who served as a policy adviser to six FCC chairmen between 1989 and 2005, said during the Powell chairmanship, "Out of the modern chairmen, Michael Powell is the most technologically sophisticated. He absolutely understands the power of technology. He invested in technology at the FCC—we hired new engineers, we revitalized the technology side of the FCC."[53]

Powell's focus at the FCC was to move the agency away from what he liked to call the one-wire problem. As he saw it, for decades telephone service was provided by a single, integrated monopoly—Bell Telephone—whose services had to be regulated to avoid price gouging. In exchange for the grant of that monopoly, the company was obligated to provide certain social goods, like making sure that everyone had a telephone connection and agreeing to serve everyone on reasonable and nondiscriminatory terms.

This was the right approach when there was only "one wire" going into each home. But Powell believed that other technologies, such as cable and perhaps wireless, would become viable competitors to the telephone, creating the possibility of multiple wires competing to provide a range of services. The problem, he thought, was that the regulatory structure had not yet adapted to this new reality.[54]

Powell's view, which he shared with many conservative economists in the early 2000s, was that when it came to Internet access, competition was not defined as different companies with the same technology vying for customers. Rather, different media—cable, wireless, satellite, and possibly "broadband over powerline" (using electrical connections to send data transmissions)—would compete, thereby providing the constraints on monopoly power that had once been imposed by regulatory structures. Instead of having the government force the key incumbent distribution network—before 1996, the telephone network—to make its poles and lines available to competitors providing Internet access, the distributors (now including wireless and cable as well as phone companies) would compete with one another to serve consumers. The result: protection for consumers against abusive pricing and monopoly-quality service without heavy-handed government regulation.

Powell's goal, then, was to facilitate the creation of multiple communications companies and technologies that would be able to reach homes and provide high-speed access to the Internet. Even a company with a monopoly over, say, cable would still have to compete with telephone and other companies. The existence of multiple deregulated platforms would drive down the price of connectivity and unleash innovation.[55]

In the long run, Powell's prediction proved wrong. Cable's advantages eventually became unbeatable: more than 90 percent of new wired Internet access subscriptions now go to the local cable incumbent, not the phone company, while wireless access is an entirely separate market.[56] But for a few years in the early 2000s, things worked out as he had anticipated: cable systems offered high-speed Internet access and made a few of their channels available for two-way transmissions running over the same hybrid coaxial fiber that brought the cable content into the home: cable-modem service. The development of the cable-modem service in turn drove the phone companies to improve their version of Internet access service over their metal lines: digital subscriber lines, or DSL. These services were clear competitors, at least initially, as they gave consumers access to the Internet at roughly similar speeds.[57]

This is where the problems began. The different modalities raised a regulatory conundrum: was high-speed Internet access via cable analogous to high-speed Internet over the phone, and therefore in need of the same common-carriage regulations? Or was it something new that should be left unregulated? Powell had another problem in creating a level playing field: if the two services were functionally indistinguishable, why should they be regulated in different ways?

The cable companies were confident they had the answer. Cable had never been regulated as a common-carriage service in the past; phone had been. It would stifle innovation, cable operators claimed, to treat cable-modem Internet access as a common-carriage system, even if the services provided were functionally the same as those of phone companies.[58]

Powell is by nature a free-market advocate, and he was frustrated by the weight of federal common-carriage regulation under Title II of the 1996 Telecommunications Act. He could not imagine why access to the Internet should be hampered by outmoded regulation. He would point out to any-one who would listen that the 1996 act took as gospel a model in which the technology of any infrastructure is understood to be integrated with the use made of the technology: if a company is running copper wires and providing voice services, for example, it falls under Title II of the 1996 act and is regulated as a common carrier; if it is running coaxial fiber wires and providing entertainment, it is a cable service and falls under Title VI; if it is a broadcaster using the airwaves, it falls under Title III. He felt that these distinctions were fine for old technologies. But they made no sense from a regulatory perspective when it came to Internet access. "When AT&T provides voice, video, and data over the same set of wires," Powell said, "you have a mess on your hands."[59]

Powell believed that when it came to high-speed Internet access via cable modems, he had a choice. He could take the existing Title II common-carriage requirements (nondiscrimination, sharing of connections) and "forbear" from—refuse to enforce heavily—the most onerous requirements, until only the portion of the regulation appropriate for high-speed Internet access was left. Or he could decide what social policies were truly needed (emergency service availability via 911 functionality, assistance to law enforcement) and apply regulations concerning them to high-speed Internet access one by one. As a free-market advocate, he was much happier "regulating up," starting with a blank, unregulated slate, than "deregulating down," starting with the multiple requirements of Title II. "Deregulating down" would require hundreds of pages of "forbearance" findings, a process he found distasteful and wasteful.

Powell had to act: cable-modem Internet access service was already in use, but it was in regulatory limbo. There had been a tussle since 1998 over how to treat it, but by the end of 2001 the Federal Communications Commission had not expressed a view except through one-off assertions in merger reviews. Powell's approach to this question set the United States on the road toward the titanic battles of 2010. Thanks to his bottom-up approach, the essential communications network of our time, access to the Internet, has no basic regulatory oversight at all.

The history of communications regulation in the late-twentieth and twenty-first centuries depended on one basic distinction: regulators have traditionally treated the transport of communications as a common-carriage service—open to all, subject to oversight to prevent discrimination, and bound by requirements to connect to other networks. Everything else, including data-processing services, was treated as a non-common-carrier "information service." When computers came into use in the 1960s and 1970s, the FCC was careful to draw a line between computer processing (information service) and the transport of data by the carriers (common-carriage service). The FCC did this as a regulatory matter to avoid giving the carriers power, in their gatekeeping role, over data processing. It would have been easy for the carriers to cross-subsidize and dominate data-processing businesses with their monopoly profits, and the FCC was trying to prevent that; it also wanted to avoid burdening the new computer services with the heavy superstructure of common-carriage regulation—rate-making, tariffs, and so on. Carriers were therefore prohibited from offering computing services. They were eventually (in 1980) allowed into this business, but only if they sold their basic transport services separately and without discrimination. The assumption was that carriers would keep selling basic transport under common-carriage rules.[60]

The 1984 AT&T divestiture was, in turn, designed to ensure that local phone companies would not be allowed to leverage their provision of local service into control over long distance. Under the supervision of Judge Greene, AT&T agreed to sell its Bell operating companies, which in turn agreed not to sell long-distance services, sell or manufacture telephone equipment, or—most important—get into the data-processing business. Then, in 1993, the restrictions on the RBOCs on providing data-processing services (or information services, as we now call them) ended (over Judge Greene's strong objections). This was a big victory for the carriers, and they wanted to cement it into statute. Shortly thereafter, drafting began on the 1996 act, which was aimed at removing communications-policy jurisdiction from Judge Greene's courtroom altogether and moving it to the expert agency—the FCC—while leaving in place the FCC definitions that had separated data processing from common-carriage transport during the proceedings in the 1970s and 1980s.[61]

From 2000 to 2002, as Powell considered how to classify cable-modem Internet access services—which seemed to have characteristics of both DSL services and traditional cable services—the courts went ahead without him. The Ninth Circuit Court of Appeals decided that cable-modem services were indeed "telecommunications service" providers under the act and so were required to not discriminate and to interconnect; in other words, they were common carriers, similar to the old telephone companies.[62]

The FCC then declared—after the court had already spoken—that cable-modem service was an information service.[63] A data-processing service. This meant it would not be regulated. The FCC asked the Department of Justice to appeal the Ninth Circuit Court's decision, hoping to get the ruling reversed, which led to a Supreme Court decision during the summer of 2005, the *Brand X* case. As a legal matter, the FCC took the view that the Commission had been handed an ambiguous statute and had done its best to interpret it; the FCC should not be obligated to apply common-carriage principles to all possible carriers, even those the public viewed as providing general-purpose communications-transport services.

The Supreme Court deferred to the FCC's interpretations of "information service" and "telecommunications," as well as its deregulatory application of those interpretations to high-speed Internet access, overruling the Ninth Circuit Court's inconvenient opinion to the contrary. (This conclusion frustrated Justice Scalia, who issued a stinging dissent, possibly informed by his service as staff to the White House Office of Telecommunications Policy during the Nixon era. He contended that transmission is transmission and that it can be seen as separate from everything else.)[64] Shortly thereafter, the FCC declared DSL Internet access service an information service, leaving DSL providers (like cable-modem providers) free to act as they pleased, even to discriminate in pricing and access. Only voice communications over copper telephone wires were still subject to common-carriage obligations—and those services were rapidly losing their popularity.[65] The upshot was that all high-speed Internet access service was completely deregulated.

This move created a risk that the carriers would be able to price discriminate—choosing which online services to prioritize based on, say, their affiliation with the service. Carriers could thus ensure that people who wanted to pay more for particular content were able to do so ("capture consumer surplus")—which, from the carriers' perspective, would facilitate investment in additional high-speed Internet access facilities around the country. But consumer advocates worried that price discrimination and prioritization could mean that the carriers would be able to decide which uses of their networks were permitted— a power that could inhibit innovation, economic growth, and competition generally. Incumbents always want to block competitors. From the advocates' perspective, the Powell Commission's regulatory gymnastics served the interests of the enormous incumbent network providers by shielding them from traditional common-carrier obligations that would have allowed upstart businesses to thrive.[66]

To mollify its critics, during the summer of 2005 the FCC issued an Internet Policy Statement that outlined "four freedoms" for Internet users: access to content, access to applications, choice of devices, and competition among service providers.[67] But two of the commissioners deemed this statement unenforceable, and the policy statement itself was subject to "reasonable network management" and the "needs of law enforcement"— unclear concepts at best.[68] Given these caveats and the lack of clarity surrounding the policy's legal status, it is not surprising that people who were already worried about the future of the open Internet were not satisfied.[69]

The "net neutrality" fights that followed Powell's deregulation of high-speed Internet access were fierce and included several prolonged and painful attempts to pass and defeat legislation. But the most important thing that happened next was a discovery by an Associated Press reporter and the Electronic Frontier Foundation (EFF).

During the fall of 2007, many Comcast users began to notice that their ability to share digital files over BitTorrent, an Internet protocol that allows people to share digital files without hosting or streaming the entire file, had been compromised. Most blamed their own computers, or the weather, or a number of other elements. Few guessed that their network access provider was blocking their ability to share video files; even if such a thing were possible, it would not have seemed right. But Robb Topolski, a barbershop-quartet enthusiast (and Intel engineer), and researchers at EFF decided to check out the disruptions more systematically.

BitTorrent works by cutting large files into pieces and allowing other users (peers) to make those pieces available across transport networks, enabling even users of devices with limited bandwidth (such as early mobile phones) to share large data files, like video. The process results in servers being contacted hundreds of times a second, a detail that Topolski and the EFF thought might provide an opportunity for someone to inter-fere. Independently setting up controlled experiments and trying to down-load a copy of the King James Bible and other non-copyrighted works, Topolski and the EFF discovered that Comcast was effectively telling both sides of a BitTorrent communication, "Sorry, I have to hang up now," and forcing the communication to terminate. Comcast was "hanging up" on attempts to use the BitTorrent protocol.[70]

When Topolski's story was published in the Associated Press, it had a sensational impact.[71] Net neutrality supporters had long suspected such corporate interference, and here was their smoking gun—and, in fact, the gun was still being fired every day. Comcast was throttling BitTorrent video traffic that conspiracy-minded technologists thought might be competing with Comcast's own video plans.

Kevin Martin, then the chairman of the FCC, was known for his relent-less pressure on the cable industry. He went after Comcast during two public hearings that further added to the uproar.[72] (Martin has become known in telecom circles more for his Machiavellian political hijinks than for his policies. This reputation doesn't do him justice; he clearly took action vis-à-vis the cable industry.) At the end of the summer of 2008, Martin announced that Comcast's practices amounted to unreasonable network management under the FCC's 2005 Internet Policy Statement. The Commission imposed no injunction or fine but insisted that Comcast promise to adopt a protocol-agnostic method of network management by the end of 2008.[73]

Comcast could have let matters stand; the Commission would have continued muddling along under its assumption that it could regulate high-speed Internet access providers (to some extent, at least) under the non-common-carriage Title I of the Telecommunications Act and its dubious Internet Policy Statement. But Comcast was bothered by having to account to the Commission for its network-management practices—to Comcast, the FCC's action appeared to be ad hoc, unprincipled, and based on little more authority than its assertion that the Commission was in charge. Comcast sued, and in April 2010 it won.[74]

The D.C. Circuit Court of Appeals found that there was nothing in the 1996 act to which the FCC's Comcast adjudication was "reasonably ancillary." Congress simply had not delegated power to the FCC to regulate network-access providers that the Commission had already labeled as deregulated. That label, it turned out, made a major difference. Powell's desire to "regulate up" (starting from scratch) rather than "regulate down" (by classifying these services as Title II and then restraining the Commission from applying rate regulation and other old-fashioned rules) had proven to be unenforceable; the D.C. Circuit Court ruled that the Commission had no delegated power over Comcast's behavior after it had expressly declined to regulate in this area. The FCC suddenly found itself to be a regulator with no clear regulatory authority over the central communications medium of the age: Internet access.

In short, the Commission had taken the basic idea in the Telecommunications Act—that general-purpose two-way networks should be labeled common carriers, obliged to treat everyone equally—and, with no direction from Congress, had relabeled high-speed Internet access as . . . something else.

The months following the decision were a frenzy of attacks and counterattacks. A difficult question confronted the FCC: could it continue to label high-speed Internet access a "deregulated" service and still accomplish its regulatory goals of achieving ubiquity, neutrality (an Obama campaign promise), and other policy ends? Or would it have to reclassify high-speed Internet access service as a "regulated" service (a Title II service) in order to tell providers what to do?

The new FCC chairman under President Obama, Julius Genachowski, was in an uncomfortable position. Since the deregulatory decisions in the mid-2000s by Michael Powell's FCC, cable companies had invested billions of dollars installing high-speed Internet access infrastructure and related facilities. Pointing out that 93 percent of the country was now reached by cable infrastructure,[75] the cable trade association argued that changing the rules governing how network access was regulated would stifle the companies' ability to attract investment that could be used to serve difficult-to-reach areas.[76]

Genachowski is not a bomb thrower. He has an eager way of speaking and a lawyerly, precise mind. He had served on the *Harvard Law Review* with

President Obama and wanted to avoid embarrassing the president; he also wanted to be seen as a business-friendly, investment-conscious centrist. Genachowski had been sworn in at the end of June 2009, and the first several months of his tenure had been occupied with creating the National Broadband Plan called for by the stimulus bill enacted at the beginning of the Obama administration. He had assembled a huge team to research and draft the plan, which was delivered in March 2010. The plan did not propose deep changes in America's broadband structure or make any substantive effort to deal with concentration in the market for Internet access. It did note that there would be a strong cable monopoly for video-speed broadband by 2015—a reasonable point, given that only cable would be sufficiently upgraded to allow for speeds beyond 50 Mbps, that the phone companies were reluctant to make the necessary investments to lay fiber, and that there would be no competition among cable providers—and it suggested that municipalities should be able to bring high-speed Internet infrastructure to their citizens. The report also suggested a lengthy transition in which the government would switch to subsidizing high-speed Internet access rather than telephone service (so-called "universal service").[77]

At the same time, the Commission had run a separate rulemaking process aimed at the president's apparent campaign commitment to address net neutrality. Hoping to keep the National Broadband Plan uncontroversial, the Commission carefully kept net neutrality out of it.

But after the D.C. Circuit Court opinion in the BitTorrent case in April 2010, that separation became untenable. The court had ruled that the FCC did not have the power to make Comcast ensure that its "network management" was reasonable—and the arguments the Commission had used to support its exercise of authority over Comcast in the BitTorrent case were the same ones supporting its net neutrality arguments. Using the same legal tactics to support net neutrality would, it seemed, run up against problems with the D.C. Circuit Court. Similarly, the FCC's "universal service" policies in the National Broadband Plan were threatened—only a Title II common-carriage service could be subsidized and high-speed Internet access now fell under Title I. The same labeling that had released high-speed Internet access from regulatory obligations meant that federal subsidies could not be provided to allow Internet access for everyone.

The FCC had hoped to keep the court focused on process, not on the substance of its authority, and both Genachowski and his lawyers were surprised by the outcome of the Comcast case. All other work stopped at the Commission as the FCC considered legal options. Genachowski and his lieutenants did not want to spark a war with the carriers. But they were deeply worried that everything they tried to do would be the subject of prolonged and painful litigation; every step would be examined to see whether it was "reasonably ancillary" to the exercise of the Commission's authorities under the Telecommunications Act, and the FCC would never be able to get anything done. The situation was a mess. And it was about to get worse.

On Monday, May 3, 2010, the *Washington Post* reported that Genachowski had decided not to reclassify high-speed Internet access as a Title II service in the net neutrality proceeding.[78] The incumbent carriers, including Comcast, must have been delighted; this is what they had been fighting for. Then, three days later, the chairman's office issued a press release. The FCC was going to suggest reclassification after all, but would restrain itself— forbear—from carrying out many of the traditional elements of common-carriage regulation under Title II.[79] A predictable firestorm of lobbying and complaints arose from AT&T and the other incumbents. How could there be a move toward regulation? Analysts called the FCC's move the "nuclear option." The rhetoric rose higher: Genachowski, the carriers said, was trying to destroy the communications industry. Even the hint of reclassification was too much for the industry to accept.[80]

The pressure on the chairman to change his position was intense: AT&T spent almost six million dollars in the first quarter of 2010 alone lobbying the Commission, the Department of Commerce, the White House, and anyone else its lawyers could think of to convince them that the FCC was planning to "regulate the Internet."[81] The company marched on the Hill, getting signatures from 171 House Republicans and 74 House Democrats for letters excoriating Genachowski for considering reclassification of the transport portion of Internet access services.[82] The campaign was reminiscent of John D. Rockefeller's attack on Theodore Roosevelt in 1907, when he proclaimed that Roosevelt's antitrust policies would bring "disaster to the country, financial depression, and chaos."[83]

Eventually the chairman changed his mind once again: in a follow-up document, he suggested that reclassification was just one of many options on the table. One of the other options, he said, was for the Commission to continue as it had been doing—relying on authority based on "ancillary jurisdiction"—the idea that whatever the FCC was doing would support one of its express statutory delegations. Rather than stating which way the Commission intended to go, the follow-up statement presented all options; everything was still on the table. A long, hot summer of lobbying lay ahead.[84]

The FCC started holding off-the-record stakeholder meetings to explore whether a deal was possible that would preserve an open Internet without strangling the carriers' ability to attract investment. Congress began its own series of closed-door sessions. The world of telecom policy seethed with rumors and discontent. In the end, after months of wrangling, the FCC agreed with the carriers in late December 2010 that they would keep their Title I classification.[85] Within this framework, the Commission applied a very light hand to wired providers of Internet access, embracing usage-based billing and the idea of "managed services" that would not be subject to neutrality requirements. Wireless providers were freed of any obligation to refrain from discriminating against online applications. For Comcast, this was good news: it could continue its vertical integration plans without having to worry (for the moment, at least) about governmental review of its control over its pipe to American homes. Verizon sued. Someone always sues.

Over several decades, the U.S. government has tried—not always successfully—to force incumbents to let new competitors have access to the materials they need to compete. Where incumbents act as gatekeepers, new technology will not emerge without regulatory help that creates a level playing field for competition and the free flow of information. The government did this for the cable industry in the late 1970s when it mandated pole-attachment sharing, for the computing industry in the 1970s and 1980s when it protected the new industry from the depredations of the telephone monopoly, for long-distance service in the mid-1980s with the AT&T divestiture, for the nascent satellite industry in the early 1990s through program-access rules in the 1992 Cable Act, and for high-speed Internet access in the late 1990s through common-carriage rules for DSL.

Incumbents will also use all available regulatory levers to protect their business models: the broadcast industry used the FCC's broad statutory power to fend off competition from cable in the 1970s; the cable industry used vague program-access rules to make life more expensive for smaller cable providers and satellite companies in the 1990s and 2000s; and the telephone companies used vague language in the 1996 Telecommunications Act to fight attempts to force them to share their local facilities.

Behavioral restrictions are difficult to enforce; structural limitations such as the separation of carriers from content are difficult to achieve politically. The pendulum swings back and forth: cable deregulation in 1984 was followed by reregulation in 1992; the structural separation signaled by Al Gore and feared by John Malone was never carried out, and vertical integration has become common and unquestioned. Genachowski's FCC was apparently not interested in diverging from Michael Powell's view that consumers and innovation would be adequately protected by the market— and that traditional regulation was not necessary.

3

A Family Company

Cable TV, over the years that we were in it directly, was a growth machine. The internal organic growth rate of the business exceeded the cost of money. And if you do any kind of present-value-of-cash calculation, that means that the equity values are nominally infinite. Which means it has high returns to equity, because you can borrow money against a growing cash-flow stream, and as long as your growth rate's faster than your cost of money it's a wonderful business.
> —John Malone, interview with Ken Auletta, October 16, 2002

CABLE HAS WON THE RACE TO SELL services to Americans seeking high-speed Internet access. People are dropping DSL service delivered over metal phone lines in droves, as those services prove increasingly unable to compete with cable for the kind of speeds that households and businesses demand. And wireless Internet access does not and cannot keep up. Wireless is great for mobility—Americans love their smartphones—but no one starting a business would depend on the wireless data speeds provided by Verizon and AT&T. Wireless is a complementary service, and only people who have no other option (usually rural, minority, or poor Americans who have no wired access where they live or work) are likely to rely on it as their sole route online. Verizon's FiOS fiber-optic Internet access service is as good as cable (better, in fact, because it allows for uploads that are as speedy as downloads), but it is available to only 14 percent of U.S. residences; from Verizon's shareholders' perspective, it is too expensive to dig up traditional phone lines and replace them with fiber.[1]

Cable, on the other hand, has exploded into an enormous market: 80 percent of Americans buying a wired high-speed connection these days sign up with their local cable incumbent.[2] The FCC has said that for 75 percent of Americans the only choice for globally standard high-speed Internet access will soon be the local cable guy.[3] Comcast is adding subscribers at an accelerating pace at the same time that its revenue per user is increasing. At this rate, Bernstein Research predicts that about 70 percent of all wired Internet access subscribers in America will be cable customers by the end of 2015.[4] And as of 2012, Comcast was getting the lion's share of these new accounts: more than four hundred thousand new subscribers for wired high-speed Internet access per quarter, amounting to a total of almost 19 million subscribers overall.[5] Time Warner Cable was a distant second, with about a hundred thousand new customers each quarter and a total of 11 million subscribers. True, Comcast lost thousands of its more than 22 million pay-TV subscribers in the first quarter of 2012 as families gave up on the crushing monthly expense of video, but the rate of loss was slow: hard-core sports fans had nowhere else to go, for Comcast owns eleven immensely powerful regional sports networks across the country.[6]

Comcast was the best at controlling city markets in America; the media-information company SNL Kagan noted in July 2011 that Comcast had won its designation for "most consolidated" markets, with 94 percent of the cable subscribers in San Francisco and 88 percent of the cable subscribers in Chicago. Comcast has done very well at home as well, with 86 percent of the cable subscribers in Philadelphia. It also has over 85 percent of cable subscribers in Houston.[7] The company had 2010 revenues of $36 billion for video and Internet access combined (94 percent of its total revenues), and most of that revenue came from expensive bundled video packages— yet the prices for all of these services continued to climb.[8] (Between 1995 and 2008, the price of "expanded basic" video packages sold by cable companies went up 122 percent, three times the rate of inflation; between 2002 and 2012, Comcast's average revenue per user per month for its video services—including high-speed Internet access—climbed 133 percent.)[9] Those pay-TV subscribers were a captive audience for bundles of services that included high-speed Internet access, and Comcast was successfully shifting its business model: the company's high-speed Internet access subscribers were signing up far faster than the video subscribers were dropping off. Comcast faced some competition from satellite for video subscriptions, but virtually none for high-speed Internet access subscriptions.

So as of late 2011, after approval of the merger, Comcast's infrastructure and distribution business was accelerating quickly and the numbers were extraordinary. Revenues for high-speed Internet access were growing by 10 percent each quarter. Comcast's investors were happy because Comcast had finished building its network and was plowing more than 30 percent of its free cash flow (operating cash flow less capital expenditures) into dividends and share buybacks—keeping the price of its shares high. Comcast's costs for high-speed Internet access continued to fall while its margins became very high—40 percent or more—as the company charged high prices for the higher-speed access that more and more of its customers wanted.[10]

Comcast's high-speed Internet access subscriptions were nearly twice as profitable as its video subscriptions because programming was expensive and cut into the profit margin. These high-speed Internet access subscriptions were growing swiftly in number at the same time that support-services costs were declining proportionally due to the greater scale at which Comcast operated—yet Comcast was still charging more per subscription.[11] High-speed Internet access, indeed, was becoming Comcast's core business, contributing most of Comcast's growth. The product is enormously profitable; when the company adds more bandwidth for consumer use this does not mean it is facing commensurate costs: the pipe is already in place. Revenue and prices continued to climb, capital spending was down, and dividends were up: all the arrows were going Comcast's way when it came to control over high-speed Internet access in the markets it dominated.

At the top of the Comcast empire stands Brian Roberts. The Roberts family, like the Gilded Age families of the late nineteenth century, possesses enormous wealth and power; Brian Roberts was one of the highest-paid executives in the country in 2010, with total compensation of about $31 million (including a cash bonus of nearly $11 million).[12] Brian Roberts owns or controls all the Class B supervoting shares of Comcast stock—an undilutable 33 percent voting power over the company, and thus effective control over its every step (though Brian controls just over 1 percent of Comcast's shares).[13]

When Comcast purchased a $40 million corporate jet for business travel related to the NBCU merger, the jet's most frequent destination (after its home airport in Philadelphia) was Martha's Vineyard, where Brian Roberts, an avid sailor, has a home. According to the *Wall Street Journal*, FAA records also showed that Comcast's new jet made a large number of winter trips to Palm Beach, Florida, where Roberts has another home. In all, nearly two-thirds of this plane's trips were to Roberts's private homes or to resorts.[14] The travel of this one corporate jet is just a proxy for deeper issues: in 2010, the Corporate Library, an independent shareholder-research organization, gave Comcast an "F" for its corporate governance practices.[15] At the time, several of Comcast's directors either worked for the company or had business ties to it, and a third of the directors were over seventy—signaling that Brian Roberts's power over Comcast's operations was effectively unconstrained.

At the Antitrust Subcommittee hearing, Brian Roberts earnestly focused on the "American icon" NBC network and its "storied past and . . . promising future."[16] But when speaking to analysts at the time the deal was announced in December 2009, Roberts struck a different and more confident tone: the NBCU transaction was about making Comcast "strategically complete."[17] That same confidence came through in March 2011, after the transaction was cleared, when Roberts told analysts that despite steady price increases in its high-speed Internet access service, to which more Americans subscribed than any other, Comcast's sales were "tremendous."[18] In each market where Comcast operated, it already controlled a third of the high-speed Internet access subscriptions. But Roberts knew that Comcast could handle more: "So," he told analysts, "the goal would be 100 or 90 [percent of high-speed Internet access subscriptions in each market]. We have one competitor."[19]

How did America get to the point where one man was within striking distance of controlling most of the major metropolitan markets for high-speed Internet access?

The family story of Ralph and Brian Roberts is often told by Comcast. The company has its epic narratives, all of which are useful on Capitol Hill, whose members love a homespun American success tale. The story has the advantage of being true, and Brian Roberts genuinely considers Comcast a family company. That said, there is a jarring contrast between this family storytelling, with its connotations of intimacy and support, and the brute strength with which the giant company wields its economic advantage. Through canny skill, dogged persistence, and political heft, Comcast has put itself in a position to squeeze all the other players. Everyone, media conglomerates and small cable companies alike, has to work with Comcast on its terms. This allows Comcast to reap the rewards of dominance in the form of ever-increasing prices for data access and content in the twenty-first century. Comcast got where it is today through clever financing strategies, clustering of its operations to take advantage of scale economies, careful and constant cost cutting, the quick embrace of new technology, and shrewd investments in content, all within an environment of regulatory passivity. The idea of "common carriage," the centerpiece of public-communications policy for most of the twentieth century, has ceased to be a credible threat to Comcast's domination. The result: wide moats around an infrastructure business that cannot be crossed by competitors, and ever-increasing power and profits. In a very real sense, Comcast now owns the Internet in America.

Yet the genial family story continues to be put on display: Ralph Roberts's presence behind his son during the Antitrust Subcommittee hearing may have made some legislators worry that they were wearying him by going on too long. Looks can be deceiving: media mogul Barry Diller, bested by Ralph and Brian Roberts in his effort, as chairman of QVC, to buy CBS in 1994, told the New York Times in 1997 not to be fooled by Ralph's appearance. "Ralph is tough," he said. "Under that bow tie and courtly manner beats the heart of one tough man. He is steel."[20]

If Ralph is steel, Brian is, by all accounts, titanium. "He's a hard guy to work with," said one former cable mogul to me who did not wish to be named. "When I did deals, we had the idea that both sides needed to succeed in order for the deal to work. For Brian, it's 'If I haven't left them dead I haven't gotten enough.'" More pithily, as one satellite company executive said to me of Brian Roberts's company, "They'll gouge your eyeballs out."

Ralph Roberts could not have imagined what was ahead for American Cable Systems, his first cable company, when he opened its doors in early 1963. After selling his men's accessories business in Philadelphia and leaving a job writing advertising copy for Muzak—run by his brother, Joe—Ralph had been looking for a place to put his money. About a year before Ralph took the leap into cable, Joe encouraged him to investigate cable franchise opportunities, which served distant rural markets that were then just taking off. (Joe's Muzak business and Ralph's cable businesses intertwined over the next few decades; having a local exclusive franchise with high initial costs and steady subscription revenue, the case with both these industries at the time, is great for business. In a July 2000 interview, Ralph described both Muzak and cable businesses as a "license to steal as recurring monthly income. . . . You put in the equipment and every month they send you money.")[21] Ralph decided to buy some cable franchises in Tupelo, and later West Point, and Laurel, Mississippi; cable services could use marketing, he figured, and he was good at that.

Ralph's Tupelo franchise covered just twelve hundred subscribers by grabbing signals from Memphis broadcasters and running them along wires to the subscribers' homes. It was a risky move: he had to put up 51 percent of the half-million-dollar franchise cost. That was the last personal money that the Roberts family ever invested in their empire.[22]

Roberts didn't go into the venture alone. Julian Brodsky, an accountant with a deep commanding voice, prominent J. P. Morgan nose, and a frank, street-smart manner, was his financial wizard (and, later, Brian's mentor in deal making). Brodsky had been Ralph's accountant before they went into business together, and he helped Ralph found the company in 1963, including setting up the Class B supervoting shares that the Roberts family still controlled absolutely as of 2011.

Brodsky was the right man to push the tiny new company along. As he describes himself, "There were people whose weapons in business are the stiletto and there are people like me . . . whose weapons are the sledgehammer. And there's no conniving, no deceit. You just say your position and that's that."[23] Brodsky had the accounting and legal finesse to make Roberts's fledgling company tick.

It was Julian Brodsky whose sledgehammer drove the big deals and who fought the franchising wars that made Comcast grow. According to Dan Aaron, Roberts and Brodsky's third partner, Brodsky was the "maniac," with his foot on the pedal, "trying to go a million miles an hour," making deals. His goal was to buy cable franchises without either taking on enormous debt or losing control of the company. "We just knew that if we could continue to make good acquisitions and find opportunities to build cable systems, then things would sort themselves out for the long haul," Brodsky said in 2009.[24]

The early escapades of Roberts, Brodsky, and Aaron (a refugee from Nazi Germany who as a young journalist had become fascinated by the cable industry) in Mississippi involved shrewd uses of Roberts's sociability—he met one new franchise holder through a newfound friend at a local craps table—and the skillful avoidance of a requirement to provide everyone with service.

From the beginning, like other cable operators, they tried to "skim a little bit off the top," in Brodsky's words, to get "better demographics."[25] Cable was expensive to build. Meridian, Mississippi, required American Cable to put up a $125,000 bond that would not be released unless the company provided service to 90 percent of applicants. This was a problem. If everyone applied, the fledgling company would have no chance of surviving—it did not have the capital to lay enough cable to serve the entire town. So instead of creating a buzz about the new cable franchise, Aaron took space in the sole high-rise in Meridian and proceeded to set up shop extremely quietly. He did no advertising, put up no signs, and used unmarked trucks. The company sent out a direct mailing to one demographically promising block at a time and deployed clean-cut college kids to follow up on the mailings. When they had enough orders, they wired up one block at a time, and thus ended up serving 100 percent of their "applicants"—because, in Brodsky's words, "it was really hard to apply."[26] Brodsky, telling the story, considered it amusing; a company that is hard to find is a company that will be able successfully to serve all its customers; and a company that cherry-picks the best areas will be successful. The bond was released. The money flowed in.

The little cable company replicated this marketing model for years. Brodsky loved the new business because it was so straightforwardly lucrative. Ralph Roberts felt the same way. "I was never, never nervous about buying a cable system," he told *USA Today* in 2001. "You have recurring billing, reasonable rate increases, you keep your costs down and it's like chicken in a grocery store. It's very nice."[27] The company rolled on, acquiring exclusive franchises in Mississippi; it charged up-front installation fees to keep cash flowing and achieved adoption numbers and monthly service rates that covered its costs with enough left over to make the business grow. Depreciation rates as short as five years on cable equipment meant that the company could avoid paying much in taxes.

But there was a limit to how far the company could go in its new territory. Cable adoption in Mississippi was a tough business because many people were too poor to commit to making monthly payments for broadcast television that other Americans received for free. So Roberts and Brodsky turned their attention to their home city of Philadelphia and its surrounding towns, acquiring a group of suburban systems. These early acquisitions allowed American Cable, renamed Comcast (from *communications* and *broadcast*) by Roberts in 1969, to consolidate its back-office operations with these other franchises, so that they could take advantage of scale economies for their internal operations—accounting expenses, legal fees, overhead— as well as their purchases from vendors.

For many cable guys in the 1960s, building and consolidating systems was exciting. "At the beginning, middle, and end, nothing is more fun than building a cable system in a town that had never had a cable system before. This is a cable company and we are all cable guys," Brodsky said. They were also talented, disciplined, and highly intelligent. "We were absolute deal junkies, and driven by a need for growth."[28]

Reminiscing in 1998 about how things had changed in his industry, Brodsky remembered that back in the 1960s, selling cable was a difficult generational issue. Older people were "not in the mood . . . to make fixed commitments to spend money." But his view then, which he conveyed to the bankers backing Comcast in the early days, was that it was "just a matter of time"; "all these people go. The young people grow up who grew up with cable, and sooner or later cable will be a way of life."[29] And Comcast would feed the demand. This was only one of many prescient calls made in the company's early years.

At the time no one thought a company like Comcast would one day try to feed all that demand by itself in every large market it entered. Cable was smalltime: despite the franchising energy, in the 1960s few firms had more than a dozen systems each; the four largest combined held just under 20 percent of all subscribers. Even though companies owning multiple systems were growing in the 1960s, there was so much territory to wire that concentration was not an issue. Today, in the areas where Comcast operates (it never tries to compete with its big-cable peers Time Warner and Charter), it routinely controls more than 50 percent of subscribers.

One of Comcast's biggest advantages in its early days was Julian Brodsky's financial and technological acumen. In a 1998 oral history, Brodsky recalled in detail the company's strategies in the 1960s and 1970s. He would fight to get long-term fixed-rate reasonably priced loans for each new system—financing the cable industry had been unable to get before— and he required each project to be self-sufficient, so that the whole operation would not be threatened if one system faltered. It was a good plan, but Comcast still nearly folded in 1969–70 when its partner at the time, McClean Publishing, pulled out. Comcast found a way to survive by stepping up its acquisitions. (Comcast learned its lesson; as Executive Vice President David Cohen said in 2011, "We're not very good partners. We like to run things.")[30]

In an early, adventurous use of technology, Comcast employed computerized cost projections to obtain the longer-term loans Brodsky wanted. "[What] gave Comcast firepower in excess to any other cable operator," Brodsky explained, "was that we got access to computers [in 1965–66]. I leased a TTY 33 teletype that was used in Western Union offices. And I subscribed to GE's time-sharing services. . . . I devised models for cable projections [that were] all externally driven. . . . I was the only person in the cable business getting computer cash flow projections in the early and mid-60s."[31] Other cable companies consistently underestimated the costs of maintaining and expanding their installations, but Brodsky could make accurate projections. Technological agility became a company hallmark.

Innovative financial structures were another strength. In addition to getting good deals on new debt, Brodsky figured out how to use the same
kinds of limited partnerships that had been popular in the real estate, oil
and gas, and trucking businesses to raise money. The equity investors in
the limited partnerships—doctors, dentists, lawyers—would get back more
than they invested and be able to take advantage of the enormous deduc-
tions Comcast would generate based on the initial losses associated with
construction of new cable systems, while they supplied the money to pay
for the building of new systems. Meanwhile, because the limited partnerships did not show up on the balance sheet, Brodsky could keep Comcast's
more traditional investors happy as well.

At the same time, Brodsky took an extremely conservative approach to
deals. Comcast was not interested in loading up its balance sheet with debt.
Each deal had to pay for itself, and those loans had to be paid off. Comcast
went public in 1972 to get access to funds that would finance its expansion,
and marched ahead to acquire franchises in Kentucky and Michigan.[32]

The 1980s saw the company accomplish a number of big deals. The key
was to get the right to operate new monopoly franchises; battles over these
rights were fierce and expensive, and involved promises of lucrative pay-
outs for cities, advanced and interactive services, and payments to favored
charities. Bidders made sure that minority groups got a stake in the resulting system. Because of the up-front costs of building the system and the
need to (legally) buy off local power brokers, these franchises were natural
monopolies, and have remained so, even though federal law since 1992 has
made exclusive franchises illegal.[33]

Brian Roberts stepped into a leadership role in the company by demon-
strating his skill at cutting costs and trimming workforces in connection
with a major acquisition of rival cable systems in 1986. The target at the
time was Group W, then the nation's third-largest cable-systems operator.
Comcast, TCI, and Time Inc. formed a consortium to acquire Group W's
systems for $1.6 billion, a huge step for Comcast, which doubled in size
with the addition of 520,000 new subscribers. Comcast moved overnight
from being the sixteenth largest cable system to the eighth. But Group W
also had 1,500 employees. Comcast thought that was too many paychecks,
and the young Brian Roberts, who had been working in Flint, Michigan,

and elsewhere around the country learning the trade and installing cable lines, reduced the Group W workforce from 1,500 to 1,200 before the companies were integrated. Brodsky said years later that in the Group W transition Brian "gained a fair amount of attention within the company" and "showed that he had potential."[34]

The company kept growing. In 1988, Brodsky was able to buy half of Storer Communications' cable systems—Comcast got eight hundred thousand subscribers and nearly doubled in size again, becoming the nation's fifth-largest cable company with two million subscribers. John Malone's TCI got the other half.[35] Other large acquisitions tumbled in. Comcast snapped up franchises in New Jersey, Maryland, and Michigan, and continued its growth in Mississippi. After a long tussle, Northeast Philadelphia became Comcast territory in the mid-1980s, cementing Philadelphia's role as Comcast's home territory (and loyal partner in resisting competitors). More important, from the family perspective, in 1990 Brian Roberts was named president and Ralph's successor. He was just thirty years old.[36]

Brian Leon Roberts's path to mogul status started early. Alone among Ralph's children, Brian, born in 1959, the fourth of five siblings and the second-oldest son, took a strong interest in the cable business. While still in grade school he spent his Saturdays putting bills together in the Comcast office. "Brian is very unique in that he made up his mind what he wanted to be when he was almost in junior high school to senior high school," said his father. "He wanted to be in the same business I was in. And he would come out to the office and sit around; he couldn't get enough of it." Brian wasn't interested in reading books or listening to music (though he excelled at squash), and his father has described him as "a one track mind . . . on how to make the business better."[37] Brian was always ready to work, and was already sitting in on deal negotiations and meetings with banks in his teens; by 1975, the summer before his senior year in high school, he was out in the field with a Comcast installation crew, and before he went off to college he managed to get Comcast listed in Standard & Poor's stock guide.

Brian graduated from the Wharton School of Business in 1981 with a B.S., played a lot of high-quality squash, and became a low-handicap golfer.[38] He could have had a comfortable life sitting on boards, dabbling in business, and playing even more squash and golf. But he had other aspirations. Things moved quickly for him; he joined the Comcast board in 1987 in the wake of the Group W acquisition, and he took part in the Storer Communications negotiations. Meanwhile, the cable industry continued to grow; cable in 1986 was in about 37 million U.S. homes, or 43 percent of all households with a television.[39]

Brian, like Ralph, had no interest in giving up control of Comcast, even for an enormous amount of money. He could see far greater profits ahead in the digital world. Given some well-timed deal making, a favorable regulatory context, and good financing, more riches were bound to come Comcast's way.

The only other cable guy whose ambition has compared with that of Brian Roberts was John Malone, former CEO of TCI, who brought down Al Gore's ire on the cable industry by his arrogance in the early 1990s. But where Malone was rough, curt, and dismissive, Brian Roberts was smooth and polite. Roberts now owns Malone's cable systems; Comcast bought them from AT&T in 2001. Malone, for his part, is proud of what Roberts has done: "Brian has really matured as a business man, as a financial expert," he told *Bloomberg News* in 2010. "I take enormous pride that he's come out of our industry."[40]

The company grew even faster after Brian's ascendance in 1990. So had the cable industry generally, following CNN's dramatic coverage of Tiananmen Square and the fall of the Berlin Wall; by 1991, cable was in 60 percent of U.S. homes with televisions.[41] Comcast aggregated its Philadelphia cluster of systems through nine separate transactions that pulled together more than 1.4 million additional subscribers;[42] it bought MacLean Hunter's systems and the Scripps systems, becoming the third-largest multiple-systems operator by 1995.[43]

Television viewers weren't the only ones taking notice. Julian Brodsky was proud of Brian Roberts for convincing Bill Gates at a dinner in 1997 that "cable is clearly going to be the way to go," the best high-speed data route into Americans' homes, far more promising than the phone companies' copper lines. Following Brian's direct pitch, Microsoft gave Comcast a major shot in the arm by buying 11 percent of the company for one billion dollars.[44] The deal was a typical sledgehammer Brodsky arrangement: "They asked about the Microsoft discount. We explained to them the Comcast premium." The Microsoft billion went right in the bank as general funds supporting Comcast, and Microsoft received no power in return.[45]

This was a turning point for Brian Roberts and for the cable industry. Gates saw that with television and the Internet becoming one thing, conduits capable of shipping massive amounts of information were going to be dominant. The cable companies could do this more cheaply than the phone companies because they did not have to dig up the streets and install a second network.

At about this time, "clustering" ("You take Philadelphia, I'll take San Antonio") became the rage for cable-systems operators. The country had been wired; there was no more room for new cabling in metropolitan areas. As a former cable mogul told me in 2010, "I thought that if cable was going to be on the technology cutting edge; if we were going to compete with the likes of an RBOC [local phone company] or a public utility, we had to own whole markets, not parts of markets." So the operators, primarily TCI, Time Warner, Comcast, and Cablevision, swapped and clustered systems during the summer of 1997—Leo Hindery, the former president of TCI under Malone, has called it the Summer of Love—so that each company could act within clusters of subscribers, a proceeding that helped cut costs.[46]

The big companies' acquisitions of smaller cable operators were also proceeding quickly. In 1996, the top five cable distributors controlled 66 percent of all subscribers: John Malone's TCI alone held a 20 percent market share. By 1999, the cable industry was dominated by just six companies: AT&T (which had bought TCI's systems for $48 billion in 1998), Comcast, Time Warner, Cablevision Systems, Charter, and Adelphia. Then, in December 2001, Brian Roberts scored a major coup by buying AT&T Broadband's cable and Internet divisions (including TCI's former cable systems) in a $72 billion quasi-hostile takeover, propelling Comcast into the top spot as the nation's largest cable company.[47] FCC chairman Reed Hundt told the *Wall Street Journal* in connection with Comcast's bid that "the Roberts don't take 'no' for an answer. They repeatedly don't take 'no' for an answer." More than a hundred million households were connected to cable wires by then, and Comcast now served twenty-two million of them, in forty-one states.[48]

RCN, a small cable provider based in Princeton, New Jersey, that has tried to compete with Comcast over the years, sharply opposed Comcast's acquisition of AT&T's cable systems in 2002, accusing Comcast of using "bullying tactics" in the form of non-compete clauses to prevent about fifteen Philadelphia-area cable-installation contractors from doing business with RCN. According to RCN, contractors were followed and photographed when they were thought to be in contact with or working with RCN, and those photographs were used as a basis to cut off the contractors from doing work with Comcast. Without access to construction and installation contractors, RCN could not offer services. The *Philadelphia Business Journal* noted in 2002 that Comcast responded by saying that it had taken four years for Comcast to obtain a Philadelphia franchise. "RCN chose to abandon its effort . . . after a significantly shorter period of time (of about two-and-a-half years)."[49]

By 2005, Comcast was more than twice the size of Time Warner, its closest national rival—but not its competitor in any major geographic market. The Summer of Love and the swaps and deals since then had ensured that no major cable-systems operator competed with any other. After family-run Adelphia, the nation's sixth-largest cable operator, went into bankruptcy in 2002, its assets were divided in 2006 between Time Warner Cable and Comcast. Comcast gave 500,000 customers to Time Warner in Los Angeles, another 500,000 in Dallas, and 100,000 in Cleveland, while Time Warner gave Comcast 750,000 customers in Houston, 50,000 in Philadelphia, and 200,000 in Minneapolis.[50] Smaller cable providers did not share in the pie—the diminishing number of huge companies ran these trades for themselves.

As a result of this unofficial non-compete agreement, although Comcast as of 2010 had only about a 30 percent share of the nationwide market for video services (far ahead of Time Warner's 17 percent share), in the local markets where it operated it had almost no video competition from a cable operator; more important, it was just about the only choice in these markets for video-quality high-speed wired data services.[51]

Comcast historically has stopped at almost nothing to get strategically located exclusive franchises and subscribers that allow it to further cluster its operations. In 2011, the Third Circuit Court of Appeals allowed a class action to proceed that charged that between 1998 and 2002 Comcast increased its share of Philadelphia subscribers from about 24 percent to about 78 percent through a series of nine swaps of systems with AT&T, Adelphia, and Time Warner; acquisitions of competing cable service providers; denial to RCN of key sports programming owned by Comcast; requiring cable-installation contractors to enter non-compete contracts with Comcast; and persuading potential customers to sign up for long contracts with special discounts and penalty provisions in areas where RCN planned to compete— all with the result that consumers in Philadelphia ended up paying a lot more for pay TV than they would have in a competitive market.[52]

The family story continued. Ralph Roberts transferred much of his voting stock to Brian in 1998.[53] And whenever additional shares are issued, the ratio of votes controlled by the supervoting shares to those controlled by ordinary shareholders is adjusted to maintain Brian Roberts's 33 percent voting power over the company.

Thus, through a well-timed series of acquisitions and swaps, as well as the helping hand of his father, by the February 2010 hearing Brian Roberts found himself at the controls of the nation's largest media company in a thoroughly consolidated marketplace. Rockefeller would have felt a twinge of jealousy.

But if other cable companies no longer were a threat, what about other technologies? Digital technology now provides the key differentiator on the high-speed Internet access side of Comcast's business, where its future growth and dominance lie: only Verizon's FiOS service, which uses fiber-optic lines (the "one competitor" Brian Roberts referred to when talking to analysts in mid-2011), represented competition with Comcast's DOCSIS 3.0 data services. But in March 2010, Verizon indicated that it was suspending FiOS franchise expansion around the country.[54] Cities like Boston and Alexandria, Virginia, that had hoped to get FiOS would be left out in the cold; in the end about 15 percent of Americans (only those in zip codes whose characteristics satisfied Verizon's fairly high target rate of return) would have access to FiOS services.

Verizon stopped expanding for a simple reason. Its existing phone lines are made of twisted copper wire. To build FiOS, it has to install a complete second network—roll in the trucks, rip up the streets, and put in fiber—essentially cannibalizing the existing network on which it still sells DSL service. That's an extraordinarily expensive procedure, and Wall Street hates steep, long-term, up-front capital expenditures. Wall Street wants to see high free cash flow, ample dividends, and frequent buybacks. Comcast, meanwhile, only has to swap out some electronics to shift its existing cable network to DOCSIS 3.0 services. Much, much cheaper. And a death knell to potential competition, even though FiOS services are objectively better because uploads and downloads across its fiber optics are evenly fast. (Comcast faces competition from Verizon's FiOS in less than a fifth of its territory; Cablevision, by contrast, is competing with Comcast in almost two-thirds of its territory.[55] Some cable companies are bigger and more important to one another than others; Comcast and Time Warner are strategically aligned in a way that sometimes leaves out Cablevision.)

Another possible competing technology, wireless access, cannot match the speeds cable lines provide. It cannot offer the same capacity unless there are towers connected to fiber lines everywhere—and that's another major up-front expense that the telephone companies don't want to incur. John Malone, among many others, has scoffed at the idea that wireless access could make a dent in cable's dominance: "The threat of wireless broadband taking away high-speed connectivity [market share] is way overblown," he said in May 2011. "There just is not enough bandwidth on the wireless side to substantially damage cable's unique ability to deliver very high-speed connectivity."[56]

Comcast has always been quick to adopt new technology. With Brian Roberts's assistance, in 1988 the cable industry created and funded a technology research center—Cable Television Laboratories, usually called CableLabs—that has played a key role in developing shared technologies and technical advances for the industry. CableLabs is an unsung hero of the cable industry; its founder, Richard Leghorn, predicted back in 1987 (before the birth of the commercial Internet) that the cable industry could become "a multi-channel, multi-format video programmer and publisher utilizing its own interactive, point-to-multipoint optical cable plant," and this is exactly what happened.[57]

In 1997 CableLabs came up with standards that could be used to deliver packet-switched, Internet Protocol–based voice services over the cable lines (nicknamed VoIP, for Voice over Internet Protocol), and Comcast quickly adopted the technology, making itself the nation's third-largest telephone company.[58] The company embraced the "DOCSIS" (Data over Cable Service Interface Specification) standard developed by CableLabs as soon as it was available, and moved its system to all digital communications in 2008–9. That freed up bandwidth inside its pipe (digital signals can be compressed more efficiently than the old analog signals) while enabling new revenue streams for convertor-box rentals (so that analog sets could continue to be attached to cable wires) and high-definition video. More recently, Comcast was the first to offer CableLabs' DOCSIS 3.0 protocol, a digital channel-bonding technique that makes possible two-way capacity of Internet Protocol traffic of at least 100 Mbps. By 2011, Comcast had covered some 80 percent of its territory with DOCSIS 3.0, on a substantially faster schedule than any other cable distributor, and was selling this high-speed access at high prices.[59] Again, only Verizon's FiOS service could hope to compete with the speeds possible with DOCSIS 3.0—and Verizon was backing off.

So Comcast was aiming to stand alone in offering truly high-speed Internet access in each of its markets. This was a sensible move: data access is vastly more profitable than video services—it takes two dollars of video revenues to deliver the same profit as one dollar of Internet access revenues—and Internet access uses only about one-sixtieth of a cable system's total bandwidth.

But technology was only part of Comcast's success. Content was also important.

Brian Roberts knew that Comcast needed to maintain, as long as possible, its power to sell subscribers large bundles of programming that included "must-have" content—particularly live sports. To do that, he needed to make sure that live sports would not be available over the Internet on demand, at attractive prices, without a subscription. The programmers and networks had to be assured that they would make more money selling to cable distributors than directly to online consumers. The Comcast-NBCU deal would stave off the day when programmers revolted; Comcast would become itself a major player in the programming market.

Content was always part of the Comcast story. In the early days, there often was not much programming available to cable operators. In an early system in Sarasota, the community could pull in stations from Tampa through rabbit ears, and local televisions could even get the ABC network from Largo, Florida, about half the time. Roberts, Aaron, and Brodsky were offering Sarasota residents just half a channel of ABC in exchange for a monthly subscription fee—not a very attractive deal.[60]

As Comcast expanded, it looked for ways to build up content. Dan Aaron thought cable would eventually be bigger than just a reception business— that, in Brodsky's words, "there should be things we can do to bring people other than broadcast television." Aaron's early attempts to offer content provide fodder for Comcast's autobiography. In Tupelo, one of the first Comcast locations, the trio was operating a three-channel system. Doing an electronic upgrade to five channels by moving amplifiers around within the system would have taken a large investment, and Brodsky worried about wasting money. Aaron said he had a feeling they would be able to use five channels. As Brodsky tells the story,

> So what does Dan do with this fourth channel, pioneer that he was, a visionary. . . . He talks to Telemation out in Salt Lake City and they built him a diorama, and he mounts a videocam, a very cheap video camera on a post that rotated 180 degrees and in the diorama he had a clock, a thermometer, a wind gauge, a rain gauge, a barometer and at the end of it was a place to put in a placard. . . . The first one was Eat at Joe's Diner, which cost Joe's Diner ten dollars a month, could have been the first local advertising that I knew of, and he played background music behind this thing, and he had [the first] time-weather channel.[61]

Telecommunications, Inc., later known as TCI, made a similar attempt at local programming in the 1960s. As Mark Robichaux puts it in *Cable Cowboy*, it was "a TV camera aimed at a news ticker service, another fixed on a thermometer and, occasionally, a camera trained on a goldfish bowl."[62]

Aaron's programming was hardly a hit, but Comcast continued to explore the content business. Its logic from the beginning has been that if you don't know whether content is king or distribution is king it is best to spread your bets. You want to be selling something that people can get only from you. When a key partner, the McLean newspaper family of

Philadelphia, dropped out, Comcast had to sell its Florida cable franchises (a decision Ralph Roberts and Brodsky regretted for years), but it continued to acquire lucrative Muzak franchises across the country. In the end, Comcast became the largest Muzak franchisee in the nation, selling off its interest to Muzak managers only in 1993.[63]

Comcast's $20 million 1986 investment in the QVC (Quality, Value, Convenience) home-shopping channel, a hedge-your-bets deal made just after its acquisition of the Group W cable systems, was one of the best moves the company ever made: QVC eventually brought in a third to a half of Comcast's revenue. For little to no cost, through QVC, Comcast was paid by its subscribers to watch content that was presented by advertisers—the sellers—and then paid again when the subscribers phoned in their orders to QVC. In 1992, Barry Diller, former second-in-command at Paramount, took over QVC; when Diller made a $7.2 billion bid in 1994 to merge CBS with QVC, Comcast blocked the sale with a $2.2 billion offer to take over QVC entirely. Comcast and Malone's TCI divided ownership of QVC (with Comcast in control), and Diller promptly left. Comcast's $250 million investment paid off handsomely; to help pay for the AT&T systems in 2001, it sold its QVC shares to Malone for almost $8 billion. Comcast continued its diversification into content by buying a majority interest in E! in 1997, as well as the Golf Channel and Versus, its main sports channel.[64]

Comcast's more important moves by far have been in sports: in the late 1990s, it leveraged its majority interest in the NHL's Philadelphia Flyers, the NBA's Philadelphia 76ers, and Philadelphia's two major sports arenas into a twenty-four-hour regional channel called SportsNet Philadelphia. Within a few years, Comcast owned exclusive rights in broadcasts by teams and regional sports networks from coast to coast, with dominion over games played in the Bay Area, central California, Chicago, the mid-Atlantic, New England, New York, the Northwest, Houston, and the Washington, D.C.–Baltimore area—ten owned-and-operated Regional Sports Networks in seven of the ten largest television markets, which became the Comcast SportsNet. Because no competing video provider can hope to survive without access to local sports programming, Comcast's refusal to license Comcast SportsNet to RCN in Philadelphia helped keep that potential competitor at bay; it did the same thing to DirecTV and Dish Network.[65] Comcast has used SportsNet as a sledgehammer in many contexts.

Brian Roberts's only public misstep came in 2004, when he made an unsolicited $54 billion takeover bid for Walt Disney in the mistaken belief that the Disney board would welcome it. He first approached then-CEO Michael Eisner with an offer, but Eisner turned him down without even consulting the board. Taking Disney under Comcast's wing would have doubled the number of Comcast employees and given it access to premium content, not to mention theme parks and merchandising. But Roberts also wanted the Walt Disney Company because it owned ESPN—the QVC of sports. The lucrative ESPN channel, launched in 1979, had become the highest-priced must-have content in the cable world, and Comcast had little leverage against it. To give Comcast a sledgehammer it could use against all other pay-TV distributors, Roberts needed ESPN. If it took acquiring the under-performing broadcast network ABC (also owned by the Walt Disney Company) to get it, he would do it.

So after Comcast's bid was rejected by Eisner, Roberts sent a letter to the Disney board, making the offer public. But whoever had hinted to him that the Disney board had had enough of Eisner's leadership and was willing to see him outmaneuvered had been mistaken. Following Roberts's hostile takeover announcement, Comcast's share price swooned while Disney's went up, making Comcast's all-stock offer—based on giving shareholders 78 percent of a Comcast share for every Disney share—less attractive to the Disney board, which publicly rejected the bid.[66] After a few weeks, Comcast backed down. Roberts claimed that stepping back from the deal showed discipline, but the reality was that he had miscalculated the board's reaction. This signal failure on Roberts's part led directly to the Comcast-NBCU merger, which gave him another chance to acquire giant sledgehammers in the form of must-have cable channels and premium sports content.

The Disney bid sheds light on the concentrated nature of the content industry. Merger mania has been widespread on the programming side since the 1970s, and by the time Brian Roberts made his attempt to buy Disney there were few media conglomerates left to choose from. In 1999, Fox, Time Warner, Disney, and John Malone's Liberty dominated the programming industry; by 2005, News Corp. (News Corporation) controlled Fox and its valuable networks and the *New York Post*; CBS and Viacom (owner of DreamWorks, Paramount Pictures, MTV, Comedy Central, BET, and Nickelodeon) were both controlled by Sumner Redstone; GE owned NBC Universal, USA Network, and its long list of popular cable channels; Time Warner owned HBO, Warner Bros., and TBS; and Disney owned ABC, Miramax, and ESPN. Since Robert's Disney bid, media conglomerates have become even more global, owning television, newspapers, magazines, publishing outlets, and sports rights in many countries.[67] Many voices speak, but there are only a few ventriloquists behind the screen.

Brian Roberts's announcement in December 2009 that the Comcast-NBCU merger made his company "strategically complete" represented a moment of extraordinary personal and professional achievement. Comcast had grown by shrewdly rolling up independent cable systems—just as the enormous railroad combinations of the nineteenth and twentieth centuries were created by buying failing systems throughout the country. Together with the other major cable operators, Comcast found a way to geographically cluster its operations to take advantage of the enormous returns to scale that characterize the cable industry. It had achieved success by embracing innovative technology and paying what it took to install upgrades that others could not match without enormous investments. It had also achieved scale and diversification by buying up content—first Muzak, later regional sports operations—that people couldn't live without. Thanks to its powerful business model and desirable sports content, among other factors, Comcast weathered the 2009 recession well: cable revenue growth rates were unaffected.[68] Comcast was becoming a high-speed Internet access company; that's where the growth was. The Comcast model was extraordinarily resilient economically, and it came with enormous amounts of free cash and a vanishingly low level of default risk.

Comcast achieved all this by keeping its costs low and targeting dense, urban centers rather than far-flung rural communities that might be more reluctant to pay high subscription fees. It consolidated its back-office and other overhead services and was extremely careful with its finances. "We were lucky, and we were good," said a wistful Brodsky as he stepped down after decades of service. "We never saw a cable company we didn't like."

Mark Cooper, one of the consumer advocates who testified against the merger in February 2010, might rail about Comcast's being among the lowest-ranked companies in America for customer service; Comcast had bigger fish to fry.[69]

The company achieved all this while maintaining the image of family management. Wall Street believes in the Roberts family story. Legislators believe that Brian Roberts is a highly competent, low-drama executive who does his best to treat his employees like family. It is a trait Brian shares with John D. Rockefeller; Rockefeller "presided lightly, genially, over his empire," according to Ron Chernow's biography of the ruthless mogul, and "placed a premium on internal harmony."[70]

In Brian Roberts's view, as he testified in early 2010, Comcast was more than ready to take on the mantle of the world's foremost media company. The NBCU acquisition would be the icing on the cake. As John Malone told *Bloomberg News* in 2010, "Comcast is so big, there's no exit scenario. They are what they are. Nobody is going to buy Comcast, the company. It's too big."[71] Malone's TCI cable-systems business had ended up in Comcast's hands, and he admired what Roberts had been able to do. As he told analysts in a conference call in 2011, "As always in the cable business, in my—whatever it is—40 years in it, it's all about government regulation and technological change. But for the moment, cable looks terrific. . . . In broadband, other than in the [Verizon] FiOS area[s], cable's pretty much a monopoly now." Malone sounded gruffly wistful. "I never should have sold to AT&T."[72]

The word *monopoly* prompted nervous laughter among Malone's colleagues. "Okay," one of them said. "Any other questions?"

4

Going Vertical

LESSONS FROM AOL–TIME WARNER

AT THE FEBRUARY 2010 SENATE antitrust subcommittee hearing, Colleen Abdoulah, the energetic president and CEO of WOW!, one of the small cable operators that competed with Comcast in the Midwest, expressed her worries about Comcast and NBC Universal joining forces. "It concerns me because the combined entity will have powerful abilities and incentives to hurt a competitor like ourselves and increase our costs," she said, her animated voice a scratchy contrast to Brian Roberts's smooth impassivity.[1]

Like Comcast, WOW! is in the business of distributing video to its subscribers. But that's where the similarities end. WOW! has superb customer service—it has earned number-one rankings several times from *Consumer Reports*—and it is serving more than 475,000 customers, but it has to pay higher prices for content than the big companies do.[2] Content negotiations are crucial for any distributor trying to sell wired data and video services, Abdoulah said, and programmers—the media conglomerates—use their market power and leverage to force competing distributors to buy take-it-or-leave-it bundles at whatever price the programmer wants to charge. "What this means is low-value networks that customers do not want, and are not asking for, are associated with high-value networks that we have to have in order to compete," Abdoulah said. Marginal channels like NBC Universal's Chiller network are bundled into packages regardless of whether the distributor wants them. There is no such thing as a market price in this context: "Many times during negotiations with both these companies and others," she testified, "rate increases can be . . . 20 percent to as high as 156 percent." With no power to fight back and few competing programmers to play off against one another, WOW! ends up having to pay more for the programming it must have to compete—like sports and local broadcast TV stations—while wasting channel space on networks that few customers want.[3]

When it was his turn to talk, Senator Al Franken (D-Minn.)—a former *Saturday Night Live* writer and performer—growled at NBC Universal's Jeffrey Zucker and Comcast's Roberts about the risks of having the same company control both content and distribution even when the company promises not to favor its own interests.

Franken's focus was on the fate of independent sources of content. Franken knew from personal observation during his time at NBC that getting a program picked up by a distributor that has an interest in making its own programming profitable can be close to impossible for an independent—notwithstanding promises from the distributor. "It is really hard to trust you guys," he said. "Look, I have had this history where I have seen NBC and I have seen other networks promise something and then do the 180-degree turn on it."[4]

It used to be that the TV networks were not allowed to own the programming they aired, but those rules were eliminated in the 1990s.[5] NBC had strongly supported erasing them, saying that since it was in the network's interest to support strong independent programmers the strictures were unnecessary. But within a few years, Franken pointed out, NBC was supplying its own prime-time programming, and no independent programmer was aired unless it gave up part ownership of its program. Franken's personal experience with NBC-the-broadcaster made him distrust the idea that a distributor could safely be combined with a programmer: "When the same company that produces the programs runs the pipes that bring us those programs, we have a reason to be nervous."[6]

Franken had fundamental concerns about the deal that ranged far beyond worries about independent programmers. Brian Roberts had called the merger "vertical," but Franken was not confident that it was as vertical as Roberts wanted the committee to believe.

As Roberts described it, the deal would merely bring together companies in two different parts of the market. Since they did not overlap, competition would not be compromised. NBC Universal had no distribution assets—cable systems—and Comcast had only minor programming assets—cable channels and rights to content. Combining the two, Roberts argued, would have little effect on competition because the same number of competitors would be in place after the merger as before. Comcast's cable-distribution system would not expand by virtue of the deal because NBC Universal had no cable systems; NBC Universal's content assets would remain virtually unchanged because Comcast had only modest programming assets. NBC Universal was in fourth place among the content conglomerates—ahead of News Corp. but behind Disney/ABC, Time Warner, and Viacom—and it would still be in fourth place when the deal was completed. The resulting new entity would have only about 12 percent of total revenues for national cable-programming networks.[7] Roberts reminded the senators of this several times. He did so for two, seemingly paradoxical, strategic reasons.

The first was that antitrust regulators have recently been much more inclined to allow vertical than horizontal mergers (such as those between two distributors), reasoning that unless the merged entity is dominant in either production or distribution, it will be unable to leverage its power in its original market into a different market. Vertical transactions do not reduce the number of competitors in either the input or the distribution markets, but horizontal mergers do: where there were two competitors in a particular marketplace, after a merger there will be just one. Also, with a vertical merger, there may be greater "efficiencies": opportunities to save money by combining distribution with production in ways that may bring benefits to consumers.[8] Emphasis on the *may*: when Comcast hired the Stanford economist Gregory Rosston to assess the consumer benefits of the NBC Universal deal, he wrote that "the actual form of the consumer benefit will not necessarily be a reduction in Comcast's prices relative to current prices or prices that might otherwise be charged, but consumer benefit could also come from increased investment by Comcast in programming and distribution leading to higher quality and more consumer choice."[9] In other words, prices wouldn't necessarily go down, but consumers might get access to more stuff.

The second reason for Roberts's emphasis on identifying the merger as vertical integration was that past efforts by distributors to get into programming (or vice versa) had not worked out. Everyone testifying that day could name examples of failed vertical mergers: Time Warner had just unwound its valuable programming properties (including HBO) from the fortunes of Time Warner Cable, leaving the cable distributor free to go out on its own as a separate company.[10] DirecTV had similarly parted ways with News Corp.[11] But the big story was AOL–Time Warner, whose much-touted (and much-feared) vertical-integration deal—in which AOL had purchased Time Warner in exchange for $165 billion in AOL stock—had dissolved ignominiously at the end of 2009 after ten fractious years.[12] The AOL–Time Warner merger had been called one of the biggest failures in American business history.

Roberts's first reason—that vertical mergers do not affect competition—argued for a light touch from regulators; the second suggested that even if the deal went through the combination might eventually fall apart, and so there was no reason for regulators to worry about its impact on the marketplace. As the University of Chicago professor Richard Epstein put it in a statement filed with the Senate Antitrust Subcommittee in March 2010: "It may well be that this merger will crater like the Time Warner/AOL deal. But that is not an antitrust concern, but a sober reminder that bigger is not always better. . . . [I]t is precisely because all mergers face economic pressures of self-correction that we should regulate them with a light hand."[13]

But there were significant differences between AOL–Time Warner and Comcast-NBCU.

When AOL and Time Warner broke up in December 2009—the same week that Comcast announced its plan to buy NBC Universal—it marked a sad end to what had seemed a match made in corporate heaven. Ten years earlier, AOL had been a new-economy powerhouse, a virtual community for early online adopters and an easy gateway to the Internet—if AOL users wanted to get there. Yet even in 1999, it could boast to potential partners that 85 percent of its users' time was spent on AOL's own content; users rarely ventured out into the Wild West of the Web itself.[14] And AOL was huge: as the *Wall Street Journal* reporter Andy Kessler put it in 2002, "As PCs and Windows grew, so did America Online—from a million members in 1994 to 10 million in 1997. Other players, Compuserve and Prodigy, were too stupid to keep up, and the only potential competitors were the phone companies. But phone companies thought online meant someone's sneakers hanging from their telephone wires."[15]

Steve Case, AOL's cofounder, was graying but still boyish, bright-eyed, and fast-talking when he appeared on a morning financial-news talk show in early January 2010 to discuss the AOL–Time Warner tenth anniversary. He was fitter than he had been a decade earlier and still enthusiastic about the AOL deal—or at least about the promise it had once held. The "deal still makes sense," he insisted. "AOL helped bring the Internet to so many people." But as the Internet spread, AOL's reliance on dial-up service was a detriment. Time Warner had seemed to have the right assets to solve Case's problem. "We needed a path to broadband," he said. "Time Warner was the largest cable operator, and also had a lot of media businesses. They needed a path to a digital future."[16] It seemed like a perfect pairing.

AOL's early success was made possible by regulation. Its business depended on having subscribers reach it by using their home phones; subscribers would attach a modem to their computer, connect the computer to a phone line, dial a local Telenet access number, and send data back and forth to AOL's servers. AOL took off only because the phone companies had no legal ability to block it. The common-carriage regulation, which required the phone companies to allow anyone to use their lines, was still alive and well.

Not that the phone companies didn't try to strangle online services in the cradle. In 1987, with the aid of the FCC, they nearly succeeded in imposing added fees on the transmission of data by telephone.[17] The phone companies themselves were not allowed to get into the data business as a result of the conditions imposed on the AT&T breakup, but they were angling to squash the IBM-backed Prodigy, one of the earliest online-access companies. They had convinced FCC chairman Dennis Patrick that Prodigy should pay per-minute "interstate access charges" for the privilege of being reached by the phone companies' subscribers, on the theory that the online database companies were, in essence, playing the same role as long-distance companies: using local phone facilities to reach subscribers.

Had the phone companies succeeded, the Internet revolution would have been stalled in its tracks; the extra charges would have made Internet access a luxury rather than a necessity. Fortunately for American innovation, they failed. In 1987, Representative Ed Markey called Chairman Patrick to a field hearing in Boston and raked him over the coals, suggesting that the FCC and its access charges would handicap the information-based infrastructure of the U.S. economy.[18] Markey was an early proponent of interactive businesses, claiming at the time that an access fee for computer users would lead to a two-tiered society: the information-rich and the information-poor.[19] Several online providers, calling themselves "videotex" services, testified that the FCC proposal would destroy their business by increasing their costs many times over.[20] Without cheap, flat-rate access to local residential users, they were sunk. It was the pole-attachment fight all over again.

Chairman Patrick, for his part, argued that it would be only fair to charge the new interactive services the prices that applied to long-distance calls that took advantage of local phone company facilities, and that failing to do so might distort the natural evolution of the marketplace.[21] Markey didn't buy it. The local phone companies, represented by Ivan Seidenberg (then of NYNEX, later CEO of Verizon), could tell that things weren't going their way and called for a delay in the ruling. But a delay, said the videotex representatives, would also destroy them; no one would invest in their services with the cloud of potential access charges hanging over them.[22]

Markey eventually won: the FCC backed down and denied the phone companies the right to apply special charges to Internet service providers (ISPs). The FCC judiciously said at the time that it was forbearing from imposing these fees ("this is not an appropriate time to assess interstate access charges on the enhanced services industry"), but the reality is that it was dragged kicking and screaming into supporting AOL, Prodigy, and Compuserve.[23] The flat-rate, inexpensive lines for Internet access that the phone companies were obliged to provide led to an explosion of consumer interest in the Internet, and success for AOL and its competitors. "Imagine the history of the Internet if I hadn't done that," Markey says now.[24]

One of the videotex providers testifying at Markey's 1987 field hearing was Philip Gross, the president of a fast-growing online service called QuantumLink that provided e-mail, chat services, and other resources to its subscribers. Its growth—zero to fifty thousand subscribers in just two years—was particularly impressive given that access to its system at the time was limited to users of Commodore 64 computers, which could be bought at Toys "R" Us. Gross testified that QuantumLink's growth was at risk, thanks to the FCC: with the threatened access-fee increase, Gross believed that the cost of transport of his interactive service would jump by 450 percent.[25]

That the local phone companies did not get their way was good for QuantumLink, and important for our story, because the mind behind QuantumLink belonged to the young Steve Case.[26] With access fees out of the way, Case went on to create the AppleLink online service for Apple and PC-Link for IBM clones; in 1991, he changed the company's name to America Online, and by 1994 his online service had a million subscribers.[27]

AOL was soon swimming in cash, or at least in stock valuations that might someday be worth cash. It was making enormous deals for sponsorship and advertising; its deal makers were infamous for their confidence, arrogance, and take-no-prisoners tactics.[28]

AOL also had the advantage of ease of use: it literally brought America online for the first time. People were hearing about the Internet and wanted to be part of this great cultural transformation, but they didn't want it to be too difficult or time-consuming to do so. With America Online, people who had grown up long before the digital revolution could easily check their e-mail, drop into a chat room, and find stories they wanted to read. And thanks to the millions of free signup disks the company mailed out, the opportunity to get online wasn't hard to find.

When I first moved to Washington, D.C., in 1992, those brightly colored disks were everywhere. They came with promotions encouraging you to sign up for a low monthly fee and proved irresistible to people who wanted to try "going online" but didn't know what online services were or how to access them. I remember looking at the Whole Earth catalog of Web sites and wondering how I could get to these things from the desk at my law firm. America Online was my answer. (It was also busy—I remember hearing the braying sound of the modem followed by static and a seemingly inevitable busy signal.)

But when people did get through, they started talking to one another. This was new for us in America; we hadn't had such easy electronic interactivity before, and making the Internet social was just what we wanted to do. Community drove AOL's growth as much as ease of access. By mid-decade it was one of the most talked-about companies in America.

The initial public offering (IPO) of the Web-browser firm Netscape in August 1995 (which gave it a valuation of two billion dollars) and the idea of expanding Internet access beyond services like AOL suggested to many pundits that AOL's days were numbered.[29] Soon people were making fun of anyone who used an AOL e-mail address—AOL was Internet for dummies and old people, the elementary, dumbed-down version of something much more exciting and current. It seemed obvious that people would soon leave AOL's walled garden for the wide-open spaces of topic-focused, global online discussions—or other kinds of interactions yet to come.[30]

Yet people who did not have time for wide-open spaces, or were a little afraid of them, stayed loyal to AOL. By the end of 1995 it had doubled its size in less than a year and was up to five million members. By the beginning of 1999, its stock had soared to an incredible valuation of $65 billion, and AOL had joined the Standard & Poor 500.[31] Its 20 million customers made it the largest ISP in the country, serving two-thirds of all new dial-up customers, 44 percent of the total dial-up market in the United States, and more Instant Messaging users than all of its competitors combined.[32]

Still, AOL was a "narrowband" company: from a technical perspective, it was a dial-up Internet service provider. Users connected via modems to their phone companies' lines and dialed in over a dedicated copper telephone line to AOL's bank of servers in order to see AOL's content (and, sometimes, the Wild West of the Internet itself). As long as the family computer was logged on to AOL, the phone line could not be used for anything else. It was busy sending and receiving data at a rate of just twenty-eight or fifty-six kilobits per second (Kbps).

This was a bonanza for the phone companies, who were secretly delighted that so many people were buying second lines so as to leave a phone line free, but it was not sustainable for Internet connections that carried anything more than e-mail text. By 1999, subscriptions to "broadband" connections to the Internet via cable were approaching one million.[33] These connections meant that consumers no longer needed AOL to reach the Internet. It was not even clear whether Internet service providers would survive. If, unlike phone companies, the cable companies were not required to be common carriers, and thus obliged to let Internet service providers use their lines, this entire category of businesses would presumably wither away.

By early 1999, the cable industry had succeeded in labeling access to competitive ISPs across their lines "forced access," and the government seemed to be accepting the argument.[34] There was little political appetite to treat broadband access to the Internet over cable lines the same way the government had treated broadband access over telephone lines. Cable companies were winning the battle against the idea of common carriage.

AOL's management saw the end approaching. Cable was the future, and the dial-up ISP model had no place there. The telephone companies had been forced to allow AOL to get rich using their lines, but the cable companies had dodged that bullet. AOL's long-term strategy, meanwhile, seemed limited to doing more deals. In 1999, it launched an "AOL Anywhere" campaign (foreshadowing Comcast's "TV Everywhere" push), allying itself with digital-video-recording companies, handheld device manufacturers, satellite companies, and PC manufacturers—all to ensure that AOL could be easily accessed from any platform.[35] But the company was treading water. Case realized that AOL needed to lock in its broadband future by reaching an agreement with a key cable distributor that had control over all-star content. This would keep the walled garden of AOL at the center of users' media experience in the new broadband world, allowing it to pull in enough advertising dollars to sustain itself. At the beginning of October 1999, Case settled on Time Warner as the target.[36]

At the time Case started looking its way, Time Warner was a cable distributor serving 15 percent of the country—about 13 million people.[37] It also owned top-flight entertainment brands: CNN, Bugs Bunny, *People* magazine, HBO, and Atlantic Records, among others. When the news of AOL's plan to merge with Time Warner broke at the end of 1999, the great promise of the Internet era seemed to be encapsulated in a single transaction. To the surprise of many, AOL's market capitalization was much higher than Time Warner's, and AOL planned to buy Time Warner for $180 billion in stock and debt, creating a company worth $350 billion, of which AOL would own 55 percent.[38] Old media would come under the dominion of the Internet model; everything was going online. The companies' leaders were hailed as visionaries and symbols of a new era. The venture capitalists and investment bankers were exulting over the grandness of the undertaking and gathering enormous fees.

Meanwhile, Time Warner could see that cable lines might be the future. As Kara Swisher reports in *There Must Be a Pony in Here Someplace,* an internal memo from Time Warner made this point back in 1994: "In the next few years, high-speed Internet connection via cable may become commercially available. It will transform the online experience, and could make dial-up services such as CompuServe and AOL, which pretend to be content services but are mainly connectivity services, vulnerable."[39] But if the cable companies' executives had any say, those cable lines would never be common-carriage pipes that allowed other providers to sell Internet access. Time Warner wanted to control the entire user experience.

The deal made sense; AOL would pull together the formidable content assets of Time Warner and bring them to people finding community online, while Time Warner's faster distribution assets would allow subscribers to enjoy graphical files—video, photographs—that would have been frustratingly difficult to see by way of dial-up connections. David Bennahum, a contributor to *Wired* magazine, made the "everything is about to change forever" point when the 1999 transaction was announced: "This [deal] has ramifications for television networks, for cable networks, for radio networks. This is the beginning of a profound transformation, and so what Time Warner gets out of this is, first, advantage, moving [to] enter the Internet. What AOL gets out of this is the incredible access of that content. And now what they both have to do, one of the many challenges they face, is to say, well, how do we then begin to create this next generation of media and content? How do we leverage all these connections in terms of marketing, in terms of relating to your audience?"[40] Both Case and Gerald Levin, Time Warner's visionary CEO, promised high revenues, with a cash flow of $11 billion a year once the companies were combined.[41] As Swisher, a technology columnist for the *Wall Street Journal,* said at the time, "No matter how you slice it, it's a moment of Internet becoming sort of an adult. It's a lot of money. It's all these fabulous personalities."[42]

Many saw a downside, too. NBC filed with the FCC seeking a "meaning-ful, enforceable commitment by AOL Time Warner to provide nondiscrim-inatory access" to Time Warner's lines by other programmers.[43] The announcement of the AOL–Time Warner deal prompted apocalyptic pro-nouncements from pundits concerned about media consolidation, and U.S. regulatory agencies erected elaborate schemes designed to avoid the evils of vertical integration.

Ten years later, the AOL–Time Warner merger was, according to Allan Sloan of *Fortune,* the "biggest takeover turkey ever that didn't end in bank-ruptcy."[44] Critics claimed that the regulatory conditions imposed by the agencies looked silly in hindsight. The two companies had not achieved the synergies their leaders had hoped for. When Time Warner launched a new broadband service, it did not even associate it with the AOL brand, calling it Road Runner instead. The two cultures had not managed to mesh; Time Warner divisions had no interest in working with the AOL cowboys. As one content executive told me, "It never occurred to us that they [AOL Time Warner] might so badly manage the integration of the companies."[45]

What happened?

To the regulators and the public-interest advocates of the day, the AOL–Time Warner merger looked like an event that would change the media landscape forever—but not for the better. The Consumers Union, in a lengthy letter to the FCC, expressed deep concern about how the merger would concentrate markets in television and online content as well as the distribution of this content through broadband and narrowband connec-tions.[46] The nationally syndicated columnist Norman Solomon was con-vinced that the AOL–Time Warner merger was the beginning of the end of the freewheeling Web:

I'm afraid that we may look back on January 2000 as the time when de facto, the World Wide Web became essentially the world narrow Web, which is counterintuitive because there's all this talk today, all this smoke being blown about how AOL and Time Warner will create these multiplicity of choices through the new media. The reality is, however, that these new media are being used to herd and goad and leverage the consumers, the media consumers into essentially cul-de-sacs. . . . So, I think this is a tremendous blow for the potential for democracy in our society through genuine wide-ranging discourse. . . . We're essentially seeing the mass distribution of corporatization of consciousness, and this step today is a big stride down that very slippery and very dangerous road.[47]

Not to be outdone, the *New York Times* published an op-ed proclaiming that the AOL–Time Warner merger could mark the end of America's independent press.[48] And the broadcasters were furious. NBC warned of dire consequences, arguing in July 2000, "Given the size and scope of the proposed merged company, AOL/Time Warner will have both the ability and the incentive to discriminate against unaffiliated content providers such as NBC." The network urged the FCC to "establish firm principles of nondiscrimination in the treatment of unaffiliated content providers in the broadband services marketplace."[49] Disney went farther, proposing that the agencies divide the merged entity into separate content and distribution companies.[50] In short, the AOL–Time Warner merger approval became a public forum for competing visions of how content would be distributed in the Internet era—the continuing battle over the future of common carriage.

One of the regulators' biggest concerns was that AOL Time Warner would have an unfair advantage because it could block competing Internet service providers from using Time Warner's high-speed cable lines. The regulators hoped to condition approval of the merger on a requirement that Time Warner let AOL's ISP competitors reach AOL Time Warner customers directly. By making this a onetime condition, they could avoid stating that all cable broadband networks should be open. (The cable distributors' "forced access" rhetoric had put that issue on the "too hard to deal with" pile for the Commission.) Three months before the deal was approved by the Federal Trade Commission (FTC) and the FCC, Time Warner announced an arrangement with EarthLink (then the second-largest ISP in the country after AOL) that would allow EarthLink to share its lines.[51] The companies agreed to a consent decree with the FTC requirement that the combined company make deals with two additional competing ISPs within ninety days of making AOL available to Time Warner subscribers in large markets. They also had to agree not to disrupt the flow of content provided by other ISPs or interactive TV services piggybacking on the AOL Time

Warner network. Meanwhile, the FCC barred AOL Time Warner from launching advanced Instant Messaging (IM) services like streaming video because the merged media giant would "likely dominate" new, IM-based high-speed services.[52]

In hindsight, the regulatory angst seems overblown, because the new company was star-crossed from the beginning. By the time the merger was approved, in January 2001, AOL's stock had lost half its value, and the merged company was worth approximately $110 billion. Things unraveled quickly from there: a scandal involving misstated revenue and backdated contracts at AOL and the crash of the dot-com marketplace in 2001–2 sent the stock lower still. AOL Time Warner reported a loss of $99 billion in 2002 (the biggest corporate loss in U.S. history at the time, according to PBS), and Time Warner dropped "AOL" from its name in 2003. Employees had been required to invest in AOL Time Warner for their retirement savings, and then they saw the stock price sag. Longtime Time Warner employees bitterly resented losing their money because of AOL's accounting antics. Time Warner CEO Gerald Levin had not consulted most of the company before the AOL deal, and employees felt betrayed.[53]

What Steve Case could not have known until the deal was done was that Time Warner was more like a stable of competing vendors than a single company. Its divisions were used to independence, fighting for their own profits and not necessarily cooperating with the others. The company had already been through two gigantic and painful mergers (Time and Warner Communications in 1990 and Time Warner and Turner Broadcasting in 1996); the addition of the arrogant, dismissive, boots-on-the-desk dealers from AOL did not help it function more smoothly. The attitude of the AOL executives grated on the Time Warner employees, who could tell that their new bosses considered Time Warner hopelessly behind the times. Following the merger, legacy Time Warner CNN employees often did not return AOL employees' phone calls. All of this jockeying hardly led to the promised synergies.[54]

And no one seemed to know what those synergies were. Ideas were thrown around: maybe AOL could be a platform for digital music sales, a repository of first-rate tunes available for download. (There was no iTunes at this point.) But being a platform would require the Time Warner employees to work closely with the new AOL group, and that seemed unlikely. Jeff Bewkes, the rising star at Time Warner and head of HBO at the time of the AOL–Time Warner merger, said in an October 2009 interview:

> The argument given for [the merger] was that somehow the content brands of *People* magazine or HBO or CNN . . . was going to go into the AOL subscription service . . . [so that] the AOL service can have content from the content company that it owns. . . . [But Time Warner content brands like] *People* or CNN, or Harry Potter, has to go . . . to all people through all avenues. That is the definition of an available content brand. And if it's on the "Internet," it needs to be available through every and all Internet platforms. If you take something like an AOL or a Yahoo! there is competition there, what they compete on is the functional ease and quality of connecting you, as a user, to any and all content or things on the Internet. So none of that . . . has anything to with rights holding, exclusivity, preferred access, or any kind of discriminatory presence for content through a distribution medium like AOL or Yahoo![55]

AOL was a distribution company, and Time Warner was a content company, but their interests did not align in a way that would make the merger work. For Bewkes, vertical integration makes sense only if the combined company has a large and powerful market share either upstream (in content) or downstream (in distribution), and the integrated AOL Time Warner had neither. Even if AOL had made itself the first screen for users' Internet access over Time Warner's cable-modem service, it would have guaranteed access to just 15 percent of Americans. Without regulations mandating common carriage for the rest of the cable-distribution landscape, AOL did not have the leverage to force the other carriers to deal with it.

At the same time, AOL remained primarily a highly profitable ISP business (both dial-up and, eventually, broadband) in a regulatory realm that did not require that cable distributors (except in the onetime merger condition imposed on Time Warner) allow competing ISPs to use their cables. (Recall that Comcast, confident that the shadow of common-carriage regulation would never fall on its operations, bought up AT&T Broadband's cable systems in December 2001—and cable-modem Internet access service was a big part of the deal's upside.)[56] Yet ironically, the cash flows from

AOL's existing business were strong enough to keep it from making the transition to another business model. And because pure distribution and pure content companies typically appeal to different kinds of shareholders, AOL Time Warner's stock was neither fish nor fowl to many investors. Add in the combined company's lack of dominance in either content or distribution, the fact that the resentful employees of Time Warner resisted helping their new AOL bosses, and AOL's own slowness to develop a new strategy, and you had a recipe for inertia and, ultimately, failure.

It took almost a decade, though, for the AOL Time Warner leadership to realize its mistake. In late 2009 Levin admitted his responsibility for the failure to convince Time Warner divisions to execute on the grand vision he and Case had articulated: "I'm really very sorry about the pain and suffering and loss that was caused. I take responsibility. It wasn't Steve Case's fault. It was taking this magnificent concept and not being able to meld it into a missionary zeal. It was not a supermarket, it was a mall." As Case put it, "vision without execution is hallucination."[57]

Bewkes, installed as CEO of Time Warner in 2007, subsequently spun off the Time Warner Cable operations in March 2009—and AOL as well. From Bewkes's perspective, both the capital-intensive needs of the cable-distribution business and AOL's inability to settle on a new business model distracted from Time Warner's content operations. By the time AOL was finally separated from Time Warner, in December 2009, the company's stock had declined 77 percent since the merger—triple the decline in Standard & Poor's 500-stock index over the same period.[58]

The regulatory conditions so painstakingly imposed on the AOL–Time Warner merger are seen today as failures. In Gerald Levin's view, the company had a "tough time with the regulatory process. They imposed conditions that are basically chimeras—I mean they don't really exist."[59] EarthLink managed to thrive as an independent actor, enlisting 445,000 new customers because of the AOL–Time Warner agreement, even as it moved from dial-up to broadband. But after the merger went through, no other ISP was able to get terms from Time Warner that would allow it to compete successfully. From a competition point of view, then, the regulations were hardly a success. (Earthlink asked the regulators to impose the same condition as part of the Comcast-NBCU merger to no avail.)

The FTC had done its best to open competition to ISPs and had hired a highly respected FCC engineer, Dale Hatfield, to oversee the ISP open-access (common-carriage) elements of the AOL–Time Warner deal.[60] But the merged company's obligations were not precisely clear, and the FTC had not had adequate technical advice in setting up the requirements. AOL Time Warner was plainly uninterested in providing the kind of access to competitive ISPs at a sufficiently fundamental technical level to allow the competitor to add value through quicker or better service; the competitor was in essence relegated to reselling the service that AOL Time Warner offered, without differentiation. (When sharing telephone wires for DSL Internet access, by contrast, a company with access to the copper wire that also had better technology on its side could do things the incumbent could not. Common-carriage requirements initially imposed on the telephone companies had made the provision of high-speed Internet access a respectably competitive business.)

But the biggest problem for potential competitors was the price squeeze: there just wasn't enough of a margin to make it worthwhile to share the pipe. Fixing this issue would have required somehow allocating AOL Time Warner's costs on a fair basis among competitors—and that, in turn, would have required major staff attention from the FTC. No one seemed to have the stomach to impose such a regime. Finally, without the ability to differentiate its services technically or charge a lot less (given the nonexistent margins), the ISP would have to prove that its service was nonetheless somehow "better" for consumers. With more and more services provided by online applications, there was little an ISP could do to stand out from the crowd. Any condition short of requiring a separation between content and distribution (something the Nixon White House had wanted, John Malone had feared, and Disney had sought in the context of the AOL–Time Warner merger) seemed to doom the future of independent ISPs.

The conditions placed on AOL Time Warner's Instant Messaging services seemed especially fanciful. The FCC had felt that AOL's IM service, with its 100 percent market share at the time, would crush the competition once it was combined with Time Warner's cable lines and content; the agency imagined a world in which IM would be the place for gaming and video, and AOL Time Warner would have an unmatchable subscription list and content library. So it required that AOL Time Warner not provide any new buddy-list video services for IM unless its subscription list were interoperable with that of another provider.[61] This quickly proved overly restrictive. By 2003, AOL was rapidly losing market share in the IM market to Microsoft and Yahoo!, which both offered attractive services, and the company pleaded with the FCC to be relieved of the interoperability requirement. FCC chairman Michael Powell lifted the condition, remarking that he had never agreed with it in the first place.[62]

Just like Comcast and NBC Universal, AOL Time Warner had had online video in mind. On January 10, 2000, the day the merger was announced, Jim Ledbetter of the now-defunct *Industry Standard* magazine zeroed in on this goal: "One of the things the two companies talked today about is streaming video through your computer . . . [but] these kinds of applications . . . right now are very difficult to do at the access speeds that most consumers have to the Internet. Time Warner, with its Road Runner service, potentially has the ability to deliver that."[63]

Arguably, AOL Time Warner was simply ahead of its time and short on some key assets that would have made the video story work out better: a stronger transition of AOL's dial-up customer base to broadband, and a stronger position in cable distribution from Time Warner, together with a willingness on Time Warner's part to tie its content fortunes to some exclusivity or priority over the AOL service. And management expertise.

Indeed, AOL had one thing at the time of the merger that has remained extraordinarily valuable in the world of online video: its reputation for simplicity. Steve Case, after all, had started by offering his service via Commodore 64s, cheap toylike devices with built-in modems, which would connect subscribers to an online bulletin board. At the time, very few people were online and very few PCs had modems installed. Simplicity was key: if you subscribed to AOL, you got access, content, and communications, all in one safe, walled-off area. AOL had hoped to use the Time Warner merger to bring that simplicity and ease of use to a faster-moving broadband world.

Today, similarly, Comcast–NBC Universal aims to make "online" experiences as accessible as possible—as long as consumers play by its rules.

The Comcast-NBCU deal suggests that Case was right but a decade too early. AOL's vision could work today in a way it was unable to ten years ago; many Americans are once again confused by the vast array of Internet options, particularly video. Limiting and protecting the online experience—making it predictable, branded, pleasant, and easy to access—might make it more appealing to more users.

The key to this walled-garden future is Comcast's embrace of TV Everywhere: allowing users to watch high-quality video from well-known programmers online as long as they are already "authenticated" subscribers to pay-TV service bundles. If you pay for HBO on your television, for example, you can watch HBO on your computer, or on a mobile device inside your house.

Like the pre–Time Warner AOL, TV Everywhere will be popular (because it is easy to use and it simplifies the search for satisfying online video) and successful (because only TV Everywhere will have the distribution leverage to keep licensing costs of popular high-quality content down for online viewing). As Case envisioned for AOL Time Warner, TV Everywhere will be able to take advantage of the libraries of content currently provided by the media conglomerates. Plus new stuff.

TV Everywhere could be what saves the content business, allowing Hollywood to move content safely online in the bundled, channeled, pay-TV format with which the movie industry feels comfortable. (The programmers have been spooked by the music industry's experience with iTunes; they want to make sure they can hang on to bundles and avoid fracturing their content into zillions of cheap bits.) TV Everywhere is easy to understand and access; and it is likely that popular TV programs and sports will be available online only through the TV Everywhere bundled service. Add a deal with Facebook, as Comcast did in 2011, and it becomes a one-stop, community-minded, well-branded, well-organized place. Just like AOL.

But there is a key difference: the TV Everywhere structure is effectively a joint venture among all the major cable distributors and most of the media conglomerates around the country. This time the cable distributors in general—and Comcast in particular—have the downstream market power in distribution that Time Warner lacked in 2001. Since then, Comcast and Time Warner have clustered their operations so that they control the "whole of the market" in which they are the providers of bundled wired-distribution services (video plus data).[64] TV Everywhere allows them to move their local physical market power online because customers must subscribe to their pay-TV service to access TV Everywhere.

As Mark Cooper testified at the Senate Antitrust Subcommittee hearing in February 2010, TV Everywhere is "a blatant market division scheme in which the two cable operators [Comcast and Time Warner] who have never overbuilt one another, never competed head to head in physical space, would like to extend that anticompetitive gentleman's agreement into cyberspace."[65]

And this time around, unlike the situation in the 1990s, the interests of the concentrated media conglomerates and the cable distributors are clearly aligned: they are all threatened by online video and interested in keeping the tens of billions of dollars in payments flowing among them—affiliate fees, retransmission consent fees, and other fees that the cable distributors kick back to programmers based on subscribership and advertising revenue—intact. All those fees will flow only if distribution of high-priced content can be carefully controlled and charged for by way of a guaranteed distribution channel—the downstream control that Bewkes says is essential for any vertical integration scheme to work. The other media conglomerates needed Comcast's goodwill for the money spigot to stay open. From the cable-distributor's perspective, a programmer was either with it or against it. A media conglomerate that put its programming online outside this framework would risk losing the guaranteed revenue that came from staying with the club. The NBC Universal deal made Comcast into a media programming powerhouse, and thus allowed it to place formidable content assets inside the TV Everywhere umbrella to kick-start efforts to fight the rise of competing online video.[66]

At the same time, TV Everywhere is a modern-day version of AOL—a safe haven from the wilds of the Internet. As an online writer said in a spring 2010 comment on a blog post:

I don't think that internet video . . . ever . . . is really going to make all that much difference. Because the way that these providers [cable distributors] are now packaging their services is so much more convenient. I go to xfinity TV [the rebranded name of Comcast's TV Everywhere product] and click a couple links and now I'm watching my HBO programming. And there's just a vast amount of other content that is part of my package that is now available as well. And best of all . . . it's all legal as well. I'm not cheating anyone. The quality . . . is superb. The speeds . . . awesome. I don't need to be a pirate surfing the open web trying to find what I want. It's all really right there. Nice and convenient. [ellipses in original][67]

Another key difference from the AOL Time Warner story was good management. Here's John Malone, talking to the *New Yorker*'s Ken Auletta in October 2002:

When the AOL merger took place, I think what was lacking was a power base that the C.E.O. had which allowed him to be somewhat dictatorial. . . . What's very hard is to force behavioral change, where you say, "We just bought AOL. We were into twenty-six million households. The music division needs to create a product that we can bundle with AOL exclusively— not exclusively, who cares, but we need a product that we can sell." And it didn't happen.[68]

Brian Roberts and Comcast might succeed where Gerald Levin and Steve Case failed: they had the management ability to turn all of NBC Universal into a smoothly functioning machine in the service of the Comcast brand, and the coordinated power in the programming-distribution market to make the whole thing work.

As John Malone put it in his interview with Auletta, "The vision [for the AOL–Time Warner merger] was taking unique content and marrying that with the Internet, and, particularly as the Internet transitions to high speed, you convince the world—that is, your dial-up subscribers—that high speed creates a value in content that wasn't there at slow speed. And so you shift AOL from being essentially a transport mechanism to being a way to receive unique content services and pay for it—a subscription-content model, as opposed to a connectivity-payment model, where little value goes to the content."[69] By owning programming and controlling access to it, and by selling "specialized services" like TV Everywhere that felt like the Internet but were treated much more favorably both technically and financially, Comcast could shift its distribution services to the all-subscription-content model, make things simple and friendly for consumers, and forestall the day when its pipes were viewed as transport mechanisms for other companies' content. In 1996, Steven Levy had scoffed at AOL for serving up a comfortable walled-garden world of content and community; Levy was confident that AOL was about to be destroyed by the advent of the wide-open spaces of the Net, and called it a "dead man walking."[70] Fifteen years later, Comcast's 2011 merger with NBC Universal, taken together with its power over high-speed distribution in its markets, looked to be the implementation of the AOL–Time Warner plan. (The next, inevitable step: in 2012, Comcast announced that its online video flowing through an Xbox would not be subject to usage caps—it would be a "specialized service" with quality guarantees—but that Netflix Internet video would be so subject, even though from the consumer's perspective the two would appear to be exactly the same.)[71] The Internet, this time around, seemed like the dead man walking.

The regulators in charge of reviewing the Comcast-NBCU deal were, understandably, haunted by memories of AOL Time Warner. Following enormous public concerns about the deal, the agencies back then had risen to the challenge by trying to make room for new marketplaces in competitive ISPs and Instant Messaging applications. But when the AOL–Time Warner merger turned out to be a fiasco, the regulators looked weak for imposing intrusive conditions that ultimately meant nothing. When the same concerns were raised about Comcast and NBC Universal, the regulators had to be worried that overzealous advocates were crying wolf once more.

Maybe this merger would also fail. Bewkes of Time Warner (now just a content, not a distribution, company) made it clear during an October 2009 TVWeek Conference that he did not think much of the Comcast-NBCU deal, explicitly comparing it to the AOL–Time Warner disaster. It was not clear to him how Comcast was going to be able to become a more successful business by buying NBC Universal. "Somebody has finally noticed that these things don't work out so well," he said, adding, "We love to see our competitors taking risks."[72] Other vertical integrations had been unwound; Bewkes split Time Warner Cable from Time Warner Entertainment in 2008–9; News Corp. went after DirecTV in 2003 but then spun it loose in 2006.[73]

Whether all vertical mergers are benign is an open question. Forty years ago, the economist Oliver Williamson argued that vertical integration had "dubious if not outright antisocial properties."[74] After years of litigation and, crucially, the defection of maverick Howard Hughes from the studio pack, the Supreme Court forced the movie studios to divest their theater chains in the 1948 *Paramount* case, even though the studios had argued that without control over distribution they would have no incentive to invest in expensive content production. (Much the same argument is made today in support of TV Everywhere models.) Studios had forced theater chains to buy films they did not want as part of packages—"block booking"—and often required them not to show films from competing studios. Independent producers had a great deal of trouble getting their films seen in major movie houses, because the theaters would say—often truthfully— that they had no open time.[75] Colleen Abdoulah of WOW! would have recognized these practices.

Before the litigation brought the system to an end, the studios had flourished within their vertically integrated format. Modern economists have asserted that block booking brought efficiency gains and that the studios' vertical integration into distribution and exhibition provided low-priced entertainment to huge numbers of filmgoers. Schemes the Supreme Court at the time saw as "devices for stifling competition and diverting the cream of the business to the large operators" are now praised by many economists as having reduced the costs of doing business, smoothing the way for high-quality mass entertainment on thousands of well-attended screens across the country.[76] The idea that there could be a public interest in decentralization—even at the risk of occasional higher costs to industry—is now out of fashion, as is the notion that an inefficient firm might want to vertically integrate in order to use its market power to foreclose change in a dynamic digital world. As the biggest purchaser of television content and the biggest broadband provider in the country, Comcast arguably had the power to influence how the most popular television programming was distributed over the Internet, and an interest in slowing the rise of online video that might replace Comcast's core transmission services' revenue stream.

In important ways, critics charged, the vertical integration planned by Comcast resembled what Microsoft had done a decade earlier: using its power in one market to move into another in order to avoid commoditization of the first.[77] In 2001, the D.C. Circuit Court found that Microsoft had violated the Sherman Act by unlawfully maintaining its monopoly in the PC operating-system market. (Other claims against Microsoft were thrown out, but this one was upheld.) How did it do that? By bundling its Internet Explorer Web browser software with its Microsoft Windows operating system, thus preventing the distribution and use of products that might threaten its overwhelmingly dominant position in the market for operating systems. The bundling created an "applications barrier to entry" because most consumers prefer operating systems for which a large number of applications have already been written, and most developers prefer to write for operating systems that already have a substantial consumer base. Bundling Internet Explorer with Windows ensured that consumers would find competing Web browsers more difficult to locate or use. As the court put it, "If a consumer could have access to the applications he desired—regardless of the operating system he uses—simply by installing a particular browser on his computer, then he would no longer feel compelled to select Windows in order to have access to those applications; he could select an operating system other than Windows based solely upon its quality and price." In other words, the market for operating systems would be competitive, and Microsoft did not want that to happen.[78]

Someone who worried about vertical integration in an era of dynamic digital change could see Comcast's plan as mapping directly onto Microsoft's efforts. Monopoly power may be inferred from a company's possession of a dominant share of a relevant market—here the market for distribution of data and video over a wire—that is protected by entry barriers, factors that prevent new rivals from responding to the monopoly firm's price increases. Ordinarily, increases in price above competitive levels get competitors interested in undermining the incumbent player. Comcast could bundle access to the most popular programming (the new market) with its existing transmission-distribution wires (the old market) in order to maintain control over wired data transmission.

Comcast's combination of live local sports and NBC Universal content with its high-priced wires, and its ability to use NBCU programming to nudge the entire programming world into the TV Everywhere framework online (unless a maverick bolted), might make it difficult—perhaps impossible—for a new player in the market for high-speed wires to show up, charge less, and compete with Comcast in any of the markets where Comcast operated. Comcast-NBCU would succeed where AOL Time Warner failed.

5

Netflix, Dead or Alive

DURING THE FEBRUARY 2010 SENATE antitrust subcommittee hearing, consumer advocate Andy Schwartzman testified emphatically about the risks a combined Comcast–NBC Universal would pose to online video. "They have every reason," he said, "to withhold NBC programming from . . . online-only competitors."[1] But Brian Roberts had a different view: of all video viewed online, "NBC has less than 1 percent; Comcast has less than half of 1 percent; Hulu [co-owned equally by NBC, ABC, and Fox at the time] has less than 4 percent; and Google has over 50 percent. It is a dynamic, rapidly changing market, but as a broadband company, we want to encourage as much video as possible because the fastest growing part of our company is broadband."[2] Who was right? Would a combined Comcast–NBC Universal help or hurt online video?

Among the many grails sought by the companies and developers behind next-generation communications, one of the holiest is online video services. Of course, not all online video is the same. Only long-form, professional online video—a series of half-hour- or hour-long shows with continuing narratives and high production values—would substitute for the proprietary bundles of cable networks offered by Comcast. (Roberts was a bit disingenuous in talking about Google's videos, which at the time amounted to a vast collection of ten-minute YouTube snippets.) But this alternative would turn Comcast's cable infrastructure into little more than pipes for someone else's moneymaking activities.

As previously separate services have converged, becoming indistinguish-able bits passing over wires, the market for the long-form, professionally produced video preferred by Americans has already moved "online." That is, the television that the vast majority of Americans watch is made up of electronic packets that are sent using the Internet Protocol, and those packets travel through the same digital pipe that the cable companies use to distribute a relatively narrow (when compared to the available capacity of the cable pipe as a whole) trickle of Internet access. Just 10 percent or fewer Americans use rabbit ears to watch television broadcast over the air.[3] But conventional television distribution as a practical matter remains a centralized, tightly controlled marketplace in which programmers and pipe owners jointly participate. True "online" services can be launched without the permission of the Internet access distributor (think Facebook in a Harvard dorm room); by contrast, access to the bundles of cable networks that Comcast sells is available only by paying the freight to Comcast in its role as distributor.

Because conventional television—a $70 billion a year advertising vehicle—offers such a lucrative marketplace,[4] the possibility of substituting online video for cable networks poses risks to both programmers and cable distributors. Cable distributors and media conglomerates have cooperative arrangements in place that channel more than $30 billion in fees paid annu-ally by the distributors to programmers, their largest source of revenue.[5] The distributors, in turn, charge individual subscription rates that keep going up: a typical cable subscriber pays more than $128 a month for video, high-speed Internet access, and phone services,[6] and the average subscription price has increased about 30 percent in the past five years, while household incomes have declined.[7] The programmers and distributors have powerful market positions that allow them to keep these flows going, and the advantage of regulatory schemes that support the status quo. As long as the distribution pipes dominate their physical locations and there is no reason-able substitute for cable networks available over the open Internet, every part of this controlled distribution chain produces enormous profits. "I think everybody is going to do well in this mix," John Malone told industry analysts in a public conference call in May 2011.[8] Online video, which threat-ens to cut out the middlemen, would disrupt this flow.

Why then did Brian Roberts say in March 2011 that he wanted to encourage online video?

A large part of the answer is that the cable industry's growth area does not come from television but high-speed Internet access, and Americans are increasingly getting their high-speed data services from their local cable monopolist. Online video, whatever it does to traditional television, will keep them signing up for data services. By mid-2011, Comcast had persuaded 17 million of its 22 million television subscribers to purchase high-speed Internet access as well as television—"incredible high penetration rates," according to Malone in the analysts' conference call. Roberts was optimistic about his company's ability to sign up additional millions of data customers over time.[9] Comcast would continue to do well even if it lost a few video customers.

The rest of the answer lies in Comcast's power, as the country's largest provider of both data and video services, to pressure potentially competitive online video providers. Netflix, an online long-form video service that became enormously popular with consumers by providing a cheap monthly subscription to streaming movies and archives of TV shows, is a prime example of an "over the top" provider of video (one that makes videos available over the Internet access portion of Comcast's pipe). The absence of any effective regulatory regime or oversight over the cable giant makes it unlikely that Netflix will ever be able to challenge Comcast. Comcast has a number of options that will make it extremely difficult for independently provided, directly competitive professional online video to challenge its dominance.

Roberts crystallized one aspect of his company's power in early 2011: "What used to be called 'reruns' on television is now called Netflix. We're not seeing it cut into our core business, but we are glad as a producer of content to see the value of that content rising."[10] His words could be seen as a reminder to Netflix that its costs were bound to go up because the dominant programmers and Comcast shared an interest in undermining competition from independent online video platforms, and because Comcast controlled the pipes.

In other words, the NBC Universal merger made online video a two-sided issue for Comcast. Comcast would be able to use its control over NBC

Universal content, its relationships with programmers dependent on money from Comcast, and its technical control over gateways to its subscribers to protect itself from any rise in the popularity of competitive independent long-form online video. At the same time, interest in online video services provided on Comcast's terms and with its permission would drive Americans' appetite for high data speeds. Comcast would be there to sell them those services and its version of TV Everywhere—over the same pipe—reaping ever-higher revenue from each user.[11] The trick would be to slow the loss of customers who were only interested in video while simultaneously selling high-priced high-speed Internet access to as many people as possible.

By mid-2011, the major cable providers had a monopoly in wired high-speed Internet access (at speeds necessary to download video satisfactorily) in areas not served by Verizon's FiOS service, and the telcos (AT&T and Verizon) had stopped expanding their fiber networks. At the end of 2011, Verizon and Comcast tacitly agreed not to compete in the provision of wired Internet access service: in a complex deal involving a transfer of spectrum worth $3.6 billion from Comcast and Time Warner to Verizon, the former competitors announced that they would jointly market each other's services. As the analyst Craig Moffett of Bernstein Research put it, the deal was "a partnership between formerly mortal enemies."[12] Tired of spending money on wired Internet access service, Verizon had essentially conceded to cable's unrivaled superiority in that arena.

The only thing that could have limited the cable industry's power, in Malone's view, was regulation. He had told the *Wall Street Journal* while the Comcast-NBCU deal was being reviewed that he was not interested in U.S. cable deals. "It is entirely feasible that government may choose to open these networks up. They could come in, for instance, and tell cable operators they can't bundle broadband with video, with telephone, that they've got to sell them all a la carte and they can't do any deep discounting, no exclusionary deals and so on. And [as they review the Comcast-NBCU deal] they can set the pattern that they would later enforce on the industry at large through rule-making."[13] But that didn't happen. The reaction of the regulators to the expansion of Comcast's power by way of the NBC Universal merger to slow the advent of competitive online video was mild. The government did not open up the cable networks, require that they separate content from conduit, insist that they provide high-speed access at reasonable prices to all Americans in exchange for their access to public rights-of-way, or meddle with the content industry's relationship with the cable distributors. Things continued to be good for Comcast.

In the highly concentrated American media business, all deals are watched closely by all the other players. Because so few actors have real power, each move that might jostle some other player is carefully examined. This is why a 2008 deal that Netflix made with Starz, a premium-cable channel, was so surprising: Netflix agreed to pay $25 million a year for the right to stream Starz content, which includes Sony and Disney movies, online. Starz sensed that online streaming would be big but had been unable to make its own online venture, under the leaden name Vongo, work. Netflix, however, already had access to millions of Americans. Twenty-five million dollars seemed like a lot of money to Netflix at the time, but the other programmers felt that the deal was a steal for Netflix and a huge mistake by Starz.[14]

In hindsight, Starz does not seem to have known what it was selling and what effect the sale might have on the programmers and cable companies. The deal made it possible for Netflix to offer cheap online subscriptions that brought consumers easy access to high-value content—twenty-five hundred movies and television shows, many of recent vintage.[15] Netflix marched on, signing a nearly one-billion-dollar licensing deal in August 2010 with the premium channel Epix that allowed it to stream current-release and back-catalogue movies from Paramount, Lionsgate, and MGM for five years. Netflix also lined up a huge range of back-catalogue television shows for online streaming from a variety of sources.[16] It announced plans to start acquiring first-run original content, beginning with a 2012 political drama called *House of Cards*, starring Kevin Spacey.[17] At the same time, its subscription numbers were surging.

Netflix, an online upstart that had not built the network it was using, had by mid-2011 built an online business that had more subscribers than Comcast, which had spent untold billions on infrastructure. According to some observers, Netflix downloads accounted for almost 30 percent of peak traffic across data lines running to residences in North America in 2011.[18] This was not the digital future that Comcast had in mind.

Netflix has long been viewed as a company that can carry out its strategies well and change direction on a dime. As high-speed data connections were rolled out in the late 2000s, it quickly pivoted from exclusive reliance on DVD by mail, which entailed $600 million in postage costs, to streaming video directly to subscribers;[19] it continued to ship DVDs, but streaming became a bigger part of its operations and grew faster. And Netflix's approach to advertising was innovative as well; its software recommended movies and shows to subscribers based on what they had already watched.[20] Consumers loved it.

The studios and programmers that licensed content were clearly pleased with the idea of an online distribution partner who could make consumers happy. And happy they were: new users embraced the idea of streaming-only subscriptions without the trouble of DVD returns.[21] Netflix went farther, embedding its software in hundreds of electronic devices—Windows and Mac PCs, Sony PS3, Microsoft Xbox, Nintento Wii, AppleTV, iPad—which gave it even greater access to American consumers.[22] For game players who were in love with their devices, having Netflix available on gaming consoles was a thrill. Even after the company deeply annoyed subscribers by changing its pricing policy so that choosing both online streaming and DVD shipping would mean a 60 percent price hike for many of its customers, Netflix retained most of its loyal followers.[23]

Jeffrey Bewkes, CEO of Time Warner, was not happy about Netflix. A gifted, frank man who had prospered through years of turmoil inside Time Warner, Bewkes was responsible for leading HBO into the twenty-first century and spinning off Time Warner's cable-distribution assets into a separate company. In response to Netflix's 2008 deal with Starz, he made some remarks, published in the pages of the *New York Times*, that could be taken as a message to the company. In a December 2010 article (published before Netflix's numbers overtook those of Comcast) headlined "Time Warner Views Netflix as a Fading Star," Bewkes noted that Starz programming would probably be many times more expensive when Netflix sought to renew its deal in 2012. "Mr. Bewkes suggested a new deal [with Starz] may not be reached," reporter Tim Arango wrote, "because Netflix's subscription streaming service, which costs about $8 a month, isn't high enough for the company to pay top dollar for movies."[24] The highly concentrated content industry might well understand by this that it would not be a good idea to give favorable terms—or perhaps any terms—to Netflix.

If consumers were satisfied with what they got from Netflix, why would they pay for Time Warner's flagship HBO content as part of a large bundle of well-branded channels sold by a cable company? Bewkes's words could be seen as a call to the rest of the industry to raise Netflix's costs. "It's a little bit like, is the Albanian army going to take over the world?" he said to Arango. "I don't think so."[25] His remarks to the *Times* appeared to be a signal: no one else had better make a low-price content deal with Netflix who wanted to continue to participate in the high-dollar cable-distribution structure—including Starz, when it renegotiated with Netflix.

In September 2011, Bewkes's confident prediction came true when Starz cut its ties with Netflix, leaving behind an offer of more than $300 million, ten times the amount of the original 2008 deal. The *Los Angeles Times* reported that Starz had wanted Netflix subscribers to pay more than Netflix's standard $8 per month for Starz content, essentially making Netflix into an online replica of a cable distributor. Starz was unwilling to disrupt its relationships with traditional distributors, who did not want subscribers to "cut the cord" and switch to online-only content. But Netflix had refused to set up tiered pricing.[26] The *Los Angeles Times* later reported that Greg Maffei, CEO of Liberty Media, Starz's parent company, had made it clear in December 2011 at an investors' conference that Starz had left the $300 million from Netflix on the table because it had not wanted to alienate its cable-distribution customers: "You just can't have a non-premium type price and offering of a premium service that doesn't create enormous channel conflict," Maffei said. "Our product is marketed through cable companies, satellite companies, telcos," he said. "You have to provide an offering that works for them. To put it into perspective, we have $1.3 billion in revenue from those guys. What can we get on the digital side?"[27]

Netflix itself may some day be overtaken by other online destinations, like Amazon's digital rental services. (In the short run, the hike of monthly rates and the end of the Starz deal triggered a sharp decline in Netflix's stock price.)[28] But what is sure is that Netflix's (or the Amazon service's) future depends on reliable access to movies and television. Netflix had made a tentative effort to get around the distribution-programming megalopolis by arranging for its own original programming, but for the television shows and movies that are its standard fare, it depends on traditional providers. Netflix CEO Reed Hastings tried to fend off destruction by the sledgehammer of the combined distributors and programmers by agreeing with Brian Roberts's assessment: Netflix was a complementary service, a non-competing provider of older television shows and movies, with no plans to tread on the cable companies' prime turf: sports, news, or current television.

But that wasn't enough for Bewkes—who, as it happens, had his own plan for online video that would keep the interests of the programmers and distributors aligned: TV Everywhere. Rather than let Netflix erode his industry's foundation, he forced Netflix to play defense.

TV Everywhere is rooted in a simple and elegant idea: large cable distributors provide the same pay-TV content online that their subscribers can get through their traditional cable subscriptions. This online product is "free"—at no additional cost—to existing pay-TV subscribers. Once subscribers have been authenticated by the TV Everywhere system, they will be able to access their particular pay-TV package online, whether on their laptop, mobile device, or Internet-ready television.[29]

The genius underlying TV Everywhere is that most pay-TV subscribers will believe that their cable provider's online aggregation of content is free, whereas they will perceive that they have to pay extra for, say, Netflix. This will presumably make those subscribers unwilling (or at least less willing) to pay a substantial fee for any competing online aggregation of content, like Netflix. At the same time, programmers will be able to ask for an increase in their licensing fees to cover the online portion of their agreement with the cable distributors. And the cable distributors can push subscribers toward bundles of pay-TV and Internet access by pricing Internet-only subscriptions at a higher rate than that of the bundle. A win-win for the megalopolis.

TV Everywhere became a major asset for the cable distributors in 2010. The ability to put all cable programming behind an "authentication wall" (you had to already be a pay-TV subscriber) would help keep the status quo in place—tens of billions of dollars in fees paid to programmers, hundreds of billions of dollars in pay-TV subscription fees paid to distributors. Broadcast network shows, which account for only a tiny portion of the media conglomerates' overall revenue, might be allowed to float online free of high-priced bundled pay-TV subscriptions, but the lucrative cable channels would be available online only via TV Everywhere, where the conglomerates' traditional revenue streams were secure. Cable distributors were also anxious to retain their revenues from Video on Demand (VOD) packages that give subscribers instant access to movies at home for extra payments; if Netflix or another aggregator had enough content, it could offer a compelling alternative to VOD.

Any independent online video aggregator like Netflix would have a tough time in this environment: if the choice is between an upstart and a behemoth, who is likely to win? If you're Disney, why risk the entire package of payments you're getting for your broadcast stations, your retransmission consent fees (more on those later), and the subscriber fees for your juggernaut ESPN from your cable-distribution partners? If you irritate those partners, they will find ways to make business more difficult— cutting the subscription fees your cable channels command, giving you less for retransmission consent. Sticking with the cable guys is an economic decision, as Greg Maffei of Starz made clear: would you earn so much from online streaming that you're willing to risk the fees you receive under the current business model? Particularly knowing that ad rates online are about a fourth of what the programming can command when it's distributed via cable? You, the media conglomerate, may need the cable distributor more than it needs you.

Moreover, cable distributors who are vertically integrated into programming—like Comcast and its regional sports networks, or Cox (another regional monopoly cable-distribution company) and the San Diego Padres—own quite a bit of important content that new subscribers to an independent online video aggregator would still want, even after giving up their cable subscription. These cable distributors have no interest in licensing to a new online video provider inside or outside their territories. Federal law does not give that independent online provider any help because the existing scheme was set up to enable competing cable providers and satellite companies to get access to programming owned by cable distributors—not online distributors. Even if Comcast is forced to give a new company access to its cable-network programming, it can make this access expensive in more ways than one—for instance, by requiring endless data-security audits. Whichever subscribers chose, Comcast or Time Warner would pocket the fee the users paid for high-speed data, but not getting their video-subscription fee on top of that payment would turn their lucrative services into a mere pipe. Comcast is unlikely to accept being treated like a commodity provider of transport, a conduit for the moneymaking operations of other people. Even if Comcast is making 90 percent-plus margins for its high-speed Internet access product,[30] it wants to be able to *also* charge for premium video services that travel across the Internet.

True, things could go a different way. Suppose Netflix moved on from the cable guys to ask content companies like Scripps, which owns the Home and Garden and Fine Living channels, directly for licenses to their cable-network content. The new online company might love to distribute Home and Garden and Fine Living to its subscribers.

But Scripps is not an eight-hundred-pound gorilla like Disney's ESPN. It needs Comcast distribution—badly—to survive. Here even before the NBC Universal merger Comcast had leverage. It could say to Scripps, "If you make your material available online, we'll make life materially uncomfortable for you. We'll move your channels to a less-widely distributed tier. We'll cut the subscriber fees we pay you. Your life will be hell."

The online aggregator might, of course, land one of the big guys. Disney might license ESPN to it, because ESPN is big enough that Disney did not have to care what pre-merger Comcast thought. Then again, ESPN would be an extremely expensive proposition for a new online video business. And it would probably come with a lot of demands: "We won't license unless the online video aggregator also has name-brand channels X, Y, and Z signed up." Why would Disney make these demands? Because it can, and because the unbundled ("a la carte") model is, from Disney's perspective, the worst thing for its overall success, which depends on selling indivisible bundles that include content the user really wants. And licensing a "Disney package" and allowing a new company to redistribute it online would smell like a la carte.[31]

Any new aggregator venturing into this swamp would soon learn what happened to AT&T and Verizon when they went into the pay-TV business. The two companies, in a hurry to launch their new video products, were mercilessly gouged by programmers. They paid enormous fees for content because they had no leverage. They needed access to programming more than the programmers needed them.[32] If these two giants could not succeed, how would a new startup online video business ever make it?

In other words, the problem with innovation in online content distribution outside the cable industry's shadow is that the status quo works too well for all the big players. If you're Disney/ESPN, you can demand that the cable operators distribute your channel to 100 percent of their subscribers (even if 25 percent or more of subscribers never watch ESPN), and you can demand that your complete bundle (not just ESPN, but the Disney Channel and Disney Junior) be carried. In exchange, you get a guaranteed large payment, year after year.[33] If you're Scripps, the model isn't working perfectly for you, but you're on your way up and you can't afford to make anyone mad at you. And if you're Comcast, you have no interest in helping anyone who would undermine your ability to command large monthly pay-TV subscription fees.

As an independent online aggregator, outside the club, Netflix needed to keep its head down and declare its pacifist nature. Direct, outright competition with the cable payment structure would have jeopardized its ability to obtain any programming at all. As it got bigger, there might come a day when the programmers and the cable distributors would need Netflix more than it needed them. But until then it was prudent for Netflix just to try to survive. Broad adoption of TV Everywhere was a persuasive argument that the status quo would stay in place.

Survival was never easy for aggregators. In mid-2011, Hulu—whose business relied on next-day streaming of broadcast content—was forced to bend to the TV Everywhere model. Fox announced that everyone but authenticated subscribers to pay-TV would have to wait eight days to watch a show online;[34] ABC was rumored to be considering a similar limitation.[35] Hulu itself looked less attractive as a destination. Things would be even tougher for new entrants; attracting investment in any new online video-aggregation businesses dependent on the media conglomerates would not be easy.

Online aggregators' problems do not end when they get access to content. A second precondition for a healthy Netflix (or any other online video service) is reliable access to high-speed Internet subscribers over a standard connection, so that the company's movies and other long-form videos will not hiccup and stall. Distribution is always an issue for any media. For newspapers, it's newspaper racks; for new online video businesses, it's high-speed Internet access. And therein lies Netflix's hidden problem and the cable industry's hidden advantage: the existing industry structure makes this precondition for success more uncertain than any business would like. There is no guaranteed level playing field for reaching an audience of cable high-speed-data subscribers.

This is where the titanic battles over the idea of common carriage during 2009–10 become relevant. The distributors won a couple of key skirmishes and, as a result, competing video providers using their high-speed data connections were in for a rough ride.

First, even though wireless connections cannot carry as much data as a wired cable connection, they are still extremely useful for getting content from cable wires to Internet-enabled televisions in peoples' houses. So Netflix would like its content to go over the wireless carriers' connections. But video imposes a big burden on wireless connections, particularly live video, and the wireless providers will therefore want Netflix to compensate them for the privilege of reaching their subscribers. And nothing in federal law or regulations establishes what rates wireless carriers can charge or how discriminatory those rates can be. Netflix will be at the wireless carriers' mercy.

Wired providers, meanwhile, have a variety of ways to charge an online video aggregator and prioritize their own services. They can underprice the aggregator by charging less for their own video packages than the aggregator can (Comcast gets the lowest prices for content because it has the most subscribers). They can charge higher prices to any data-transmission network the aggregator works with to get its programming to their gateways. They can charge users for the data usage involved in getting access to the aggregator's programming, while keeping their own material on "specialized services" portions of their own pipe, which aren't subject to the same pricing schemes. There are a thousand ways to turn the knife.

The investment community has had long debates over whether distribution or content is king. Where are the best businesses? Where should we put our money? The genius of the cable industry model, when it comes to the future of online video, is that Comcast and the other cable distributors win either way. They are making tremendous, unthreatened margins on their data services. At the same time, the cable operators want to provide online video to their users because they know that video availability will drive adoption of high-speed data service. It already has. The only catch is that they would prefer users to embrace their TV Everywhere financial model, which requires an authenticated pay-TV subscription. Only through the TV Everywhere umbrella do users get "online" access to sports, news, new television series, or cable-network programming. Consumers can make an economic decision: they can buy an "extra" subscription to a new online aggregator (if it can promise them interesting programming) and stream a connection across an "open Internet"—that part of the cable pipe that is subject to the weak and probably unenforceable nondiscrimination rules adopted by the FCC, where the cable operator caps usage—or they can buy from the cable operator and play "free" online video that is not subject to caps. But they make their decision within a carefully controlled context. The cable operator can decide what the prices are by controlling the reliability and amount of Internet access, prices for content, and the price paid by the subscriber for Internet access without a cable subscription.

Here's the kicker: if Comcast sells Xfinity (its TV Everywhere–model service) in other cable distributors' territories, what is the result? The major players have divided up the country.[36] Let's say that Comcast decides to market TV Everywhere in Time Warner territory. Then it will be using Time Warner's infrastructure. If that happens, Comcast can easily undersell Time Warner's own TV Everywhere package because, again, Comcast pays the least for this content. It will have the best and cheapest video package in America.

So Comcast wins either way. Inside its own territory, it can turn all the dials—access to content, access to a guaranteed connection—to block any online video package seeking to compete with its own products. Outside its territory, it can underprice the other operators' packages. John D. Rockefeller would love such brutal elegance.

6

The Peacock Disappears

Jack Donaghy: Then what do you want with NBC? Why do you even want me?

Dave Hess: Well, buying NBC counts as a charitable donation for tax purposes.

—*30 Rock*, March 18, 2010

WHEN THE ANTITRUST POLICY FIREBRAND Senator Herb Kohl (D-Wis.) launched the Senate Antitrust Subcommittee hearing on the Comcast merger in February 2010, he was clearly focused on the programming assets NBC Universal would contribute to the deal: "NBC Universal . . . includes the family of NBC broadcasting and cable networks, 25 local NBC and Telemundo stations in some of the nation's largest cities, and the Universal Pictures Movie Studios. NBC has some of the most popular programs on television—from the Olympics, to NFL football, to NBC news programming, to entertainment programs ranging from 'The Tonight Show' to 'The Office,' to give just a few examples." With such a trove of assets, Kohl, like Senator Al Franken, was worried about the power the combined company would have. He asked that the witnesses from Comcast and NBC Universal "explain to us . . . and the American people how the creation of this media conglomerate will serve the interests of the American people, not just the interests of your companies."[1]

The witness for NBC Universal was its president and CEO, Jeff Zucker. Seated next to Brian Roberts, he was a study in Hollywood earnestness, prepared to back up whatever Roberts had to say. He had joined the network right out of college, answering a phone call from NBC during his graduation ceremony at Harvard in 1986 that landed him a job as a researcher for the 1988 Seoul Olympic Games. For Zucker, NBC Universal was both an "iconic" media company and his emotional home; he had been, in rapid succession, executive producer of the *Today Show*, president of NBC Entertainment, CEO of NBC, and, since 2007, the head of NBC Universal.[2]

Nevertheless, most people watching the hearing saw Zucker as a doomed man. Brian Roberts had steadfastly denied that he had plans to send Zucker to career Siberia, telling UBS analysts right after the deal was announced: "We are big believers in decentralization. We are not going to run NBC Universal; Jeff Zucker is."[3] But no one bought it. Just months after the hearing—and a full four months before the deal was approved by the regulators and the Department of Justice—Zucker was out, telling friends (according to the *New York Post*) that he was taking an exit package of $30 million to $40 million to leave NBC Universal following completion of the merger; in his place would come longtime Comcast chief operating officer Steve Burke.[4]

With NBC running fourth in ratings among the four networks and Zucker himself the subject of public disdain for his management record (including his disastrous decision to replace late-night host Jay Leno with Conan O'Brien), it was pretty clear that Comcast saw him as a liability.[5] As *PaidContent*, a news and information source focusing on subscription-based media businesses, put it, "Not since Gerald Levin [former CEO of AOL Time Warner] destroyed about $200 billion in shareholder value has a more maligned executive emerged from the media world, which is really saying something."[6]

Zucker apparently didn't see his ouster coming. His testimony that day was characteristically upbeat: "I could not be more excited about the future of this company," he said, his chin up, rimless glasses flashing, and bulldog voice resounding in the hearing room. "This deal will give us the resources and the tools to innovate and adapt in an unpredictable media world and meet the needs of 21st century consumers."[7] That "us" would not include Zucker, but he had already played his part in laying the foundation for a successful post-merger company. He had presided over NBC Universal as it had built its strength as a cable network—which is what the deal was about—not the NBC broadcast peacock but the clutch of powerful cable channels controlled by NBC Universal, holdings that generated mountains of cash at margins of more than 50 percent. At the end of 2011, the NBC Universal cable channels (including USA, Syfy, CNBC, and Bravo) were providing the profits for the division, increasing in value each quarter, while the broadcast network's revenue continued to descend—swooning by 7 percent for the year.[8] As the media analyst SNL Kagan put it in late 2011, the cash flow margin of cable networks was "amazing."[9]

Thomas Edison made mass communication possible. He invented the phonograph and the telegraph and figured out how to distribute electrical power. He also founded General Electric, which commercialized his inventions and is today one of the largest publicly traded companies in the world. General Electric made everything from microwaves to jet engines—and thanks to its 1986 purchase of RCA, it owned NBC, too.[10]

When deal discussions began in 2009 between Comcast and GE over NBC Universal, Edison's old company, for all its size and breadth, was not doing well. Profits were down, losses within its finance arm, GE Capital, were enormous, and, as part of the constellation of businesses that had profited from elaborately complicated securitizations of subprime mortgages, GE was being blamed as a participant in the country's financial near-collapse. GE Capital had been started in the 1930s as a middleman operation, smoothing transactions between factories and consumers on durable goods like washing machines; eventually it moved into turbines, real estate, and a host of other areas. By 2009 it was deeply involved in the subprime credit market and needed $50 billion in bailout assistance.[11]

Following a 56 percent drop in revenue in 2008, trust in the company was eroding fast.[12] Jeffrey Immelt, General Electric's CEO, needed to show that his company had a plan, that it was slimming down and exchanging assets for strength on its balance sheet. Although he had emphatically asserted in March 2008 that offloading his company's key media asset was unthinkable, as the financial world crumbled around him in 2009 selling NBC Universal began to make sense.[13]

Jack Welch, for two decades GE's famous CEO, had made the deal back in 1986 to bring NBC within the GE family. Later, Immelt bought up $21 billion in additional assets, tripling the size of GE's entertainment business in 2004 by buying cable, film, and Universal theme-park assets from Vivendi, which became a minority partner in the new company, NBC Universal.[14]

But being in the media business did not make sense for GE, and being inside GE's giant world of turbines, jet engines, commercial loans, and air conditioners did not make sense for NBC. NBC employees had little to offer when they were summoned to be part of annual GE Imagination shows, and GE's factory floors were a universe away from the set of *Saturday Night Live*. As NBC faltered—moving from first place among the networks in 1996 to a seemingly permanent fourth spot starting in 2001–2, its position as part of General Electric made even less sense.[15] In the first nine months of 2009 NBC made 27 percent less profit than in the same period in 2008. Even though overall profits for the entertainment division remained healthy—bolstered significantly by NBCU cable-channel revenue from CNBC, USA, and Bravo—and NBC Universal as a division contributed about 12 percent to GE's enormous bottom line according to *Bloomberg* data, analysts considered the division the odd man out within GE.[16]

General Electric kept NBC Universal partly out of corporate vanity and a desire for political influence. Executives seemed to revel in their power over NBCU editorial decisions, which rankled NBC employees. During the summer of 2009, GE allegedly directed an MSNBC journalist not to criticize Fox, and, as the parent company aimed to capture lucrative stimulus funding for green energy developments, allegedly ordered NBC to cover President Obama's health-care summit.[17] Rumors flew about GE's role with the administration; Immelt was reported to be making calls to Capitol Hill supporting Ben Bernanke's renomination as chairman of the Federal Reserve.[18] The same week the Comcast-NBCU merger was approved by the Obama administration in January 2011, Immelt was appointed to lead President Obama's Council on Jobs and Competitiveness, replacing former Federal Reserve chairman Paul Volcker.[19]

But NBC Universal was also pursuing other options. Zucker considered encouraging Vivendi to go public with its 20 percent stake (if Vivendi decided to exercise its option to sell, which was available each year from November 15 through the first full week of December). He brought in a parade of bankers, who probably discovered what Comcast's team found out at about the same time: NBC Universal's books were in shabby shape. It was hard to tell how things added up. An IPO seemed unlikely.[20]

However much Zucker may have dreamed of independence, in 2009 Immelt needed a comeback story for investors. Shedding NBC Universal would give him a $30 billion headline and let him claim a large deal that would make GE's operations more coherent. He could then move on with GE's enormous core businesses in power generation, aviation, and medical imaging; save his reputation; and divert attention from doubts about his standing as CEO.

By early 2009, with GE stock at a fourteen-year low,[21] Immelt was ready to sell. The investment banker Jamie Dimon, head of JPMorgan, met with Brian Roberts and Steve Burke on March 3, and in July JPMorgan Chase's vice chairman James B. Lee set up a meeting with both Brian and patriarch Ralph at the annual Allen & Company Sun Valley media conference. By December, Ralph had signed off on the deal, saying, according to the *New York Times*, "I've done a lot of deals in my life. Every deal has its time. This is the right time."[22]

Talks between General Electric and Comcast during the summer of 2009 were volatile and irritable. The goalposts kept moving as valuations shifted and GE intermittently demanded more cash. Comcast wanted to put as little cash into the deal as possible, and argued that its existing programming properties were highly valuable; meanwhile, GE was having trouble getting Vivendi to sell its stake at a reasonable price.[23] The television comedy *30 Rock* lampooned the negotiations in 2011:

> Liz Lemon: Hey, what's going on with Jenna's dressing room?
> Pete Hornberger: Jack rented it out to an IT company. The Kabletown board is meeting this week to approve buying NBC, and he's doing everything possible to make us seem profitable. He turned the green room into an NBC experience store. And we have to schedule our rehearsals around the Bat Mitzvahs Jack has booked in the studio.[24]

At particularly difficult moments, Comcast's chief financial officer, Mike Angelakis, met with Keith Sherin, his GE counterpart, to rescue the relationship and solidify the basic terms on which NBC Universal and Comcast would join forces. During all those months, NBC Universal network executives, including Zucker, were left out of the negotiations.[25]

And the deal worked. Sort of. The news leaked the day NBC Universal executives were told about it at the end of September 2009; the leak made it seem as though NBC Universal wanted to scuttle the talks by making Comcast's investors balk at the company's apparent plans to spend $30 billion for NBC Universal. If the investors were sufficiently spooked, they would sell and lower Comcast's share price—making it more likely that NBC Universal could strike out on its own. NBC Universal may have been nervous about being a tiny part of a cable-distribution company; there was still a broadcasting cachet that did not mix with the cable-guy cowboy culture. Zucker sent a proud e-mail to NBCU employees the day after the leak was published in *The Wrap*, a trade blog: "Given the attractive nature of our assets," he wrote, "there is always significant interest in NBC Universal. That has been amplified lately by the annual discussion with Vivendi about its 20 percent ownership of our company. Vivendi . . . have not yet made us aware of any final decisions about their future with us; should they choose to exit, there are a number of possible things that could happen."[26]

Brian Roberts was furious at the leak: he did not want investors thinking that Comcast was putting its own money at risk in buying NBC Universal. Before the deal terms were made known, the headlines might have trumpeted that Roberts was off on another Disney-like detour. Comcast held its collective breath, and its stock price stayed firm. When the deal was formally announced, in December 2009, analysts applauded Immelt's focus, but Comcast's institutional investors were puzzled. There seemed to be a lot of hot air in the numbers, making the $30 billion fanfare overstated. There were no particular synergies—since Comcast could get access to NBC Universal programming through contracts, why did it have to buy the company?[27]

On the whole, however, the logic of getting NBC Universal out of GE overwhelmed the media industry's hesitations over putting it into Comcast. In particular, making NBC-the-network more successful might help the rest of the broadcasters. Keeping media companies together might be good for the overall ecosystem.

But interest in NBC-the-network was not driving the deal: after decades of media leadership, the network's most valuable assets were likely to be its federal licenses to use spectrum and its rights to be transmitted by the cable company. As a programming entity, it was not worth much.

Still, if the NBCU sale made sense from Immelt's point of view in 2009, it remains to be asked: how did NBC-the-network, once among the most powerful media entities in the world, get to be fodder for the chopping block? What changes in the media and communications landscape had made it an unwanted asset of an American manufacturing company, almost lost in the rounding? What had happened to the proud NBC peacock?

NBC, the Radio Corporation of America's broadcasting arm, became the first television station to transmit broadcasts in the country when it covered a speech by President Franklin D. Roosevelt launching the New York World's Fair in 1939.[28] After World War II, the television industry boomed: in 1948 there were 350,000 television sets, primarily along the eastern seaboard; six times that many were sold in 1949.[29]

RCA had started its television broadcasting operation as a way to sell RCA television sets, but it came into its own as a broadcaster in the late 1940s, when stars like Milton Berle and programs like *Texaco Star Theater* gripped the popular imagination.[30] Sports rights were already expensive: according to *Television History—The First 75 Years*, an online cataloguing project, in 1948 television rights in the New York City area for baseball games cost $700,000, or the equivalent of $7.7 million today.[31]

RCA-NBC was also first in color programming, transmitting a *Dragnet* episode in Technicolor. NBC competed strongly with CBS in sports programming in the 1950s and was "all color" by the summer of 1966.[32] Although the early 1970s were not good years, as it fell behind ABC and CBS, NBC restored much of its former magnificence in the 1980s with several major hits—*Cheers, Golden Girls, Miami Vice,* and the *Cosby Show* among them.[33] In 1986, General Electric bought NBC's parent company, RCA, for $6.3 billion.[34]

In the tussles between distributors and programmers that have shaped the American media narrative, NBC initially played the role of distributor. As Senator Franken reminded Zucker at the February 2010 hearing, until the 1990s, the FCC's Financial Interest and Syndication (fin-syn) Rules prevented broadcast networks from owning long-term rights in the programming they aired. The Commission was concerned that vertically integrated networks—controlling production as well as distribution—would have an incentive to favor their own programming, and it wanted to shore up independent (and thus diverse) programming by allowing independent producers to run the lucrative market in syndication.[35]

In the early 1990s, the fin-syn rules were taken off the books after NBC and others argued that getting rid of them would not lead the networks to favor their own programming.[36] As Bob Wright, then president of NBC, said at the time, "It is in our self-interest to do everything we can to promote a strong independent production community." NBC pointed out that it was unfair to allow media companies like Time Warner to be vertically integrated while locking broadcasters out of the game. But the attraction of favoring its own programming proved to be too great.[37] By 2005, NBC was the largest supplier of the shows aired over the network; more than 75 percent of NBC's prime-time programming was produced by companies owned or controlled by its corporate parent.[38] In exchange for the privilege of broadcast distribution, the networks were asking for at least part ownership of any show they put on the air.

As Senator Franken said to me in September 2010, "As soon as they got what they wanted, they just let it out, they let it be known to the creative community that they were interested in owning as much of the programming as possible. And they let it be known to their affiliates and everybody, that they were going to have—and I was at NBC, so I saw it at affiliate meetings—they were basically saying, NBC is going to own at least half its own programs. I mean, they were very blatant about it. Then the creative community in Hollywood and to some extent New York were basically told that if you want a get a good time slot, you want to get on, you might want to sell us, or give us, essentially, a piece of your show."[39]

Getting rid of the fin-syn rules led to substantial media consolidation: Disney bought ABC TV; Paramount bought CBS.[40] The broadcast networks ceased standing alone; it made much more sense, now that they could vertically integrate, to fold them into larger conglomerates that could funnel product down the distribution chain with total control.

Zucker, testifying in 2010, had the same challenge as Bob Wright had faced during the fin-syn discussions of the early 1990s: assure legislators that a mega-distribution company would continue to act in the best interests of capitalism and consumers once it controlled valuable content. When Zucker was asked by Representative Charles Gonzalez (D-Tex.) whether the new merged entity would have any "advantages as to other providers that may not have the access to the content that you are going to have," Zucker replied: "It is in our interest to make sure that our programs are as widely distributed and seen by as many people as possible. So that is the way that we will recoup the tremendous investment that we make in entertainment, news and sports. And so from our perspective, we want to make sure that our programs are as widely distributed as possible."[41] (The phrase "it is in our interest" is usually a warning flag.)

Since the elimination of the fin-syn rules, the NBC broadcast network had been on a bit of a roller-coaster ride. Ratings surged with *Friends* and *Seinfeld* in the 1990s but collapsed in the 2000s. On the plus side, NBC bought Telemundo, the nation's second-largest Spanish-language television network, in 2002.[42] Its news and sports operations remained strong, with *Nightly News*, *Today*, and *Meet the Press* on the news side and the Olympics, the Super Bowl, and *NFL Sunday Night Football* at the top of the sports list. But as a whole, NBC broadcast faltered.

NBC seemed to be symbolic of the broadcasting business generally. As Craig Moffett, an analyst for the investment firm Bernstein Research, said in 2009, "Broadcasting is the sick man of media and NBC is ailing worst of all." In the fourth quarter of 2009, the NBC broadcast network saw its revenue fall by 2 percent and its operating profit sharply decrease. Meanwhile Universal, the movie studio, lost 25 percent of its revenue in the fourth quarter, mostly because of a huge fall-off in DVD sales—64 percent lower than the previous year—and money-losing movies like *Land of the Lost*, *The Incredible Hulk*, and *The Mummy: The Tomb of the Dragon Emperor*. Although Brian Roberts testified in early 2010 that "at the heart of NBCU's content production is the National Broadcasting Company, the nation's first television broadcast network and home of one of the crown jewels of NBCU, NBC News," the fact was that NBC-the-network was a small, cold, and distant planet in the NBCU galaxy of content.[43]

The traditional broadcast networks' business model was based for decades on big brand-name advertisers buying millions of dollars' worth of bulk advertising. Advertisers spent that money because the Nielsen ratings agency told them that people were watching particular shows—and Nielsen collected its data by tracking a few thousand households and scaling up the numbers.

But now that market is no longer functioning the way it used to. CBS and ABC have weathered the change better than NBC has, thanks to cannier programming choices, but the trend is unmistakable: except for political ads and prescription drugs, spending on broadcast-television advertising has markedly and steadily decreased. Even the Olympics do not give much return for advertising dollars on broadcast: GE spent $2 billion in 2003 for rights to the 2010 Winter Olympics and the 2012 Summer Games, but ended up losing at least $250 million on the former, in part because advertising revenues did not live up to projections.[44]

Cable channels, meanwhile, are getting a bigger share of the total ad dollar; by 2008, they had $21.6 billion in total advertising spending, up 15 percent from just ten years earlier, and drew in 39 percent of all television advertising dollars.[45] (The Internet, meanwhile, has grown nearly twice as fast as cable television, as measured by ad revenues.)[46] According to Nielsen, ad spending on national cable networks went up 16 percent, to $19.1 billion, in 2009, while broadcast network advertising fell around 10 percent, to $20.3 billion.[47] Even though each cable network may attract only a small slice of the audience, cable as a whole has the broadest scope and is the easiest way to reliably reach a mass audience. Meanwhile, broadcasters' costs remain extremely high: NBC labors under at least $3.5 billion in annual program production costs.[48] So with advertisers moving to cable, broadcasters are looking for other sources of revenue.

That means that NBC Universal's traditional flagship, the broadcast network, has taken a backseat to the company's cable offerings, including USA (the number one–rated cable channel), Bravo, Syfy, CNBC, and MSNBC.[49] These are enormously popular brands with a huge market share; collectively, they represent 80 percent of NBC Universal's value.[50] USA is available in 82 percent of all U.S. homes (about 90 million households) and is a hugely popular source for original series, movies, and sports events. Syfy provides what it bills as "imagination-based entertainment," including a strong dose of horror, science fiction, and fantasy. Bravo is seen in 75 million households, is the fastest growing Top 20 ad-supported cable entertainment network, and is the home of both *Top Chef* and *Real House-wives* programming. CNBC has 85 percent of the market for business news and is seen in more than 340 million homes worldwide, including more than 95 million households in the United States and Canada. MSNBC, launched in 1996 as a joint venture between NBC and Microsoft, is a mar-ket leader in news, particularly online.[51] During the fourth quarter of 2009, NBC Universal's cable networks grew by 8 percent in both revenue and operating profit, with Syfy, Oxygen, and Bravo all growing operating profit by double digits, and CNBC by 7 percent.[52]

Comcast saw NBC Universal's cable channels as a new cash cow: the NBCU cable programming would generate torrents of cash while giving Comcast control over a product that all video distributors—the telcos, satellite companies, and competing cable companies—would need to resell. The rest of the company—the NBC network *and* the theme parks *and* the movie stu-dio *and* movie library holdings—amounted to less than 25 percent of the deal's announced $30 billion value. Although the NBC TV Network generates 67 percent of NBC Universal's broadcast segment revenues, it generates only 8 percent of the division's profits.[53] It may be surprising to many Americans over forty who grew up in the era of the grand television networks, but NBC itself was almost lost in the rounding. As the writer John Dillon told Brian Stelter of the *New York Times* when the deal was announced, "in the 2,742-word press release about the deal, the broadcast network was not mentioned until word 2,170."[54]

The reason NBC Universal makes so much more from its cable offerings is not just a shift in advertising; it is also a shift in the relationship between broadcasters and cable providers—between content providers and content distributors. And it is this shift, which has been taking place over the past twenty years, that made the NBCU-Comcast deal so compelling and consequential.

As discussed in Chapter 2, the FCC must-carry requirement means that a local broadcaster must permit its signal to be carried on cable systems, and a local cable system must carry it—but the local broadcaster is not paid for this automatic carriage. Under existing law, local broadcasters can, instead of must-carry, opt for "retransmission consent," which under the

1992 Cable Television Consumer Protection and Competition Act gives the broadcaster the right to negotiate with a cable-systems operator every three years for carriage of its broadcast programming. (The choice is with the broadcaster, not the cable system.) The broadcaster (or the network, if it owns the local broadcaster) can make a deal with the local cable-systems operator for any form of compensation.[55]

Larry Tisch, the head of CBS when retransmission consent was set up in 1992, claimed at the time that it would be the salvation of free broadcast television because local broadcasters stood to make a billion dollars a year. The day after the act was passed, John Malone, then head of cable giant TCI, growled that he wasn't paying a cent; "I don't intend to pay any money," he said. "I will scratch backs." All the cable operators followed suit in refusing to pay for retransmission consent. As a result, broadcasters that chose retransmission consent received no cash; they got, instead, permission to distribute additional new cable channels and some advertising concessions.[56]

This new model of compensation-in-kind led to the creation of a number of new cable channels as broadcasters elected to be "paid" for their network programming by ensuring that their new cable channels had a slot in the cable lineup. In the 1990s, ABC used retransmission consent to get ESPN2 carried, NBC used it to get *America's Talking* (now on MSNBC) carried, and Fox used it to get cable operators to carry FX.[57]

Even though the broadcasting business itself is in a terminal slump, since this scheme was set up in 1992 the balance of power has, paradoxically, shifted in favor of broadcasters. They have more distribution outlets for video than they had before—they can get their programming out through satellite (Dish, DirecTV) or telco (Verizon, AT&T) video offerings as well as cable. In fact, video subscribers are often drawn to satellite or telco pay-TV packages instead of cable, because their prices are lower; the cable companies have unbeatable data and broadband offers, which is their comparative advantage, but they are slowly losing market share in video. A broadcaster can thus credibly threaten a cable company with withdrawing its signal unless a deal is made in the broadcaster's favor. Put simply, even though the cable distributors won't carry independent cable channels without exacting a pound of (equity) flesh, the cable distributors need the

Big Four network broadcasters more than the broadcasters need the cable guys.

As a result, in a major change in the broadcaster-cable relationship, broadcasters are now hoping to get actual retransmission fee revenue or "affiliation fees"—cash, not carriage, on a per-subscriber basis—and they have the power to ask for it. They no longer need to rely on must-carry regulations for free, or in-kind deals involving distribution of more of their channels over cable (deals that, in many cases, gave them slots for channels that did not yet exist). Now they can demand money.

So if Comcast or Time Warner has a broadcast network (like, say, ABC) on its lineup, it will be asked to pay the broadcasters. The only statutory constraint on both sides is that they have to negotiate in "good faith," and it is entirely unclear what that means.[58] Every once in a while, a broadcaster and a cable distributor play a game of chicken over their deal terms, and sometimes they actually drive over the cliff, and the cable operator, with no agreement in place, stops carrying the broadcast signal. Cable subscribers get upset, particularly when the programming they lose access to is something like the Emmys or the Super Bowl. Cable systems and broadcasters each try to direct the consumer uproar against their opponent, while legislators and the FCC express deep concern (but do nothing). Eventually, the two sides make a deal.

Cablevision and Fox went through this routine in 2010, when Cablevision refused to pay more than $150 million a year for Fox programming— reportedly a doubling of Fox's fee.[59] The same year, Cablevision also fought with Disney, and Time Warner Cable fought with Fox.[60]

Broadcasters are happy with the retransmission consent scheme because they have been able to convert their advertising-only business model into one based on subscriber fees in addition to advertising. Just like a cable channel. As of mid-2011, CBS was planning to double its retransmission consent revenue to one billion dollars a year. As CBS's chief financial officer, Joe Ianniello, said, the revenue was pure profit: "There is no cost against it. . . . Whether [the billion dollars] happens in three years or five years, we can debate about the time frame, but nobody is debating that it's there. We know every contract when it expires and what we need to get in those negotiations."[61]

After some high-profile scuffles, cable-distribution companies have conceded, after a fashion: they have decided simply to pass on the cost of retransmitting broadcast networks to consumers by masking the fee payments as license fees for cable networks owned by the broadcaster.

The creation of the retransmission consent scheme may have helped to make it much more difficult for independent programming to survive. After that point, broadcasters created new cable networks using the leverage that retransmission consent gave them. Allowing the broadcasters to charge cable distributors for their content made the cable distributors look for alternative ways to "pay" the broadcasters with in-kind space for programming—space that otherwise might have been available to new independent channels. Everything became a deal with existing players rather than a search for new content.

As a result of such maneuvers, retransmission-fee compensation—that is, the fees paid by distributors to broadcasters—is rising by about 20 percent a year; SNL Kagan estimates that retransmission fees paid by all distributors of broadcast networks (telephone and satellite companies as well as cable operators) grew from an estimated $487.5 million in 2008 to almost $1.14 billion in 2010 and will grow to $3.6 billion in 2017.[62] Life is good for broadcasters: CBS CEO Leslie Moonves has said that these subscriber fees (whatever the cable distributors call them) should add "hundreds of millions of dollars to revenues annually" for broadcasters, and so far he has been right: the amount doled out in 2011 adds up to roughly 50 percent of the total amount of retransmission compensation ever generated from video distributors, most of which will be passed on to consumers. Indeed, cable fees have gone up since 1996 at more than double the rate of inflation.[63]

The advertising-only model of broadcasting no longer works. It is the cable programming model—yielding subscription fees in addition to advertising revenues—that makes the most sense for media conglomerates, including NBC Universal. And the entire system of payments—retransmission consent for broadcasters, affiliate fees for cable networks, advertising revenue for content owners—works only if cable distributors have sufficient market power to maintain the prices that consumers pay. Cable distributors thus have an interest in both achieving massive scale and vertically integrating with broadcasters; once distributors and programmers are on the same team, the scuffles over particular retransmission fees paid to broadcasters will disappear. Just as John D. Rockefeller, according to Ron Chernow, saw competing oil producers as a "rabble of wild, excitable men, waiting for a war-cry to rush into the arena with a suitable noise" and sought to ensure steady prices and adequate returns on investment by imposing an orderly marketplace, the cable distributors have an interest in smoothing out the programming marketplace to avoid holdups and disruptions.[64]

In a signal to broadcasters that it would not abandon them, Comcast signed a ten-year deal for carriage of CBS's content even as the Comcast-NBCU merger was pending in Washington.[65] In a further appeal to broadcasters, Comcast agreed with NBC affiliates (in a filing with the FCC) not to seek repeal of the retransmission consent regime. It suggested to legislators and the FCC that because the NBCU transaction would put it *on both sides* of the ongoing retransmission consent fracas, the company would be able to help fix the situation. Comcast, Roberts said, would "have a role, to help come up with constructive solutions of how—for the industry, how should [retransmission consent disputes] get resolved in the future." He was confident that the other broadcasters would benefit once he was wearing both hats. And he felt certain that there was no chance the FCC would intervene. In effect, he was proposing to take the burden of regulation off the shoulders of civil servants.[66]

At the time it announced the NBCU deal, Comcast already had programming assets, but except for the regional sports networks these weren't nearly as successful as NBC's cable networks. E! Entertainment Television, which Comcast bills as "television's top destination for all things entertainment and celebrity," was its leading cable channel, famous for *Keeping Up with the Kardashians*.[67] Versus, Comcast's sports channel, broadcast hockey, auto racing, college sports, and some baseball and other games. Comcast's other properties included the Golf Channel (which reached a hundred million households) and FearNet. None of these held a candle to NBC Universal's cable holdings.

Still, it was widely believed that NBC Universal was not worth $30 billion—at most it should have cost $25–$26 billion. But Comcast wanted control and was willing to accept the broadcaster's inflated number to get it; Comcast wanted to build its stable of cable networks without paying the whole sum for NBC Universal's properties up front. The bankers helped layer on a premium to get to $30 billion based on claims of synergies that would be created by vertical integration.[68]

The only issue was how to structure the payments. In exchange for about $1.4 billion down, Comcast was able to make a deal with a protected structure. Along with the cash, it contributed its own channels, which were assessed by the bankers using the same formulas used for NBC Universal's cable channels—leaving these properties possibly overvalued at $7 billion. The first half of the deal would create a content joint venture between General Electric and Comcast, with Comcast in control. The second half of the deal was left to the future: Comcast could buy out GE's interest in the joint venture using the venture's cash flow, but the amount to be paid to GE was stated at the start of the deal.[69] Comcast was saddled with a binding commitment, but at the same time it was getting all the value of the upside of the venture's success—for just $1.4 billion in cash.

Analysts and some of Comcast's institutional investors quietly suggested that Roberts was making the NBC Universal deal simply to diversify his personal portfolio; if investors had wanted programming assets they could have bought stock in those companies separately. Instead, as the primary holder of Comcast's supervoting stock, Roberts had an incentive to mitigate his own personal exposure to the vagaries of the distribution marketplace—and he didn't seem to worry that regulators might place onerous conditions on the deal if they felt that Comcast would wield its market power to abuse its relationship with programming.[70]

Roberts had good reasons for wanting to hedge against the power of the other cable programmers. Sixty percent of the money Comcast spends each year already goes into programming, much of whose cost Comcast can pass along directly to consumers. But only so much can be passed along immediately—price hikes take time, and consumers are feeling the pinch these days. Meanwhile, programmers keep demanding more for their product. As a result, as John Malone says, "In the video area, the big issue for [cable distributors] is margin squeeze."[71] With powerful cable networks under its control Comcast would be able to run its distribution operations more cheaply (with less margin squeeze for the programs coming from NBC Universal!) and then use its programming to squeeze other distributors.

Small cable companies and satellite companies found the prospect alarming. For Comcast, it would be just a matter of hedging its bets.

In 1998, Congressman Billy Tauzin (R-La.)—who had pushed for the 1992 cable act—noted, "In 1992, we awakened to the sad realization that we had forgotten one crucial element, and that was that cable controlled programming. And that controlling programming was a way of making sure that there would be no competitors. If a competitor couldn't get the programming, it certainly wasn't going to launch the satellite or put up the antenna. Or, in fact, even build another cable system in the same community to compete with the incoming [incumbent] cable company." In the newly converged world, Comcast had even more ways to use its control over programming—and, most important, over cable networks—to make it more expensive for potential competitors to stay in business. As upstart RCN said of Comcast, cutting off or impeding the flow of programming is "one of the most powerful ways an incumbent cable operator can kill off competition."[72] Comcast now could wield USA, Syfy and Bravo, cable news outlets CNBC and MSNBC, Universal Studios, a library of films and television shows, Telemundo, and the NBC Sports empire in support of its plans to dominate its markets. Oh, and NBC.

Even if some Americans dropped their cable subscriptions, Comcast would be able to continue raising its video prices for those who hung on. At the same time, facing little or no competition in its markets as it added many more high-speed Internet subscribers to its rolls, Comcast would be able to stave off the growth of successful long-form online video through its TV Everywhere scheme. And the much-maligned Zucker's team had served up the programming that Comcast could deploy in this rout; his cable division, run by Bonnie Hammer, was steaming ahead.

Yet Comcast would continue to point to the existence of other video distributors—telephone companies, "overbuilders" (which in any other reasonable marketplace would be called competitors), and satellite companies—as evidence that it was operating in a competitive marketplace.[73] As President William Howard Taft had written of Standard Oil in the early twentieth century, "It was indeed an octopus that held the trade in its tentacles, and the few actual independent concerns that kept alive were allowed to exist by sufferance to maintain the appearance of competition."[74] None of the other video distributors had Comcast's overwhelming advantages in wired high-speed Internet access in its markets. And none of them had Comcast's power in programming. Comcast's bundle—including, most importantly, its live sports programming—was going to win.

7

The Programming Battering Ram

The idea of a new sports TV network gets all the headlines, because it involves a lot bigger dollars spent and generated. But much more efficiently, the new [Comcast-NBCU] company can massively expand its existing footprint online, bringing together all of these various (and valuable) assets—along with a couple quick acquisitions—to become a leader in emerging sports media, not just televised sports media.

—Dan Shanoff, ESPN columnist

BRIAN ROBERTS'S FAVORITE SPORT MAY BE SQUASH, but as a businessman he knows the real value in American television entertainment lies in controlling rights to football, basketball, and baseball games. If there was a guiding ethos to Comcast's pursuit of NBC Universal, it was to gain control over more sports programming. Live sports is the one thing that people can get almost nowhere else—not on DVD, not online—the only options are pay-TV or a stadium seat. Leo Hindery, a thoughtful former cable guy who has played leadership roles in TCI, AT&T Broadband, and Liberty, thinks that the winners in the media world will be those with a devoted audience. "If you own audiences viscerally, deep in their core . . . [that's] a relationship that has value," he told *Bloomberg* in mid-2011. John Malone, interviewed in late 2009, sounded impressed by Comcast's NBC Universal strategy: "There's no question that if you have a strong position in sports, and you have distribution, you're kind of in the catbird seat. . . . Because if your competitors don't carry it, you're going to gain market share in your distribution. If they do carry it, you're going to charge them a lot of money for it. So either way, it's kind of a nice position to be in. Trust me, I used to be there."[1] No form of programming is more visceral, addictive, and loyalty creating than sports.

In an era of disaggregation and fragmentation, watching cable sporting events is a shared pastime. Our brains love this kind of stimulation—indeed, the brain circuitry that makes us successful operates on the same kind of learning, memory, and motivation signals that sports programming provides. For a sports fan, the salient focus of any room in which a cable sports channel is playing is the screen, and we're all wired to focus on the most salient stimuli. Sports fans care intensely about access to sports programming.

The complex interplay among teams, broadcasters, cable sports channels, and video distributors over the past ten years has led to a perfect storm: content that people (particularly men aged 18–49) crave, available only over pay-TV services at ever-higher prices. In many ways, the subject of sports programming crystallizes all the convergence stories of the twenty-first century—and sports provided the motivation for the NBC Universal deal.

You might think that the league commissioners were the most influential people in sports. You would be wrong: the leaders of companies that distribute sports content call the shots. They dictate how all of us see sports and how we think about what we are seeing. (Sometimes the distributors own the teams, which further simplifies the chain of influence.) Sports fans may even prefer to watch their teams on television than in person because they want all the content that accompanies a televised game. This is why the former CBS Sports president Neal Pilson told a reporter that the Comcast-NBCU deal was "the biggest thing that's happened in my 40 years in broadcasting. No question."[2] As Rupert Murdoch told News Corp. shareholders in 1996, ownership of long-term rights to major sporting events can be used "as a battering ram" in all pay-TV operations.[3] Comcast now has more battering rams in its armory.

As the FCC observed in 2004, "The basis for the lack of adequate substitutes for regional sports programming lies in the unique nature of its core component: regional sports networks typically purchase exclusive rights to show sporting events, and sports fans believe that there is no good substitute for watching their local and/or favorite team play an important game."[4] This is true "must-have" programming. According to the Congressional Research Service, "the programming for which consumer demand is both broadest and most intense is major sports programming."[5] The effect is so strong that in the places where there is real competition between video-distribution companies (satellite, cable, telco) most viewers choose their distributor based on the availability of sports content. The numbers are eye-popping, particularly where a subscriber's home team is involved. One survey showed that "some 40–48% of cable subscribers would be less likely to subscribe to cable service if it lacked local sports [programming]." An additional 12 percent of respondents were unsure whether the absence of sports programming would affect their decision, ensuring that at least 40 percent, and possibly as many as 70 percent, of potential video-distribution subscribers would not subscribe to a service that did not have local sports programming.[6]

So a video distributor's ability to gain access to local sports content, and the price and other terms of conditions of access, are important factors in its ability to survive. A satellite, cable company, or phone company that drops local sports programming risks subscriber defections. Video distributors, the FCC recognizes, "will drive hard bargains to buy, acquire, defend or exploit regional sports programming rights."[7] Comcast has driven some of the hardest bargains of all; it has evolved over the years from a mere distributor of other peoples' games to a sports-rights juggernaut.

Even before the NBC Universal transaction, Comcast had gone beyond traditional programming to become a powerhouse in sports. By August 1997, it controlled several local teams in Philadelphia as well as the rights to distribute their games—Flyers hockey games, 76ers basketball games (Comcast sold the team in 2011 but retained the rights to televise and distribute the team's games and retained ownership of the building in which the team plays), and Phillies baseball games. Across the country, it acquired extensive broadcast rights to local sports content, allowing the company to build a dizzying array of regional sports networks: Comcast SportsNet (CSN) Bay Area, CSN California, CSN Chicago, CSN Mid-Atlantic, CSN New England, CSN Northwest, CSN Philadelphia, CSN

Houston, CSN Southeast, and CSN Southwest. Comcast also holds partial ownership interests in SportsNet New York, Comcast/Charter Sports Southeast, and MountainWest Sports Network.[8]

Comcast has used its ownership of sports rights (and, in Philadelphia, the teams as well) to make life more difficult for its competitors. The best-known example of this is in Philadelphia, where it has denied satellite companies—competitors with Comcast for video subscriptions—access to CSN Philadelphia. Yet as described in Chapter 2, the 1992 Cable Television Consumer Protection and Competition Act forced cable distributors to give the nascent satellite companies access to their programming.[9] So how was Comcast able to withhold the most important programming of all?

It did this by using a loophole in the legal structure for programming, which was interpreted by Comcast to mean that cable operators did not have to give satellite companies access to programs that originally came to the cable provider over a wire in the ground. At the time when Congress mandated that cable operators treat all their competitors fairly, most programs arrived at central cable-distribution facilities (the "headends") by way of satellite. So Congress focused on practices by the cable distributors that would prevent a competitor (like a satellite-distribution company) from providing "satellite cable programming," and the FCC's program-access rules initially followed that lead: if programming arrived by satellite at a cable headend, the cable operator had to make it available.[10]

The rules were originally written to make it possible for satellite pay-TV distributors to compete with the cable companies, and they were modestly successful along those lines: nationally, satellite distributors have about 30 percent of the video-distribution market. But programming that arrived at a headend by way of a wire was not within the scope of the program-access rules. Comcast argued that it did not need to be: from the cable company's perspective, boxing satellite companies out of access to sports programming that it owned and that came via wire should be permitted because exclusivity would enhance innovation and programming diversity.

Yet Comcast as a vertically integrated cable operator controlling rights in sports programming now has the incentive and ability to use its programming to block competition. At any rate, Comcast has made sure to transmit its sports programming in Philadelphia only through terrestrial means.

Same programming, different delivery mechanism, different access rights for satellite competitors.

Comcast's withholding of sports content has been an enormous problem for satellite video-distribution companies because they have nothing to offer subscribers who want regional sports shows in the Philadelphia area. The harm is significant: according to the FCC, Comcast's refusal to provide sports to the satellite companies has reduced satellite adoption by 40 percent in that region.[11] You might think that Comcast as a rights owner would want the fees that would accompany distribution of its teams' games, but there is more value to Comcast in foreclosing competition: directly charging 60–70 percent of video subscribers high prices for sports content is worth more to Comcast than licensing that content to its competitors. People really want sports, and satellite companies can't sign up customers without it.

Competitive wired video providers—other cable companies and telephone companies—have also suffered. At the February 2010 Senate Antitrust Subcommittee hearing, Colleen Abdoulah of WOW! was clearly frustrated by the bundles of programming Comcast required WOW!'s customers to buy in order to get access to the sports they actually wanted. "It is very difficult to compete without that kind of transparency, without that kind of market-rationalized pricing," she said, "and it is wrong for consumers. They do not have the choice because we are told [by Comcast] how to deliver the product. We are not able to deliver it in the way the customers have asked us to deliver it." Getting to the heart of her subject, Abdoulah went on: "Specifically, sports, if people want to just watch sports and pay more for it, we would love to put that on a tier [sell only sports programming to consumers who wanted only sports]. We are not allowed to do that."[12] But WOW! has to sell the bundles, because the mere threat that sports shows won't be available will keep subscribers from choosing its services.

Comcast sales representatives in Philadelphia told RCN subscribers several years ago that RCN might not be able to provide Comcast's local sports network (CSN Philadelphia) in the future. (RCN, the small company from Princeton that was trying to get a toehold in Philadelphia, is what is called an overbuilder by the cable industry: a small cable-distribution company that tries to compete with the big guys.) RCN alleged that Comcast limited it to untenable short-term contracts for CSN Philadelphia, knowing that a sudden loss of this crucial local sports programming would decimate RCN's subscriber base. Comcast only stopped doing this when the Department of Justice intervened to ensure that competitors (at least, wired competitors) would have access to CSN Philadelphia. As with satellite, it is apparently more valuable to Comcast to withhold programming from its competitors than to reap the increased fees that would come from licensing the content.[13]

Comcast has long taken the position that the rules under the 1992 act that require it to give competitors fair access to its sports programming are no longer necessary given the success of these competitors over the years. There are dozens of ways for Comcast to redefine its obligations under the act, but for Comcast it would be even better for those obligations simply to disappear.

In order to use sports rights as a sledgehammer, Comcast has to acquire them in the first place. Hardball tactics come into play here as well. Comcast initially acquired rights to the Portland Trail Blazers in 2007, when it paid approximately $120 million for a ten-year carriage contract. Although it vowed at the time to "dramatically increase exposure for the Trail Blazers," Comcast has not licensed CSN Northwest to its rivals, including two satellite providers and the cable system Charter Communications. Comcast has announced plans to "expand" Trail Blazers coverage by making Trail Blazers games available online—for Comcast's cable subscribers only.[14]

But the most colorful rights-acquisition story comes from football. Comcast has always wanted rights to more football games, and in late 2005 and early 2006 the company applied for a license from the NFL to carry a package of eight live NFL games on Versus. Versus was shown on Comcast's expanded basic tier to 21 million subscribers. But NFL did not want to license to Comcast. Instead, it wanted to license games to the NFL Network.

Comcast retaliated. Saying that "a state of war existed" between itself and the NFL, it moved the NFL Network from its digital tier, seen at the time by approximately 11 million subscribers, to a special "sports" tier that carries an additional charge and is seen by only 2 million Comcast subscribers— Siberia for sports. Former NFL commissioner Paul Tagliabue testified to the FCC that "Mr. Roberts warned me that, as a result of the League's failure to license the eight-game package to Comcast for Versus, '[our] relationships with the cable industry are going to get very interesting.'" The NFL's senior vice president also testified that Roberts "threatened that, if the NFL did not license the package to Versus, Comcast would drop the NFL Network from the 'D2' [digital] tier and shift it to an undesirable premium sports tier" delivered to just a fraction of the Comcast households that then received the NFL Network.[15]

Comcast said that it had decided to reduce NFL Network penetration to save its subscribers money. Yet as NFL officials pointed out, Comcast did not actually reduce its subscribers' fees when it retired the NFL Network; rather, it continued to charge them the same price for fewer channels.[16]

These tactics have clearly won Comcast some advantages. In the end, it negotiated a price for NFL Network (approximately fifty cents a subscriber per month) that was far below the rate it had previously paid or the rate paid by most other cable systems. Comcast's friends also did well in this transaction—large cable systems that do not directly compete with Comcast (including Time Warner and Cablevision) had their contracts renegotiated to lower prices.[17] As Andy Schwartzman, one of the consumer advocate witnesses at the February 2010 hearing, told the Senate Judiciary Committee: "Even the NFL, with its vast resources, couldn't crack the Comcast stranglehold without lawsuits, FCC proceedings, and years of uncertainty before it reached a negotiated settlement which was less than what it wanted."[18] As a result of a settlement in 2009, the NFL Network ended up on a lower-penetrated digital tier that reached about 11 million customers. This was better than the Siberia of a premium sports tier, but not what the NFL had sought from Comcast.

The sports industry has learned its lesson. When MLB started its own network in 2008, five years after the NFL launched its network, it gave equity to Comcast right away while asking for distribution. No one needed to be beaten up twice.[19]

When Comcast acquired rights to show NHL games in 2011, the company paid an enormous premium—$200 million, far more than the $60 million ESPN was willing to pay. It was, in a sense, a foreclosure premium, a bet that hockey would be a prize that ESPN eventually would not be able to do without. (Rupert Murdoch made the same bet when he bought exclusive rights to NFL broadcasts on behalf of Fox—and lost $350 million—in 1994. He dismissed the loss, calling it "an investment" in altering audience perceptions of his then low-rated network.) Comcast chief operating officer Steve Burke must not have been worried about the NHL's low ratings or concerned that Comcast paid more than ESPN would have for the same rights. Hockey has a deep, passionate fan base, and Comcast was game to challenge ESPN with hockey as its anchor sport. With the NBC Universal merger, hockey has paid off: Thanks to a two-billion-dollar deal with the NHL, the new NBC Sports Network cable channel will have up to a hundred regular-season games to air in primetime each year for the next ten years. NHL television ratings in the United States climbed 84 percent between 2007 and 2011, and the league's seasonal revenue is up to nearly three billion dollars.[20]

According to an article published in the *Sports Business Journal* in 2010, "If the [Comcast-NBCU] deal is approved, the sports industry stands to be one of the biggest beneficiaries," because Comcast will "become even more aggressive buying up sports rights."[21] That's exactly what has happened. Even more than run-of-the-mill sports rights, which are unique and valuable, Comcast wants rights to once-in-a-lifetime signature events because those are even more valuable. Just months after the merger between Comcast and NBC Universal was approved, Comcast spent $4.4 billion— outbidding Disney-ABC and News Corp.–Fox by a billion dollars—to acquire rights to the Olympics through 2016.[22]

Once Comcast has the rights it wants, its clustering strategy allows the company to charge higher prices for its sports content than non–vertically integrated regional sports networks can command. Portland is a good example. Before Comcast signed its ten-year deal, Fox Sports (FSN Northwest) held a five-year television contract for the sports rights in the area. At the time the Fox contract was signed in 2002, Comcast had little presence in the Portland area; it soon acquired AT&T Broadband and became the dominant pay-TV provider in that city. When the Trail Blazers television rights contract came up for bid for the first time after the AT&T-Comcast merger in 2007, Comcast offered *three times* the annual price (approximately $14 million per year) that Fox was willing to pay. Once it had the rights, Comcast reportedly asked competing pay-TV providers to pay more than two dollars per subscriber per month in Portland for the same programming—substantially more than FSN Northwest had previously charged. Predictably, no other major pay-TV provider in Portland was willing to pay such high prices.[23]

Same thing for the NFL content. Although Comcast has not been able to exclude other pay-TV providers from NFL programming altogether, it has achieved its goal of forcing competing distributors (satellite, overbuilders, and telephone companies) to pay higher affiliation fees than it pays. When it comes to sports programming, Verizon, for one, is willing to stand up and talk about Comcast's abusive pricing and strategic withholding practices. In a 2011 document filed with the FCC, Verizon stated that Comcast had a "long history" of withholding access to regional sports networks.[24]

The same thing will undoubtedly happen with Olympics programming. Comcast is planning to make money by charging other video distributors, such as Cablevision and DirectTV, more for its Olympic-content channels (NBC-the-network, and Versus—now, predictably, renamed the NBC Sports Network—and any special Olympic channel created by Comcast), raising advertising rates, and charging for access to Olympic events through tablets, mobile devices, or whatever else somebody comes up with.[25] It is a big play, but it is not surprising.

It is no wonder Comcast focused on sports in acquiring NBC Universal: the company could lock in long-term customers for its general-purpose pipe and high profits by locking up additional local, national, and international sports programming. And it could try to expand the sports dollar-extraction marketplace. In 2008, Brian Roberts was not considered one of the top hundred most influential people in sports—but in 2009 he and Steve Burke shared fifth place and Steve Burke alone was named the most influential person in the sports business at the end of 2011 by *Sports Business Journal*. The reason was the NBCU transaction.[26]

Murdoch was right: sports could be a battering ram. But this wasn't a one-sided joust. Comcast needed its own defenses against ESPN. ESPN was a Goliath, a master at extracting fees from customers, and Comcast needed leverage on its side of the deal.

Sixty years ago, sports helped television take off, and NBC led the pack: the first network television sporting event was NBC's *Gillette Cavalcade of Sports* in 1944. After several years in prime time, televised sports eventually moved to the weekends. There it attracted substantial advertising and sponsorship, and fees for broadcast rights skyrocketed. The 1970s rights for NFL, NBA, and MLB broadcasts cost $50 million, $2 million, and $18 million respectively; by 1985 those same rights cost $450 million, $45 million, and $160 million. Players were paid more, and sports was getting to be an enormous business.[27]

If the twentieth-century paradigm was sports driving television—people buying televisions in order to watch games for free—the twenty-first-century-paradigm is sports working with pay television to charge subscribers. These days satellite and cable providers can charge for both advertising and subscriptions, earning two streams of revenue, money that allows them to pay the sports leagues more for the rights to their games. In turn, the distributors can charge consumers to watch.

The pay-TV sports story starts with ESPN. Launched in 1979 by an unemployed sports announcer named Bill Rasmussen, ESPN began on a flyer, taking advantage of unused capacity on an RCA satellite. Initially, its all-sports programming was advertising supported and free to the many independent cable systems then in existence, reaching about 5 percent of all subscribers. After a change in management in the early 1980s, ESPN decided to start charging cable operators a small monthly fee. The major cable companies went along, setting the stage for an enormous twenty-first-century marketplace: today, pay-TV distributors pay on average between twenty and fifty cents for most cable channels they carry, though ESPN may be getting as much as seven dollars per subscriber.[28]

ESPN quickly became the largest cable network in the country, distributed to almost 29 million households by 1983. Its purchase by ABC in 1984 drove the story farther, because having distribution across the ABC-TV network as well as through the cable channel gave ESPN the negotiating strength (and cash) to sign up all the major sports leagues for broadcasting rights: NBA, NHL, NFL, and MLB all held long-term broadcasting contracts with ABC-ESPN during the 1980s. ESPN's rights to Sunday night NFL football and the Major League Baseball playoffs made it the top cable channel starting in 1999. This trend has continued, with ESPN broadcasting all college football Bowl Championship Series games and many other major league events. ESPN makes about $6.3 billion a year, up from $1.8 billion a decade ago. It can bid for and win whatever game rights it wants.[29] Or, at least, it could.

After witnessing ESPN's success, Comcast began its own efforts to build a sports portfolio. By buying the broadcast rights from sports leagues, it could then charge competing distributors to show the leagues' games. Another strategy was to buy up teams and existing sports networks. Comcast moved to control Chicago by taking over Fox's regional sports network there, and replicated this strategy across the country. It now owns eleven regional sports networks (RSNs) that control all or most of the rights to carry local professional teams in baseball, basketball, soccer, and hockey in particular areas.[30] As Richard Sandomir of the *New York Times* puts it, RSNs are now "the primary local outlets on which to see professional teams play."[31] Comcast has control over RSNs in seven key regions across the country, all of them in markets where the company has 60 percent or more of the area's cable customers.[32] Fans who want to watch their teams will have to sign up with Comcast, and Comcast's strength in video raises even higher barriers to entry for any business that wants to compete in providing wire for Internet access into homes.

Comcast's next move was its abortive attempt to purchase Disney, including Disney's ABC and ESPN channels, in 2004.[33] According to Steve Burke, then president of Comcast Cable, Comcast's primary motivation for the deal was to gain control of ESPN, the only major national sports network. Burke described ESPN (and presumably sports programming generally) as a business with tough entry barriers: "ESPN is a great castle with a very big moat."[34] When the Disney deal failed, Comcast had to find other ways to reduce the pressure of ESPN's high fees. As the *Wall Street Journal* reported in 2011, Comcast's Versus cable channel premerger was small compared to ESPN: it was seen in only 80 million homes, while ESPN was seen in more than 100 million, and "Versus costs cable operators about 28 cents per month per subscriber . . . compared with more than $5 for the full lineup of basic ESPN channels."[35] Comcast executive Jeff

Shell said in 2009 that expanding Comcast's sports business was the "top of our list over the next five years."[36] NBC Universal provided the path.

The NBCU deal allowed Brian Roberts to do several things. It gave him the standing to win rights to broadcast the Olympics, thus keeping them out of ESPN's hands; he can bid up the cost of rights in sports events, thus raising ESPN's costs; he can pay less for ESPN, which he claims now receives about a quarter of Comcast's revenue, or $6 billion a year, by showing that he has substantial programming rights that ESPN needs; he can demand that competing video distributors pay more for new bundles of programming; and he can be far more aggressive in buying up rights to NFL, MLB, and NBA games.[37] According to sports media analyst Dan Shanoff, Comcast can take all this content online under the TV Everywhere umbrella and instantly become a top-tier online site "with massive growth potential in local media and social/mobile media."[38]

What's more, because none of the program-access rights discussed in Chapter 2 apply to the online world, and because the FCC's jurisdiction to impose that kind of structure online is unclear, ESPN, which accounts for 75 percent of Disney's cable networks earnings and nearly a third of its overall earnings, may not be able to run footage from Comcast-NBC events on its online site. Comcast can simply move its buffed-up NBC Sports Network (formerly Versus) online, with all the NBC content and all the regional sports networks added to it, and then put these shows behind a firewall, allowing only Comcast cable subscribers to see certain games or events. Even if Comcast-NBC decided not to block content entirely through authentication, it could still use it to charge other cable providers higher prices for NBC content than the network currently does. These higher prices would be passed on to subscribers. There is a precedent for this behavior: NBC put certain Olympics events behind a firewall in 2010.[39]

The most obvious thing Comcast could do to hurt ESPN, though it is not likely to do so, is refuse to carry the channel or threaten to move it to a higher tier with lower penetration. Such threats would be useful in price negotiations for ESPN programming. But there are many other incremental steps Comcast could take. For example, what if ESPN's sports events were less interactive than Comcast sports events? Comcast already provides interactive access to *Sunday Night Football* games by way of Xfinity.com, feeding viewers online chats, statistics, and analysis while streaming the games. As the owner of the pipe, it would be within Comcast's power to reduce interest in ESPN by slow-rolling access to similar functions accompanying access to ESPN content. Another scenario is that whatever sports content Comcast-NBCU acquired, like the Olympics, could be exclusive to Comcast-NBCU.

All the fees for advertising and subscriptions Comcast-NBCU can now charge will support the overall strength of Comcast's sports operations—allowing it to outbid other networks for future rights and, in turn, think of ways to raise its rivals' cost of access to that programming. Comcast-NBCU's sports operations may not be bigger than ESPN, but the cable company may be able to squeeze CBS and Fox out of the game. And with hockey, *Sunday Night Football*, and the Olympics, it can put pressure on ESPN on a national scale.

More generally, the sea of revenue and exclusive arrangements that Comcast now commands will allow it to transform its premerger sports operations into must-have content (the NBC Sports Network) for most of the households in its regions—thus locking in those subscribers for the long term. This is the apotheosis of the TV Everywhere model: streaming sports content on an iPad to users who have paid for a cable subscription.

Comcast wants a share of the enormous revenues ESPN is now commanding. It wants its own quasi-online version of ESPN, but bigger, and it wants to be the only source of the sports content that it controls. As ESPN vice president Damon Phillips told the *Chicago Tribune* in 2008, with broadband Internet today, "people base their decision on speed and price. We think that will change, with content being the deciding factor."[40] The ability of a wire distributor to decide what content goes to which consumers carries with it the ability to monetize that content—charge differentially for it—and Comcast is unquestionably looking to have these additional revenue flows in place. As long as people are willing to pay a lot for sports, Comcast will keep making money.

There are lots of synergies here: Comcast grows sports, sports grows Comcast, and consumers are apparently willing to pay more every year for Comcast's sports packages. You might think that competition between Comcast and ESPN would drive prices down. But because Comcast controls distribution, Comcast can bid more for rights and pass those increases on to consumers; ESPN then has to bid more and pass those increases on to Comcast. The competition is over revenue share between ESPN and Comcast, and it is the sports lover who pays. The daily cost of bundled programming is about the same as a nice lunch. And who wouldn't enjoy a nice lunch, even if the only restaurant in town keeps raising its prices?

The Comcast-NBCU merger is probably only the first of a series of transactions that will integrate content—particularly sports content—with distribution networks. In that way, Comcast-NBCU now resembles Rupert Murdoch's News Corporation. That giant media conglomerate says proudly that it communicates with 70 percent of the world's population on a daily basis. In the United States, News Corp.'s profits from its Fox cable channels alone amount to around $700 million a year, and it also controls sixteen RSNs, 20th Century Fox, vertically integrated satellite distributors in Italy and the United Kingdom, the *Wall Street Journal*, and 45 percent of Hulu, among many other holdings.[41] News Corp. has been clear from the beginning of the convergence era that it sees subscription models as the future. It is not enthusiastic about ad-supported online content: "Good programming is expensive," Rupert Murdoch has told shareholders. "[It] can no longer be supported solely by advertising revenues."[42] Free content, to Murdoch, is a joke. Only the 2011 phone-hacking scandals involving Murdoch and his *News of the World* stopped News Corp. from buying BSkyB and its premium sports channels, and using them to squash competition from other pay-TV distributors.

As Comcast gets as big as News Corp., how will regulators in the United States react? When free broadcast of sports has been completely replaced by pay TV over a big Internet Protocol pipe, what will constrain the market-powerful distributor from raising prices every six months? Without rate regulation, and in the absence of competitive pressure, what can any federal agency do about ever-increasing prices being charged to loyal consumers? How will competing distributors get access to this programming without rules that govern what happens online, where the FCC's jurisdiction is highly uncertain? Will any programmer put sports online on a one-off basis, faced with almost certain retribution from the giant cable distributors?

With NBC Universal's sports content under its tent, Comcast is now in a position to direct the future of subscription sports in the United States—or at least to give ESPN a run for a lot of money. Comcast's control of its own distribution network changes its incentives and gives it more ways to beat down competitors than ESPN has: it can refuse to supply programming to rival distributors on reasonable terms; deny carriage of independent sports networks so new sports channels cannot reach Comcast's subscribers; extract equity in any channel that wants carriage; ensure that anyone signing deals with Comcast makes sports content available online only through the TV Everywhere authentication scheme, which requires that the viewer subscribe to Comcast pay-TV services; and force everyone else to pay exorbitantly for Olympics content bundled with a lot of lower-value programming. Sports is the battering ram.[43]

8

When Cable Met Wireless

BY 2012 THE WORLD WAS GOING MOBILE, with major consequences for the data and video industries. People around the world love their handheld devices and prize mobility; in dozens of countries, there are more mobile subscriptions than there are people. For billions, a handheld device is always within reach. By 2011, Apple had logged 15 billion downloads of its apps; nearly 90 percent of all app downloads were of Apple-approved applications, and Apple had sold nearly 55 million iPads by the end of that year. By March 2012 the company was sitting on $100 billion in cash reserves.[1] Some analysts have predicted an eighteenfold growth in wireless data from 2011 to 2016, as young people who want next-generation entertainment and information services come into their own.[2] The Comcast-NBCU deal is wholly compatible with the way things are done in the wireless world and fits neatly with Apple's aspirations as well.

All the big carriers—Comcast, Time Warner Cable, AT&T, and Verizon—are happy with the existing regulatory environment, which amounts to no supervision at all, and they are all doing well as scale businesses with no serious competition. But the two groups, wired and wireless, also do not compete with each other. The cable industry and AT&T/Verizon seem to have divided up the world much as Comcast and Time Warner did; but instead of "you take Philadelphia, I'll take Minneapolis," it's "you take wired, I'll take wireless." At the end of 2011, the market-allocation relationship between Comcast and Verizon became explicit when the two giant companies agreed to market each other's services jointly.[3] Comcast, as well as Time Warner Cable, will promote Verizon Wireless services as part of its bundles, and by 2015 the cable companies will have the option of selling mobile services under their own brands. "We do not believe it is feasible to enter the wireless market as a freestanding new entrant," Time Warner Cable CEO Glenn Britt wrote in a blog post about the Verizon deal.[4] Comcast, Time Warner, and Verizon Wireless will work together to shape the future as well, forming a joint venture to develop advanced wireless/ wireline integration technologies. The deal came about because, with Time Warner, Comcast owned a substantial amount of spectrum that the company had bought during an auction held by the FCC in 2006; Verizon Wireless gets that spectrum for $3.6 billion in exchange for intertwining its business with that of Comcast and Time Warner. As Comcast CFO Michael Angelakis put it to analysts in September 2011, "We have no desire to own a wireless network. We have no desire to write large checks, but we would like to find a way where we can offer that kind of mobility for our products in a strategic way that makes sense."[5]

This cooperation indeed made eminent sense. In most areas served by Comcast and Time Warner, Verizon's FiOS—the only real competition the two face for wired Internet access—is not present. (Comcast and FiOS overlap in just 15 percent of Comcast's physical market; Time Warner and FiOS overlap in 11 percent of Time Warner's.) By cooperating, Verizon Wireless is implicitly promising that the FiOS service will spread no farther; Comcast and Time Warner, for their part, are implicitly promising that they will not go into the wireless business. At the same time, much-smaller Cablevision is in for a rough ride: it overlaps with Verizon FiOS installations in at least 40 percent of its market and will have to keep competing.[6]

But the most important thing about the cooperation between Comcast and Verizon is that it sheds light on the fact that the wired truly high-speed access sold by Comcast and the wireless services sold by Verizon are not direct substitutes for each other. They are, instead, complements. Competitors would not agree to market one another's services.

Before we get into the differences between these two access networks— cable and wireless—let's consider their similarities. Both are highly concentrated and highly profitable realms. On the wireless side, AT&T and

Verizon Wireless together control two-thirds of the marketplace and generate 80 percent of its revenues, while enjoying (like Comcast) margins of roughly 40 percent. Sprint and T-Mobile, the third and fourth national players, trail far behind, lacking access to key infrastructure inputs—making their operating costs much higher.[7] The barriers to entry for any new national player are insurmountable.

The major wireless carriers, like the major cable distributors, have market power that allows them to raise prices at will: AT&T and Verizon often raise fees in concert, as they did in early 2010 by requiring all of their customers using feature phones to adopt data plans.[8] In 2011–12, first AT&T and then Verizon Wireless, looking to boost their average revenue per user, ended unlimited data plans for new users and instituted overage penalties. As a result, AT&T and Verizon subscribers buying new Apple iPad tablets found that they were using up their monthly data allotments within hours and paying hefty additional fees.[9]

Devices are also central to this story. Smartphones (handsets used to process data and access the Internet as well as make phone calls) and tablets have different DNA from the personal computer and the World Wide Web. To most consumers, a smartphone's computing power makes it feel like a personal computing device, and about half of American mobile subscribers had one by 2012.[10] But the whole idea behind the classical model of Internet access was that any device could "speak Internet" and contribute to the network of creativity and invention that is the Internet as long as it followed a few simple rules. When Michael Bloomberg switched his proprietary news business network from devices hooked up to private telephone lines to terminals connected to the Internet, he did not have to ask anyone's permission to launch a new "service," or check whether his terminals complied with anyone's idiosyncratic technical specifications. The owners of the telephone lines that Bloomberg's terminals first connected to in the 1980s were required to let his new business go over their wires without "editing"—interference of any kind. He could innovate while assuming that the network—the common-carriage telephone network—would not interfere with his plans.

The personal-computer model of communications comes from a tradition of nondiscriminatory commodity transport of information, in which the network provider is not in charge. As discussed in Chapter 2, in the 1970s and 1980s, the FCC, worried that phone companies might control nascent data-processing services, drew a line between transport—conduit— and content, and instructed the phone companies to stay in the transport box.[11] The network providers' job was to make the tubes available and get out of the way; they were tasked with providing information-transport service to all comers without unreasonable discrimination and at reasonable rates, terms, and conditions. The FCC also required that any devices meeting published technical standards be allowed to attach to the communications network without asking permission from the network-service provider.[12] This model made the Internet and World Wide Web possible.

The smartphone/tablet explosion began in a radically different environment. Although wireless phone companies are labeled common carriers by statute, the FCC in early 2007 deregulated Internet access services provided by those same companies.[13] (Wireless voice services, which are accessed by the same devices using the same towers and other facilities, are still formally provided on a common-carriage basis, but the FCC has avoided imposing most of that regulatory scheme—particularly price regulation—on voice services.) Since then, both Verizon and AT&T have found a variety of ways to ensure that only smartphones and tablets of which each company approves can be used on their networks, that each device is tied to a particular authenticated subscriber, and that no device can easily be used on a different network.[14] The December 2011 joint venture between Verizon and Comcast represented another step down this walled-garden path: the spectrum Comcast sold Verizon allowed Verizon to consolidate its position so that it was operating only outside AT&T's frequencies. The device marketplace result: Apple's new 4G iPad, introduced in 2012, came in two flavors—one version that worked on Verizon's system, and one that worked on AT&T's.[15] Although smartphones and tablets may have great reservoirs of processing capability, the network operator— for the most part Verizon or AT&T—decides whether they will be permitted to use that capacity on its network.

This carrier-centric walled garden includes applications as well as devices. The smartphone you carry in your pocket is part of an ecosystem in which the network provider acts as a gatekeeper in deciding which communications move across its network onto users' (authorized) hand-sets. Verizon does not allow wireless subscribers to download applications or software of which it does not approve. As one online commentator put it in 2012, "It's like saying heres this 2000$ laptop. You can't remove or install any software unless you get proper authorization. You can't even upgrade your OS [operating system] until we deem that your computer can handle it without any issues."[16] Verizon says that it does this in order to avoid harm to its network—which is just what the old pre-divestiture AT&T used to say.

All this behavior is the opposite of the common-carriage idea now fighting for existence in the arena of high-speed access to the Internet. Common carriage separates content from conduit by requiring the pipe to be only a pipe. Since the early 1990s, wireless networks, like high-speed Internet access generally, have been subject to less and less government oversight. Verizon and AT&T have managed to rejoin content to conduit, making themselves into very powerful vertically integrated entities uncon-strained by either competition or regulation; they can set prices, decide what uses and users of their networks they will allow, control what handsets are permitted on their networks (and what features those hand-sets can have—sometimes requiring manufacturers to cripple features that the carrier does not want), sell highly subsidized phones attached to long-term contracts, and make the switching costs involved in moving to another carrier prohibitively high.[17] The wireless carriers, in short, are just like cable pay-TV distributors leasing set-top boxes to customers: they think of themselves as editors.

The big differences between wireless and cable lie in how these networks are actually used. Mobile wireless communications are a separate product, clearly distinguishable from the wired data-distribution marketplace that Comcast dominates in its U.S. regions. No one at the Senate Antitrust Subcommittee hearing in February 2010 even mentioned wireless.

When people want to download a lot of data—say, to make a video call—they overwhelmingly opt for high-speed wired connections. Wireless can never match wired in this regard; the laws of physics constrain the amount of data that a wireless connection can carry through the harsh environment of the outside air. As Sanjay Jha, chairman of Motorola, said in 2011, a wireless platform "just isn't big enough" to support the huge amounts of video that people want to watch. "That is why the [high-speed Internet access–equipped] home will be the central hub" for all the bits people consume.[18] A fiber (or cable) wire is twenty to a hundred times as fast as a 4G wireless connection, and those wireless connections will slow down as they are shared by more people.[19] The only way out of this trap for the wireless carriers is to add enormous swaths of spectrum to their holdings (in an environment in which all the relevant frequencies have already been allocated to others) or build cellular towers everywhere, at enormous expense. Neither of these things will happen.

Once you leave your cable-wired home, the quality of your wireless video will degrade sharply. Small screens with low-resolution images will be the norm, and you'll be able to carry out a video call on a large screen with a high-resolution image only if you're standing near a tower fed with fiber. Wireless could probably do about the same job as a DSL connection over a copper wire, but, as AT&T's CEO Randall Stephenson said in a moment of frankness during the summer of 2011, DSL is now "obsolete" in comparison with Comcast's DOCSIS 3.0 wired speeds.[20]

But the telephone companies are not trying to compete with DOCSIS 3.0. That's not where their profits are. Even though most of their business assets are wires, America's dominant phone companies, Verizon and AT&T, are walking away from their residential wires and focusing wholly on wireless.[21] As Americans have dropped their landline phones, and as the moat around the cable companies' high-speed wired data-distribution product has grown wider, investing in digging up streets and putting fiber into consumers' homes appears to be a losing proposition for the phone companies. The telephone companies would be savaged by Wall Street if they tried; high capital expenditures would drive down free cash flow, dividends, and buybacks, making their stock far less attractive.

The phone companies are safe with wireless: the distribution product that Comcast sells, the wired transmission of large amounts of data, is not directly threatened by handheld devices. And there is growth in wireless; in fact, it is the source of *all* the phone companies' growth. (AT&T's and Verizon's wireless margins are much higher and more resilient than their wireline margins; their wireless revenue growth is positive and relatively strong, in comparison to stagnation and decline on their wireline sides.)[22] The companies know they're on solid ground with wireless: cable distributors can't provide mobility outside of a narrow range around a subscriber's house without reselling the wireless carriers' services. Both markets— wired and wireless high-speed Internet access—are extraordinarily profitable, and by and large they do not intersect.

The programming-distribution cycle on the wireless side will be as it is on the wired side: Verizon and AT&T have the incentive and ability to charge content providers for the privilege of reaching their subscribers with the "premier" compressed and curated video services they offer. Watching more video by way of the carriers' handheld devices will also trigger overage charges as users hit their monthly allotments and end up paying more. As Lowell McAdam, CEO of Verizon, told the *Wall Street Journal* in March 2012, "On the wireless side, I think the bill will probably go up because people are going to be using [a handheld device] a lot more [to watch video]."[23] In time, it may make sense for a large wireless carrier to merge with one of the media conglomerates to capitalize on the efficiencies of scale and scope that such a deal will make possible. Until then, joint ventures will have the same effect.

Given the capacity problems of their wireless networks, Verizon and AT&T will claim (and have claimed) that it is essential that they curate and prioritize the tidal waves of data flowing to users' wireless handsets. They have to be choosy, they say, because their networks can handle only so much video traffic. This is why Verizon fought so hard against the extension of common-carriage-like network-neutrality mandates to wireless Internet access in late 2010; the company was planning on charging for online video and other "premium" services and did not want to have to treat all bits of data equally.[24] From Verizon's perspective (which Google joined in August 2010 in order to forward its own plans for the Android wireless handset operating system), imposing common-carriage-like rules on wireless networks would be job-killing, cost-raising, innovation-crushing, anti-investment regulation.[25] Worse, it would get in the way of Verizon's business plans. And Verizon and Google won.

Though the two groups of massive carriers are not competing with each other, they have shared interests. In the wireless world, as in the cable-distribution marketplace, it is clear that the carriers will favor some data over others, using their power in the wireless Internet access marketplace to reap additional returns and shape speech. And like the cable distributors, the wireless carriers will have two streams of revenue: subscription fees and payments from programmers of various kinds for the right to reach those subscribers. Additional fees may include up-front payments by subscribers for network activation of their phones and early termination fees if they quit the carrier's network before the end of the contract period. In return for signing a contract, customers receive subsidized phones. Both groups are accustoming their subscribers to usage caps and overage fees. They have every reason to cooperate.

Just one other oligopolist keeps the carriers on their collective toes: Apple's wildly popular devices, permitted to attach to the wireless network by the grace of the carriers, allow only rigidly circumscribed communications through preapproved apps—and Apple takes a 30 percent cut of the revenue those apps generate.[26] At the same time, Apple routinely closes the iPhone/iPad world to apps that would compete with its core default device functions.[27] Control and monetization are layered on control and monetization.

There is currently a standoff of sorts. AT&T's essentially unconstrained ability to act as an editor gives it power to decide how its network is used, and it has enough subscribers to demand (at least in limited ways) that Apple treat it well. That explains why Apple's iPhone was for so long (2007–11) available only through AT&T; AT&T, the network provider, had the legal power to decide which devices were allowed to attach to its network, and was able to use its enormous number of wireless subscribers as leverage to get an exclusive deal from Apple. At the same time, AT&T spent a great deal of money subsidizing iPhone purchases so that consumers would lock themselves into long-term contracts.[28] Apple needed AT&T as much as AT&T needed Apple.

Wireless provides a friendly environment for the supply side of the transaction as well: the iPhone and iPad app store, with its appealing graphics and wealth of choices running on extraordinarily beautiful devices, has been a treasure trove for consumers and developers alike. The guaranteed distribution mechanism, discrimination in "carriage" decisions, and resistance to piracy made possible by the Apple environment mimic what the cable operators have created on the wired side, but with even more diversity of programming and ease of use. Apps for iPhone and iPad use a single payment mechanism, look great, and have all been rigorously checked for security issues.

This private-carriage wireless model appeals to more than just consumers and developers—old-line industries are jumping in too. When Rupert Murdoch launched the *Daily*, an iPad-only newspaper, in February 2011, there was a bit of a kerfuffle from both journalists and Web enthusiasts: the *Daily* had great graphics and its own staff, could not be accessed via a Web browser, and had an attractive gee-whiz newness, but Apple was taking its 30 percent cut, subscriptions cost just ninety-nine cents a week (which seemed to undermine traditional print journalism), and it was available only in America.[29] Was this the future of newspapers? Murdoch thought he was on to a good thing, predicted confidently that the iPad would lead to "the end of the laptop" (meaning the end of the common-carriage, PC-based model of communications), and hoped aloud that Apple's cut would go down after the first year.[30] Whether the *Daily* itself survives, it could be a sign of things to come.

Indeed, because of the careful control embedded in the iPad and iPhone, media companies have seen these devices as potential saviors. Not just newspapers but music, film, and book publishers have fallen in love with their possibilities. The advent of the Internet has rumbled through their business models, making ad-supported businesses (particularly newspapers and magazine publishers) tremble and decimating the recorded-music industry. Search engines permit users to find exactly the news they want rather than being forced to buy a bundle of disparate bits of information in the form of a hard-copy newspaper. The easy availability of single-song digital files online in unencrypted form has made it extraordinarily difficult for CD producers to persuade people to buy an entire physical album.

Book publishers, television studios, game developers, and film studios all needed some way to reintegrate their content with a guaranteed delivery network that could track, bundle, and charge for access. The wide popularity of the iPad, together with its control over unauthorized uses of media and its facilitation of online video, seemed like the answer. The private-carriage model of mobile, controlled, authenticated, billed-for transactions has been overwhelmingly successful, to the point that Morgan Stanley suggests that in 2014, more people—more than 1.6 billion—will be accessing the Internet from their mobile device than through their desktops.[31] Revenue from mobile apps for iPad tripled between 2010 and 2011, to $15 billion according to marketing research firm Gartner, and will climb to almost $60 billion by 2014.[32]

The cable distributors, particularly Comcast, were watching the wireless world carefully in 2010. Although they were not competing head to head with wireless and were not expert in wireless technology, they did not want to be left behind. As John Malone put it in 2009, "The whole strategy for those of us in the distribution business is to be able to deliver it over multiple distribution channels. If you're a cable company right now, you're busily trying to increase the speed of your Internet offering. You're already delivering digital voice. You're trying to give people a device that will allow them to store [programming] and play it back in very high quality. You're probably now experimenting with a thing called Slingbox, or technology that allows you to take [programming] off of your device and put it on the Internet and receive it somewhere else. You're trying to evolve with the digital technologies and the wave as it comes in."[33] Comcast found a way to ride the wave by hanging on to subscribers who wanted to watch television on sleek new tablets that were not plugged into sockets but were physically near a Comcast cable connection.

Comcast was not planning to get into the wireless business. It was essentially a wire-distribution company, and the majority of its growth would always come from high-speed data subscriptions. But Comcast needed some connection to the wireless world in order to maintain its edge as a digital leader for the young and to slow its loss of video subscribers for as long as possible. The answer: dump the Comcast brand, re-label its TV Everywhere service (as well as everything else Comcast sold) Xfinity, employ Comcast's lowest-cost rights to use content to extend its model onto wireless devices in the form of Xfinity apps for the iPad, iPhone, Fire, Xbox, and whatever else came along, and tell Comcast pay-TV subscribers that they were getting even more value for their ever-higher monthly bills: a "free" iPad app. Result: a seamless, Comcast-branded, unified experience across TV, mobile, and the Web.

Subscribers to Comcast's pay-TV services took to the Xfinity TV iPad application at once, with more than a million downloads in a few months. David Pogue's March 2011 review in the *New York Times* must have warmed hearts in Philadelphia: "[The] new Xfinity app for iPad is a thing of beauty. Frankly, it's a lot smoother, better-looking and easy to understand than the Web site."[34] Devices using the Android mobile operating system would also have Xfinity TV apps available. Xfinity would be everywhere.

Moving the cable model onto tablets and phones in the form of a jazzy point-and-click app made sense for Comcast; the company could be part of the mobile world, using its existing programming levers in a bid to continue satisfying consumers while keeping in place the bundles and authentication requirements it had deployed so successfully across wires. Comcast had the heft to persuade programmers to extend its rights to stream content online to rights to stream content via the iPad; a relatively easy sell, given the security the iPad promised to media companies.

Time Warner Cable experienced a few more hiccups with in-home wireless streaming. Some programmers raised strong objections to being part of Time Warner Cable's iPad app and had to be coaxed into making licensing deals.[35] Comcast, meanwhile, with greater leverage stemming from its enormous subscriber base, steamed ahead.

While the first generation of the Comcast Xfinity TV app was designed to function only inside pay-TV subscribers' houses, Comcast will be able to hedge its bets: if consumers eventually decided that the speed of a conventional wired cable Internet connection was not worth the amount Comcast charged for it and moved to a cheaper, second-best wireless data connection, Comcast would still be represented by its popular content—as long as consumers continued to subscribe to its expensive pay-TV services. So the deal with Verizon Wireless in late 2011 gave Comcast a reliable source for reselling wireless access as part of its bundles of services, so as not to alienate customers who craved mobility as well as fast wired connections. Bundling resold wireless access with Comcast's wired connections tied customers even more tightly to the company; Comcast's average revenue per subscriber was up to an astonishing $143 a month by early 2012, an increase of nearly 140 percent over ten years. It will inevitably go higher.[36]

With its huge subscriber base, Comcast will get the lowest prices of any distributor for rights to use programmers' content, and with Verizon Wireless's help it will be able to stream programming nationwide via iPads and other mobile devices at lower prices than providers in any region of the country. No longer limited to its service areas, Comcast will be able to play both sides of the online video marketplace: charge for traditional pay-TV fees in its service areas as a wired provider (with iPad streaming a "free" add-on) and charge streaming fees outside its service areas as an online video company.

In other words, because Comcast has the most subscribers for pay TV, it can enter the territories of other pay-TV providers with an over-the-top (Internet) product (or app product) that will systematically underprice all other over-the-top products. Comcast has more sports. Comcast has more top cable channels. It can win from any angle.

"Live streaming and the play now feature on our Xfinity TV app are two important pieces of our strategy to deliver any content to any device, any time," Roberts said in January 2011, just after the deal was approved.[37] And all this mobile activity could take place in the controlled, safe world of apps. Comcast had nothing to lose: Xfinity on the iPad and Microsoft's Xbox applications (and Microsoft's Windows operating system for smartphones and tablets) would protect Comcast's traditional distribution model while allowing the company to experiment with mobile streaming video. The Xbox deal, in particular, would help block competition from Google TV and Apple TV, which lacked the 50 million–strong worldwide fan base of Xbox.[38] Time Warner's Jeff Bewkes, the originator of the TV Everywhere idea in 2009, sounded triumphant by mid-2011: "If you look at the television business . . . TV viewing is up, time spent viewing is up, the number of channels and the quality is up—more than films, actually. And the programming investments are up, the profits are up. There's nothing in it that isn't up. And when you say, is it TV vs. the Internet? No, it's TV on the Internet."[39]

Steve Case's prediction that people wanted safe walled gardens of well-designed interaction was coming true; the AOL–Time Warner deal had foundered, but the mobile environment was providing the perfect set of affordances for everyone involved. And U.S. regulators have made this possible: on the wireless side, there are two dominant carriers, AT&T and Verizon. Neither is constrained by competition, both are subject to little governmental oversight, and both have an interest in snapping up whatever slivers of gold will come from prioritizing particular bits of digital information from their friends. This makes Comcast, AT&T, Verizon, and Apple "frenemies": they have overwhelming strength in their own arenas and a shared interest in a future world that looks a lot like a collection of large, expensive, well-groomed theme parks. Private carriage, not common carriage, is the regulatory approach they are interested in. As the industry heads toward convergence—packets of video, voice, and data over multi-purpose communications networks taking the place of single-purpose cable, broadcast, and telephone networks—it is becoming clear that the carriers' desired model of control, discrimination, and premium services is winning the battle on both the wired and wireless sides.

In fact, the communications industry is at a point of equipoise with all these major actors. Each of them (AT&T, Verizon, Comcast, Time Warner, Apple, Google, and Microsoft) is too big for any of the others to swallow up or crush. They all have achieved enormous scale. So they tacitly cooperate by carving out their separate areas of expertise, much as tough kids will find separate playing areas and stay there when they know equally tough kids occupy the other parts of the room. Comcast gets wired distribution and stays out of the wireless distribution and device marketplace—and the other guys don't stop it from streaming its content wirelessly across iPads and Xboxes. Comcast's strength gives it room to maneuver in negotiations for transport over wireless networks and through wireless devices, getting better rates than its satellite competitors on the video side. AT&T and Verizon get wireless distribution and avoid having to install fiber lines into Americans' houses—and Comcast does not try to take over their wireless marketplace. Comcast does not need to control the last mile of a wireless transmission: 95 percent of any wireless network is a wire, and Comcast is in a position to sell the wireless companies its "backhaul" products—carrying the data generated through wireless uses over Comcast wires from cell towers to Internet access points. Comcast and Apple are similarly strong enough to collaborate while flourishing financially: as long as people love high-speed Internet access and the design of

Apple devices, they'll buy products from both Comcast and Apple that work well together.

Everyone is doing well: profits are climbing, allowing the communications giants to pay ever-higher dividends even as worldwide economic woes mount; free cash is piling up; investment in infrastructure is down because there is no competitive pressure in either the wireless or the wired sector to increase it; and all the companies have been increasing dividends or buying back stock (or both) in an effort to concentrate each stakeholder's profit—boosting their earnings per share and driving up the popularity of their equity in a virtuous cycle. Inequality grows, as poor and rural people are left behind completely or are relegated to second-best wireless "substitutes" for high-speed Internet access. But those zippy iPad apps look just great.

9

The Biggest Squeeze of All

In the end, the distributors are really the middlemen. It's the American public that's going to end up paying.

—John Malone

AS HE OPENED THE SENATE ANTITRUST SUBCOMMITTEE hearing on the Comcast/NBC Universal merger in February 2010, Senator Herb Kohl was clearly worried: "We must pay particular attention," he said, "to the effects of this merger on a new and promising form of competition—video programming on the Internet."[1] Later in the proceedings, consumer advocate Andy Schwartzman chimed in: "NBC and Hulu have denied access to NBC programming to existing over-the-top video provider Roku. That is not hypothetical. That is a fact. So there is every reason to expect that the combined entity will have even greater reason to . . . withhold NBC programming from . . . online-only competitors."[2] Hulu.com, a free online video site launched in 2008 by NBC Universal and Fox as a competitor to YouTube, had become a popular locus of online television content accompanied by advertising. Hulu's owners had become concerned in 2009 that people would use the video-watching software Boxee (which gives a computer screen the appearance of a television media center) or a Roku device (allowing users to stream online video directly to television screens) to access Hulu video. Hulu had therefore denied Boxee and Roku access to its content; as CEO Jason Kilar had explained it, "Our content providers requested that we turn off access to our content via the Boxee product, and we are respecting their wishes." The worry then from NBC Universal's perspective had been that the line between Hulu's online videos and the cable industry's video business would be blurred, and the programmers—and the cable industry—did not want that to happen. Hulu's CEO, in turn, felt his company had no choice but to block Roku and Boxee: "Without [the programmers'] content, none of what Hulu does would be possible," he wrote in 2009.[3] NBC Universal wanted Hulu to be an addition to its pay-TV business, not to undermine advertising sales on NBC.com. Following the blocking fracas, Hulu marched on, adding a monthly payment plan and climbing to a million paying subscribers (and 30 million viewers overall) by 2011.[4] Schwartzman was clearly worried that a combined Comcast-NBCU would have even greater incentives to block competing consumer products.

Brian Roberts took a different view, pointing out that Hulu was responsible for less than 4 percent of video online and had revenue of just $108 million in 2009; Netflix had revenue of more than $1 billion. From Roberts's perspective, online video was a "dynamic, rapidly changing market" over which the new Comcast-NBCU could not possibly exert control.[5] Indeed, by the fall of 2010 Hulu, a joint venture among Fox, NBC Universal, Michael Powell's employer Providence Equity Partners, and Disney, was being described (not by Roberts) as "the unloved bastard offspring of a doomed tryst among three aging TV giants."[6]

The two camps seemed to be talking past each other: Kohl and Schwartzman were worried about the future distribution of long-form video (NBC programming) online, but Roberts was including ten-minute YouTube videos in the online video category. Kohl and Schwartzman seemed to think Comcast-NBCU would have an interest in withholding long-form video from competitive distributors. Roberts (and NBC Universal's Jeffrey Zucker) repeatedly claimed that it was in Comcast's and NBC Universal's interests to ensure the widest possible distribution for the merged entity's programming.[7] Comcast probably saw Hulu primarily in defensive terms—as an online platform that would allow the traditional programming-distribution complex to retain its pricing power while neutralizing any over-the-top competition.

Meanwhile, in the world outside the hearing room, the pay-TV industry (including Comcast) was finding its former unchecked growth beginning to slow down.[8] Distributors kept passing along higher programming costs to consumers, but some Americans were growing tired of cable rate increases that were running at about triple the rate of inflation.[9] A few, ground down by the worsening economic situation, were cutting the cord—discontinuing traditional pay-TV subscriptions in favor of low-priced online video alternatives. In mid-2011, SNL Kagan estimated that 4.5 million of more than 100 million pay-TV subscribers would have discontinued their subscriptions in 2011.[10] It seemed likely that people under thirty would find life without a cable subscription easier than their elders did.

Who was right? Was online video threatened by the merger, or was cord-cutting threatening the future of the pay-TV model? The answer, it turned out, was yes. Comcast saw the numbers of cord-cutters and knew that long-form online video threatened its video business model. But it also saw that cord-cutters were still a small group—somewhere between 1 and 4 percent of the adult population of America. There was time to delay the advent of successful online competition for Comcast while increasing the advantages that would give Comcast an overwhelming head start in high-speed Internet access services.

As Roberts put it in early 2011, "If you think about Comcast, I believe that the best business we may well be in is our broadband business."[11] Comcast's almost unchallenged hold on the high-speed Internet access market in the areas it serves puts it in a position to make even greater profits in the years to come. Comcast's service areas cover 50 million U.S. television households, or about 45 percent of households nationwide, but only half of those households (23 million) subscribe to at least one Comcast service.[12] When it comes to high-speed Internet access, the company has a lot of headroom and no real competition. As *SNL Insurance Daily* reported in September 2011, Comcast CFO Michael Angelakis has told analysts that Comcast has captured only a third of the market in high-speed Internet access in its coverage area, but he "expects the figure to eventually hit 85% to 90%, as consumers clamor for higher speeds to watch such things as [high-definition] video."[13]

Reaping ever-higher revenue per user for high-speed Internet access alone—even in the absence of a viable traditional pay-TV business—would still be a profitable pursuit. While overall revenue might fall (because high-speed Internet access revenue by itself would be less than the traditional video-plus-access bundle), costs would fall even farther and faster if Comcast no longer had to pay for content. Comcast faces high programming costs from other actors—particularly in sports, where ESPN is rumored to charge as much as seven dollars per subscriber for its content.[14] On the whole, Comcast's margins in video are being squeezed by the demands of other programmers—its programming costs rose 7 percent in 2010, to $7.5 billion.[15]

If Comcast someday became simply a conduit pipe, it would still be in a good position: customers would continue to buy their favorite programming, and they would get much of it from Comcast online. Comcast would have even more cash on hand and could stop spending money on set-top boxes. Even if pay-TV swooned, Comcast would continue making torrents of cash, and if all went well, in 2014 Comcast could buy out General Electric's 49 percent stake in the Comcast-NBCU joint venture.[16]

Meanwhile, Comcast needed to slow the development of successful long-form online video-distribution businesses so as to control the timing of the transition to a mostly online video ecosystem and get Americans accustomed to the TV Everywhere authentication model. Comcast and its programming allies had many dials to turn, many ways to make sure independent professional distribution of long-form online video did not thrive. Online video distributors needed Comcast-NBCU: access to its programming, access to its pipes on a predictable basis, and access to its subscribers. Comcast-NBCU neither needed nor wanted competition.

As Steve Burke, Comcast's second-ranked executive, said in May 2011, "What we really bought when we did the deal for NBC Universal was a bunch of very, very well run, very strong cable channels."[17] As we have seen, Comcast can use its ownership of NBC Universal cable channels to protect itself against losses to traditional video-distribution competitors: by bundling and pricing its programming offerings at the wholesale level, Comcast can make these channels more expensive for competing distributors.

Comcast can do even more against new kinds of online video-distribution competitors. Here's Roberts again, speaking to investment analysts two months after the closing of the NBCU merger: "As more and more applications require bandwidth, as the bits per home go up, the bet we're making and the bet you're making, if you own us, is that over the next 10 years, people will want more bits in their house over a wire than ever before. And whether that is called Xbox Live, whether that is Skype, whether that is Netflix, whether that is Comcast, Xfinity, streaming, whether that is some kid in the garage inventing an application that we all wish we'd thought of, Facebook Junior, next Google—I like that position."[18]

Comcast's position as pipe provider gives it a bristling armature of techniques for squeezing independent online video aggregation that might increase cord-cutting. It can withhold programming—because the program-access rules that helped the satellite industry take off do not apply online.[19] It can prioritize its TV Everywhere programming by calling it a specialized service over which the FCC has said it has no power to require even the weakest common-carriage obligation.[20] It will thus make any independent Internet-based video seem jittery, less reliable, and subject to long buffering periods by comparison because the independent video (say, Netflix) will be available only over a "best efforts" Internet connection that the cable company will have every incentive to narrow and, ultimately, refuse to offer. The company's "specialized service" will "feel" just like the Internet and will take up a growing share of the company's digital channels, but will be devoted to the distributor's own Video on Demand services and its partners' online communities—similar to, say, Facebook. A cable company like Comcast can enhance its own video with innumerable digital add-ons and make independent online video harder to find. And it can simply charge consumers more for watching movies that come from anyone other than Comcast.

The bottom line: policy makers might be thirsty for a new source of competition to discipline accelerating price increases for content coming from the cable companies, but Comcast's interest is in neutralizing the possibility of online competition. Netflix, for its part, has long since been forced into complementarity: given the policy makers' inability to constrain the pipe owners and all the vertical advantages those pipe owners have,

Netflix has never had the ability to compete directly against Comcast in the video realm. The battle ended before the first shot was fired; without sports or broadcasting content, and without a guarantee of fair treatment by the pipe owners, neither Netflix nor any other online video shop will ever provide a full substitute for cable's pay-TV services.

At the time this chapter was drafted, Netflix was the closest thing to a viable online competitor to Comcast's video services. It was moving toward becoming a cable channel; *Reuters* ran a story in early March 2012 reporting that Netflix was in negotiations with the cable incumbents to be part of their Video on Demand packages.[21] If Netflix as an independent over-the-top service has disappeared by the time you read this book, crushed by the forces I have described here and its own missteps, just insert the words "any new online video-distribution company" every time you see the word "Netflix."

Even in offering complementary services, Netflix's powers are constrained. As a pipe provider, one important lever available to Comcast in its efforts to slow the advent of competitive online video is "usage-based billing" or "consumption billing." Usage-based billing sounds innocuous enough: charge consumers additional fees if their network usage exceeds a set level. Network operators have often claimed that these overage fees are necessary to allow them to invest in upgrading their networks to handle the high volumes of bits needed for consumers to access the video they love and that they need the flexibility to charge higher fees to heavy users who are congesting their networks. When you dig into the details, however, usage-based billing rates bear little relationship to actual network costs or to solving the problem of congestion. It is purely a way to raise revenues.

Network operators justify usage-based billing by arguing that light users should not be subsidizing heavy users. If your neighbor is paying a hundred dollars a month but streaming high-definition movies every night, and you use the same service just to send e-mail, why should you both have to pay the same rate? It sounds like a simple fairness argument. What's more, the network operators argue, they have to do something since their networks are becoming congested: it is expensive to build networks, the high volume of use of data is clogging the pipes, and no one should expect them to build more networks if they cannot charge the biggest users more.[22]

While these arguments have a superficial appeal, usage-based pricing is a crude instrument with which to manage traffic congestion. If your hoggish neighbor is streaming those high-definition movies during the day, you probably don't care. The real problem for cable broadband networks, which are shared within neighborhoods (and so subject to "contention," which means that you are battling with your neighbors for the flow of bits you want, in a context in which the cable distributor has no incentive to invest in better connections to increase the flow of bits), is the traffic during peak usage time, not the total amount of usage.[23]

Charging for peak-load usage, or congestion pricing, might take care of these contention issues. If the cost to deliver a bit to a particular house during key evening download hours were higher, users would probably change their behavior. But that would involve tinkering with all subscribers' bills, not just the hogs', and—to be cynical—might not discourage people from subscribing to the online video services that could cause them to exceed the network operator's cap. Providers are not interested in this solution.

Because the United States has given up on rate regulation for high-speed Internet access services, and the reporting requirements that go with it (number of subscribers, revenues, costs, service outages, quality of service), regulators have no reliable data about how pricing is computed.[24] No regulator seems to know what it costs to deliver the extra gigabyte the operators want subscribers to pay for. The actual cost of delivering bits over the last mile is probably pretty low; according to Netflix, an Internet service provider's cost to "deliver a marginal gigabyte, which is about an hour of viewing, from one of our regional interchange points over their last mile wired network to the consumer is *less than a penny*, and falling, so there is no reason that pay-per-gigabyte is economically necessary."[25] But overage charges (per-gigabyte charges imposed once the user has exceeded the network operator's cap) can be two dollars per gigabyte or more; Canadian ISPs have been known to charge five.[26]

In the absence of concrete information, regulators are stuck: carriers claim they need to charge overages, and the government—needing to encourage the building of infrastructure by these private parties—has no choice but to agree. And given the concentration in the marketplace for network operators, users have no choice but to pay.

According to the FCC, network operators in the past have routinely advertised "up to" speeds that are twice as high as the speeds subscribers actually experience; part of the reason for this phenomenon may be the prevalence of shared (contended-for) connections. Cable operators, in particular, routinely oversell their services.[27] If everyone is downloading a movie between 6 P.M. and 9 P.M., those shared networks burden the bitrates that everyone gets. The same amounts of bits go through the pipes, but they go more slowly. Between six and nine, you're battling your neighbor for bandwidth.

As a result, online video distributors face the prospect of being squeezed out: users won't sign up for independent online video if they believe they will end up paying more for Internet connectivity as a result.

To see how this might play out, consider our frozen neighbor to the north, where usage-based billing has been a major consumer issue. In 2010, Bell Canada convinced the Canadian telecommunications regulator, the Canadian Radio-television and Telecommunications Commission (CRTC), to approve a rate structure that it could impose on buyers of its wholesale data services—entities that planned to resell Internet access to their retail customers. The wholesale offering would have a number of options, ranging from a "Lite" rate of up to two gigabytes per month, with a $1.87 surcharge for every gigabyte over the cap, to a "Basic" plan of up to sixty gigabytes per month with a $1.12 overage fee.[28] Those are pretty meager usage rates before the surcharges kick in: by streaming video you could use up the Basic monthly allotment within six hours.[29]

Bell Canada argued that it had to impose caps to deal with fast-rising usage of video that had caused a 25 percent uptick in the volume of data carried over its networks.[30] But the real targets were Netflix and other online video providers. Netflix had launched services in Canada in 2010. Rather than build out its networks to allow consumers to watch video more readily, Bell and the other Canadian network providers had decided to enforce scarcity.[31]

Bell's technology, though, seemed incapable of accurately measuring how much subscribers were using, and the resulting overcharges and undercharges caused a furor. More than five hundred thousand people signed an online petition to the Canadian government demanding an end to usage-based billing.[32] Both Michael Geist, Canada Research Chair of Internet and E-commerce Law at the University of Ottawa, and Cory Doctorow, a Canadian-British futurist and author, pointed out that Bell had conceded that the rates it was charging for overages had nothing to do with the actual costs of providing services. The fees, instead, were designed to constrain users' behavior by making it unattractive for them to do things that required a lot of data. "In other words," Doctorow wrote, Bell had "set out to limit the growth of networked based business and new kinds of services, and to prevent Canadians experimentation that enables them to use the Internet to its fullest."[33]

Government officials called for an end to the practice and asked the Canadian regulator to reverse a ruling that would have forced retail ISPs using wholesale services from the large Canadian incumbents to adopt usage-based billing.[34] In March 2011, Bell Canada backed down from applying mandatory caps to independent retail ISPs buying its wholesale services, but it continued to charge hefty overages to its own subscribers who exceeded its bandwidth caps.[35]

Netflix quickly sent its own political signal, declaring that it would automatically compress its Canadian online video services into a third as much data in order to avoid the Canadian caps. Thirty hours of streaming film or television typically uses 31 GB of data; under this default compression setting, only 9 GB would be coming across users' wires. But this resulted in measurably reduced video quality.[36]

According to Geist, usage-based billing only helps the large Canadian telecom companies squeeze out their small competitors and squelch innovation. "The effect extends far beyond consumers paying more for Internet access," he has said. "There is a real negative effect on the Canadian digital economy, harming innovation and keeping new business models out of the country. Canada is not competitive when compared to most other countries and the strict bandwidth caps make us less attractive for new businesses and stifle innovative services."[37] Jesse Brown of the news Web site Macleans .ca wrote, "Yes, that's innovation in Canada: new players can indeed compete, by grossly degrading their product to a level beneath anything they'd dare offer to Americans. True, it may be a publicity stunt on Netflix's part, a calculated move to embarrass Canada into getting with the times.

If so, it's a brilliant one."[38] Netflix, for its part, argued that Bell Canada's wholesale usage-based billing rates provided margins in excess of 99 percent.[39] In late 2011, Netflix's arguments carried the day: the Canadian regulator required large providers like Bell Canada to sell access to independent ISPs at set rates based on actual costs plus a reasonable profit, and prohibited the incumbent from limiting the plans that the independents could sell to their customers.[40]

American network providers would like to charge for consumption of bandwidth based on rates that they choose, but following a disastrous attempt by Time Warner Cable to impose a cap of 75 GB in 2009, the American companies have been cannier about implementing usage-based billing. Protests over Time Warner Cable's proposed cap forced the company to reverse its policy, prompting Senator Charles Schumer (D-N.Y.) to issue a proud press release: "By responding to public outrage and opposition from community and elected officials, Time Warner Cable made the right decision today."[41] The message to the rest of the providers: be extremely careful about how you set your limits.

But it is not clear that U.S. regulators will follow Canada's lead in this area. A major development was the FCC's agreement in late 2010 to let network providers use their discretion in charging additional fees for exceeding caps that the providers themselves would establish. Julius Genachowski, the FCC chairman, had warm words of support for usage-based pricing just weeks before the Comcast-NBCU merger was approved: "Our work has also demonstrated the importance of business innovation to promote network investment and efficient use of networks, including measures to match price to cost such as usage-based pricing."[42] The rumor in Washington was that the FCC had promised to praise usage-based pricing in order to garner AT&T's support for its "open Internet" rules in December.[43] Comcast was then required as part of the merger not to treat "affiliated" broadband network traffic differently from unaffiliated traffic when it was implementing caps, tiers, metering, "or other usage-based pricing."[44] But Comcast could get around this limitation by calling its own Video on Demand services something other than "broadband"—again, "specialized services" are not subject to neutrality obligations, and the FCC's authority to say anything about neutrality in the first place is tenuous.

Following the approval of the merger, in March 2011 AT&T announced caps for both its DSL and U-verse fiber-to-the-neighborhood services. The caps would kick in at 150 GB per month for the DSL service, and at 250 GB per month for U-verse. Users exceeding the caps would be charged ten dollars for each additional 50 GB of use. AT&T already had in place a dramatically low cap for its wireless services: new mobile consumers can no longer access unlimited data and have to choose between a 0.2-GB-per-month plan and a 2-GB-per-month plan.[45]

Given Americans' appetite for television, the AT&T caps seemed to be designed to discourage the substitution of online video for traditional television; anyone watching more than two high-definition movies a day would be subject to the wired cap.

Most of the other high-speed Internet wired access service providers were expected to follow suit. Comcast has had a cap of 250 GB in place since 2008, terminating users who consume more data than that per month, and plans to raise this to 30 GB and charge for additional data transfer.[46] And the iPad mobile plans were clearly focused on limitations: 2 GB for a flat fee, and then ten dollars per gigabyte after that.[47] In short, American distributors have learned from their own early mistakes and, aided by the permissive statements of regulators, have brought usage-based limits to the market without consumers even noticing, let alone protesting. Usage caps have allowed American carriers to impose scarcity (so that average revenues can continue to increase), while other countries have focused instead on providing abundant bandwidth for new ideas and new ways of making a living.

Raising the cost of Netflix's access to programming, as described in Chapter 5, was one way the cable complex could keep Netflix in a box. Another would be to make it more expensive for Netflix's users to stream its content, and imposing caps would do the job: high-definition streaming movies on Netflix, at five gigabytes each, would almost certainly become a luxury if usage-based pricing became the norm in America. Usage-based pricing would be a useful tool for cable distributors, giving them an opportunity to leverage control over their giant IP-enabled pipe to discriminate against competing offerings, using their position as the only conduit for content companies to reach their subscribers.

Usage-based billing would not apply to the portion of the pipe that the cable distributors could label specialized services, such as their own proprietary video or gaming services—data using the Internet Protocol that the network operator could prioritize—but Netflix would be subject to the caps imposed by the network operators if it remained a pure online video distributor. Comcast could use its control over access to the last mile to collect a toll that would not be collected from its own content services.

Consider how powerful Comcast's position is: it can label TV Everywhere a specialized service or say that it has to prioritize its own video for reasons of "reasonable network management." The FCC has said it will consider *on a case-by-case basis* whether "specialized" video services offered by cable distributors are an end run around its light-touch common-carriage (net neutrality) rules; under these circumstances, what investor would take a risk on a new online video-distribution company?[48] David Cohen, Comcast's executive vice president, has argued in the past both that without reasonable network management "these networks collapse" and that it is very difficult to put into words just what reasonable network management means.[49] Welcome to the land of uncertainty, where new online businesses go to die.

What's more, Comcast already has the hammer in place. The company installed meters for all its subscribers that can be triggered if it decides to switch to finer-grained usage-based billing for high-speed Internet access. And although it swears that it has no immediate plans to start billing separately for each service used over its Internet access connection, Netflix is not missing the signals. Comcast can implement more stringent usage-based pricing—which might dissuade more people from signing up for Netflix—at any time. At the same time, it can expand the portion of its pipes used for Internet-like interactive services—"specialized services"—over which it has unquestioned control.[50] Comcast will have the power to ensure that users reach only online sites with which Comcast has some form of relationship.

Netflix is thus engaged in a game of chicken with Comcast. It is banking on the fact that users who take a while to reach Comcast's caps will stay loyal to Netflix until this happens, and that by the time the caps began to bite, users will have started protesting. Not that this will happen immediately:

Netflix's own 2011 report showed that the average user streamed Netflix at just over 2 Mbps—much slower than the 50 Mbps or 150 Mbps of which Comcast is capable.[51] When it came to the last mile, Americans are just starting to buy the very highest speeds in large numbers.[52] Netflix's hope must be that in time—when the inevitable showdown comes—Comcast will need Netflix more than Netflix needs Comcast, and that Netflix's loyal subscriber base will give the company protection from Comcast's high charges.

But the threat remains. Cable's response in this game of chicken means that investors in Netflix (or future purchasers of the entire company) may be discouraged by the deeply contingent nature of Netflix's plans. Usage-based billing poses risks to all kinds of new online businesses. As Stacey Higginbotham of *GigaOM* puts it: "In the broadband arena where there is little competition among providers and a tendency to avoid investment in networks because of pressure from Wall Street and . . . a lack of competition, usage-based pricing could lead to expensive broadband and stifle burgeoning technologies such as online video and HD video conferencing."[53]

In the end, the FCC's "specialized services" category creates a business development opportunity for operators like Comcast. Comcast can say to a company like Facebook—the ESPN of the Internet—that its traffic won't be subject to a cap or the limits of best-efforts transmission because it will be treated as part of a specialized service. Facebook, in turn, will have to share revenue with Comcast or pay a premium in exchange for this treatment. (Or, perhaps, because Comcast needs Facebook, Facebook will be able to get this categorization for free.) A cable-distribution company that "rates" Facebook sessions in this way could effectively avoid the threat of the Internet. Kids these days don't use e-mail or phone calls, but they do use Facebook, which provides them with an AOL-like walled garden of media content and intimate interactions with friends. To avoid being hit by high overage charges, customers might choose to avoid buying Internet access altogether or limit themselves to packages that allow for limited Web browsing. After all, they'll still have Facebook.

Even if usage-based billing did not slow the arrival of competitive online video services right away, Netflix faces other squeezes from last-mile network providers. Because other networks have no other means of reaching Comcast subscribers, Comcast can charge any networks Netflix signs up that try to send traffic to Comcast's gateways—let's call them "connecting networks." And that would raise Netflix's costs.

Traditionally, the big pipes crisscrossing the country "peered" (or connected) with one another at interconnection points and swapped traffic for free. The major actors were AT&T, Sprint, and Verizon, and while they sold wholesale traffic carriage to smaller companies, they traded traffic at no cost among themselves. They also used a technique called hot-potato routing, in which data traffic was handed over to other carriers at the point closest to the point of origination.[54] This may sound technical, but it's not: if you are a pipe provider with network interconnection points in Los Angeles, New York, and Miami and a peer pipe, and your customers in Pasadena are sending out traffic that is destined for that peer's network subscribers, hot-potato routing would have you handing over that traffic in Los Angeles.

In that traditional environment, if you started to hot potato a lot more traffic to the other network, and the other network was carrying your traffic from Los Angeles to its destination in New York City, the other network might start arguing that you should pay if you were sending, say, twice as much traffic to them as they were sending to you. Your relationship with that network might switch from a free exchange of traffic to a paid exchange.

The problem for these traditional free peering relationships is that, unlike the days when most network usage consisted of telephone conversations, consumers today are no longer sending and receiving the same amount of traffic. Instead, with so much more video online, they are receiving a lot more traffic than they are sending. Comcast can argue that the traffic with connecting networks is out of balance—they are getting a lot of traffic, but they are not sending as much—and so the connecting networks should pay Comcast.

But connecting networks—pure-play, no-retail pipe providers like the company Level 3—argue that the hot-potato aspect of the traditional equation no longer applies. Rather than drop off traffic to Comcast at the point where it originates, they are portaging traffic as close to the relevant consumers as possible—taking it to the New York metro area, in our example, instead of handing it off in Los Angeles—and so the connecting networks should not have to pay Comcast.[55] In fact, Comcast should pay the connecting networks for bringing so much content that Comcast's subscribers want almost the entire way. And by the way, the connecting networks argue, Comcast's *outgoing* traffic has no way of reaching subscribers of Verizon and Qwest without going through them—another reason Comcast should pay them, rather than the other way around.

At bottom, the connecting networks are irritated that Comcast appears to be asking them to subsidize its local network when it is sitting on huge profits and should have the incentive to improve its local network infrastructure on its own. From their perspective, it appears that Comcast would rather have an inefficient network and charge everyone for it than have interconnecting networks carry traffic to Comcast in the most efficient way. Comcast has the power to protect its business by preventing any infrastructure provider from building facilities closer to Comcast's subscribers. Comcast can require that interconnecting networks be built only to its designated "meet points" at its network boundaries.

This dispute has grown into a major business and policy problem because the carriage of traffic to Comcast subscribers is not competitive. Content providers have no other way of reaching Comcast customers. So Comcast has an incentive to constrain its interconnection capacity with other networks and to charge for interconnection in ways that will raise its rivals' costs. If Comcast decides not to play nice at the edge of the network, there is no way to route around it.

In November 2010 a battle royal over Internet interconnection broke out when Level 3 made a deal with Netflix to carry its traffic to Comcast's retail, last-mile network. Although the details are unknown, Comcast apparently demanded that Level 3 pay for local distribution, which had the effect of raising Netflix's costs. Level 3 felt that Comcast was making up its rates arbitrarily and planning to disadvantage Netflix through its interconnection arrangements. But Level 3, which carries the most Internet traffic of any network in the world, also felt it had little choice but to pay up—while complaining to the news media.[56] Coverage of the fracas was swift and confused. A few months later, Level 3 announced that it would buy another connecting network, Global Crossing; the betting was that Level 3 needed even greater scale and power to control its own destiny in the face of ever-consolidating last-mile providers.[57]

Complicating the story further, content companies like Google have begun building their own pipes and connecting directly with last-mile networks like Comcast, thus avoiding having to buy connectivity from Level 3.[58] To prepare for the coming battles, everyone is bulking up and consolidating, hoping to achieve advantages of scale and scope that will give them the upper hand in disputes over payments.

In effect, Comcast and the other major cable distributors, unconstrained by competition, are segmenting the market for wired Internet access in America. The rich will get moderately high (by global standards) speeds at very high and incrementally increasing prices (or for incrementally increasing revenue per user as Comcast's costs go down and users sign up for impenetrable bundles of services); the poor will often not be served at all; and the state will be left to fill in the gaps, at a higher cost for everyone. Comcast's plan seemed to be to provide high-data traffic speeds (up to 105 Mbps) to major markets at a very high price—an initial cost of $105 a month as part of a bundle, or $200 a month a la carte, with a $249 installation fee.[59] Stand-alone data access was twice as expensive on its own; to avoid being treated as a mere pipe Comcast wanted to be able to ensure that consumers were paying for its video and voice services.

A 300-GB monthly cap—Comcast's analogue to the controversial Bell Canada formula—will remain in place. That cap would be reached in several hours with steady use at Comcast's highest speed or, perhaps more realistically, in a week by watching one high-definition movie a night at 30–40 GB each. Tim Beyers of the financial-services company Motley Fool noticed the tension in Comcast's announcement of its initial 250-GB cap: "Anyone notice the conflicting messages? Here, have a Maserati. All we ask is that you stay within the 25 mph zone."[60] The costs were very high indeed: by contrast, in Paris consumers have 100 Mbps service for $40 a month, in Lisbon the same service costs $63 a month. And Comcast's expensive services were available only in major markets like Seattle, San Francisco, Portland, Denver, Salt Lake City, Baltimore, and Philadelphia.[61]

Meanwhile, for less well-off areas, nonurban areas, and poorer consumers, high-speed Internet access is simply not available. Towns fifty or sixty miles away from downtown metropolises often cannot get cable, and even "obsolete" DSL is hard to obtain. The FCC says that as many as 26 million

Americans live in areas unserved by even very slow (4 Mbps) broadband, and a third of Americans (roughly 80 million adults) do not subscribe even if they can.[62] By contrast, over 90 percent of people in South Korea and Singapore subscribe to high-speed Internet access.[63] Why has this happened?

The third of Americans who do not subscribe say that cost is a major obstacle to adoption.[64] A thirty-dollar-a-month offering of one gigabit per second (Gbps) service, to be available throughout South Korea by the end of 2012, is unthinkable in America today.[65]

The Americans who are not served suffer from the country's lagging deployment of high-speed access. Wall Street frowns on major capital expenditures by the carriers, preferring companies that have large amounts of free cash and pay handsome dividends. Outside major markets where they can cluster and charge high prices to city dwellers, the carriers doubt there is a business case for high-speed Internet access, and the situation is particularly hopeless for Americans in rural and tribal areas. It looks like we will all end up paying for federal subsidies of high-speed data service in those areas. The resulting connections will still probably be substantially slower than those provided to urban dwellers. We will have created two digital Americas, at tremendous expense to all involved.

At the same time, when it comes to usage-based billing and interconnection fees (not to mention monthly subscription fees charged to consumers in urban areas), Comcast and the other cable distributors have the market power to raise these at will, without regard to actual costs—and in clear service of their own corporate goals of avoiding just-pipe treatment for as long as possible so as to delay the advent of competitive services. So far, would-be regulators have shown little initiative or seemed to lack the information necessary to change the situation. At the Cable Show in May 2012, Julius Genachowski praised usage-based billing, calling it "healthy and beneficial" for broadband and high-tech industries.[66]

Pure communications transport services like those offered by Comcast have historically been subject to extensive regulatory oversight. The government has always, in the past, imposed common-carriage and universal-service obligations on these companies so that they would offer service to all comers without unreasonable discrimination at reasonable rates, terms, and conditions. Regulators have recognized that these transport services are expensive to build and that it makes no sense to build more than one in a given area, so they have given out franchises in exchange for promises to serve the entire licensed area for reasonable rates—which the government then monitored. Those rates have allowed the creation of cross-subsidization schemes that made it possible to provide all Americans (even those in remote areas) with communications transport. Result: a large national market to sell to, commercial and personal freedom based on the inability of the monopoly carrier to discriminate in its own favor, and a single basic facility on which all Americans could depend that knitted them together as a country.

But to the country's detriment, America has wandered far from this model. As Representative Ed Markey says, "As a nation, in constructing our economic strategy, we should be saying that we should be number one in speed and access. We need to be Number One, looking back over our shoulders at Number Two."[67] But we are not, and the costs to innovation, economic growth, and national competitiveness—not to mention fair treatment of new businesses and ordinary citizens—are great. How is Netflix doing today?

10

Comcast's Marathon

THE FEBRUARY 2010 HEARING BEFORE THE Senate Antitrust Subcommittee was more about politics than policy. The senators were there to put the witnesses through their paces, and they had the ability to raise the political stakes, but the merger would ultimately be reviewed by the Antitrust Division of the Department of Justice and the Federal Communications Commission. Opposition was strong from the public advocates' side, but it was a vertical merger, and suing to block it would be an uphill battle for the Justice Department, given a string of cases in which vertical deals had received favorable reviews. Senator Herb Kohl, opening the hearing, saw his role as setting the political stage: "So the role of the antitrust regulators at the Justice Department and the FCC will be vital to preserving competition," he said. "Should these agencies decide to allow this merger, we believe it is essential that they insist on strong conditions to protect consumers."[1] The signal was clear: most of the people at the hearing considered the merger a done deal. Some conditions might be imposed, but it was going to go through. Eleven months later, it did.

Comcast's run through the process was a marathon, not a sprint. The company prepared a battle plan in 2009, anticipating months of maneuvering. The Comcast government affairs office prepared (and inadvertently sent to me) a spreadsheet of "priority 1" contacts the company planned to make as it rolled out the merger announcement. These were people or entities who might oppose the merger, listed with contact information and a designated Comcast (or NBC) employee tasked with keeping in touch. Public-interest groups, networks, sports teams and leagues, and unions were all on the list.

The campaign started off with a bang. The initial FCC filing was a hefty document—almost 150 pages long—laying out the structure of the transaction and the benefits and synergies it was expected to create. These benefits included an increase in the amount of content available to consumers, more and better local programming, and the fostering of innovation. And there was more: "the Applicants propose to enhance those benefits by offering an unprecedented array of specific and verifiable public interest commitments to expand the amount, quality, and diversity of programming across multiple platforms."[2]

These public-interest commitments included promises to maintain free over-the-air broadcast and to provide the same amount of local news on NBC-owned stations that the stations were currently offering.[3] But the beneficiaries were strategically chosen as well; for example, commitment 5 was targeted at a pet charity of FCC chairman Julius Genachowski, Common Sense Media, whose board he had helped to form years earlier: "In an effort to constantly improve the tools and information available for parents, Comcast will expand its growing partnership with Common Sense Media ('CSM'), a highly respected organization offering enhanced information to help guide family viewing decisions. Comcast will work to creatively incorporate CSM information in its emerging On Demand and On Demand Online platforms and other advanced platforms, and will look for more opportunities for CSM to work with NBCU." Whether Genachowski saw through the ploy or not, he must have had to smile at the giant company's personal touch. Another friendly dart aimed at the chairman: "Comcast is currently in discussions with CSM about a broader partnership to be launched on completion of the transaction"—in other words, provided Genachowski's FCC approved the merger. "Comcast will devote millions of dollars in media distribution resources to support public awareness efforts over the next two years to further CSM's digital literacy campaign." Common Sense Media honored Genachowski with its Newt Minow Public Policy Award for Outstanding Leadership on Behalf of Children and Families in February 2010; Comcast was a "benefactor" of the Kennedy Center event at which the chairman received the honor.[4]

Genachowski's connection to Common Sense Media had existed long before Comcast announced its commitment to the nonprofit; in turn, Common Sense Media's honoring of Chairman Genachowski was no doubt equally heartfelt, based as it was on a long friendship between Genachowski and Jim Steyer, CSM's energetic chairman.[5] Still, recognizing the connection was a brilliant move on Comcast's part.

Genachowski was not the only target. Commitment 12 was aimed at FCC commissioner Michael Copps, a progressive Democrat who was expected to have concerns about the merger. The company promised to develop new approaches to the distribution of public, educational, and governmental programming. Commitment 16, a promise to maintain the journalistic integrity of NBC News, was likewise aimed at Copps.[6]

This isn't speculation: David Cohen, the man in charge of Comcast's merger strategy, acknowledged the importance to the merger of these kinds of commitments, saying, "We've proposed a series of conditions that we think make sense and that we think are appropriate. . . . We have things [in the joint venture agreement] that are near and dear to Copps's heart, including commitments to maintaining local news coverage at NBC owned and operated stations."[7]

Comcast's list of public-interest commitments focused importantly on broadcast, even though NBC-the-network was not at the heart of the deal's value. The company committed to maintaining free over-the-air television and to preserving NBC News's independence. Minority groups also received attention—Comcast would expand Hispanic broadcasting—and unions' concerns were addressed: Comcast would honor NBC Universal's collective-bargaining agreements.[8]

The Washington onslaught thus began with an effort to convince commissioners and traditional interest groups (minorities and unions) that Comcast was a good corporate actor. The consumer advocacy groups Free Press, Consumers Union, and Consumer Federation of America complained that none of Comcast's advance "'concessions' [were] meaningful commitments beyond what Comcast is already doing, is likely to do anyway, or is bound to do by law."[9] They were right: for all its largesse,

Comcast was not committing to lower prices for cable or high-speed Internet access, or to provide globally relevant Internet access to all Americans, or to open its networks to competitors. Conditions that would address the fundamental competition and social contract concerns raised by the transaction would have to come from the regulators. And that's what the main fight was about.

The Comcast lobbying story centers on David Cohen, Comcast's executive vice president of policy and the man who oversees its government relations office. Cohen is a likeable man with an unpretentious way of speaking. He has played an important role in the Democratic Party for a long time, and he is an irresistible force on behalf of Comcast. "If I had to negotiate with him, I'd be really worried," one Hill staffer told me. "I believe David Cohen is the driving genius behind Comcast"—and Comcast must agree, since it pays him more than $10 million a year.[10] He's a dynamo, a multitasker with as many as twenty people waiting to see him at any given time, a sender of e-mails at 5 A.M., a man of enormous energy, efficiency, and organization. He has thousands of names on his BlackBerry. Rhonda Cohen once told the *Philadelphia Inquirer* that she sees so little of her husband that "we've been married for 30 years, but in terms of time, we're still on our honeymoon." The Cohens, who have two sons, met at Swarthmore, where she was editor of the school newspaper and he "slept half the day."[11] Things have changed.

According to *Philadelphia Magazine*, "he's so genial, and tends to speak to everyone in such pleasant baths of words—he's so naturally embracing—that it's easy to miss how purely competitive he is." Indeed, Cohen is something of a street fighter; if a Hill staffer brings up issues that challenge his version of events he will bristle, turning from a diplomatic pussycat into a tiger. But above all he has discipline and control.[12]

In a sense, Cohen has been smoothing the way for the Comcast merger for his entire career. He is originally from New York, but he made his name in Pennsylvania Democratic politics. He has been described for years as the gateway to Pennsylvania politics and in 2010 was named by *Politics Magazine* as one of the "Top 10 Democrats" in the state. He was Philadelphia mayor Ed Rendell's enormously effective chief of staff from 1992 to 1997.[13]

Buzz Bissinger's *A Prayer for the City* (1998), based on four years of wide-open access to Cohen and Rendell, chronicled in adulatory terms Cohen's unflappable, almost unearthly ability to stay focused despite little sleep for months on end. Bissinger wrote that Cohen, "like Radar on M*A*S*H, had the ability to be in the right place well before anyone even knew there was a right place."[14] The *Pennsylvania Report*, naming Cohen to its list of the seventy-five most influential figures in Pennsylvania politics in 2003, noted that "no one—in or out of government—is closer to Ed Rendell than Cohen. No major policy decision, personnel, political or other decision will be made without his imprimatur or veto."[15] When then-Governor Rendell held an impromptu press conference in May 2010 on the occasion of Arlen Specter's loss of his Senate seat, David Cohen—"Rendell's Karl Rove," according to the *Philadelphia Inquirer*—was at his side.[16]

Cohen and Rendell turned Philadelphia around by focusing on waste in government spending; Cohen went from one department to the next, instructing managers to stick with the revenue they had and prioritize their spending. In the end, the Rendell-Cohen team balanced the budget, implemented major structural reforms, and rescued the city from financial oblivion. As Cohen said to Bissinger, they proved that "you could cut taxes, increase revenues, and operate the city reasonably and responsibly."[17]

Cohen's influence on Rendell and Philadelphia continued after he left government in 1997. Less than a week after he departed the mayor's office to rejoin the prestigious Philadelphia law firm Ballard Spahr, Andrews & Ingersoll, he was asked by Mayor Rendell to co-chair, with Comcast's Brian Roberts, the city's effort to attract one of the 2000 party conventions to Philadelphia. The committee succeeded in bringing the Republicans.[18] The entire convention was a hymn to Comcast branding; buttons reading "Welcome to Comcast Country," with "Republican National Convention" in tiny print, were handed out to conventioneers, who met in the Comcast Arena near downtown Philadelphia; the arena was ringed with enormous letters spelling out "WELCOME TO COMCAST COUNTRY."[19]

Cohen quickly became the go-to Democratic fundraiser in the state. He chaired the board of directors of the Greater Philadelphia Chamber of Commerce and the University of Pennsylvania's board of trustees, and served as an adviser or board member for the CEO Council for Growth, the

National Urban League, the National Council of La Raza, the Jewish Federation of Greater Philadelphia, the United Way of Southeastern Pennsylvania, and the Pennsylvania chapter of the American Red Cross. In 2008 *PolitickerPA* ranked him second among the state's top fifty political power brokers.[20]

Comcast, a Ballard Spahr client, had also had a strong influence on Philadelphia politics. When the small cable company RCN applied in 1998 for a license to provide cable services in Philadelphia, Rendell openly derided the attempt. After the city council dragged out the process for two and a half years, RCN gave up and left town, saying that it had been forced to respond to "Comcast-scripted" questions. This is the same RCN, recall, that claimed that Comcast had bullied independent contractors in the Philadelphia area to keep them from working for RCN, had carried out an elaborate predatory pricing scheme, and had "demonstrated both the inclination and the wherewithal to use their market power to crush broadband competition in their local markets"—in short, that Comcast's ability "to choke off nascent broadband competition" was becoming "unstoppable."[21]

Exclusive franchises had been illegal under federal law for years, but Philadelphia was and is Comcast country. The company poured money into Rendell's campaigns and into Philadelphia for a decade before RCN showed up, and the city and the mayor were grateful for Comcast's good works and millions of dollars. These same civic techniques would prove extremely effective during the 2010 merger discussions.

After leading Ballard Spahr for a little more than four years, during which time the firm had also hired Ed Rendell (who was running for governor at the time), Cohen left the firm to join Comcast in 2002 with a job invented specifically for him.[22] As he describes it, as executive vice president for policy, he is part of a troika charting the company's strategic direction. All external and administrative functions report to him. But Cohen's ties with Rendell seem to have only strengthened since he left Rendell's side, making Rendell and Comcast close allies as well. Comcast's acquisition of NBC Universal, Governor Ed Rendell said, would mean more jobs in Philadelphia, where Comcast is headquartered. "The prestige is enormous," he added. Asked if he expected the merger to encounter any federal regulatory hurdles, Rendell responded, "I have confidence in David

Cohen." Not surprisingly, Rendell was expected to join the Comcast board when he left the governor's mansion in 2011. Even before he left public office, Comcast had the governor doing post-game analysis for Philadelphia Eagles games (Rendell donated the money to charity).[23]

Cohen's Democratic ties have grown during his time at Comcast. Cohen made about $180,000 in contributions to Democrats between 2006 and 2011, compared to $12,000 to Republicans, according to OpenSecrets.org. Cohen also personally helped raise more than $6 million for President Obama's election campaign in 2008; during the 2008 election cycle, Comcast's political action committee raised more than $2.5 million. At a fundraiser for then-Democratic senator Arlen Specter on September 15, 2009, just months before the Comcast merger was announced, President Obama called out the "luminaries" in the room—Governor Rendell, Mayor Michael Nutter of Philadelphia, various congressmen, and the chair of the Democratic State Party, T. J. Rooney. He reserved particular praise for Cohen: "And I want to acknowledge a special friend, somebody who is a great supporter of mine and is the chairman of this event, David Cohen is in the house. Please give him a round of applause." Obama had good reason to single Cohen out: in late 2008 Cohen had hosted a fundraiser for candidate Obama featuring rocker Jon Bon Jovi, also an Obama supporter, that raised millions. (For 2012, Cohen has committed to raise $500,000 nationwide on behalf of Obama's reelection committee.)[24]

Cohen is not just an Obama supporter; he held a fundraiser to help Hillary Clinton retire her campaign debt in early 2009, with Vice President–elect Biden, Governor Rendell, Senator Bob Casey, and Mayor Nutter in attendance. Cohen had been enthusiastic about Clinton, giving her the maximum permitted individual donation, and Rendell had boasted that if Clinton had become president he would have recommended David Cohen to her for deputy chief of staff.[25]

Donors to the 2009 Specter events were required to write a check for ten thousand dollars or raise a minimum of fifty thousand, even though Specter was already trailing his Republican opponent by a substantial margin. "We would like to generate a literal outpouring of financial support for Sen. Specter," Cohen said in a letter to Democratic fundraisers.[26] All good things come around: Specter had hired Ed Rendell forty years earlier to work in the district attorney's office, Rendell had hired Cohen, and Cohen, now a very powerful man in Philadelphia, was willing to try to save Specter's career. And it was a subcommittee of the Senate Judiciary Committee, of which Specter was a member, that held the hearings on the Comcast merger the following year.

Specter was broadly useful to the Comcast team; staffers told me that he set up meetings between senators and Brian Roberts. Although the decision on the merger was made by the Department of Justice and the FCC after Specter left office, his friendly presence at the subcommittee hearing in February 2010 could only have helped. He told those in the hearing room that he "approach[ed] the hearing with a little different perspective because I know Comcast and I know Brian Roberts and I know his father, Ralph Roberts. So I am in a position to attest to a number of critical factors evaluating whether this merger ought to occur. One factor that I can attest to is they are really very good corporate citizens." Warming to his theme, Specter noted that the Comcast tower distinguished the Philadelphia skyline and, on a personal note, remarked that his son had teamed with Brian Roberts to win the gold medal at the Maccabiah Games squash tournament.[27]

Cohen is esteemed for his judgment and ability. Legislators and policy makers respect him. In 2008 he moved adroitly to soothe Rep. John Dingell's ruffled feathers at a time when Dingell (D-Mich.) chaired the House committee with jurisdiction over communications. Comcast had planned to move Michigan public, educational, and governmental (PEG) channels to digital-tier Siberia, in the 900s—a shift that would have forced approximately 450,000 analog subscribers in the state to get digital set-top boxes or new televisions in order to receive them. After officials in Dearborn and Meridian Township sued Comcast, a federal court in Michigan ordered the company to leave the PEG channels where they were. Dingell was irate and held a hearing on the matter—and it is not a good thing for any company to have the leading legislator with jurisdiction over its activities angry at it. Cohen flew to Washington, assured Dingell that the whole thing was a mistake, reversed the company's plan, and somehow remained on Dingell's good side throughout the entire affair. "I am pleased that Comcast, which had announced changes detrimental to the way it delivers PEG services in Michigan, has agreed to make a good-faith effort to work out a settlement with the affected communities," Dingell said. "I want to commend them for that."[28] Cohen was prepared to apologize publicly, saying, "In retrospect, we failed to communicate adequately our goals and to work cooperatively with our local partners to produce a win for everyone."[29] Only Cohen could have pulled that off.

After having been battered by then-FCC chairman Kevin Martin, who was widely viewed as hating the cable industry, Cohen was determined to change the perception of the cable guys in Washington. The National Cable & Telecommunications Association, the cable trade association (now headed by former FCC chairman Michael Powell), jumped in generously to help with the nation's transition to digital broadcast television after Obama's inauguration in early 2009, providing extensive assistance with call-center aid and other efforts to prepare people for the switch.[30] And once the new administration was in place, Cohen praised Martin's successor, Genachowski, as "the most qualified person ever to be appointed" FCC boss: "He brings a great intellect, great experience, tremendous organization and a commitment to run fair, data-driven processes that will underline the decisions the commission makes under his leadership."[31]

Cohen was Brian Roberts's right-hand man for the merger. In meetings with Hill staff, Cohen routinely interrupted Roberts and took over the discussion. Roberts did not seem to mind; he understood that Cohen knew what he was doing. Roberts wanted the scale and scope that the NBC Universe content would bring Comcast; Cohen was trusted to run the politics and to know where the next right place to be was.[32]

As Robert Huber wrote in *Philadelphia Magazine* in 2009,

> For a long time, the Robertses were viewed as civically unengaged and stingy when it came to giving back. So it's quite helpful to Brian Roberts and Comcast that David L. Cohen is a big wheel at Penn Med, and . . . chairman of the board of the university trustees, and head of the Chamber of Commerce, and still close to Rendell, and a fund-raiser for Barack Obama. Whatever he's doing out in the world, he's *executive vice president of Comcast*. The David L. Cohen brand has become embedded with the Comcast message. . . . Cohen's the guy next to *the* guy. The guy who makes things go, the guy people come to, to help them get things done.[33]

But even Cohen wasn't ready for what came next.

That February, during a House Judiciary Committee hearing held the same day as the Senate Antitrust Subcommittee meeting, African American members of Congress complained that NBC programming was not sufficiently diverse; the network had not a single African American–targeted show. When Rep. Maxine Waters (D-Calif.) asked NBC Universal president Jeff Zucker why this was, he replied, "we have not found that [African American] show." When Waters continued pressing, Zucker assured her that NBC was continuing to look for a good African American program. "Let me say that it is very difficult to accept that you cannot find the kind of program I'm talking about," Waters said. "It is unacceptable to say you don't know . . . when it could happen. . . . I don't think black viewers would like to hear that kind of answer." The same went for the news: Rep. Sheila Jackson Lee (D-Tex.) noted that there is no diversity on the Sunday morning talk shows, including NBC's *Meet the Press.* Waters and Jackson Lee also asked Brian Roberts why Comcast had just one woman and one African American man on its board; Rep. Luis Gutierrez (D-Ill.) noted that the board had no Hispanics. Roberts was forced to admit that he didn't have a good answer.[34]

A few months later, things heated up considerably: Waters and sixty-eight other members of Congress, many of them members of the Congressional Black Caucus or the Congressional Hispanic Conference, asked the FCC to extend its public comment period and hold public hearings on the merger.[35]

Hiring policies, board membership, and programming diversity had no relevance to the competition and concentration issues raised by the merger, but these comments hurt Comcast's public image and were important to the larger public-interest concerns at the FCC. Comcast needed to avoid the kind of interest-group politics that could destroy reputations and scuttle carefully laid plans; indeed, it had attempted to forestall objections through the public-interest commitments in its original filing. Apparently those were not enough.

After the FCC declined to hold the hearing Waters wanted, John Conyers (D-Mich.), chairman of the House Judiciary Committee, arranged for a field hearing in Los Angeles in June. It was Waters's hearing; it was well-attended, raucous at times, frequently interrupted by applause, and nearly four hours long. Taking NBC to task for not having adequate diversity among its executives, Waters said, "If you're telling me how many janitors you're hiring, how many clerks you're hiring—that's not good enough. We know we can always get some numbers at that lower level. So having said that, let's just understand each other. This is about ownership, this is about programming, this is about executive management, this is about advertising."[36] Roberts and Zucker were conspicuously absent, but less senior Comcast executives listened politely. (John D. Rockefeller also made it a practice not to show up at hearings that promised to be unpleasant.)

During that same hearing, Stanley Washington (representing a new group called the National Coalition of African American Owned Media, which appeared to have been formed by the law firm where former FCC chairman Kevin Martin worked) described Comcast as a "plantation" and charged that the company had not done enough to ensure the viability of African American–owned channels. He called for a minority boycott of Comcast.[37]

There was some question of whether Comcast was carrying any African American content. An earlier effort, the Black Family Channel, had not wanted Comcast to take a stake in its operations as a condition of carriage and had ended up shutting down, leaving just one American cable network with significant black ownership: TV One. "While Comcast carries the network on its most widely distributed tier," Waters said, "it is worth noting that Comcast owns a 33% stake in TV One." Washington's group asserted that African Americans make up as much as 40 percent of Comcast's subscriber base but that none of the 250 channels Comcast offered was 100 percent African American owned.[38]

Comcast had made many contributions to minority charities, and the charities—hundreds of them—sent in letters and calls of support to lawmakers and agencies. ("It is crumbs, and they know it is crumbs," said Washington at the L.A. hearing.)[39] Waters was not moved. "And while we take the opportunity to say to Comcast, we appreciate the donations," she said at the field hearing, "that has nothing to do with the competition or ownership that we're talking about today. So they should continue to give the 50 cents to the Boy Scouts. But we're talking about competition or ownership. So if there's anybody here today who wants to talk about how much money you have given to the NAACP, the Urban League, to Al Sharpton, to anybody else, this is not the place to do it."[40]

The hearing was so striking that NBC's *30 Rock* commented on it a few months later, with Queen Latifah playing a fictional congresswoman who chastises NBC for its lack of diversity.[41] Waters seemed to think the merger could be blocked: "We have worked long enough at this, we have enough self-confidence to look Comcast in the eye, NBC in the eye and say, not this time, not this time."[42]

Waters also said that Comcast had contacted her to ask how the company could satisfy her demands; the *Los Angeles Times* suggested that she was hinting that she had been offered a bribe. And she intimated that people were afraid to testify: "As some will note, there are a few people who are missing from the panel who were previously scheduled to attend. It is somewhat troublesome that many independent and minority programmers, producers, writers and directors have been afraid to voice their concerns for fear of blacklisting or other forms of retaliation within their industries."[43]

Comcast was briefly rattled. Representatives of the company swiftly called legislative offices to take the temperature of the leadership. Would these issues be a problem?

David Cohen had apparently learned from experience that the way to work with interest groups was to continue making promises. To cool the criticism following the Los Angeles field hearing, Comcast prepared for the next hearing—to be held in July 2010 in Chicago under the leadership of Rep. Bobby Rush of Illinois—by making more public-interest commitments. It would add two new independent cable networks to its lineup for three years, with substantial minority ownership for at least one of them each year.[44] At the Chicago hearing, Jesse Jackson, president of the Rainbow Push Coalition, called for Comcast to commit to making at least 10 percent of its basic tier consist of minority-owned networks and to set "aggressive benchmarks" to get more minorities both in front of the camera and running budgets and shows.[45] Okay, Comcast said—how about four cable networks whose majority owners are African American? It would create "diversity advisory councils" that would meet with Comcast-NBCU executives. *Broadcasting & Cable* reported that the company had made unspecified pledges about employment, programming, procurement, governance, and corporate giving to a host of Latino organizations. Comcast pledged to add a Hispanic member to its board; expand training, internship, and scholarship programs for minority students; and extend carriage of current African American programming "in key market systems" within six months of the deal's close. Most important, it would pay $20 million into a new venture fund for expanding opportunities for minority entrepreneurs.[46]

Comcast had turned a bug into a feature while diverting attention from the central issues of market domination: it had managed to make the public's review of the merger focus on diversity instead of market power. The Hispanic groups were on board. Bobby Rush, well known for receiving contributions from the telecommunications industry, announced that he was for it, noting his enthusiasm about the deal's prospects for minority media owners and entrepreneurs. Will Griffin of Hip Hop on Demand asserted that Comcast had the best "infrastructure of inclusion" to build upon in the media industry, and that African American consumers and policy makers had more potential leverage with Comcast than any other media company.[47]

Some observers noticed Comcast had not promised to provide diverse content; when Rep. Rick Boucher (D-Va.) asked about specifics guaranteeing such content in primetime slots, Comcast's Joseph Waz could only say that he was "hopeful," and NBC Universal's Paula Madison pointed to a "positive trend" in diverse content.[48]

Waters was having none of it; she noted that Comcast's commitments to diversity were only being made—and very quickly—because she had raised the issue. In her view, Comcast was making concessions only to obtain approval for the merger.[49]

But none of this mattered. The two-hour hearing was really an occasion to present the press release from Comcast: $20 million was coming, and the groups had signed off. Waters continued to press against the deal from time to time, saying in October 2010 that the proposed $20 million capital fund for minority entrepreneurs was "a marginal amount considering the scale of modern media ownership and associated operational accounts."[50]

But in the fall of 2010, she had her own ethics problems to deal with: a House investigation began into whether Waters and Mikael Moore, her chief of staff, had acted inappropriately when they attempted to assist a minority-owned bank, OneUnited, during the 2008 financial crisis. The investigation was postponed in November 2010 and was revived in early 2012, but it appears to be moving slowly in the face of recusals by Ethics Committee members.[51]

But in the months after the $20 million went on the table, together with Comcast's other commitments, minority opposition to the deal—the only thing that worried Comcast during the yearlong review of the merger— melted away.[52] David Cohen and Comcast had made friends and influenced people.

Comcast was nothing if not flexible when it came to small, nonstructural favors. At the House Judiciary Committee hearing, Jean Prewitt, president of the Independent Film & Television Alliance (IFTA), testified that "what is good for Comcast and NBC is not good for the American public." For Prewitt, the merger was about "the very future of creative life, cultural expression and the free exchange of ideas." The merger "places at risk the opportunities for diverse, original and independent programming to reach the public through traditional media and new platforms." The government should not approve the merger, she argued, without strong commitments that independent filmmakers would be able to distribute their works through the new network.[53]

Comcast listened. About a month later, NBC Universal announced that it would increase support for independent programming under an agreement made by NBC Universal, Comcast, and Prewitt's IFTA. The deal called for NBC to spend one million dollars annually and NBC Universal's cable networks to spend another half million for four years after the merger closed. The companies also said they would find ways to smooth licensing of independent programming for new-media distribution. Jean Prewitt was happy: the agreement, she said, "has the potential to create business opportunities for independent producers that have long wanted to produce for television in the United States again."[54]

No more opposition from IFTA.

Another group that could have caused problems for Comcast was the 210 NBC network affiliates, the stations not owned by NBC that carried its programming. The affiliates worried that the Comcast-NBCU merger would cost them advertising revenue since direct-to-cable distribution of high-value NBC programming—sports coverage, for example, which made the affiliates millions in ad revenues—would mean that cable customers would get Comcast's best shows and the local affiliates would not get a cut. (Networks used to pay their affiliates to air network shows, but these payments have gotten smaller over time; now the affiliates are more likely to broadcast shows for free and make their money through commercials. If affiliates are not allowed to sell commercial slots by the network owner, their margins will dwindle and their existence will be threatened.) Affiliates also wanted to ensure they could continue to charge fees for the local programming—mostly news—they allowed the cable networks to redistribute.[55]

It might seem that the affiliates had little leverage. But if a local news station had been angry enough about losing profits because of the merger, it could have complained to the FCC and Justice Department; such a complaint could have made the merger approval process much more difficult. And the NBC affiliates were not the only ones looking to start a fight— ABC, CBS, and Fox affiliates also stood to lose and were willing to push for a better deal. All the affiliates commanded a microphone in their local areas, and if they decided to yell, the public would have noticed.

Again, Comcast deftly smoothed the waters. It promised the NBC affiliates that NBC sports programming would not move to cable and that NBC's overall signal would be available for rebroadcast. It also promised these affiliates—as well as those at ABC, CBS, and Fox—that it would keep its negotiations over fees for programming separate from its negotiations over the terms under which a particular station could become an NBC affiliate and that it would not discriminate in programming-fee negotiations based on a local station's affiliation or lack of affiliation with Comcast. This appeased the affiliates, who had been worried that Comcast would be wearing both hats as a network owner (jealous of an affiliate's ability to command any fees for programming) and a cable distributor (anxious not to pay high fees for programming) and that it would force the affiliates to accept unfavorable deals for programming as a condition of remaining affiliates.[56]

The affiliate agreement was a coup; while giving very little in return, Comcast took the affiliates out of play as a source of vocal opposition to the merger.

As thousands of comments came in to the FCC about the merger, predictable patterns emerged. Public-interest advocates like Public Knowledge and Free Press had prompted individuals to file tens of thousands of one-page comments opposing the merger. (Although many of these comments were individually drafted, many used language provided by Free Press: "A merger of this size would give one company unprecedented control over media content and platforms. It would allow the largest cable and Internet access provider to control one of the nation's largest media companies.") These letters helped build the impression of widespread public opposition to the merger, something the FCC, Justice, and especially the Senate were likely to take seriously.[57]

But Comcast was ready for this move, too. It had a sturdy reputation as a generous and civic-minded company, and it had already encouraged letters from more than a thousand nonprofits, government officials, and community activists. Hundreds of state legislators supported the merger. Community centers, rehabilitation centers, civil rights groups, community colleges, sports programs, senior citizen groups—hundreds wrote in, saying that Comcast had been a partner in time of need. These too were prewritten; a typical letter read, "[Name], Comcast's Vice President of Customer Care, serves on our board, and has not only provided leadership, but has been a constant voice of support for our cause. Comcast has been a major funder of our services. . . . It has also established a yearly presence at our most important fundraiser. . . . Being able to count on Comcast's annual support is a big help to our organization."[58]

The sole FCC field hearing on the merger, held in Chicago in July 2010, was attended by a single commissioner out of five: Michael Copps. Chairman Genachowski pleaded other commitments and sent a video statement. The hearing finished up with a two-hour open-mike session dominated by nonprofit beneficiaries of Comcast's largesse. As John Eggerton of

Broadcasting & Cable reported: "A representative of an afterschool program called Comcast a wonderful supporter; a diagnostic treatment center rep called Comcast an angel; a drug prevention center got carriage of programming by Comcast that others would not. . . . After a couple of plugs for FCC protection for public access channels, the parade of fans continued, including a Hispanic civil rights group, a community college foundation, a dance program for at-risk youth. The tenor of those comments could be summed up by one: 'Comcast epitomizes ethical corporate citizenship.' " Even FCC staff could not help chuckling privately when one of the groups speaking for Comcast turned out to be an organization whose mission involved supporting "companion animals." Comcast had helped them out as well.[59]

Comcast's gifts of more than $400 million in cash and in-kind contributions (mostly public service announcements) in 2009 to charities around the country had an impact not only on the community groups that got the money directly but on the legislators whose districts and favorite causes were supported. These contributions, amounting to $1.8 billion between 2001 and 2010, were a creative way to get closer to lawmakers.[60] Comcast got a tax deduction, the causes got support, and the political relationships so critical to Comcast's success were strengthened.

Of course, Comcast is hardly the only practitioner of this art. As the *New York Times* reporter Eric Lipton said in 2010 on CNN, politically motivated charitable donations demonstrate that "Washington is really a creative place . . . everyone, to some extent, is served." Mickey Edwards, a former Republican Congressman from Oklahoma, told Lipton that through charitable contributions, a company "can make that person identify with me, have a relationship with me, feel that I am somebody who shares their concerns. . . . It's a way of trying to build that relationship between a member and a funder, to the mutual advantage of both." For example, Jay Rockefeller (D-W.V.), the chair of the Senate Commerce Committee and a tremendous fan of Johann Sebastian Bach and the Washington Bach Consort, was happy to see communications companies, including Comcast, Verizon, and AT&T, give the group more than three-quarters of a million dollars in 2009. Do such contributions influence the positions taken by Rockefeller and others? "Absolutely," said Edwards.[61]

The Comcast-NBCU merger provided a classic case study of the influence of nonprofit contributions. Comcast's own influence-buying campaign was big, if not novel; the company applied enormous resources and sheer force to ensure that support for the deal was widespread. Whether the resulting support had anything to do with the public-interest merits of the deal itself, it was vocal and widespread. And it was high-level: Governor Rendell wrote in, and so did Governors Schwarzenegger of California and Paterson of New York.[62]

Even hearings unrelated to Comcast became a platform for praise. On the last day of Supreme Court nominee Elena Kagan's confirmation hearings during the summer of 2010, Sen. Al Franken began to express concern about Comcast and pressed Kagan for her views. "Comcast is already extremely powerful," Franken said. "It's the nation's largest cable operator and also the largest home Internet service provider. If it owned both the pipes and the programming it would have the ultimate ability to keep others from publishing." Specter, who also sat on the confirmation panel, was moved to respond: soon after Franken's comment, he introduced into the record a letter from himself saying that the merger was a good deal.[63]

Comcast had been paving the way for these favorable statements for years, playing a very long game of indirect and direct political contributions. Between 2002 and 2010, it had laid out more than nine million dollars in direct donations to congressional members' campaign and political organizations—with most of that coming during the 2008 and 2010 election cycles. One Hill staffer told me that there was no political reward for members in opposing the merger. Indeed, opponents would have had to meet with a host of Comcast-hired consultants asking questions about their opposition that members might not have been prepared to answer. Another obvious cost of opposition could come in the form of campaign contributions to election opponents. (Things have become more subtle since the old Standard Oil days; in the late nineteenth century Standard Oil simply bought a guarantee—in the form of state legislation granting an ironclad exclusive charter to Rockefeller—that no other refinery would be able to route around Rockefeller's business plans in Maryland.)[64] But money was not the only incentive: members were worried about how the Iraq and Afghanistan wars would affect their reelection efforts, and unless other large companies started making arguments

against the merger, it was hard to find a good political reason to say anything in opposition. The air of inevitability about the deal was hard to miss.

And yet a few members of Congress spoke out. Sen. Herb Kohl of
Wisconsin was of one of the wealthiest senators and the most fiercely
independent, having been elected in 1988 on the slogan "Nobody's Senator
but Yours." Campaign contributions from the cable carriers were meaning-
less to him. As chair of the Antitrust Subcommittee of the Senate Judiciary
Committee, Kohl had been raising alarms for years about the consolidation
of American industry. He had sent letters and worried aloud about antitrust
immunity for airline alliances and had taken on the exemptions from
antitrust laws enjoyed by the railroad industry and health insurance companies. He had vocally opposed the Sirius–XM satellite radio merger that
the FCC approved in 2008, and he did not consider the Comcast-NBCU
merger a good idea either.[65]

Kohl publicly proposed in May 2010 a long list of conditions that he
thought should be imposed on the merger, including divestiture of
Comcast's stake in Hulu and a requirement that Comcast not prohibit
programmers with whom it dealt from distributing their content independently online. Sen. Bernie Sanders (I-Vt.) voiced outrage throughout the
merger review, saying at one point, "Once we allow companies to become
this powerful, the FCC does not regulate them. They regulate the FCC."[66]

But it was Al Franken, with his gravelly drawl and persistent spark of
humor, who was by far the most publicly outspoken about the problems
with the merger. In an April 2010 hearing about the activities of the
Antitrust Division, Franken expressed his concern to Attorney General Eric
Holder. "I'm concerned because I see the potential here for the consolidation of media in a way that is, to me, very frightening," he said. Would the
merger lead to a world in which "five companies are going to be controlling
all the information that we get?" Franken suggested that the Comcast-
NBCU merger could also affect consumers' cable bills. Holder, who had
been answering Franken's previous points with bland statements about
"putting into place a variety of conditions," snapped to attention:

> Holder: Well now I care. I'm a—a Comcast subscriber, and the fact that you
> point out it could have an impact on my cable bill has awakened me . . .
> Franken: I knew I could reach you somehow.

When Franken said that he was unhappy with regulator-imposed behavioral conditions on mergers, arguing that they were hard to enforce and "inevitably expire[d]" after a few years, Holder replied, "I think we can make those conditions ones that are enforceable. . . . It involves having . . . access to . . . experts in the field." Franken wasn't convinced, arguing at a Minneapolis session in August 2010: "We don't just have a competition problem. We have a First Amendment problem. Justice Hugo Black once said that "[f]reedom to publish is guaranteed by the Constitution, but freedom to combine to keep others from publishing is not. . . . Yet if this merger goes through, Comcast and NBCU will have an unparalleled ability to keep others from publishing. And it will mean a poorer marketplace—and a poorer marketplace of ideas—for everyone."[67]

Throughout all this David Cohen moved smoothly ahead. He had hired Kohl's former chief of staff, Paul Bock, to lobby on behalf of the deal.[68] Kohl's letter and the opposition of Sanders and Franken would not stop it. All was going well.

Taken together, the hearings on the merger showed Comcast in top form, defusing one potential landmine after another. Roberts had easily stayed on message, reminding legislators that NBC would be better off inside Comcast than with General Electric. The Los Angeles field hearing had thrown off more heat than light, with the diversity worries raised by witnesses and Maxine Waters assuaged by Comcast's quick promises. The first Chicago field hearing, convened by Rep. Bobby Rush, had been an opportunity for Comcast to present those promises in public, and the second Chicago field hearing, convened by the FCC, had ended up as a farce, with dozens of public commenters attesting to Comcast's corporate generosity. No one seemed to be listening to Franken, Sanders, or Kohl, and Franken was aware that his energetic opposition to the deal might dim his own reelection prospects.[69] Then again, the decision was not up to Congress: it belonged to the agencies. And that's where the lobbyists focused their real firepower.

11

The FCC Approves

THE COMMUNICATIONS MERGER PROCESS at the Federal Communications Commission, one content-industry employee told me, is "just awful."[1] It's a game: the companies that plan to merge know that if they can get the regulators to spend enough time considering the deal, it will probably go through. There may be a brief struggle with underfunded public-interest groups, but if no other large companies oppose the deal, the feds' invest-ment of time in working with the merging parties, coupled with their interest in moving on to other items on their agenda, generally overcomes any private concerns about consolidation of market power. Just two major media–telecommunications mergers have been rejected by the FCC in the twenty-first century: the proposed combination of the country's two major satellite video providers, EchoStar and DirecTV in 2002, and the proposed merger between AT&T and T-Mobile in 2011.[2] Both rejections were unusual. In 2008, by contrast, the FCC approved the merger of the two providers of satellite radio, Sirius and XM, even after it became clear that the combined entity (Sirius XM) would, in fact, monopolize the satellite radio market.[3]

The merger-approval dance requires a series of steps. What is called a "record" of filings with the FCC is created over a period of months, amount-ing to hundreds of thousands of pages. Deals are struck before and during the process to make stakeholders (such as interest groups and trade associations) who might object feel that they have gotten something out of the process. In the Sirius-XM merger, for example, the Commission pointed to the new combined satellite radio company's voluntary commitment to offer lower prices for a three-year period as a public-interest benefit that would outweigh the long-term monopolistic harm generated by the transaction.[4] Yet after all the filings and the hundreds of meetings, the last phase is often an unseemly scramble for concessions. "At the end," the content-industry employee told me, "people will all be in the room trying to get something. It will matter who is in the room."[5] Mergers are fact-dependent—particular companies are involved, particular market power issues are at stake—but the final decision sets the stage for broad future policy even though only a few key actors are "in the room" at the end of the process.

For instance, after their last-minute struggles to merge at the end of 2005 with SBC and MCI, respectively, AT&T and Verizon voluntarily agreed to subject their DSL Internet access businesses to the FCC Broadband Internet Access Policy Statement, which entitles consumers to run applications and use services of their choice.[6] The companies' agreement made a nonbinding policy statement by the Commission appear suddenly binding—but for only part of the high-speed Internet access industry and not for the cable companies. The same 2005 merger approvals were used to pressure the phone companies to sell ten-dollar-a-month DSL services separately, divested from bundles of services, for two years. Commissioner Kathleen Abernathy felt that the Commission was overstepping the appropriate scope of its merger review by exacting these agreements, noting that "[i]t should not be standard operating procedure to craft company-specific merger conditions to address unknown and hypothetical competitive threats," and urging the FCC to use its "customary administrative weaponry" of rulemaking and enforcement actions, rather than merger reviews, to shape policy.[7] As Thomas Koutsky and Lawrence Spiwak of the Phoenix Center asked in a 2007 article, "Are consumers really well-served by backroom, closed-door negotiations between the regulator and prospective merging parties over important public issues?"[8]

Part of the reason for the somewhat chaotic process at the FCC is the interplay between its statutory public-interest mandate and the belief of some commissioners in the power of "intermodal competition." Former chairman Michael Powell largely deregulated the information-transport industry beginning in 2002 because he was convinced that different pipes and wires and airwaves would compete with one another, and this competition would protect consumers better than any regulations. Phone companies would battle cable, cable would battle satellite, and wireless and "broadband over powerline" would take on all comers. Given this policy focus, a wave of mergers had inevitably followed among the competitors in each industry.[9] The result was extraordinary consolidation in the telephone world (both wireless and wired) and the cable arena but, ultimately, none of the anticipated competition.

At the same time, the FCC has broader authority over mergers than the antitrust division of the Department of Justice (DOJ). The Commission is charged with determining how the public's long-term interest will be served by any merger transaction, and so it takes into account traditional public-interest values like diversity of broadcasts and localism—considerations that are not relevant to DOJ review, in which the agency looks at the effects on competition.[10]

The Commission thus has the difficult task of addressing the concerns of innumerable groups about the effect of a given transaction on a wide range of public values while tacitly encouraging telecommunications companies that have sufficient scale and scope to survive—so as to avoid the need to regulate. What is fascinating is that this "awful," detailed, back-room drafting of broad voluntary conditions routinely leads to deal points that are trumpeted by the commissioners approving the merger as wins for consumers but that in the end are either unenforced or unenforceable.

In 1999, the FCC conditioned a merger between SBC and Ameritech on SBC's commitment to enter into thirty markets outside its region. But no one defined "entry"; SBC sold service to some of its Boston employees and then shut down the Boston operation.[11] The "separate $10/month DSL" offering required by the Commission of AT&T and Verizon in 2005 was buried in the phone companies' Web sites. The FCC had not said anything about *publicizing* the offering. Adherence to the FCC Broadband Internet Access Policy Statement (giving consumers free choice of applications and services) was meanwhile limited to slow DSL services and did not apply to the companies' fiber communications—or to Comcast, Time Warner, and Cablevision.

Here is how the process at the FCC works: The merging companies figure out whom they have to please in order to avoid controversy and set to work persuading those groups or companies to support their transaction; the FCC, after much negotiating, creates conditions that it feels will serve the public interest and outweigh the anticompetitive harms created by the deal; the merging parties complain bitterly that the conditions are not specific to the merger but are broad attempts to make policy; a long series of meetings and filings is followed by a last-minute scramble for concessions; and on the day the deal is approved, the parties and regulators both issue press releases claiming victory.

This was the course taken by the Comcast-NBCU merger. The deal faced high hurdles because of its sheer size and the opportunity for abuse the arrangement provided. But thanks to years of positioning, lots of deftly distributed cash, and the organizational brilliance of Comcast's David Cohen, it went through with relative ease. There were a few hearings, but any concerns about the deal were overwhelmed by the orchestrated political support coming from all over America, as well as by the fact that the cable industry was already so concentrated that this single transaction would not by itself change the picture appreciably.

The theater of the deal, the march of posturing, lobbying, arguing, and persuading, followed the usual pattern. It was grand in scale and scope, perhaps, but it was not surprising or even particularly Machiavellian. And following a last-minute flurry of activity, it set the stage for future policy. There were conditions carefully worked out by the FCC (together with the Department of Justice's Antitrust Division) aimed at reducing the distributor's power to raise prices for its rivals and, particularly, its nascent online rivals.

The day the merger was approved, Cohen said that the conditions imposed by the reviewing agencies would not impair Comcast's ability to operate its business or disadvantage its competitiveness.[12] The conditions Comcast had accepted did not seem likely to make any difference to media market structures in the United States—and particularly to the overwhelming dominance of local cable incumbents in the market for high-speed Internet access. Four months later, one of the FCC commissioners who had voted to approve the merger left to work for Comcast.[13]

As communications behemoths routinely consolidate, the public could be left with the impression—if it were paying attention—that nothing much happens between the announcement of a proposed deal and then, a year or so later, its approval by the relevant agencies. But this is not the case. For the gargantuan Comcast-NBCU merger, the staffs of the Federal Communications Commission and the Antitrust Division of the Department of Justice pulled large teams together to review documents, hold meetings, and agree on conditions. So did the company and industry lobbyists.

Comcast hired almost eighty former government employees to help lobby for approval of the merger, including several former chiefs of staff for key legislators on congressional antitrust committees, former FCC staffers and Antitrust Division lawyers, and at least four former members of Congress: Reps. Robert Walker (R-Pa.), William Gray (D-Pa.), and Chip Pickering (R-Miss.), and Sen. Don Nickles (R-Okla.). Many Comcast vendors were hired who did not need to register as lobbyists because they were strategizing in the background rather than meeting directly with agencies or legislators.[14] Such profligate hiring had two advantages: in addition to attracting talented lobbyists who could speak meaningfully to former colleagues inside government, every lobbying or economic consulting firm whose employee was retained was effectively barred from offering objections to the deal because the firm would have a conflict of interest. To get the merger approved, Comcast spent many times what it had lavished on its last major deal, the colossal 2002 purchase of AT&T's cable systems, which had made Comcast the largest cable provider in the nation. David Cohen was rumored to have joked, "Let me know if there's anyone I haven't hired."[15]

To avoid internal turf battles and ensure that its wide-ranging review process had a single manager, the FCC hired John Flynn, a former Supreme Court clerk, general counsel at a satellite company, and partner at a large Washington law firm.[16] By all accounts the poker-faced Flynn kept a steady if not charismatic hand on the tiller at the FCC and was an extraordinarily quick study, something a deal with this many angles needed. He approached his task with humility and a low-key intensity. He had come to do this single job and would be gone when it was over.

On his arrival in the spring of 2010, Flynn was almost immediately presented with a demand from FCC management that the review go faster than the staff had initially thought possible. The broad scope of the FCC's public-interest standard for reviewing mergers meant that the agency had to consider a host of issues beyond antitrust matters, including broadcasting, children's programming, diversity, and localism. Flynn's charge was to harness the staff's expertise in all these areas while ensuring that every secondary issue had economists and lawyers assigned to help, and to get the work done as quickly as possible. At the same time, he would be acting in public: summaries of meetings at the FCC and comments submitted on a merger are posted online; although these summaries are often unhelpfully superficial, the fact that X has met with Y will probably be known. Flynn and his team set to work, creating clear lines of responsibility and dividing up tasks. The Comcast-NBCU process would be the most intense review the FCC had ever run for a single transaction.[17]

Meanwhile, at the Department of Justice, the Antitrust Division assigned more than thirty lawyers, plus a group of economists, to its review process. The DOJ review would be more narrowly focused on whether the transaction had the potential to strangle nascent markets and raise competitors' costs of doing business. The department is a law enforcement agency with a broad mandate rather than an administrative agency focused on a single industry, so it is less of a hotbed of gossip and public-private intrigue than the FCC; its lawyers tend to be discreet, and its documents and meetings are not made public. Lawyers within the Antitrust Division hoped to use their relative confidentiality to reassure companies and individuals who were worried about retribution from Comcast if they spoke up or handed over documents. Christine Varney, the division chief, quickly zeroed in on the merger's potential effect on online video, and the team met with scores of people (more than 125 companies in all) and sent out extensive and detailed demands for information to small and large cable operators, broadcasters, online video providers, and many other companies. The division ultimately reviewed more than a million business documents from the merging companies.

The Antitrust Division and the FCC closely coordinated their analysis. They held several key meetings jointly, pooled their economic and telecommunications expertise, and simultaneously announced harmonized conditions for the deal when the merger was approved. Such close coordination differed from past procedures, and agency personnel told me that they thought their joint work had made it harder for the companies to play the agencies off against each other.[18]

At the same time, the coordination made some companies nervous: they were leery of talking to the DOJ for fear their discussions would leak out through the FCC and irritate Comcast. As one content-industry person told me, "You can't overstate the amount of fear people have in dealing with Comcast. The programmers are terrified, and they don't want to give things to DOJ that will then go to FCC. Even if a programmer has a multi-year contract with Comcast, things come up all the time—ambiguities—and they have to re-negotiate. So having a long-term contract doesn't give a programmer any comfort. They're still completely stuck with Comcast."[19]

Months of meetings and filings followed. Varney regularly met with Genachowski; she was said to be urging Genachowski to be firm. It was a rough time for the FCC chairman. While the Comcast-NBCU review was going on, the net neutrality issue was raging and staff were holding ten meetings a day internally trying to resolve policy and technical questions. By mid-2010 Genachowski's careful effort to consider all points of view, take a thoughtful centrist position, and not risk having President Obama attacked as hostile to business appeared to be backfiring. The carriers knew that Genachowski was considered thin-skinned, someone who could not abide the politics of personal destruction that prevail in the telecommunications and media sector; they figured that all they had to do was rattle his cage, and they would probably get what they wanted. The same dynamics seemed to apply to the Comcast-NBCU review, and Varney and her staff may have worried that when push came to shove, the FCC would be unable to stand up to Comcast.[20]

The public narrative of the Comcast-NBCU transaction remained largely the Comcast-shaped story. Major media would have jumped on the news if any major companies had spoken up about the deal, but the telephone companies (Verizon, AT&T, Qwest), large cable companies (Time Warner, Cablevision), media conglomerates (News Corp., Disney, Viacom, CBS, Turner), and large online companies (Google, Amazon, eBay, Facebook) were mostly not saying a thing. The media and telecommunications world had become sufficiently consolidated that no large company saw much upside to opposing another large company's deal—their positions might be reversed soon enough, and all of them needed to deal with Comcast. They talked to the Department of Justice and provided information about their practices, but they did not make noise; when it came to Comcast-NBCU, the media community maintained an appearance of equipoise.

Public-interest groups did their best to kick sand in the gears. Free Press in particular agitated for blocking the deal entirely; Executive Director Josh Silver issued statements and wrote blog posts throughout the year of the FCC review, and wrote after the deal was approved that "the Comcast-NBC merger is truly a disaster for anyone who hopes the American public might someday emerge from the propaganda morass that is embodied by cable television, and now threatens to consume the internet."[21] Andy Schwartzman of the Media Access Project testified vehemently against the deal.[22] Public Knowledge's Harold Feld wrote comments and blog posts.[23] All these groups joined the Communications Workers of America and Common Cause in opposing the merger as filed and asking for detailed conditions that would, in their view, curb Comcast's market power.[24]

But in the absence of opposition from another large corporation, the tens of thousands of comments filed in support of the public advocates' views were outweighed by the hundreds of supportive comments from Comcast allies—state and local officials, business groups, and nonprofits.[25] Sensing a draw complicated by a lot of tricky details, reporters saw little to write about. National coverage of the deal was surprisingly thin considering the size of the participants.

Meanwhile, Kathy Zachem, an engaging, forceful, and well-liked Comcast employee charged by David Cohen with managing the company's relationship with the FCC, virtually camped out at the Commission's offices, holding court on the eighth floor, where all the commissioners have offices. The entire Comcast team was viewed by staff as good to work with and professional; the Comcast people worked hard and did not leak information.

The FCC and DOJ had a lot of ground to cover, even if the public was not hearing about it. This was the Obama administration's first mega-merger, and the reviewing agencies had mountains of information to absorb and analyze. The basic concerns were obvious: would the addition of NBC Universal content to the assets already under Comcast's control give the company the power to demand better terms for programming and for carriage of other peoples' programming? Would Comcast be able to use this power to move the subscription cable model online while suppressing competition from new forms of online video? What effect would the merger have on the future of Internet businesses and Internet access? The merger review took more than a year, in the end, because each of these issues had to be understood and then explained in writing to the public in the final order, which was filed online.

From the start, blocking the merger was unlikely. The agency economists took the view that there were positive gains from vertical integration between content and distribution; "double marginalization" (overhead overlaps triggered by the involvement of multiple companies) could be reduced, innovation could be enhanced by coordinating work on content with work on new forms of distribution, and overall costs could be cut through economies of scale and scope. Case law supported the idea that vertical integration was less worrisome than horizontal mergers; the antitrust agencies had not successfully litigated a vertical merger challenge for decades.[26]

Besides, Comcast was already in the content business: its regional sports networks were powerful engines driving the company. The Antitrust Division staff, given the scope of their review, felt they did not have a good enough analytical reason to challenge the merger as a whole; the FCC wanted to limit itself to merger-specific harms, and staff members believed that it would be difficult to make a strong case that the merger would make the existing situation worse. And the political dynamics clearly favored the merger; with most legislators, minority groups, and state officials from across the country in favor and no large businesses opposed, there was little reason to contest a vertical merger. Six months before the final decisions were released, John Malone said of the deal, "Absolutely it'll happen. I don't think there's any question. And I don't think they'll [Comcast and NBC Universal] have to make a lot of commitments to get it through. They'll make some." Malone predicted that other distributors would see clues in the deal's approval that would prompt them to vertically integrate as well, in order to protect themselves.[27]

The skirmishing was over the conditions for the deal. Competing providers of pay TV wanted to ensure that they would have fair access to programming that would be owned by Comcast. Although AT&T did not seem overly concerned—CEO Randall Stephenson told the press that he expected his company would have the same access to programming following the deal— small cable companies complained that the existing program-access rules allowed Comcast innumerable ways to make life hell for them. Enforcing the rules was costly and time-consuming, and Comcast could always claim that it was merely using standard volume discounts and (secret) "most favored nation" provisions in its contracts to favor larger distributors.[28]

Other programmers wanted the chance to be distributed through Comcast's enormous pipes. Without this distribution, they would not be able to sell advertising effectively so that they could become bigger, and without distribution on Comcast they would not be viewed as important enough to get distribution from Cablevision, Cox, or Charter. The big cable companies routinely act in parallel. Comcast had been denying independent programmers access for years; the FCC had just one judge dealing with carriage complaints, and Comcast had been able to avoid or wear down most complainers. *Al Jazeera* may have been able to trigger the fall of governments, but it could not get carriage on Comcast; no programmer independent of the media conglomerates has managed that reliably.[29] With the addition of NBCU content, programmers argued, Comcast would have even more reason to shield its marquee brands (USA, CNBC, NBC Sports) from competition by keeping independents out of its pipes. *Bloomberg*, in particular, wanted special treatment from Comcast: "neighborhooding" of all business channels so that it could be found next to CNBC.[30]

Online video-distribution companies worried that Comcast could make things especially difficult for them; with control over more programming and no obligation to allow competing broadband companies to use its pipes, Comcast could deny new online companies a platform. Comcast's ability to offer its own online video with TV Everywhere would make the situation even worse; the cable bundled subscription model would be successfully moved online.[31]

Toward the end of the process, the FCC paid glancing attention to the issue of high-speed Internet access and the power of Comcast (and other cable incumbents) to dominate wired access in its market areas. Earthlink, the Internet service provider that had been allowed onto Time Warner's cable system as a result of the AOL–Time Warner merger a decade earlier, strongly argued for wholesale stand-alone broadband access so that it could compete.[32]

Public-interest groups trooped to the FCC offices about once a week. Like some of the companies, they wanted rules to ensure Comcast's rivals access to programming, better rules covering Comcast's obligation to carry programming from independent programmers, and a requirement that Comcast make its high-speed Internet access services available on a wholesale basis.[33] To the end, the public-interest groups thought that wholesale access to high-speed Internet services was a strong possibility.

Comcast, for its part, kept asserting that the review was certain to be settled in 2010—the company was expert at creating an air of inevitability, and it had financial reasons for wanting to get the deal done that year. It had seen an opportunity in a business-friendly administration and had gone forward. But approval of the merger on Comcast's schedule would not be possible, given the work that had to be done on net neutrality and the compromises the staff had to get through in order to complete that order. Approval would have to wait until January 2011.

Some outsiders to the process found it hard to believe that public policy would permit the deal to go through. "If the framers could see what has happened to their First Amendment, they'd be shocked," one commenter told me. "It now protects corporations. . . . Comcast owns the Internet now."[34]

But the unthinkable had become commonplace. At the end of 2010, after months of work, the FCC staff was nearly ready to circulate its proposed conditions for a vote. There was, predictably, a last-minute scramble to add on conditions that had personal appeal for one actor or another. The commissioners all had their own requests. Commissioner Mignon Clyburn had already made hers known; she wanted to ensure that the deal was used as an opportunity to provide low-income Americans, as well as schools and libraries, with better access to low-cost broadband.[35] Commissioner Michael Copps, after a period of disengagement, submitted a host of requests at the end, including requiring Comcast to sell Internet access on a wholesale basis as well as putting in place much stiffer rules about programming—both access to Comcast's programming and carriage by Comcast of independents' programming.

The Republican commissioners, McDowell and Baker, had had little involvement in the process beyond preliminary briefings; now, however, they insisted that the conditions on the merger expire as quickly as possible. And they wanted to be sure that the Commission did not say anything about either net neutrality or the terms under which Comcast would make programming available online; the FCC had never extended its program-access rules to the Internet.[36]

Brian Roberts and David Cohen came in to see Chairman Genachowski on Thursday, January 13, 2011. The results would be announced the following Tuesday. Genachowski told them that the merger would be approved, and Comcast was comfortable with the conditions that had been proposed. The Republicans had gotten some minor language tweaks but had not otherwise prevailed; Commissioner Clyburn's concerns had largely been addressed and she would support the merger; Commissioner Copps's end-of-process list of requests had not made it into the deal, but his nay vote would not affect the final outcome.[37]

Investment analysts looking at the announced conditions saw a positive outcome for Comcast. Although competing distributors got the ability to trigger "baseball arbitration" for programming (in which both sides are obliged to make a last best offer, one of which will be chosen by the arbitrator), Comcast could still bundle at will—which would make any arbitration extremely difficult to win.[38] And online video distributors would get access to Comcast-NBCU content, but there were enough exceptions and details and expenses involved to keep lawyers busy for a long time; the most potentially disruptive condition required Comcast-NBCU to license to an online video distributor (OVD) broadcast, cable, or film content comparable in scope and quality to the content the OVD received from one of the joint venture's programming peers. There would be fights over the meaning of "comparable," and in order to trigger the obligation at all one of the four peer conglomerates would have to break ranks with the others in making programming available online outside the TV Everywhere umbrella, a situation that left ample room for maneuvering and litigation. Little had changed with regard to Comcast's ability to protect its own programming from independent competitors (the "program carriage" issue), and the net neutrality obligation did not apply to IP-based services Comcast carried over its own "private network." This exception effectively negated the rule because Comcast would be the source of the definition of its "private network."[39]

On the plus side for the public, Comcast was obliged to offer a retail stand-alone high-speed Internet access service at $49.95 a month for 6 Mbps speed—a service it was already selling. It would have to bring data services to an additional four hundred thousand homes (but could impose whatever terms it wanted) and would be obliged to promote greater broadband adoption by 2.5 million low-income households through a $9.95 per month service—information the FCC tried to ensure would be more public than AT&T and Verizon's ten-dollar-a-month DSL offer had been a few years earlier. The FCC adopted Comcast's low-cost broadband suggestion nearly verbatim, but although the program looked like a public benefit, it would not be easy for customers to apply for it.[40] Means-tested plans were not going to affect Comcast's existing services, and, as the company had found back in Meridian, Mississippi, in 1963, when it is difficult to apply for something, customers won't. The company would not be offering the program to anyone who had recently been a customer of Comcast. In effect, the merger condition opened new business opportunities to Comcast without creating any pressure on the company to offer the same deal to its existing customers. And when the program ended, families would be forced to choose between canceling their access or paying Comcast's higher rate for the same services. Most important, the voluntary nature of the program substantially lowered the risk that Comcast would be regulated by the FCC: if the Commission tried to wield power, the company could threaten to withdraw its voluntary assistance. In the meantime, the program would give Comcast essentially free advertising facilitated by government and nonprofit organizations.

As one experienced Comcast watcher told me, the merger conditions would be completely ineffective in limiting Comcast's ability to use its market power; there are a number of ways for Comcast to legally wriggle out of every condition imposed by the DOJ and FCC. "I would take structural competition any day," he said, "over trying to regulate behavior. The Comcast [merger] conditions are regulating behavior."[41]

His prediction came true just months later. *Bloomberg* had succeeded in getting a condition included in the merger approval that appeared to require Comcast to carry *Bloomberg*—and other independent news and business channels—in the same neighborhood of business channels as MSNBC, CNBC, and Fox News. The interpretive lawyering had begun. Comcast chose not to comply and claimed that it did not have to. As David Cohen's subordinate Sena Fitzmaurice argued: "Bloomberg simply misinterprets the 'neighborhooding' condition in the FCC's Comcast NBCUniversal transaction order. It does not 'neighborhood' news channels in the way Bloomberg seeks to be repositioned." *Bloomberg* responded, "This is something of a test case of how serious Comcast is about implementing the conditions set by the FCC order," and filed an enormous record of documents aimed at convincing the FCC that Comcast was deliberately misinterpreting the condition in order to harm *Bloomberg*'s ability to compete with CNBC. Comcast responded with enormous filings of its own.[42]

The day after the merger was approved, with the disappointed FCC commissioner Copps offering the lone voice of dissent, Cohen talked about the government conditions for the deal. His argument now pivoted: his audience was no longer the regulators, whom he had been praising for more than a year, but the investment community. "None of these commitments or conditions will prevent us from operating these businesses the way our business plans call for us to do so," he said, "and none of them will prevent the businesses from being competitive in all of the markets in which we do business."[43] Cohen knew better than to sound triumphant, but he clearly was. Comcast had not been pinned down by the regulators, and it was now ready to move ahead as one of America's four media powerhouses.

Meanwhile, the company continued to bulk up its Washington lobbying force. FCC commissioner Meredith Attwell Baker, a Republican and the daughter-in-law of former secretary of state James Baker, announced that she would leave at the end of her two-year term to join Comcast. A well-respected former Department of Commerce official with a substantial telecom legal background, Baker had been seen as a shoo-in for reappointment by the Obama administration, so her departure seemed sudden. More important, her quick transformation from regulator to voice of the regulated struck many observers as inappropriate.[44]

One of Comcast's nonprofit grantees, a small media nonprofit organization in Seattle called Reel Grrls, sent out a tweet expressing shock. A Comcast manager wrote to Reel Grrls: "Given the fact that Comcast has been a major supporter of Reel Grrls for several years now, I am frankly shocked that your organization is slamming us on Twitter. I cannot in good conscience continue to provide you with funding." Following an outcry, Comcast quickly apologized and said the whole thing was a mistake; it "reach[ed] out" to Reel Grrls to let the organization know that its funding was not in jeopardy.[45]

After a couple of weeks of bluster, the issue died down; Baker hadn't broken any laws. Comcast hired a slew of other Washington notables. *Politico* characterized the spate of hires as "a veritable tour de force of Beltway know-how—and a possible sign that the company anticipates some big battles on the policy horizon."[46]

Aftermath

AFTER ITS $13.8 BILLION PURCHASE OF 51 percent of NBC Universal in January 2011, Comcast moved professionally ahead.[1] A cheerleading town meeting for NBCU's thirty thousand employees was sent via Webcast from the *Late Night with Jimmy Fallon* studio at 30 Rockefeller Plaza, with Ralph Roberts, emcee Ryan Seacrest, and *Saturday Night Live*'s Seth Meyers onstage; during that event, according to *Daily Variety*, the ordinarily calm and reserved Steve Burke told the crowd that "whatever we do, we should be in it to win it. . . . We got big for a reason." A new logo was revealed: no more peacock, just lettering. And Jeff Zucker was gone; after nearly a quarter century presiding over the extraordinary growth in the company's cable business he had been replaced by Burke.[2]

Shortly after the merger was approved, President Obama appointed Brian Roberts to the newly restructured Council on Jobs and Competitiveness headed by General Electric CEO Jeffrey Immelt. In a blog post expressing pride in his appointment, Roberts invoked family lore: "My father Ralph is one of America's great entrepreneurs; he started Comcast as a small business with just a few hundred customers in Tupelo, Mississippi. With the recent completion of the NBCUniversal joint venture, we now have over 127,000 employees."[3] Comcast's tradition of public-private service continued.

Following the merger, Comcast remained predominantly a distribution company: its non-content operations generated 80 percent of the company's

$55 billion in annual revenues and accounted for 70 percent of its employ-
ees. Its growth area, high-speed data services, was picking up steam, just
as Roberts had predicted.[4] Profits were soaring. Americans in Comcast
Country—which included people living in twenty-two of the twenty-five
largest cities in America—were signing up for Comcast's very expensive
highest-speed data offering.

And the profit margin was getting better and better. The cable-television
advertising market had weathered the economic downturn without much
of a dip; ad revenues were up more than 9 percent in 2010, the average
price of a pay-TV subscription had risen 29 percent between 2005 and
2010 (despite a decline in average household income), and cash-flow
margins for the top cable networks were climbing over 50 percent as
Americans continued to watch more television.[5]

Comcast's ability to bundle its offerings was undiminished; subscribers
were getting dozens of channels whether they wanted them or not. To
hedge against video losses, Comcast started testing the waters with triple-
play packages (high-speed Internet access, Voice over Internet Protocol,
and television) that were a little cheaper and included smaller bundles of
video channels—but true a la carte offerings were still unavailable. And the
TV Everywhere model was flourishing, as viewers kept their cable accounts
even as they streamed movies and shows over iPads.

Comcast and the rest of the cable industry were successfully boxing
Google and Apple out of the set-top-box marketplace; when the FCC suggested that it might make sense to require standardized video connections
to which any device could be attached without permission, former FCC
chairman Michael Powell, now leading the cable industry trade association,
called the idea a classic example of "jobs-killing, cost-raising, innovation-
crushing regulation."[6] The cost of providing data services was dropping,
but revenues per user for the cable distributor's bundles were going up.
Comcast's investment in its networks was essentially over for the time
being, and equipment—modems and gear—was getting cheaper. All the
arrows were heading in the right direction. John Malone predicted in
November 2009 that whatever restraints Comcast had to agree to as a
condition of the transaction going through would provide "clues to other
distributors as to whether they need to go vertical, and have something to

fight back" with against Comcast; more vertical integration deals (AT&T and DirecTV?) might follow in the path of Comcast's success.[7]

Comcast's Video on Demand strategists were feeling confident; consumers would clearly want to watch high-production-value, long-form video anytime, anywhere, and on multiple devices, and Comcast was ready to rent programming to capture users who might have bought DVDs in the past. If users cut out their cable company, they would not be able to watch pro sports or popular network programs. Comcast even introduced a sixty dollar one-time video service in late 2011 that would allow consumers to watch movies while they were still playing in theaters—showing that the company believed that consumers would pay a premium to watch something as soon as it became available. "The [$60] pricing is insanity," jeered *TechDirt*, a blog that reports on the business and economics of technology companies.[8] Comcast backed down but vowed to figure out another way to get first-run movies to customers' homes.[9]

Netflix, meanwhile, was struggling in late 2011, having apparently outraged subscribers and shareholders alike by focusing single-mindedly on its streaming business rather than its shipping DVDs business. It was also having trouble getting access to first-run content. Comcast's CFO, Michael Angelakis, was questioning as of late 2011 whether licensing current NBC Universal shows and movies to Netflix made sense: "You have to be really careful about what the value of that current content is," he said. "I think we are more comfortable monetizing the deep library."[10] Translated: Netflix, as Brian Roberts so pungently said, was for reruns. Maybe it had a future as a cable channel.

Meanwhile, the only potential competitor for customers looking for high-speed data services was backing down. In 2010, Verizon cut FiOS expenditures by two-thirds, and company executive Francis Shammo explained that "wireline will continue to come down year over year"; Verizon had already announced that it would not be extending FiOS to new cities.[11] DSL connections to the Internet were obsolete, could not compete with cable services, and were being dropped by customers in huge numbers. Roberts sounded understandably gleeful: "We really do start 2011 on a positive note," he said. "Our competitive position has never been better. Now it's really all about execution, in order to maintain our momentum and drive profitable and sustainable growth."[12] Responding to the news that Comcast share prices were rising sharply, Roberts said, "Hallelujah."[13]

But there was a slight softening in one part of the Comcast universe: video customers were dropping off slowly and were being picked up by AT&T, Verizon, and the satellite companies. Cable still had the lead in the pay-TV market, however, and Comcast could slow its video losses using sports and its new NBC Universal channels.[14] Meanwhile, Americans' appetite for data was growing. In the areas it served, Comcast had little or no competition for these high-spending, high-speed data customers; it was pivoting to focus on higher-spending subscribers in data to offset its losses in video. For Roberts, all the numbers pointed to "an exciting new beginning." Comcast was adding broadband subscribers in droves while steadily increasing its revenue per user.[15]

The merger seemed to be going well, too. Although, as Cohen said in a speech to the Chamber of Commerce of Southern New Jersey in mid-2011, "Comcast is not a Hollywood culture," Steve Burke showed that he could make the two companies work effectively together.[16] He promptly launched "Project Symphony," aimed at using cross-promotion opportunities across the Comcast megalopolis to support key programming. Burke, determined and no-nonsense—his father once headed Johnson & Johnson—made clear to the *Wall Street Journal* that Comcast-NBCU employees would be thinking of their jobs "not as programming Bravo or the lead story on NBC .com" but as working to better Comcast-NBCU.[17]

And Comcast was carefully centrally managed. John Malone, recalling the failure of the AOL–Time Warner integration, had said: "When the AOL merger took place, I think what was lacking was a power base that the C.E.O. had which allowed him to be somewhat dictatorial."[18] Comcast-NBCU would be no soap opera of conflict and turf battles; the cable guys were in, and they would systematically wring the inefficiencies out of the merged company, just as Cohen had wrung out the waste in Philadelphia's spending. Some of the broadcast stars, including the fabled Dick Ebersol of NBC Sports, were out.

When asked by *Bloomberg* about the NBC Universal joint venture, Malone had responded that the merger was probably good for Brian Roberts. "He gets to be king. It's good diversification of risk for Comcast.

It's a good economic deal for GE to avoid a big check to Vivendi. And the market power Comcast will achieve by owning NBC will allow Comcast to extract higher economic returns. The open question is, 'Will they be allowed to do that without some regulatory restrictions?' Because in the end the distributors are really middlemen—it's the American public that will end up paying."[19]

Had adequate regulatory restrictions been put in place? Both the FCC and the Department of Justice's Antitrust Division argued strongly that they had done a good job in constraining the possibilities for abuse. The FCC's chief economist, Jonathan Baker, wrote that he viewed the Commission's merger review process with pride: "The FCC worked with the applicants and other parties to craft an order that protects the public interest," he said, "without restricting the applicants' ability to accomplish their legitimate business objectives." Baker went on to quote (approvingly) David Cohen's post-approval statement: "I don't think any of the conditions is particularly restrictive."[20]

Keeping track of all the details of the Philadelphia city budget and safeguarding the welfare of the metropolis takes a pretty smart lawyer, and there is no question that Cohen is that. Although the FCC and DOJ had done their best to ensure that the merged company was obliged to allow in new competitors—a nondiscriminatory Internet and online video—it looked to the outside world as if the regulators had been outlawyered by Cohen and his team. Every requirement imposed by the agencies was subject to interpretation, and none of the obligations dealt directly with the consequences of Comcast's overwhelming dominance in high-speed Internet access.

There was no change to Comcast's obligation (or not) to carry independent programming. *Al Jazeera* would not get any help. Comcast was confident that program carriage rules were unnecessary; from its perspective, the company told the FCC in 2011, it was facing intense competition from the two satellite companies, traditional telephone companies, and "overbuilders" and had "every incentive" to carry unaffiliated programming "that is valued by subscribers."[21] But that meant that programs not owned by any of the media conglomerates would continue to have a tough time getting carriage.

What's more, the program-access rules were not extended online; Netflix (or whatever other online video distributor wanted to claim the benefit of the rules) would have to show that it had a deal with a peer for "comparable content" and for the "same business model" that it wanted for Comcast content. A good lawyer could run rings around those open-ended definitions. Comcast assured the Commission that it had "strong incentives to seek the broadest possible distribution of its networks," and that all NBC Universal networks, "including RSNs," were "available to all distributors that are willing to pay a fair market price for the network at issue."[22] That might not be a price that any online video distributor could afford.

The other route for online video distribution allowed the requestor to ask for NBC Universal's entire scheduled lineup of programs. Cohen asserted the day after the condition was set up that Comcast would be asking for *not only* the full-freight charge for that programming (the charge it assessed against the smallest overbuilder ineligible for volume discounts from Comcast) but also any retransmission or other fees it traditionally requested *plus* any amount it was going to lose in advertising because the programming was going online.[23] Comcast could gently suggest that the requestor had misunderstood the condition, and schedule another meeting. And another meeting. And then stop responding to the requests for meetings.

Given its ability to strangle online players by withholding NBC Universal content, and its incentive to do so to protect its own video subscription business, Comcast was likely to find ways to avoid the obligation to provide NBCU input to online video distributors. And the "peer" obligation might never be triggered at all. If all the programmers wanted to keep the tens of billions of dollars they got in fees from traditional video distributors, they would not jeopardize that structure by licensing to an online actor; and unless one of them moved toward independent online distribution, Comcast would not have to hand over NBCU content.

Comcast's bet was that the TV Everywhere model and the company's ability to stream programmers' material to iPads and other devices would satisfy consumers' needs for online video long enough to forestall the development of true online competitors. Programmers (now including Comcast) could withhold content, and pipe providers (still Comcast) could make the rules about connections and prices. As Malone put it, "On the video side, you have a pretty robust, pretty profitable, pretty predictable business. And those who kind of undermine it—I think are playing at their own peril."[24]

One condition that could have made a difference to Comcast's future power over online innovation generally was that proposed by Earthlink: a requirement that Comcast provide wholesale stand-alone high-speed data access to companies, which would then be allowed to resell that service. Wholesale access, the thinking went, would allow competition to emerge, driving a wedge into Comcast's domination of high-speed Internet access. This remedy had been imposed in the AOL–Time Warner deal and was the basis for much of the telecommunications structure in the rest of the developed world. As Yochai Benkler wrote on behalf of Harvard's Berkman Center in a February 2010 report, "In countries where an engaged regulator enforced open access obligations, competitors that entered using these open access facilities provided an important catalyst for the development of robust competition which, in most cases, contributed to strong broadband performance across a range of metrics."[25] In other words, figuring out a predictable and fair structure under which competitors could share infrastructure has led to faster, competitive Internet access at lower costs around the world. When the distributors cease to have gatekeeping power, they become providers of a commodity input to other businesses, similar to the electrical utilities.

For Comcast, such a condition was unthinkable. Cohen explained in a 2009 interview with C-SPAN that the idea of wholesale access was a serious mistake: "Any requirement that our networks—built with private dollars, with no guaranteed taxpayer return—would have to be opened to anyone who wanted to retail or wholesale those services at a governmentally regulated rate, that is not a very good way to stimulate ongoing investment in the private network." The threat seemed plausible to regulators: if the government pushed for wholesale access, the cable industry would never build faster networks. (John D. Rockefeller had often made a similar point: "To justify Standard's plush earnings," Ron Chernow writes, "Rockefeller cited everything from fire hazards to the vagaries of drilling to the need to invest in new fields.")[26]

Moreover, the agencies were anxious not to repeat the failures of the AOL–Time Warner merger; they were convinced that wholesale access would have been complicated (how much of Comcast's costs for the network would the retail provider have to bear? who would work out the details?) and ultimately fruitless. And, again, the company was strongly opposed to the condition. Even though the public-interest groups thought that a wholesale condition was right around the corner, the leadership of the agencies was not ready to impose it.[27]

The Commission did not seem anxious to pressure Comcast or any other cable incumbents on their ability to route around the FCC's weak net neutrality rules by labeling online video services "specialized"; when asked whether an online video service would be permitted to make a business arrangement to be carried on a provider's "managed" network (whatever that meant), an FCC official said in late 2011 that the issue would have to be decided "on a case-by-case basis."[28] Translation: the idea of common carriage was gone. Comcast was free to prioritize TV Everywhere and to make special deals that allowed online videos in which it had an economic interest to look better and be more interactive with other services. If there were complaints, they would have to be litigated.

To be fair to the regulators, they were presented with a highly concentrated market, and it was not clear how much difference the merger would make to it. The transaction illuminated the state of communications in the United States: high-speed Internet access was dismally uncompetitive and getting more so; the potential for offline/online tying arrangements by the media conglomerates—in ways that would prevent competition from disruptive online video—was high, and it looked as if TV Everywhere would be the model for all programmers; there were very few programmers, and they were all cooperating within the cable-distribution structure; the transaction threatened net neutrality as a huge combination of content with a pipe that had many incentives to differentiate in favor of its own business plans; there were concerns about the future of media and innovation generally.

But these industry-wide issues had existed before the deal was announced. So the regulators did their best, created a new category of actors called "online video distributors," and tried to limit Comcast's occasions for abuse.

In the end, what they had over Comcast was oversight authority. The Department of Justice, in particular, had put itself in a position in which it would monitor every programming contract, both for traditional pay TV and online distribution. There might be compliance actions in the future; there might be enforcement; the story wasn't over. In terms of law enforcement oversight, Comcast was a more regulated company after the merger than it had been before.

But absent some kind of public blowup leading to a call for new legislation or antitrust investigation, Comcast was not worried. It had a new stable of content with which to pressure competitors. It had its pipes in place and it could charge whatever well-off Americans could afford to pay. Profit margins were increasing, and Comcast was buying back its stock in order to increase its earnings per share—and thus the attractiveness of its equity. (None of this activity served to generate positive spillovers that would help the country's economic recovery.) Both TV Everywhere and usage-based billing had been enthusiastically embraced by the FCC despite pleas from Netflix chief counsel David Hyman to consider the "anticompetitive aspects of consumption-based billing."[29] And Comcast did not have to share its pipes.

Comcast was also confident that it could defeat any call for government action that would materially affect its business. Any attempt to implement the Nixon-era idea of separating content from the pipe would be nothing more than an irritant, a gnat buzzing uselessly around the giant company's ears.

Labeling cable a utility based on its natural monopoly tendencies and its benefits from decades of effectively exclusive government franchises and favorable treatment would be an uphill battle in the political context of the merger. Breaking up cable was not under consideration: legislators and the executive branch were not focused on telecommunications. Senator Herb Kohl was retiring; Al Franken could be dismissed as a crank; and no one else had an interest in sticking his or her neck out, particularly when the telecommunications industry was being so generous with its contributions.

As David Cohen said in 2009, "If you were to take a poll of 435 members of Congress and 100 U.S. Senators to name the five top issues you think this Congress has to deal with over the next two years, you will be hard-pressed to find a telecommunications issue in the list of the top hundred that would come out of that polling. And I think that's right, by the way. I think we, Comcast, the cable industry, the telecommunications industry, deserve some credit for that. I think that we're conducting ourselves in appropriate ways and we're pursuing agendas that are working for the American consumer and for the country."[30]

Senator Franken, in particular, knew that opposing the giant carriers would be politically destructive to him. He knew the political risks he was taking by being so outspoken about the risks of control over Internet access to society. "They [the carriers] are very powerful interests, and . . . you have a situation where corporations can really put unlimited money into campaigns or into defeating people, and I suppose that they might look at me as Public Enemy No. 1, and they don't have to disclose where the money is coming from. So I think this could be seen as foolhardy and inviting a tremendous amount of money to be spent to defeat me the next time." But he was undeterred: "I came here to do what's right, and I really don't have any choice, because it's the way I see it. I see pretty clearly what the battle is here, and I think it's partially because of my experience in the business that I see it, where others don't." Then he turned contemplative. "It's ironic, because I'm on the Judiciary Committee, so I'm on the Antitrust Subcommittee, and even though I'm not a lawyer and I've only been in this business for a little while, I found myself being the only one who was seeing this." Franken thought he saw a good deal of self-delusion in the statements and actions of the legislators around him.[31]

Meanwhile, most people in the United States were not getting leading-edge Internet access. Fewer Americans, as a percentage of the population, had high-speed Internet access than in South Korea, Japan, or most of Europe. Speeds for uploading data, necessary for "cloud computing," were at a crawl compared to other countries. About a hundred million Americans had no high-speed Internet access at all.[32] The major reason: cost. And none of the cable companies was under any obligation to serve all Americans with globally relevant high-speed Internet access, much less at a reasonable price.

The Comcast-NBCU merger had shed light on concentration and market power in high-speed Internet access, programming, and devices, but after it was over there was scarcely a ripple; Comcast continued on its path, strengthened.

The investment bankers were already hard at work on the AT&T–T-Mobile merger.

13

The AT&T–T-Mobile Deal

"We don't believe for a moment that [a rejection] will occur. We're a very careful and cautious company in our strategic decisions," [James] Cicconi said. He added that the company has no need for a backup plan, such as filing suit against the government if regulators nix the deal. "We understand the antitrust laws . . . and we've examined all these with great care. We wouldn't be doing this deal if we did not expect approval."
—*Washington Post*, March 23, 2011

FEDERAL REGULATORS HAD BARELY recovered from their efforts to understand the cable industry when they were confronted with AT&T's plan to merge with T-Mobile. AT&T and its grand strategist James Cicconi made David Cohen and Comcast look junior league. Imagine creating a spectrum crisis, getting the commander in chief to warn the nation about it, and then claiming to solve it—and America's Internet access crisis—through a proposed merger. You had to admire these guys.

There are many similarities between the AT&T–T-Mobile and Comcast-NBCU mergers. Both were designed to achieve greater scale and thus lower the carrier's costs. Both involved an extensive political push to make any opposition to the deal look like antibusiness rhetoric. Both efforts employed narrative strategies (Comcast: "We're saving the NBC Peacock!"; AT&T: "We're saving rural America!") that turned out to be tangential to the business reasons for the transaction. Both took place in highly concentrated communications markets. As suppliers of high-speed Internet access, both dominant players (Comcast and AT&T) routinely cherry-pick their areas of service, sell as many bundles as possible, and seek to retain as much pricing power and discretion in choosing customers as possible.

Like the Comcast-NBCU merger, the AT&T–T-Mobile deal helps shine a light on the enormous overall consolidation in U.S. communications-access providers. There are, in essence, two big markets: cable wired and telecommunications wireless. The few dominant companies in both sectors share an interest in making content available everywhere on a prioritized, fee basis. And all are threatened by disruptive moves in Internet content and applications as well as by the risk of the introduction of devices that they cannot control.

But AT&T's deal looked, on the surface, more horizontal than Comcast's did. AT&T also had the burden of following Comcast. By the time the Antitrust Division got to the AT&T deal, the department knew that it needed to shore up its antitrust bona fides—and it sued to block the transaction, shocking a confident AT&T.[1] But whether the AT&T deal with T-Mobile went through or not almost didn't matter: AT&T won either way.

In America, wireless data is a separate marketplace from the cable wired data world. The physical-capacity constraints on wireless networks mean that wireless services cannot be substituted for wired connections. In order to build a wireless network that could be used by everyone and that would perform as well as wired high-speed Internet services, there would have to be a wireless tower on every rooftop—connected to a wire—that no user shared with any other. Each tower in a wireless network has to serve, on average, 436 times as many homes as a cable network, which connects to just one home at a time; each wireless network access point has one-thirty-seventh the information-carrying capacity as a cable wire; and there is vanishingly low interference inside a cable network.[2]

If the United States ever moves to ubiquitous fiber connections, as other countries are doing, the distinction between wired and wireless will become even clearer: the inherent capacity of fiber-optical links greatly exceeds that of wireless communications. Laser-transmitted information carried inside glass fiber-optical strands travels at the speed of light across great distances and carries millions more pieces of data per second than radio waves, without interference. The result is consistently high speeds, with no delays. Wireless radio signals, by contrast, carry much less information, are easily interrupted by trees or buildings at high frequencies, and decay sharply over distance. As noted earlier FiOS and DOCSIS 3.0 speeds as of 2010 were twenty to a hundred times as fast as optimistic projections for 4G wireless speeds.[3]

But as a complementary service, wireless is very popular. Americans like the convenience of mobile devices and are willing to compromise on the quality of Web browsing or data access in exchange for mobility. The phone companies are happy to serve this preference because wireless is far more profitable than wireline. It is cheaper to build, for one thing; rather than string and maintain copper wires, wireless companies can locate their equipment at towers (base stations). And they can charge premiums for voice and aggregated data services because U.S. customers now expect to pay individually for each expensive service from their wireless company (even though online Internet-based voice and data services would probably be far less expensive than they currently are if the companies faced true competition).[4]

The wireless world in the United States has many of the same economic characteristics as the wired world; it is extraordinarily concentrated, with just two dominant players nationwide—Verizon and AT&T—and those two players have the power to segment the market much as Comcast and Time Warner do in wired services. Monthly wireless service plans (post-paid subscriptions) for smartphones and other devices can cost more than traditional high-speed Internet access; the carriers charge overage fees for large volumes of data, and users incur many additional fees (including activation fees and early-termination fees). But while well-off Americans can afford these services, poorer Americans often depend on government-subsidized "pre-paid" wireless plans. The fastest-growing segment of the wireless marketplace in mid-2011 was Universal Service Fund federally subsidized wireless services for the poor offered by companies like Trac-fone. As Bernstein Research put it, "The top is trading up, the bottom is trading down, and the middle is being hollowed out."[5]

But what is worth noting is how neatly the characters in this story have divided up their roles. The telephone companies stick to the wireless part of high-speed Internet access and have ceded the wired territory to Comcast and Time Warner. Verizon and AT&T are no longer investing in fiber beyond their current commitments. AT&T made clear in 2011 that the company would not be installing any more U-Verse "fiber to the node" service and that 40–45 percent of its customers would be left with copper wires.[6] (AT&T's U-Verse was not competitive with cable's services anyway because it brings fiber only to nodes or neighborhoods and runs last-mile communications over copper wires.) Here's AT&T CEO Randall Stephenson in early 2012: "Our U-verse build is now largely complete. . . . We have been apprehensive on moving, doing anything on rural access lines because the issue here is, do you have a broadband product for rural America? And we've all been trying to find a broadband solution that was economically viable to get out to rural America and we're not finding one to be quite candid." AT&T is planning instead on selling expensive "LTE" (Long Term Evolution: a wireless high-data-transfer technology designed to support data access by way of handheld devices) services in rural areas. As we have seen, Verizon stopped expanding FiOS outside of franchise agreements already in place in big cities, leaving about 40 percent of its wired customers without upgrades. While FiOS is the only kind of last-mile infrastructure that could compete successfully with cable's DOCSIS 3.0, Verizon's investors do not want the company to pay for expensive fiber installations, for which the payoff will be slow.[7] For both of these companies, there is no financially compelling reason to upgrade millions of Americans to globally competitive wired data access. The result, according to Columbia University telecommunications scholar Eli Noam: areas of the country relegated to AT&T's 4G wireless access will be limited to "little 4G mobile screens or tablets while their metropolitan brethren enjoy 2-way, 3D, 4K, 5.1 sound, and 6-foot screen televisions."[8] Relying on wireless access for rural and other "unserved" areas means forcing millions of Americans to use compressed, highly curated information over a second-best network characterized by lower speeds and higher prices. And thus, a racial and economic digital divide is emerging in America: Hispanics, rural Americans, African Americans, and low-income Internet users disproportionately rely on wireless connections for access to the Internet. The online world of the rich—who can afford truly high-speed wired Internet access—is growing increasingly divorced from the online world of the poor, who generally have only mobile access. This new digital divide has significant consequences for the country's future, as health services, educational opportunities, and economic life migrate online. As the Media Action Grassroots Network put it in April 2011, "Many everyday Internet needs such as applying for a job, conducting research, registering for classes, or accessing government or social services are difficult or impossible on a mobile device."[9]

Wireless is the near-term growth area for both Verizon and AT&T, and to please Wall Street, both companies have to focus their energies there, where they are wringing out profits. But even in the wireless realm, both AT&T and Verizon face enormous challenges. Their margins for voice services are ten times higher than their margins for data services, but Americans prefer data services, and data usage is skyrocketing. AT&T and Verizon need to keep wireless data usage as low as possible for as long as possible by managing scarcity: imposing usage-based billing and not installing fiber to their towers (or building additional towers) unless they have to. To keep their average revenues per user as high as possible, they need to spread their costs across as many users as they can. Faced with the unassailable advantages of scale and scope, the wireless companies have chosen to combine rather than compete.

And so AT&T in 2011 made a big play for T-Mobile, its scrappy, low-price national competitor. T-Mobile was pushing an open platform for development of new applications (the Android operating system), had great customer service, and was backing policy positions in Washington aimed at increasing competition. It had not been able to get access to the spectrum it needed in order to compete effectively with AT&T and Verizon, but discussions were under way with the third-place wireless carrier, Sprint, about joining forces. Then AT&T swooped in and proposed its own deal, and T-Mobile's investors could not turn it down; who wanted to partner with the number 3 company when they could do a deal with number 1?

How did AT&T and Verizon Wireless become the dominant providers of mobile wireless services in the United States? Accidents of history, combined with multiple mergers, led to this state of affairs.

When the cellular phone emerged as a consumer product in the 1980s, it operated in 800 megahertz (MHz) frequencies, for which the FCC initially gave away two licenses for 40 MHz of spectrum in each of the 306 market areas in the United States—one to a wireless provider and one to a wired provider. Small-market licenses frustrated the buildup of viable nationwide wireless infrastructure; companies in urban areas had only a few voice channels, which did not provide enough capacity to serve demand, and companies in rural areas could not earn enough revenue to survive. No one could operate at the scale needed to make the business worthwhile.[10]

The 1980s licensing process led, predictably, to quick consolidation and market-division agreements among the applicants.[11] This desirable "beachfront" low-frequency spectrum—so-called because of their desirable properties: these frequencies travel well over long distances and inside buildings, which means operators can build 20 to 25 percent fewer towers as they do in areas which require higher frequencies—went to the corporate ancestors of today's AT&T and Verizon.

Two big breakthroughs came in the 1990s. First, the government had grown increasingly concerned that a decade of a wireless duopoly had led to too little competition and innovation in the mobile marketplace. Lack of competition and high interconnection charges made wireless calls about ten times more expensive per minute than wireline, turning them into tools for the rich. After the General Accounting Office (GAO) and others criticized the lack of competition, Congress and the Clinton White House allowed the FCC to auction additional spectrum to break up the wireless duopoly.[12]

The second big breakthrough was the development of digital standards, vaguely referred to as second-generation or 2G standards, that could compress audio signals and use spectrum more efficiently than the old analog standards, and across cheaper and smaller components. Though all were developed to use frequencies more efficiently, these 2G standards were often incompatible. They were based on different basic ideas, like separating users' transmissions by frequency and time (users communicate using the same channel but have different time slots) and particular encryption codes (users use the same channel, but their communications travel within varied envelopes of encryption). This latter, CDMA (Code Division Multiple Access), standard was widely adopted in America, and was based on many redundant communications across a wide range of frequencies and careful power control over all mobile units within a particular cell.[13] At around the same time the European Groupe Spéciale Mobile developed its own standard based on dividing up the channel by both frequency and time. This standard was called GSM—later Global Systems for Mobile Communications—and had been adopted by consensus across 103 countries by 1996.[14] In sum, this second digital generation of wireless service was more efficient, but users could not roam between standards or easily among countries.

The United States quickly stepped into the lead as it implemented the GAO's suggested legislation to allocate more spectrum at higher frequencies to more competitors for use in digital communications.[15] The government auctioned these bands for billions of dollars beginning in late 1994—the so-called PCS, or Personal Communications Services, auction. The government was hoping to avoid the paperwork, delay, and deal-making associated with the spectrum licensing and lottery systems it had tried earlier. It also sought to break up the Bell wireless duopoly (the two licenses in each market that had been issued at no cost to the Bell Operating Companies and other providers) that had limited competition and innovation and left consumers with the worst wireless network of any developed nation. The goal was to increase the number of competitors in every market. The incumbent wireless operators tried to block the effort and forestall new competition, but Congress and the White House prevailed. The ensuing auctions sparked new competition, innovation, and investment, and wireless moved from being a tool for the rich to an affordable way for families to connect. The corporate ancestors of Verizon, Cingular, and AT&T Wireless paid billions for spectrum, as did Voicestream, the corporate ancestor of T-Mobile.[16]

After the auction, consolidation proceeded apace. Bell Atlantic absorbed NYNEX in 1996 and then merged with GTE; then in 1999 the company merged with Vodafone to become Verizon. South Western Bell became SBC, bought Pacific Telesis in 1997 and Ameritech in 1999, and finally merged with Bell South in 2000 to become Cingular.[17]

Prices did go down for cell service during the late 1990s because of the new competition, the breakup of AT&T in 1984, and increased efficiencies from better technology. Spurred on by the breakup and by its technological advantages, AT&T introduced the Digital One flat rate in 1998 for wireless service, which was wildly popular with both consumers and businesses.[18]

Still, by 2003, enough companies had consolidated that Americans were left with just three large wireless providers. Verizon had a nationwide CDMA network and 30 percent of the market; Cingular had a GSM network that covered urban areas and a 15 percent share; and AT&T Wireless (the former McCaw Communications) had a 13 percent market share from an old-fashioned standard (D-AMPS) that was unable to produce sufficient bit rates for Internet access. Sprint PCS, T-Mobile, Nextel Communications, Alltel, and others divided up the rest of the market.[19]

Then something big happened: Cingular bought AT&T Wireless (and adopted its name) in 2004 for $41 billion. The new AT&T Wireless got the GSM standard and a new lease on wireless life.[20]

Meanwhile, technical innovation continued. Again the government found additional spectrum, this time for the third generation of wireless phones, and held another round of auctions in 2008. The goods were again beachfront property—low-frequency spectrum that had been reclaimed from TV broadcasters and was perfect for building out wireless phone systems. The problem was that the established licensees had no incentive to allow new entrants into the market, and could afford to bid high enough to keep them out. Verizon paid $9.6 billion to win a national allocation of 22 MHz in a single contiguous nationwide block. AT&T spent $6.6 billion for more than two hundred 12-MHz licenses in mostly small geographic areas around the country, amounting to 35 percent of these available licenses. It also bought two smaller blocks in private purchases. Between them, the two companies accounted for about 85 percent of the $19.6 billion raised by the auction.[21]

Even before this auction, the low-frequency spectrum that the corporate ancestors of today's AT&T and Verizon had bought in 1993 represented a significant windfall advantage that Sprint or T-Mobile could not replicate. As a result, an enormous gap had existed between AT&T/Verizon and everyone else in terms of subscribers, revenues, profit margins, and cash flow.

This gap increased following the 2008 sale. Because it was clear that the value to the two giants of keeping a new competitor out of the arena would exceed any reasonable market value for the spectrum, and because the

giants were allowed to bid even though they already had enormous holdings in beachfront low-frequency spectrum, T-Mobile did not even enter
the auction.

And so in some ways by 2011 the wireless marketplace was even less
competitive than the wired market: it had been a concentrated field since
1995, and it was growing more concentrated every year. If AT&T were
allowed to merge with T-Mobile, the combined company, along with
Verizon, would control 80 percent of the national market.[22] But even without the merger, Verizon (31 percent) and AT&T (32 percent) divided most of
the market between them in terms of both spectrum holdings and revenues,
with Sprint (17 percent market share) and T-Mobile (11 percent) barely hanging on as distant third and fourth players, with uncertain ability to constrain
the prices charged by Verizon and AT&T.[23] And by 2011, AT&T and Verizon
had done an impressive job of shaping the federal government's policies
for the future of high-speed data access along lines that favored their own
business plans.

The federal government's problem was that almost a third of Americans
were not subscribing to high-speed Internet access (often because of price),
and many of those nonsubscribers were rural, minority, or low-income
residents.[24] In 2011 an estimated 18 million Americans had no wired access
at all; it was unavailable where they lived.[25]

To solve this problem, AT&T and Verizon offered a compelling proposal
to policy makers and journalists. Arguing that wireless access would help
close the broadband gap in rural areas, they pointed out that data usage was
exploding across wireless networks. Wireless had become so popular that
their networks were buckling under the strain. The carriers helpfully
pinpointed the source of the problem: given this popularity and the greatly
increased use of data services by way of smartphones like the iPhone,
limitations on the frequencies available to them for data access were
constraining their ability to serve U.S. consumers—particularly in rural
areas, where Internet access adoption was low.[26]

The Obama administration, seeking to spark innovation, investment,
and competition in the wireless market, took seriously the talking point
about a "looming spectrum crisis." The administration proclaimed that
spectrum reallocation and auctions of the resulting freed-up spectrum for

high-speed Internet access use were the keys to the future of mobile Internet access in America. If spectrum were reassigned from old-fashioned, inefficient uses like broadcast television, the argument went, more companies and more people would have access to broadband. And if some of that spectrum were auctioned off, it would bring billions into the U.S. Treasury. Other reallocated spectrum could be made available to public safety officials, and based on the explosive benefits of technologies like WiFi (which uses unlicensed radio waves at low power to connect to access points), some could be reserved for unlicensed uses. At the same time, a lot of money could be made by Americans manufacturing devices and selling wireless applications to be used across the newly available broadband spectrum.[27]

Spectrum reform became the focus of the administration's approach to mobile high-speed Internet access: the FCC's March 2010 National Broadband Plan relied on revenue obtained by reallocating and auctioning off spectrum to fund its recommendations and asserted that improving wireless access was the best way of solving the country's high-speed Internet access deficit.[28] The Justice Department went along, saying, "Given the potential of wireless services to reach underserved areas and to provide an alternative to wireline broadband providers in other areas, the Commission's primary tool for promoting broadband competition should be freeing up spectrum."[29]

It sounded like a win-win-win: wireless would fix the nation's high-speed access problems, auctions could raise billions of dollars for the Treasury, and the administration could solve a public safety problem by using the auction proceeds to fund the development of interoperable networks and devices. The administration could help make more wireless high-speed Internet access possible by releasing more spectrum. And all this could be done without a dime of federal spending.

There were just two problems. First, AT&T and Verizon had plenty of spectrum—the spectrum crisis did not exist. But their investors did not want them to spend money improving the wires and adding the additional towers that facilitated better wireless communications. Without a high-capacity wire and a tower in close proximity to the wireless communicator, a wireless transmission cannot go very far. Capital expenditures would obviously reduce the companies' return on capital—bad for investors.

Second, unless the administration set auction rules that limited who was allowed to bid for spectrum—something it had little interest in doing given the deficit-reduction anxiety sweeping the nation—AT&T and Verizon would again spend whatever they needed to keep competitors at bay. Releasing spectrum under these conditions would have no effect on the duopoly's power to charge more for services and to pick and choose service areas. Without competition forcing prices down, lower-income Americans would still find high-speed Internet access too expensive; adoption would not increase, even if more spectrum was out there.

But having worked with the administration to frame both the policy problem (more spectrum capacity!) and its solution (take spectrum away from the broadcasters and give it to broadband!), AT&T found the perfect way to capitalize on the administration's messaging: merge with a company that had spectrum. The result, it promised, would be more capacity for AT&T and a solution to the nation's telecommunications failures.

On April 21, 2011, AT&T told the FCC that it was seeking permission to acquire T-Mobile for $39 billion.[30] JPMorgan Chase had put up a $20 billion loan to support the deal.[31] It was like watching Humpty-Dumpty being put back together again: Ma Bell would reappear in the form of Ma Cell. AT&T claimed that the synergies inherent in merging with T-Mobile would instantaneously free up new capacity that was the "functional equivalent of new spectrum." With T-Mobile's spectrum holdings and cell-tower placements, AT&T said, it would be able to avoid dropped calls and frustrating iPhone experiences in New York and San Francisco and build out a higher-speed wireless network to 97 percent of the country within six years.[32]

In making this last claim, AT&T banked on Americans' lack of interest in telecommunications issues. Verizon and AT&T had already said that this level of coverage would be reached by the two companies together almost as quickly.[33] AT&T also conveniently ignored the fact that its rural infrastructure overlapped almost completely with T-Mobile's; rural Americans would get no help from the merger.[34]

But AT&T argued forcefully that the deal would give more Americans access to broadband and would spur innovation in devices and applications. Not only that, the merger would be so helpful to AT&T's ability to do business—it would create so many synergies in the form of complementary network infrastructure, reduced advertising and marketing costs, and complementary retail store and customer support—that it would end up adding as much to AT&T's business as it cost. And the broadcasters had been irritated at having to give up their spectrum; with the merger, they would not have to.

AT&T pointed out that the president himself, in his 2011 State of the Union Address, had placed great emphasis on all these points: he had vowed to "make it possible for businesses to deploy the next generation of high-speed wireless coverage" throughout America, not only to produce a "faster Internet" and "fewer dropped calls" but also to "connect every part of America to the digital age." Given that its goals for the merger aligned neatly with the administration's goals for the country, the company asserted to the press that regulatory approval was all but certain.[35]

The American telecommunications chattering class was briefly surprised; would such a major consolidation be allowed? But within a week after the merger was announced, the deal began to seem likely. Only Sprint Nextel, a company that had hoped to buy T-Mobile to bolster its own market share in the United States, protested strongly, saying that the acquisition would harm consumers and jeopardize the country's future.[36] But Sprint was in an awkward position; it was a direct competitor complaining about a rival's possible success. Jim Cicconi, AT&T's senior executive vice president for external and legislative affairs, countered that Sprint was being hypocritical: just a few months earlier, as he had sought to bolster the administration's focus on spectrum policy and lay the groundwork for Sprint's possible merger with T-Mobile, Sprint's CEO, Dan Hesse, had called the wireless sector "hypercompetitive" and said that some consolidation would be healthy.[37]

Cicconi held his ground, even as the sense of the deal's inevitability began to dissipate. "Opposition is not growing," he told the *Wall Street Journal* that May. "If anything, it seems fairly confined to the usual people and the usual organizations and does not seem to be growing beyond that."[38] Cicconi had already lined up letters of support from eleven state governors. He also had the backing of the Communications Workers of America, an influential voice among Democratic elected leaders, which issued a press release lauding the deal within hours after it was announced.[39] Support also came quickly from the NAACP and the Hispanic Federation, a familiar ally for large communications companies.[40] And since T-Mobile's parent company was Deutsche Telekom, AT&T could claim to be transforming a German company's holdings in America into an American operation run by unionized workers.

The deal was designed to work out well for AT&T from every direction. The company offered Deutsche Telekom a $3 billion breakup fee and some high-frequency spectrum if the deal didn't go through. But if the adverse effects of regulatory conditions (like divestitures) added up to more than $7.8 billion, AT&T could back out and not pay the fee.[41]

AT&T's own canny assessment of its risks were expressed in the breakup fee: that three billion dollars was more than Sprint could hope to put on the table in any counteroffer. Even if the deal did not take place, while it was under consideration AT&T had not only kept Sprint and T-Mobile from joining, it had taken T-Mobile out of the game. With its low pricing plans, policy aggressiveness, support for an open-source operating system that gave developers a competing outlet for their applications, and dreams of its own high-speed wireless network, T-Mobile had been a maverick, a threat to the AT&T (and Verizon) model. No matter what it meant for American consumers, in oligopolist's terms, the deal was genius.

AT&T argued that the deal should be scrutinized on the basis of local markets, many of which have three or four carriers from which consumers can buy service, and it claimed that this meant wireless service was highly competitive.[42] But this is like asserting that Washington, D.C., has several football teams: the NFL Washington Redskins, the Georgetown University Hoyas, and the Gonzaga College High School Eagles. Only AT&T and Verizon provide reliable nationwide service. They own the physical lines that connect to the wireless towers and carry data to the Internet backbones. Smaller carriers like Sprint and T-Mobile have to pay AT&T and Verizon for the privilege of roaming services in areas where they do not have their own towers. But AT&T went on hiring scores of influential lobbyists, muscling its way through Washington, and repeating the mantra that all relevant markets were local.

Its timing and political planning seemed to be pitch-perfect. The Obama administration, busy touting the vital importance of wireless access to

America's future, was put into an even tougher position than it had been with the Comcast-NBCU merger. Blocking the deal would allow Republicans to paint the administration as antibusiness. Given that no large businesses other than Sprint publicly opposed the deal, that it seemed to dovetail with the administration's own interest in improved wireless high-speed data access, and that the administration could use the deal to exact public policy improving conditions, it looked initially as if AT&T would win the day.

Why did T-Mobile decide to sell itself to AT&T? One word: spectrum.

Comcast can keep competitors at a distance because it has snapped up exclusive franchises—given by the government—around the country, and then clustered its operations so that it owns the whole of market where it chooses to sell services. The programming it controls—most important, sports—is another barrier to entry; Comcast's competitors have to have this content, and Comcast can charge whatever it wants for it. No one is likely to have the resources to enter the market to compete seriously with Comcast in the distribution business—a competitor would have to offer great video programming and, at the same time, shoulder the enormous up-front costs of building a network.

AT&T has its own ace, and it also came from government. Instead of licenses to do business (like a cable franchise), AT&T has licenses to transmit signals, granted by the FCC.

AT&T and Verizon inherited an enormous amount of beachfront—lower frequency—spectrum from their corporate ancestors. T-Mobile acquired its spectrum holdings through Deutsche Telekom's acquisition of Voicestream, which had bid successfully in the FCC's 1994 PCS auctions, and through its own $4.2 billion bid in a 2006 AWS (Advanced Wireless Services) auction. Both PCS and AWS are higher-frequency bands than AT&T and Verizon's 700 MHz spectrum (for which they paid a combined $15 billion in 2008) and 850 MHz spectrum (granted free to AT&T's and Verizon's corporate ancestors).

The amount of information that can be conveyed goes up with higher frequencies, but the distance data can travel goes down, and the data are more easily interrupted by physical objects in the way. The high-frequency bands can thus indeed carry gigabits of information, but they require cell towers every hundred yards or so. This is what makes WiFi faster than commercial wireless but limits the signal to the area around your house. A carrier with licenses to lower-frequency spectrum can thus serve a territory better than a carrier with higher-frequency spectrum, because it can build far fewer base stations. This is a major cost advantage held by AT&T and Verizon. It would take significantly more cell sites to serve T-Mobile's customers using its spectrum than to serve the lower-frequency spectrum customers of AT&T and Verizon, and even then, indoor coverage would probably suffer.

These spectrum issues have created a gap between T-Mobile (and Sprint) and the two big wireless carriers, with their broad, unchallenged holdings in the 700 MHz and 850 MHz bands. Nonetheless, T-Mobile's management told investors in a January 2011 conference call that the company was "a very good asset" that was generating positive annual free cash flow of between $2.5 billion and $3 billion a year. T-Mobile, claimed its management, had a strong network architecture in which half its towers were already fed by fiber, terrific smartphones, the best value for consumers, great customer service, and higher (and growing) margins on revenue than Sprint. Why the optimism? T-Mobile's management also said during that call: "We're absolutely positive and optimistic about [the] commercial option in [the 700 MHz] D block."[43] T-Mobile, in other words, was hoping to buy additional beachfront, low-frequency spectrum that the FCC had planned to make available: the nationwide "D block" of 10 MHz within the 700 MHz overall allocation. If it got access to that spectrum, it could catch up with Verizon and AT&T. And there was another block of federally used spectrum that T-Mobile planned to pair with its own existing holdings. More spectrum would give T-Mobile a chance to compete.

When the administration failed to follow the FCC's lead and appeared likely to take another auction for commercial use of the 700 MHz D block off the table, Deutsche Telekom apparently could not see a path forward and decided to pursue a merger. In a sense, the Obama administration itself caused T-Mobile to seek a deal. The company could see the writing on the wall: it would never have the beachfront spectrum holdings or scale to enable it to compete effectively with AT&T and Verizon, so it might as well fold its tents.

The merger announcement had an immediate effect on the viability of Sprint, the other also-ran wireless carrier. Talks between Sprint and T-Mobile had been going on for months before AT&T swooped in. Given the deal's apparent inevitability, Sprint's market valuation plummeted. John Delaney, research director with the analyst firm IDC, noted, "With Sprint's position looking increasingly difficult, and with one of Sprint's options for improving its position, a merger with T-Mobile USA, now off the table, the US looks like it is heading towards a duopoly of national mobile operators."[44]

AT&T is fond of pointing out that devices like smartphones and iPads generate twenty-four times more data than conventional wireless phones, and that AT&T's mobile data volumes climbed by 8,000 percent from 2007 to 2010. AT&T's networks cannot bear the strain, and the company says that the answer—the only answer—is more spectrum.[45] Eager to help, the Obama administration in 2011 launched a search for 500 MHz of spectrum to be reallocated to wireless data use from less efficient uses.[46] Every closet in every federal agency is being scoured for spectrum. This process will take years—on average, it takes six years to identify, reallocate, and distribute spectrum—and a scores of civil servants will invest a great deal of energy in the spectrum hunt.[47] (Prediction: the Department of Defense will fight giving up any spectrum it has been allocated using every lobbying tool it has available. The military-industrial complex in this country is enormously effective at avoiding sharing its spectrum assets with commercial actors.)

In the meantime, it is worth continuing to ask whether the problem is solely, or even mostly, spectrum. The large wireless carriers could also increase the information-carrying capacity of their networks by building more towers and connecting them to fiber rather than copper wires. Today, even though 97.8 percent of the U.S. population has 3G coverage, more than 80 percent of cell sites are still connected to copper wires.[48] But since the goal of any private company seeking Wall Street investment is to achieve the same levels of revenue (or more) while laying out less money, spending on "backhaul" (connections between towers and Internet access points) has not been a high priority. The problem in wireless transmission, therefore, is probably the wires and the towers, not spectrum. Executive compensation and quarterly results trump higher-quality service every time.

Avoiding capital-intensive fiber installations where possible will both please investors and continue to shape users' expectations; Americans will be used to slow, crippled, heavily curated, and compressed mobile services. AT&T can also use the usage-based billing model to ration usage of its network while reducing the attractiveness of potentially competing data services and other nonaffiliated products crossing its wireless networks; consumers will not want to use competing services, even if they technically can, because they will thus be subject to large overage charges, service cut-offs, or other remedies imposed at the carrier's discretion.

All in all, AT&T's effort to merge with T-Mobile made sense; it was trying to force a utility communications service (similar to the water and electricity companies), with its extraordinarily high up-front costs and sharply declining cost curves, into a private, profit-making, model that would be attractive to investors, and the only way to do that was to continue to scale, tightly ration capacity, employ price discrimination, keep capital costs down, and eliminate competitive ideas that would undermine the model. T-Mobile's low-priced services and open development platforms were one such disruptive idea. Acquiring T-Mobile would have eliminated that alternate mindset while letting AT&T add subscribers without increasing its employee headcount.

Thus, although "more spectrum!" became the call of all of the carriers in 2010, it was unclear whether spectrum was the problem—just as it had been unclear in the Comcast-NBCU transaction whether "saving the NBC Peacock" was a strong enough reason to approve the deal. T-Mobile had hoped that new spectrum would be made available for it to bid on so that it could compete. AT&T and Verizon already had a lot of spectrum. AT&T had more than anyone else in the top twenty-one markets in the United States, and it was using less than a third of what it had.[49] Verizon said it did not need any more.

But with Jim Cicconi shaping the story line, "more spectrum" would take the form of more capacity offered by the same player. The merger between AT&T and T-Mobile would solve the country's broadband problem.

When the Department of Justice sued to block the merger in August 2011, arguing that the national market was relevant and that getting rid of T-Mobile would reduce horizontal competition, AT&T was shocked. The company had been supremely confident of approval, and its response was remarkable: "We are surprised and disappointed by today's action particularly since we have met with the Department of Justice and there was no indication from the DOJ that such an action was being contemplated."[50]

If anyone in AT&T's enormous communications–public relations shop had known the story of J. P. Morgan's meeting with Theodore Roosevelt, the company would not have made that statement. It echoes Morgan's words when Roosevelt's attorney general sued his railroad trust under the Sherman Act. AT&T, like Morgan, apparently thought of itself as the government's equal.

What made the difference between the Comcast-NBCU and AT&T–T-Mobile cases? AT&T had brought even greater political pressure to bear on the administration: even more letters from state governors and nonprofits had been filed in support of the merger, even more lawyers and lobbyists had been deployed, and even more adept political messaging had taken place at the highest levels. But this time the merger-specific merits of the antitrust case seemed clearer; the Antitrust Division's objection to the increase in horizontal concentration seemed more likely to be upheld by a court. Besides, the department had just been through the deep political waters of the Comcast-NBCU deal and wanted to remind the country that it was a law enforcement agency. AT&T's CEO, Randall Stephenson, took a slap on the hand as a result of the failure of the deal, losing $2 million of his total compensation for the year—which left him with $22 million in his yearly pay package.[51] AT&T took a charge on its books to cover the breakup fee ($1.4 billion after the tax write off).[52] But its stock price had gone up more than 8 percent since the deal had been announced—more than Verizon's had climbed. AT&T had also won: it had severely damaged T-Mobile, undermined Sprint, gotten access to a lot of T-Mobile's strategic planning documents, and stalled any potential change in the regulatory structure for its sector.

Better regulatory policy on the wireless side would help foster competition, innovation, and lower prices: the government could make spectrum available to more players for less money by capping participation in auctions or charging fees for spectrum; it could require existing carriers to share their towers, thus lowering the costs of doing business for new competitors; it could make more unlicensed spectrum available; and it could oblige wireless providers to act as common carriers when it comes to the Internet data passing over their airwaves. But there is little or no impetus for government intervention in wireless. And at the same time the government is relying heavily on wireless as the answer to America's Internet access problem.

Will wireless access help America reach the president's goal of one gigabit to every community? No. It bears repeating: wireless access cannot be a direct substitute for high-speed wired services (other than the legacy DSL services, which have already become irrelevant). Ever since the dawn of the digital age, wireless-technology speeds have lagged behind wired speeds by substantial margins. Published data rates of post–third generation standards—Verizon claims peak speeds of around 25 Mbps, and average speeds of around half that—seem high. But these numbers need to be understood in context. They assume optimal (and unlikely) conditions, such as a single user or a few users who can use all the available bandwidth without sharing and are in close proximity to a base station. In addition, it is possible to achieve these rates only by using large amounts of spectrum, generally more than is available for current 3G systems, and by using relatively small cell sizes—which means building lots of towers or deploying many base stations and serving them with fiber, which AT&T and Verizon have not done and are experiencing no competitive pressure to do. The laws of physics make it extremely unlikely that wireless connections over long distances will ever be capable of delivering the hundreds of gigabits per month that users will want to consume over their data connections.

True, wireless is and will remain a useful complementary mobile service. Many Americans who either cannot afford the cable companies' high-priced offerings or prize mobility above quality of communications will depend on it. Americans love their smartphones, and they are buying more of them all the time.

But the country is headed toward a complete duopoly, in which wireless access will be like having a portable cable network: consumers will choose subscription-based premium bundles of content and click on highly compressed, favored applications in which the carrier has an interest. AT&T has never pretended that it planned to provide nondiscriminatory Internet access across its wireless connections, or to allow devices to connect to its network without permission.

And there appears to be no appetite in the federal government to change this state of affairs. To the contrary: the "open Internet" rules the FCC proposed in December 2010 shielded wireless carriers from any obligation to treat communications or devices equally. Americans will be able to entertain themselves only on the carriers' terms; every pixel of the screen and keyboard real estate will be managed in some way by AT&T and Verizon. But this relatively slow and hyper-controlled data world is nothing like the fast and open Internet based on wholesale fiber availability that other countries demand for their citizens. It is much more like the Comcast experience.

The AT&T–T-Mobile transaction, like Comcast-NBCU, showed that the country's communications providers are actually competing with access to the Internet. They would like to ensure that a private-carriage mindset prevails that allows them to favor their own business partners and enormous profit margins over access to online applications that might be available to Americans at lower cost. So far, they face almost no regulatory oversight. There is no competitive pressure that would drive them to install next-generation fiber networks to make America globally competitive.

To be sure, the blocking of the AT&T–T-Mobile deal in 2011 ensured that a single company would not be controlling 45 percent of the U.S. wireless market. The day after the Department of Justice sued to stop the deal, Mike Isaac of *Wired* quoted a T-Mobile user: "I'm so happy I don't have to be an AT&T customer."[53] But it was not clear that the two companies left in charge of the marketplace—AT&T and Verizon—would be lowering prices or providing better services any time soon thereafter. Sprint and T-Mobile did not appear to have the financial wherewithal or spectral resources to exert competitive pressure on the two behemoths. In February 2012, AT&T senior vice president John Donovan floated the idea of charging sources of content for the privilege of reaching AT&T subscribers: "Reverse billing," a "1-800" structure for applications, would provide a path for developers of applications to pay for the consumer's bandwidth usage so that use of favored applications would not count against a consumer's data plan.[54] As Colin Weir, a telecommunications analyst, noted when Donovan suggested this plan, "When AT&T introduced toll-free long distance calling back in the late 1960s, its rates were regulated by the FCC and in many cases 800 Service—which was offered under a bulk usage pricing arrangement—was actually cheaper than by-the-call outbound long distance rates."[55] AT&T would be subject to no such constraints. Bernstein Research asserted that the idea of reverse billing signaled that duopoly pricing power might be just ahead: "If reverse billing 'sticks'—and bear in mind that it hasn't even been tried yet, so the public policy debate really hasn't yet begun—then there is perhaps hope for the carriers yet; at least for the lucky two duopolists."[56] AT&T would have the power to ensure that only its content partners reached AT&T's subscribers reliably while imposing steep overage charges on consumers who exceeded their data caps; both sides of the market, supply and demand, would pay tribute to the carrier. Unregulated duopolies do well when they are selling services that Americans cannot live without.

14

The Costly Gift

TERRY HUVAL IS A LARGE, FRIENDLY MAN with a lilting southern accent who plays Cajun fiddle tunes in his spare time. He is also the director of utilities in Lafayette, Louisiana, where the system is owned by the local government. "Our job is making sure we listen to our citizens," he says. In recent years, the citizens of Lafayette have been asking for speedier Internet access.[1]

In 2004 the Lafayette utilities system decided to provide a fiber-to-the-home (FTTH) service. The new network, called LUS Fiber, would provide everyone in Lafayette with a very fast open Internet connection; the plan was also to use the system to bring down electricity costs by allowing people to monitor and adjust their electricity usage.

Perhaps predictably, there was immediate push-back from the local telephone company, BellSouth, and the local cable company, Cox Communications. Huval faced a deluge of efforts to stop the public utility service from serving its public. The private carriers, he said, "tried to pass laws to stop us from doing it, passing laws to make it more difficult for us to do it, suing us." BellSouth even forced the town to hold a referendum on the issue, in which the people voted 62 percent in favor of the project. But the fight was not over. "Then those private companies sued us again, then they found someone to sue us on their behalf." Finally, after weathering five civil lawsuits opposing the idea of a city's offering fiber communications to its residents, in February 2007 the Louisiana State Supreme Court voted

7–0 in favor of the project. "That opened the doors for [LUS Fiber] to be able to afford to borrow money for the project, which we did."[2]

A less resilient public servant might not have made it through the long fight between announcement and service to his customers. "We had to go through a long haul, legally, in our state," says Huval. "I think it's going to be difficult for anyone to jump into [a service like] this without having themselves prepared."[3]

Because Cox, the local cable incumbent, offers voice-video-data packages (but at much slower speeds for data than LUS Fiber), Huval and Lafayette have felt it necessary to provide cable channels to Lafayette customers. LUS Fiber applied to join a cooperative of cable systems, the National Cable Television Cooperative, so that it could be part of a larger group negotiating with the programmers for content, but after Cox joined the cooperative, LUS Fiber's application was denied.[4] Huval told the *Lafayette Advertiser* that this denial was "totally unanticipated." Huval and LUS Fiber are thus on their own when it comes to making deals with programmers—and this has proven to be a very expensive and uncertain proposition. All the same, LUS Fiber estimated in mid-2011 that people in Lafayette had saved $5.7 million on telecommunications services since 2007—because of LUS Fiber's cheaper services and because Cox cut its rates (though only in areas around Lafayette where LUS Fiber was not providing services, so as to keep LUS Fiber from expanding).[5]

Since Lafayette went down this path, other communities have followed suit, and many have fought similar battles. According to the Institute for Local Self-Reliance, a group that advocates for municipal fiber networks, these community-owned networks are generally faster, more reliable, and cheaper than the private carriers—and provide better customer service.[6] It's not free: it costs between twelve hundred and two thousand dollars to connect fibers to individual houses from a network node, and often business buildings need retrofitting so that their wiring will bring the fiber inside to serve tenants. It can thus take two to three years for revenues from any given customer to offset the up-front investment. But the advantage is that fiber lasts for decades.[7] These days, municipal networks that are providing the fastest speeds at the lowest costs are seeing very high (more than 50 percent) adoption rates.[8] At the same time, scores of communities are discovering that the new networks have brought new jobs to their areas.[9]

In Chattanooga, Tennessee, the municipal utility offers FTTH along with "smart meter" services for businesses, allowing companies to use lightning-fast communications connections to schedule their energy-intensive activities at times when utility prices are low. Residents of Chattanooga can sign up for excellent fiber service that is installed for free and is much cheaper than that offered by Comcast or AT&T (DSL, a hundred times slower than fiber).[10] Some businesses based in Knoxville—a hundred miles to the northeast—are adding jobs in Chattanooga, where they can save on connectivity.[11] But when the utility tried in 2011 to expand its fiber services to towns outside Chattanooga, the area's private carriers launched a lobbying assault and defeated a bill that would have allowed the expansion.[12]

Also in 2011, six Time Warner lobbyists, working full-time, successfully persuaded the North Carolina legislature to pass a "level playing field" bill that will effectively make it impossible for cities in that state to launch their own municipal high-speed Internet access networks.[13] Time Warner, which reported $26 billion in revenue in 2010, donated more than $6.3 million to North Carolina politicians over four years.[14] Eighteen other states have laws that make it extremely difficult or impossible for cities to provide this service to their citizens.[15]

Other experiments are beginning to emerge. When Google announced an FTTH pilot project in 2009, more than eleven hundred communities applied. As of mid-2012, people in the Kansas City area, which was chosen for the project, were looking forward to the launch of a fiber network—the standard communications medium, and the fastest and most reliable way to access the Internet—that will spur economic development for their citizens.[16] The alternative fiber story is still being written; hundreds of communities are interested in serving their citizens with inexpensive fiber connections and routing around the incumbent high-speed Internet access providers.

Electricity, provided by largely reliable, taxpayer-supported entities, is crucial to the economic and social health of the country. It is an essential public good, something that no neighborhood or private company would have an incentive to provide on its own to everyone at reasonable prices.

Providing electricity is also an economic activity, though hardly ever a profitable one. It is a social service because it is a platform for other economic activity.

No one seems to think the country would be better off if a purely private, wholly deregulated operator were in charge of electricity. Such a service would be unsatisfactory in many ways; the company might find it worthwhile to provide service only in New York and Washington and other big cities, at very high rates for those who could afford it, and refuse to serve small towns and less-successful areas even though the absence of electricity there would damage the overall economy. Needing to attract short-term attention from Wall Street, a private service would have little incentive to invest in upgrades with only long-term payoffs. Looking for higher revenue per customer, it would carry out as much price discrimination as possible to ensure that it captured as much profit as the market could provide.

This is exactly what happened in the 1880s, when privately owned electric companies served big cities and the homes of the rich, and everyone else intermittently if at all. Electricity was a luxury, synonymous with wealth and power. Glenn Fleishman of *Publicola* found this October 24, 1905, statement from lawyer Henry Anderson in the Richmond, Virginia, *Times-Dispatch:*

> The ownership and operation of municipal light plants stands upon a different basis from that of the ownership of water works, with which it is so often compared. Water is a necessity to the health and life of every individual member of a community. . . . It must be supplied in order to preserve the public health, whether it can be done profitably or not, and must be furnished, not to a few individuals, but to every individual.
>
> Electric lights are different. Electricity is not in any sense a necessity, and under no conditions is it universally used by the people of a community. It is but a luxury enjoyed by a small proportion of the members of any municipality, and yet if the plant be owned and operated by the city, the burden of such ownership and operation must be borne by all the people through taxation.[17]

The private electrical companies consolidated, wielded enormous influence in state and national legislatures, cherry-picked their markets, and mounted huge campaigns against publicly owned electrical utilities, calling them "un-American." At the beginning of the twentieth century, private power companies electrified only the most lucrative population centers and ignored most of America, particularly rural America. By the mid-1920s, fifteen holding companies controlled 85 percent of the nation's electricity distribution, and the Federal Trade Commission found that the power trusts routinely gouged consumers.[18]

In response, recognizing that cheap, plentiful electricity was essential to economic development and quality of life, thousands of communities formed electrical utilities of their own. Predictably, the private utilities claimed that public ownership of electrical utilities was "costly and dangerous" and "always a failure," according to the November 1906 issue of *Moody's Magazine*.[19] Now more than two thousand communities in the United States, including Seattle, San Antonio, and Los Angeles, provide their own electricity.[20] And electricity is a regulated public utility, not a luxury.

As a result of the depredations of the electrical utilities, we came to understand that public goods like electricity (and railroads and highways) must be overseen by the public (and funded by the public) if they are to remain publicly useful and generate increasing economic and social returns for all. Why have Americans stopped applying this thinking to communications?

After the Great Depression, the Federal Communications Commission was given the job of providing America with a high-quality, general-purpose communications system at reasonable rates. For fifty years, the state oversaw the development of phone service. Providers were prohibited from entering into other businesses and were obliged to serve the public on nondiscriminatory terms. Phone lines used narrow bandwidth to make telephoning cheap for conversational use. Everyone, by and large, had the ability to make a phone call to everyone else.

In the 1970s, communities began handing out exclusive franchises to cable companies that could bring remote entertainment into homes. Over the next twenty years, the cable companies consolidated and swapped system franchises so that they would each control certain markets. By the mid-1980s, the phone companies, anxious to get into the long-form entertainment business, asserted that they could not attract the capital needed to expand their bandwidth to allow video delivery unless they were released from the conditions imposed on them by the AT&T breakup.

As communications companies converged on bundled phone and entertainment services, legislators and regulators struggled to constrain the companies' potential gatekeeper control and ability to raise prices. The arrival of commercial Internet communications in the mid-1990s posed a threat to both the phone and cable companies; eventually, pummeled by endless litigation, cajoled by well-paid lobbyists, and spurred on by the promise of consumer-protecting competition among various modalities of Internet access—cable, phone, wireless, satellite, broadband over powerline—the FCC deregulated the entire sector over a five-year period beginning in 2002. The belief animating deregulation was that competition would protect Americans, and in 2002 there was indeed rough parity—speed and price—between the cable companies and telephone companies providing Internet access.

But cable companies soon found a technical way to upgrade their networks to provide far higher bandwidth—perhaps a hundred times faster than what was possible over copper wires—at much lower expense than the phone companies incurred replacing their phone lines. Now Comcast, like all the cable distributors, is providing a single, all–digital communications, all–Internet Protocol pipe. A small portion of that pipe, four out of hundreds of channels, is devoted to the public communications platform that is now the common medium around the world: the Internet.[21] Comcast has the incentive and ability to minimize the impact of Internet-based communications on its video packages, and to control, constrain, and cripple any Internet business that threatens its plans.

For their part, the phone companies are riding a wave of explosive growth in wireless data, and the two largest have carved off this separate marketplace for themselves. If anything, the wireless situation with regard to Internet access is even worse. Wireless carriers have no obligation to refrain from discriminating in favor of their own business plans.

Here is the problem: The American copper wire telephone system is becoming obsolete, as consumers move to cellphones for voice service and the physical switches used in that network reach the end of their useful lives. The telephone companies who built that regulated network are hoping to get rid of the obligation to maintain it now that cable has decisively won the battle for high-speed wired communications in America. Some municipalities are trying to install fiber-optic networks for themselves, but their efforts are routinely squelched by lobbying campaigns and other tactics launched by incumbent network providers at the state level. Because America has deregulated the entire high-speed Internet access sector, the result is expensive, second-rate, carefully curated wired services for the rich, provided by Comcast and Time Warner; expensive, third-rate, carefully curated wireless services (or no services at all) for those who cannot afford a wire; close cooperation among the incumbent providers of wired and wireless services; and no public commitment to the advanced communications networks the rest of the developed world is adopting. At the same time, the longtime consensus in the United States that basic, nondiscriminatory, affordable utility communications services should be made available to all Americans is being dismantled, state by state—just as America's peer countries are coming to the view that it is a national priority to replace copper with fiber for all of their citizens as soon as possible. As Bernstein Research noted in a 2012 report, "What is most remarkable, in our view, is how little attention [the end of the copper phone network] has received. When confronted with the question 'Will we still operate a national scale low-bandwidth wired network in 20 years?', most investors and policy makers quickly acknowledge that the likely answer is 'no.' But when faced with the question of 'what should be done about it?'—one draws blank stares."[22]

None of this is good news for consumers or for American innovation.

The sea change in policy that led to the current situation has been coordinated over the past twenty years by legions of lobbyists, hired-gun economists, and credulous regulators. The cable companies have no incentive to upgrade their core network hardware to ensure that advanced fiber connections are available to every home throughout the country. Communications companies describe globally competitive high-speed access as a luxury, just as the private electricity companies did a century ago.

Yet communications services are now as important as electricity. Today if you asked American mayors what technology they most want for their city, the majority would say, "affordable high-speed Internet access." And they want these networks not simply for the jobs created to construct them but because the Internet brings the world to their community. High-speed Internet access gives towns and cities online commerce and services, the ability to reach world markets, to invent and innovate, to learn and communicate. It brings a wealth of economic activity and information. But despite these manifold benefits, Americans continue to treat such services as the exclusive domain of private monopolies and as luxuries obtainable only by the wealthy.

Not coincidentally, the United States has fallen from the forefront of new developments in technology and communications. It now lags behind countries that long ago defined communications as a public, and publicly overseen, good. America is rapidly losing the global race for high-speed connectivity, as fewer than 8 percent of Americans currently receive fiber service to their homes.[23] And the country has plateaued: adoption gains have slowed sharply, even though nearly 30 percent of the country is still not connected.

Not surprisingly, cost is the most commonly cited reason people in America do not subscribe to high-speed Internet access, and nonadoption is closely tied to economic status; lack of data access reinforces other inequalities.[24] Meanwhile, the future of start-up businesses, independent programmers, the computing industry, the quality of life of many Americans, and free expression online are all in jeopardy; neither businesses nor people can count on fast, open access to new markets, new ways of getting an education, new ways of obtaining health care, and new ways of making a living.

It is clear from extensive evidence around the world that this publicly supervised infrastructure should be made available to everyone and provided on a wholesale basis to last-mile competitors in order to keep speeds high and prices low. Yet vertically integrated incumbent monopoly communications providers have every incentive to discriminate in favor of their own information and content—to the detriment of innovation coming from the rest of us, and to the detriment of the flow of information generally. America has emerged decades after the breakup of AT&T with a communications system that has all the monopolistic characteristics of the old Bell system but none of the oversight or universality.

Yet this inequality is not irrevocable. It is not a product of "market forces" absent human intervention. But to fix it, a new approach is needed.

The first step is to decide what the goal of telecommunications policy should be. Network access providers—and the FCC—are stuck on the idea that not all Americans need the high-speed access now standard in other countries. The FCC's National Broadband Plan of March 2010 suggested that the minimum appropriate speed for every American household by 2020 should be 4 Mbps for downloads and 1 Mbps for uploads. These speeds are enough, the FCC said, to reliably send and receive e-mail, download Web pages, and use simple video conferencing. The Commission also said that it wanted to ensure that by 2020, at least 100 million U.S. homes have "affordable access to actual download speeds of at least 100 megabits per second and actual upload speeds of at least 50 megabits per second."[25]

Such rates would not be difficult. Comcast is already selling its hundred-megabit service in the richest American communities, but it costs $200 a month (or just $105 if you buy the bundle—a 50 percent discount for keeping the company's business model in place).[26] In a sense, the FCC adopted the cable companies' business plan as the country's goal. Its embrace of asymmetric access—far lower upload than download speeds—also serves the carriers' interests: only symmetric connections would allow every American to do business from home rather than use the Internet simply for high-priced entertainment.

Other countries have chosen different goals. The South Korean government announced its plan to install one gigabit (Gb) per second of high-speed symmetric fiber data access in every home by 2012. Japan, the Netherlands, and Hong Kong are heading in the same direction. Australia plans to get 93 percent of homes and businesses connected to fiber, ensuring download speeds of 100 Mbps; the other 7 percent, in more remote areas, will get a 12 Mbps wireless or satellite service. In the United Kingdom, a 300 Mbps fiber-to-the-home service will be offered on a wholesale basis. As we have seen, even some U.S. communities (Chattanooga, Kansas City through Google) have made this leap, believing that their citizens want and will need 1-Gb symmetric connections in their homes.[27]

The current 4-Mbps Internet access goal is unquestionably shortsighted. And when the public agencies' lack of technical foresight is combined with the carriers' incentives to keep their incumbent market structures in place, the 4-Mbps prediction for minimum universal Internet access service in America takes on a darker hue.

If this speed remains the country's goal for 2020, only the carriers' interests will have been served. They can already provide 4-Mbps wireless service to most of the country, and they can extend it to the rest without much effort. (Though they are likely to demand heavy subsidies from the state to do so.) If investing in high-speed Internet access can be compared to the Eisenhower administration's investment in freeways, a promise of 4 Mbps is like a promise to surface all dirt roads with asphalt; it will make the ride smoother, but drivers will still be stuck in a single lane behind the feed truck. It won't give them multi-lane highways.

At the same time, a 4-Mbps goal gives corporate America a pass; it allows the cable distributors to assert that they have already made all the necessary investments. They are poised to provide the richest Americans with profitable asymmetrical high-speed access while leaving ample wiggle-room for their own "premium" bundled services.

As a result, the firmly entrenched digital divide, with rural, poor, and minority areas poking along with publicly subsidized 4-Mbps services while urban and suburban residents pay as much as they can spare to access high bandwidth, will remain the status quo. And there America will stagnate, while other countries rocket ahead.

What does America really need? For starters, most Americans should have access to reasonably priced 1-Gb symmetric fiber-to-the-home networks. This would mean 1,000-Mbps connections, speeds hundreds of times faster than what most Americans have today. The copper-based lines are not up to the gigabit task because they cannot handle additional data. As we have learned, wireless connections work well for small screens carrying low-resolution images but cannot support the data rates that will be needed for each home. Only fiber will be able to cope with America's exponentially growing demand for data transmission.

Put it this way: using dialup, backing up five gigabytes of data (now the standard free plan offered by several storage companies) would take twenty days. Over a standard (3G) wireless connection, it will take two and a half days; over a 4G connection more than seven hours; and over a cable DOCSIS 3.0 connection an hour and a half. With a gigabit FTTH connection, it will take less than a minute. And if the fiber needs to be upgraded, all it takes is upgrading the electronics.

If America's communications infrastructure were the subject of concerted investment resulting in a fully fiber-based network, shipping large files to the cloud would be trivial: Hollywood blockbusters could be downloaded in twelve seconds; real-time video conferencing would become routine; gaming applications could become even more immersive; 3D and Super HD images could be in every household. Imagine businesses, both large and small, being able to run their enterprises using HD video conferencing or making online backups that took hours instead of days. Americans could be connected instantly to their co-workers, their families, their educational futures, and their health-care monitors.

But for this, America needs reliable, symmetrical gigabit-level connections to residences and business sufficient to support three or more two-way video streams. And America needs it now: the computing industry is working toward a data deluge that the country's slow, fixed-line connections will be simply unable to handle. Right now, the nation's backward-looking infrastructure is a bottleneck for the future of computing. Amazon and the online backup service Mozy have to send backup disks through the mail because the country's infrastructure is not up to the task of shipping large amounts of data. Services are becoming cloud-based—remote from users. But rather than update their core networks, carriers are imposing usage-based billing schemes that allow them to parcel out artificially scarce bandwidth; rather than expand, they're propping up their share prices and extracting more money from consumers.[28] All of this is good for the 1 percent but not for the 99 percent.

Opponents of a minimum fiber-to-the-home requirement will say that no one needs such a fast connection. But when municipal networks make fiber available, adoption rates for these connections are very high; even though fiber is a new (and rare) commodity, 50 percent of customers routinely sign up.[29] America is a nation of fast adopters and innovators, given the chance; if the infrastructure is there, the American market will find uses for it. But without that fast nationwide fiber infrastructure, America will not be the country that produces the next big idea, the next Google, for the world market of fast connections.

Just as the Nixon White House staff suggested, U.S. policies should require separation between wholesale and retail access facilities and between wholesale transport and content. The government should support municipal networks and ensure the freedom within which local initiatives can operate, so that the next Terry Huval can install a city network without slogging through years of exhausting litigation.

This support should include upgrading core networks to make truly high speeds possible throughout America's communications ecosystem, preempting state laws that make municipal networks impossible, making available the long term, low-interest financing independent actors need to build and maintain fiber, and regulating the prices of wholesale transmission facilities so that competitors can count on this input when planning their own services. Municipally controlled fiber networks will route around the second-best installations now sold to residents by the incumbent cable companies.

To do this, though, America needs to move to a utility model. This is not to say there is no role for private industry. AT&T's early-twentieth-century chief Theodore Vail was right when he said in 1915 that only large corporations with extensive resources are capable of initially mass-producing communications infrastructure at low prices; economies of scale are needed. The tradeoff, as Vail recognized, is that public supervision and control are needed to encourage "the highest possible standard in plant, the utmost extension of facilities, the highest efficiency in service, [and] rigid economy in operation" by the private actors providing the public service.[30] Higher adoption of high-speed Internet access will require dramatically higher capital spending. Wall Street hates this; falling returns on capital are anathema to private investment markets. But without universal fiber access, America's private market for innovation and ingenuity will cease to compete. Americans need to stop treating this commodity as if it were a first-run art film—expensive, luxurious, high-margin, and available only in urban areas. In urban areas, providers of fiber must allow competing network access operators use of their systems at fixed and reasonable rates, and the providers should be allowed to earn returns at a set percentage above their investments. They could charge the retail operators a fixed fee per unit of data; in exchange, they would need to build a sufficiently robust fiber baseline. In rural areas, independents should have easier access to capital to serve all Americans.

And these physical connections to homes must be open to all Internet service providers, so that customers have choices of operators. The rates charged can support building network hardware in difficult to reach areas. Where public subsidies are needed, they should be given in the form of reasonably priced "middle mile" optical fiber backbone installations that do not provide Internet connectivity themselves. Capacity via these middle-mile links can be leased to other carriers, local governments, schools, hospitals, and other businesses. Less-speedy wireless connections should be the permitted minimum connection only to towns of fewer than twenty thousand people and remote areas.

Moving from a high-speed Internet access model based on overcharging rich, urban residents for bundles of services while letting the state subsidize slow access for poor and rural residents to a model based on the assumption that America requires fast, standard, reliable, and unbundled fiber-optic Internet access at reasonable prices will present many challenges. But the paradoxical lesson Americans learned from both the antitrust suit against Standard Oil and the breakup of AT&T is that government intervention is necessary to ensure unfettered competition. Voluntary services from private carriers are costly gifts that do little to move the country forward.

The incumbent communications companies have no interest in switching to fiber deployments that will cannibalize their existing revenues, and they will resist this move with every tool they have. There will be years of litigation; the carriers will claim that any attempt to regulate basic high-speed Internet access is an expropriation of their property. They will claim that their rights as "speakers" under the First Amendment have been trampled on. They will attack whoever is president at the time, saying (as John D. Rockefeller did of Teddy Roosevelt) that he or she was "venturing with rash experiments" and "impeding prosperity" by "advocating measures subversive of industrial progress."[31] They will make it extraordinarily difficult to investigate their practices and books. They will embroil the transition toward coherent Internet access policy in a long, slowly moving grind. The government may need to settle some disputes with hefty payments, and carrying out the cut-over to the new system will be a multi-year effort. America will need an army of Terry Huvals.

How much would it cost to bring fiber to the homes of all Americans? Encouraged by the wireless industry, the FCC estimated in March 2010 that it would take about $350 billion. According to the Bill and Melinda Gates Foundation, all anchor institutions across America—schools, libraries, hospitals, and government buildings—could be wired with fiber for just $12 billion. Thus the $350 billion estimate seems wildly high, and the $12 billion would not cover individual residences and businesses. Corning, the American glass manufacturer, and others have estimated that the real cost of bringing fiber to most Americans is between $50 and $90 billion.[32]

Think about what $90 billion means in terms of the total U.S. budget. Security agencies were given a combined total of $682.8 billion in discretionary funding during 2010. The Defense Department was given $80 billion in FY 2010 just for research, development, testing, and evaluation of new weapons systems. For the same amount that the country spends on defense research in one year, America could bring access to fiber networking to all Americans for generations. Eighty percent of the cost would be labor—which is good for job growth.[33] The payback to the operators would be slow; in exchange, the economy would be stimulated via a massive national infrastructure project that would set the stage for strong economic and cultural health for generations to come.

Regulation of utilities has had a long and difficult history in the United States. Every once in a while, Americans get it right. In the Progressive era, farmers who were furious at the limited opportunities to get their goods to market rose up and persuaded the country to regulate the railroads and Standard Oil. The country was networked with taxpayer-financed freeways under a Republican president, Eisenhower; when cloverleafs became crowded, the nation re-built the freeways with stacked levels. Someone's ox is always gored by government involvement; when the freeways were installed, the railroads were undermined. But it was worth it.

The government standardizes, regulates, provides tax subsidies, and puts price supports in place every day. By abdicating that task with regard to the utility service of high-speed Internet access, federal agencies have enabled a situation in which a few companies control America's informational destinies and policies.

Americans must rest their hopes on the generation after mine—people now in their twenties and thirties. My generation, which came of age after the breakup of the New Deal consensus, has succumbed to the idea that markets fix everything and that the government has no business intervening in things like privately provided high-speed Internet access. The very rich among my generation, the people who have the time to be involved in politics, often don't care about public infrastructure; as one of my media-industry interviewees said to me, "I don't know anyone who rides the subway."

America needs more people who can calmly and rationally oppose the free-marketeer rhetoric. People who don't have the knee-jerk response that "we tried regulation in the 1996 Telecommunications Act and it didn't work." People who see the public provision of high-speed Internet as a vital role of the public sector, who are willing to fight for years against vested interests to make it happen. People who can understand this issue and then channel their understanding into useful, long-term political engagement. People who will make this an electoral issue for all public offices.

The country's current political leaders operate with a sense of constraint. Convinced that they have little freedom to act, they find it increasingly difficult to act at all. Even though a core function of the modern state is to provide certain goods and services that are in the public interest—such as transportation, communication, clean water, sewage systems, and electricity—the complexities of modern-day applications and devices, and the enormous market and political power of both wired and wireless carriers, have been allowed by U.S. policy leaders to create a spectacularly dismal national communications infrastructure.

American leaders need to insist on the nation's shared interests. They need to have conviction and authority as well as a coherent set of principles and policies. At the moment, the carriers themselves seem to be in charge. Like J. P. Morgan in 1902, they view government as—at best—a peer; at worst, they have no respect for government save as a client for their surveillance and networking systems. Without a strong, sympathetic, authoritative policy, the development of widespread, low-cost, very-high-speed Internet access will not happen. Without it, America will have no free market for new investment in uses of the network. America needs a plan. The incumbents have their plan, and it is working well for them. But it is not working for the rest of the country.

Without government intervention, there would have been no Internet in the first place. Sen. Al Franken knows this. At a morning meeting with me at his office in September 2010, he sat on a couch looking a little sleepy, and recalled a speech he had recently made. "I was at an FCC meeting in Minneapolis, a public event out there," he said, where "some folks said, 'Keep the Internet the Way It Is.'" He laughed briefly. "You want to say, 'That's what we're doing.'" Franken shook his head. "They'd say, 'Get the government out of the Internet, it was developed by free enterprise.'" Franken answered himself, with humor, "'No, it wasn't, it was developed by DARPA [Defense Advanced Research Projects Agency, a federal agency].'"

He went on. "Aside from . . . having to deal with people who . . . are just reflexively anti any kind of regulation—even if it's regulation to make sure that the Internet is the way it is and it has been from the very beginning, it's the much much bigger issue of making sure that we have a free and open Internet, free for innovation, free for freedom of speech, it's desperately important to our first amendment rights and to the functioning of a democracy." I asked him what he thought would happen in the next five years on this issue. He sat up on the couch, bristling with earnestness. "I think they'll write of this period: this was the moment in which the Internet was saved by a few brave souls who had the vision to see what was happening and took tremendous political risks and summoned up an amazing amount of courage to save not just the country but the world as we know it." And then he laughed, self-mockery taking its turn. "Not to be self-serving."[34]

Since America last tried to regulate the cable industry, in 1992, the world of communications has been transformed. The Internet has taken the place of the telephone as the world's basic, general-purpose, two-way communication medium. All Americans need high-speed Internet access, just as they need clean water, clean air, and electricity. But they have allowed a naive belief in the power and beneficence of the free market to cloud their vision. The enormous private cable distributors—particularly Comcast— on whom the country increasingly depends for high-speed Internet access have a giant conflict of interest. Comcast is a great American success story, but its interests are not necessarily aligned with those of the country as a whole. Their interest is in keeping their profit margins as high as possible by exacting tolls from any independent company or entrepreneur seeking to use their wires, and from bundling and pricing their services so that Americans pay a lot of money for products they're not sure they need. No competitive pressure will force these companies to act otherwise. Traditional wisdom dictated that competition would protect consumers from the cable companies' abuses and obviate the need for regulation, but things did not work out that way, and now America has the worst of both worlds: no competition and no regulation.

Incumbents always have an interest in slowing down developments that might disrupt their plans. Comcast has an interest in slowing the advent of fast, cheap, reliable, universal Internet access. The only threat it faces is action by the government to force it to respect the valuable tradition of common carriage. While concerned citizens continue fighting that battle in the courts—which will take time—all Americans can work on another idea that is as old as the electrical cooperative: encouraging towns and municipalities to oversee their own open-access, nondiscriminatory, fast fiber networks. When it comes to bringing high-speed Internet access to all Americans, the country cannot afford to fail.

NOTES

Introduction

1. As of May 2012, Comcast was the largest high-speed Internet access provider in the nation, with nearly 19 million subscribers—a nearly 14 percent gain over the previous two years. The company added nearly half a million new subscribers during the first quarter of 2012, its best quarterly result in four years. The Associated Press, "Subscriber Data from Internet Service Providers," May 8, 2012. As will be clear from this book, Comcast is rapidly gaining subscribers as telephone companies Verizon and AT&T steadily and steeply lose copper-phone-line customers and cease expanding their fiber installations. With more people using the Internet to access bandwidth-consuming services such as Spotify, Netflix, and Major League Baseball games, copper high-speed Internet access (DSL) does not provide adequate service.

2. As of June 2011, the Organisation for Economic Co-operation and Development (OECD) ranked America fifteenth among developed nations for wired Internet access adoption.

3. Governments that have intervened in high-speed Internet markets have seen higher and earlier levels of adoption and lower subscriber charges. Many have required their telecommunications providers to sell access to parts of their network to competitors at regulated rates, so the competition will lead to lower prices. See Berkman Center for Internet and Society, "Next Generation Connectivity: A Review of Broadband Internet Transitions Around the World," February 2010. Meanwhile, they are working toward, or already have, fiber-optic networks that will be inexpensive, standardized, ubiquitous, and equally fast for uploading and downloading. Many countries, not only developed nations like South Korea, Sweden, and Japan but also less-developed ones such as Portugal and Russia, are already well on their way to wholly replacing their standard telephone

connections with state-of-the-art fiber-optic connections that will even further reduce the cost to users, while significantly improving access speeds. See Susan Crawford, "The New Digital Divide," *New York Times*, December 7, 2011.

4. David Folkenfilk, "Comcast to Buy 51 Percent Stake in NBC Universal," NPR, December 3, 2009, http://www.npr.org/templates/story/story.php?storyId=121046318.

5. Peter Svensson, "Verizon Winds Down Expensive FiOS Expansion," *USA Today*, March 26, 2010, available at http://www.usatoday.com/money/industries/telecom/2010-03-26-verizon-fios_N.htm.

6. "What if the cable operators are forced to rebuild their networks with fiber to the home? The best answer is perhaps a question. Who would force them to? . . . With no competitor other than Verizon FiOS (which exists in just 14% of the US) able to offer speeds that are even remotely competitive, there seems little risk that the cable [distributors] would feel compelled to widely upgrade" (Bernstein Research, "U.S. Telecommunications and U.S. Cable & Satellite: Nature Versus Nurture," May 2012, 139).

7. Senate Committee of the Judiciary, Subcommittee on Antitrust, Competition Policy and Consumer Rights, The Comcast/NBC Universal Merger: What Does the Future Hold for Competition and Consumers? 111th Cong., 2d sess., February 4, 2010, 8–10.

8. Folkenfilk, "Comcast to Buy 51 Percent Stake in NBC Universal."

9. Letter from Al Franken, United States Senator, to Marlene Dortch, Secretary of the Federal Communications Commission, Washington, D.C., June 21, 2010, available at http://apps.fcc.gov/ecfs/document/view?id=7020510670.

10. David L. Cohen, "Comments on Comcast NBCU Joint Venture Due Today at FCC," Comcast Voices: A Place for Conversations with Comcast (blog), June 21, 2010, http://blog.comcast.com/2010/06/comments-on-comcast-nbcu-joint-venture-due-today-at-fcc.html.

11. David L. Cohen, "The Intersection of Politics, Business, and Public Policy," posted by "SwarthmoreCollegePA," December 5, 2008, Thomas B. McCabe Lecture at Swarthmore College, http://www.youtube.com/watch?v=oZ2y2hcKHQM, at 18:56.

12. *"Competition in the Media and Entertainment Distribution Market": Hearing Before the H. Comm. on the Judiciary*, 111th Cong. 63 (2010) (Testimony of Jean Prewitt, President and CEO, Independent Film & Television Alliance).

13. Cecilia Kang, "Landline Rules Frustrate Telecoms," *Washington Post*, April 12, 2012, available at http://www.washingtonpost.com/business/economy/landline-rules-frustrate-telecoms/2012/04/12/gIQAG2XvDT_story.html.

14. Brian Stelter, "With Verizon's $3.6 Billion Spectrum Deal, Cable and Wireless Inch Closer," *New York Times*, December 2, 2011, available at http://mediadecoder.blogs.nytimes.com/2011/12/02/with-verizons-3-6-billion-spectrum-deal-cable-and-wireless-inch-closer.

15. Alex Sherman, "Watching Netflix Could Lead to Higher Cable Bills," *Bloomberg*, November 30, 2011, http://www.bloomberg.com/news/2011-11-30/netflix-viewing-seen-swelling-u-s-cable-bills-next-year-tech.html.

16. "Canada Joins Global Ranking of FTTH Countries," Fiber to the Home Council press release, February 16, 2012, http://www.ftthcouncil.org/en/newsroom/2012/02/16/canada-joins-global-ranking-of-ftth-countries.

17. Diffraction Analysis, November 2011, on file with the author.

18. Brendan Greeley and Alison Fitzgerald, "Pssst . . . Wanna Buy a Law?" *Bloomberg Businessweek*, December 1, 2011, http://www.businessweek.com/magazine/pssst-wanna-buy-a-law-12012011.html.

19. Manuel Roig-Franzia, "Brooksley Born, the Cassandra of the Derivatives Crisis," *Washington Post*, May 26, 2009, available at http://www.washingtonpost.com/wp-dyn/content/article/2009/05/25/AR2009052502108.html.

20. U.S. Department of Commerce, *Exploring the Digital Nation: Computer and Internet Use at Home* (Washington, D.C.: U.S. Department of Commerce, November 2011), available at http://www.ntia.doc.gov/files/ntia/publications/exploring_the_digital_nation_computer_and_internet_use_at_home_11092011.pdf

21. Josh Barbanel, "Comcast Chairman Digs In," *Wall Street Journal*, May 6, 2010, available at http://online.wsj.com/article/SB10001424052748703961104575226831270560658.html.

22. Josh Barbanel, "Co-op Triple Play for Chief at NBC," Wall Street Journal, July 6, 2011, http://online.wsj.com/article/SB10001424052702304760604576428363664891984.html.

23. Bernstein Research, "Comcast: Torrents of Cash," April 28, 2010.

24. Ron Chernow, *Titan: The Life of John D. Rockefeller, Sr.* (New York: Random House, 2008), 208.

25. Yinka Adegoke, "Malone: DirecTV Would Be 'Compatible' with a Telco," Reuters, November 19, 2009, available at http://www.reuters.com/article/2009/11/20/industry-us-libertymedia-malone-idUSTRE5AJ06K20091120.

26. Ron Chernow, *The House of Morgan: An American Banking Dynasty and the Rise of Modern Finance* (New York: Grove, 2001), 56.

Chapter 1. From Railroad to Telephone

1. Ron Chernow, *Titan: The Life of John D. Rockefeller Sr.* (New York: Vintage, 2004), 71.

2. Charles Perrow, *Organizing America: Wealth, Power, and the Origins of Corporate Capitalism* (Princeton: Princeton University Press, 2002), 134.

3. Frank Dobbin, *Forging Industrial Policy* (Cambridge: Cambridge University Press, 1997), 44–45.

4. Lewis Henry Hany, *A Congressional History of Railways in the United States, 1850–1887*, Bulletin of the University of Wisconsin no. 342 (Madison: University of Wisconsin, 1910), 49.

5. Dobbin, *Forging Industrial Policy*, 54.

6. Edward Winslow Martin, *Behind the Scenes in Washington* (New York: Continental, 1873), 271–74.

7. Dobbin, *Forging Industrial Policy*, 58.

8. Clarence D. Long, "Chapter 1: Introduction," in *Wages and Earnings in the United States, 1860–1890* (Ann Arbor: UMI, 1960), 4, available at http://www.nber.org/chapters/c2495.pdf.

9. David A. Skeel, *Debt's Dominion: A History of Bankruptcy Law in America* (Princeton: Princeton University Press, 2001), 51–52.

10. Peter Tufano, "Business Failure, Judicial Intervention, and Financial Innovation: Restructuring U.S. Railroads in the Nineteenth Century," *Business History Review* 71, no. 1 (Spring 1997): 28–29.

11. William G. Roy and Philip Bonacich, "Interlocking Directorates and Communities of Interest Among American Railroad Companies, 1905," *American Sociological Review* 53, no. 3 (June 1988): 368–79.

12. Louis D. Brandeis, *Other People's Money: And How the Bankers Use It* (New York: Frederick A. Stokes, 1914), 36.

13. Chernow, *Titan*, 136.

14. Worth Robert Miller, "Farmers and Third-Party Politics in Late Nineteenth Century America," in *The Gilded Age: Essays on the Origins of Modern America*, ed. Charles W. Calhoun (Wilmington, Del.: Scholarly Resources, 1996), 235–60.

15. Dobbin, *Forging Industrial Policy*, 74.

16. Paul Teske, Michael Mintrom, and Samuel Best, "Federal Preemption and State Regulation of Transportation and Telecommunications," *Publius* 23, no. 4 (Autumn 1993): 73.

17. Dobbin, *Forging industrial Policy*, 48.

18. Robert Rabin, "Federal Regulation in Historical Perspective" *Stanford Law Review* 38, no. 5 (May 1986): 1189–1326 (see esp. 1199–1202).

19. William G. Thomas, *Lawyering for the Railroad: Business, Law, and Power in the New South* (Baton Rouge: Louisiana State University Press, 1999), 84–99; Dobbin, *Forging Industrial Policy*, 78.

20. Ripley, *Railroads*, 452–53.

21. Teske, Mintrom, and Best, "Federal Preemption," 26.

22. Peter George, *The Emergence of Industrial America: Strategic Factors in American Economic Growth Since 1870* (Albany: State University of New York Press, 1982), 155.

23. "Populist Party Platform (1892)," available at http://www.wwnorton.com/college/history/eamerica/media/ch22/resources/documents/populist.htm.

24. Theodore Roosevelt, *Presidential Addresses and State Papers: December 3, 1901 to January 4, 1904*, vol. 2 (Whitefish, Mo.: Kessinger, 2006), 556–57.

25. Rabin, "Federal Regulation in Historical Perspective," 1227–28.

26. Sherman Antitrust Act, 15 U.S.C. §§ 1–7 (1890).

27. Ron Chernow, *The House of Morgan: An American Banking Dynasty and the Rise of Modern Finance* (New York: Grove, 2001).

28. Chernow, *Titan*, 131–33, 226.

29. Mitchel P. Roth, *Crime and Punishment: A History of the Criminal Justice System*, 2d ed. (Belmont, Calif.: Wadsworth Cengage Learning, 2010), 199.

30. Brandeis, *Other People's Money,* 135–47.
31. Jerry L. Mashaw, "Federal Administration and Administrative Law in the Gilded Age," *Yale Law Journal* 119, no. 7 (May 2010): 1370.
32. Edmund Morris, *Theodore Rex* (New York: Random House, 2001), 60.
33. "Private Divestiture: Antitrust's Latest Problem Child," *Fordham Law Review* 41, no. 3. (1973): 581; Carl N. Degler, *Out of Our Past: The Forces That Shaped Modern America* (New York: Harper and Row, 1984), 272.
34. Chernow, *Titan,* 433.
35. Sherman Antitrust Act, 15 U.S.C. §§ 1–7 (1890).
36. Morris, *Theodore Rex,* 91–92.
37. Chernow, *House of Morgan,* 106.
38. Milton Handler, "Industrial Mergers and the Anti-Trust Laws," *Columbia Law Review* 32, no. 2 (1932): 184–85.
39. "1904: A Retrospect," *New York Times,* January 8, 1905; Morris, *Theodore Rex,* 313–16.
40. Carl Helmetag, Jr., "Railroad Mergers: The Accommodation of the Interstate Commerce Act and Antitrust Policies," *Virginia Law Review* 54, no. 8 (December 1968): 1493–94; A. J. County, "Consolidation of Railroads into Systems: A Review of Some of the Financial Considerations and Processes That Consolidation Under the Transportation Act Imposes." *American Economic Review* 14, no. 1, Supplement, Papers and Proceedings of the Thirty-sixth Annual Meeting of the American Economic Association (1924): 73–74.
41. Helmetag, "Railroad Mergers," 1495; Transportation Act, ch. 722, 54 Stat. 898 (1940); http://www.bnsf.com/about-bnsf/our-railroad/company-history/pdf/hist_overview.pdf.
42. Morris, *Theodore Rex,* 316.
43. Ernest Hamlin Abbott, "Introduction," in Theodore Roosevelt, *The New Nationalism* (New York: Outlook Company, 1910),vii–xxi.
44. Theodore Roosevelt, "Fourth Annual Message" (speech to Congress, December 6, 1904), available at http://www.presidency.ucsb.edu/ws/?pid=29545.
45. *Modern Business: A Series of Texts Prepared as Part of the Modern Business Course and Service of the Alexander Hamilton Institute,* vol. 14 (New York: Alexander Hamilton Institute, 1917), 237–43.
46. Samuel Huntington, "The Marasmus of the ICC: The Commission, the Railroads, and the Public Interest," *Yale Law Journal* 61, no. 5 (1952), 467–509.
47. Interstate Commerce Commission Termination Act, 49 U.S.C. §§ 101–6, 201–5 (1995). Railroad mergers and acquisitions are exempt from antitrust law and are reviewed by the Surface Transportation Board. The National Rural Electrical Cooperative Association claims that "the railroads' antitrust exemptions are antiquated, have no public policy justification and allow anticompetitive conduct. The resulting lack of competition, together with the Surface Transportation Board's past ineffectiveness, has allowed freight railroads to reap huge profits from electric cooperatives and other industries with no marketplace consequences or legal

accountability for their unreliable service and exorbitant rates and fees" (NRECA Fast Facts, May 2012, http://www.nreca.coop/press/fastfacts/Documents/Fast FactsRailCompetition.pdf).

48. Kimberly A. Zarkin and Michael J. Zarkin, *The Federal Communications Commission: Front Line in the Culture and Regulation Wars* (Westport, Conn.: Greenwood, 2006), 5.

49. Interstate Commerce Act of 1887, ch. 104, 24 Stat. 379 (1887) (current version at 49 U.S.C. §§ 501–7, 522, 523, 525, 526, 20102, 20502–5, 20902, 21302, 21304, 31501–4 [1994]). In *Munn v. Illinois*, 94 U.S. 113 (1876), the Supreme Court upheld Illinois state laws establishing minimum railroad rates and preventing rate discrimination, stating that private property "affected with the public interest . . . must submit to being controlled by the public for the common good."

50. Phil Nichols, "Redefining 'Common Carrier': The FCC's Attempt at Deregulation by Redefinition," *Duke Law Journal* 1987, no. 3 (June, 1987), 508–11.

51. Alfred Dupont Chandler and James W. Cortada, *A Nation Transformed by Information: How Information Has Shaped the United States from Colonial Times to the Present* (Oxford: Oxford University Press, 2003), 94.

52. Leonard Reich, "Industrial Research and the Pursuit of Corporate Security: The Early Years of Bell Labs," *Business History Review* 54, no. 4 (Winter 1980), 511; David Gabel, "Competition in a Network Industry: The Telephone Industry, 1854–1910," *Journal of Economic History* 54, no. 3 (September 1994): 543, 558; John Brooks, *Telephone: The First Hundred Years* (New York: Harper and Row, 1976), 122, 134.

53. Tomas Nonnenmacher, "History of the U.S. Telegraph Industry," *EH.net*, February 1, 2010, http://eh.net/encyclopedia/article/nonnenmacher.industry. telegraphic.us; John Brooks, *Telephone: The First Hundred Years* (New York: Harper and Row, 1976), 134.

54. Nonnenmacher, "Telegraph Industry," 248; "Loses on Its Messages: The Postal Accuses the Western Union of Discriminatory Methods," *New York Times*, February 7, 1911. As reported in the *Times*: "For messages thus transferred the Postal is obliged to pay the Western Union full rates and a further charge is exacted for additional words which indicate the transfer point and the date. By this arrangement the Postal loses about 10 cents on each message transferred."

On November 14, 1911, the New York Public Service Commission prohibited Western Union from imposing these additional charges ("Postal Telegraph Co.," *Wall Street Journal*, November 14, 1911). On February 9, 1912, Postal again complained that Western Union was charging for additional words ("Postal Again Complains," *New York Times*, February 10, 1912; "Postal Versus Western Union," *Wall Street Journal*, February 12, 1912). On January 16, 1914, the New York Supreme Court affirmed the New York Public Service Commission's decision to forbid Western Union from charging for additional words for telegraphs forwarded for Postal ("Western Union-Postal Telegraph," *Wall Street Journal*, January 16, 1914).

55. "Theft of Messages Charged by Postal," *New York Times*, April 1, 1912.
56. Gerald W. Brock, *The Telecommunications Industry: The Dynamics of Market Structure* (Cambridge: Harvard University Press, 1981), 155; Brooks, *Telephone*, 136.

Chapter 2. Regulatory Pendulum

Epigraph. Paul Starr, *The Creation of the Media: Political Origins of Modern Communications* (New York: Basic Books, 2004), 193.

1. Patrick R. Parsons, *Blue Skies: A History of Cable Television* (Philadelphia: Temple University Press, 2008), 121.
2. Ibid., 122.
3. Ibid., 122–25.
4. Ibid., 104. In a 1986 oral history, Smith noted that in 1949, when he first learned about cable, he thought it might be a common-carriage service. "It occurred to me that it might be considered to be a wire communications service for hire and, therefore, possibly a common carrier service subject to the jurisdiction of the FCC." After all, as he put it, "the subscriber paid the system owner to receive signals intended for reception and use by the public and to communicate the signals to the subscriber's television receiver. There were certainly other theories which could be argued but at the time I was a common carrier lawyer." He then drafted a report for the FCC noting that the Commission could classify cable this way. But after he left the FCC, Smith changed his mind: "Later, after I had left the FCC and was in private practice the existence of that report came to light while I was representing the National Community Antenna Association in hearings before the Senate Interstate and Foreign Commerce Committee where I was arguing that community antenna services were not common carriers or any form of public utility. When teased about this apparent turn around by Kenneth Cox, who was special counsel to the Senate Committee, I told him that when I wrote the report I thought I was right, but that this time I knew I was right" (Ed Parsons, interview with E. Stratford Smith, March 31, 1986, the Cable Center, Barco Library, Hauser Oral and Video History Collection, available at http://www.cablecenter.org/content.cfm?id=667).
5. Parsons, *Blue Skies*, 195.
6. Ibid., 171, 173–90, 196–206.
7. *United States v. Southwestern Cable Co.*, 392 U.S. 157 (1968); Parsons, *Blue Skies*, 247–48.
8. *Teleprompter Corp. v. Columbia Broadcasting System, Inc.*, 415 U.S. 394 (1974); Parsons, *Blue Skies*, 238–46, 350–51.
9. Cabinet Committee on Cable Communications, "Cable: Report to the President" (1974), 20. Two other studies at about the same time argued that cable should be treated as a common carrier of some kind. See Committee for Economic Development, *Broadcasting and Cable Television: Policies for Diversity and Change* (New York: CED, 1975), and Sloan Commission of Cable Communications, *On the Cable: The Television of Abundance* (New York: McGraw-Hill, 1971).

10. Parsons, *Blue Skies*, 344–46.

11. Monroe E. Price, "Requiem for the Wired Nation: Cable Rulemaking at the FCC," *Virginia Law Review* 61, no. 3 (April 1975): 572.

12. Walt Mossberg, "Show Me the Money," *Wall Street Journal*, June 2, 2009.

13. Parsons, *Blue Skies*, 227, 260.

14. Representative Ed Markey, interview with the author, January 2011.

15. Parsons, *Blue Skies*, 90, 92–96.

16. *In the Matter of the Associated Bell Sys. Co.'s Tariffs for Channel Serv. for Use by Cmty. Antenna Television Sys.*, 6 F.C.C.2d 433 (1967); *In the Matter of California Water & Tel. Co. Tariff F.C.C. No. 1 & Tariff F.C.C. No. 2 Applicable to Channel Serv. for Use by Cmty. Antenna Television Sys.; In the Matter of the Associated Bell Sys. Co.'s Tariffs for Channel Serv. for Use by Cmty. Antenna Television Sys.; In the Matter of the Gen. Tel. Sys. & United Utilities, Inc., Co.'s Tariffs for Channel Serv. for Use by Cmty. Antenna Television Sys.*, 22 F.C.C.2d 10 (1970).

17. Memorandum Opinion and Order in Docket 16928, 37 Rad. Reg. 2d (P & F) 1166 (July 28, 1976); Parsons, *Blue Skies*, 360.

18. Parsons, *Blue Skies*, 360; Communications Act Amendment of 1978, Pub. L. No. 95–234, Sect. 6 Stat 33–35 (1978) (codified as amended at 47 U.S.C. § 224).

19. Parsons, *Blue Skies*, 298–320, 365–69.

20. Paul Baran, "Convergence: Past, Present, and Future," lecture presented at CableLabs Winter Conference, February 9–11, 1999.

21. Parsons, *Blue Skies*, 404–15.

22. Ibid., 473–79. Cable Communications Act of 1984, Pub. Law 98-549, 1984 98 Stat. 2779, codified at 47 U.S.C. sec. 521 et seq.

23. Parsons, *Blue Skies*, 498–501, 544–46.

24. Ronald Goldfarb, *TV or Not TV: Television, Justice, and the Courts* (New York: New York University Press, 2000), 137.

25. Ken Auletta, "Annals of Communications: John Malone, Flying Solo," *New Yorker*, February 7, 1994.

26. Parsons, *Blue Skies*, 469–71; "Cable Rate Hikes Anger Residents of Oregon City," *Multichannel News*, October 24, 1988 (citing "indifferent service, unanswered telephone calls, arbitrary programming changes and rate increases" by TCI). In 1988, Congress held hearings into citizen complaints about cable customer service. Problems included "poor signal quality, inadequate service, decrepit system infrastructures, escalating subscriber rates, with monopolistic cable operators behind the whole scam," as reported in K. Van Lewen and R. Stoddard, "What's Wrong with the Cable Act," *Cable Television Business* (March 1, 1989): 58–61.

27. Mark Robichaux, *Cable Cowboy: John Malone and the Rise of the Modern Cable Business* (Hoboken, N.J.: Wiley, 2002), 95.

28. Parsons, *Blue Skies*, 544, 569–75; Andrew Kupfer, "The No. 1 in Cable Has Big Plans," *Fortune*, June 28, 1993, available at *CNN Money*, http://money.cnn.com/magazines/fortune/fortune_archive/1993/06/28/78011/index.htm.

29. Robichaux, *Cable Cowboy*, 104–8; Parsons, *Blue Skies*, 581–83, 540–41. John Malone today is the largest private landowner in America, with more than two million acres of land. See "2011 Land Report 100," *Land Report*, available at http:// www.landreport.com/americas-100-largest-landowners/.

30. General Accounting Office, *Report to the Chairman, Subcommittee on Telecommunications and Finance, Committee on Energy and Commerce, House of Representatives, 1991 Survey of Cable Television Rates and Services*, GAO/RCED-91-195 (July 17, 1991), 4–5.

31. Parsons, *Blue Skies*, 577–78.

32. Ibid., 554–62, 567–68, 570–72.

33. Robichaux, *Cable Cowboy*, 117–18, 570–72.

34. "Company News: House Gets Cable TV Bill," *Reuters*, March 26, 1992.

35. William M. Kunz, *Culture Conglomerates: Consolidation in the Motion Picture and Television Industries* (Lanham, Md.: Rowman and Littlefield, 2007), 174.

36. *Broadcasting and Cable* (September 14, 1992): 6.

37. Parsons, *Blue Skies*, 578.

38. *"Competition in the Telecommunications Industry: Hearings Before the Subcomm. on Communications of the H. Comm. on Interstate and Foreign Commerce,"* 94th Cong., 2d Sess. 23 (1976) (Testimony of John DeButts).

39. Parsons, *Blue Skies*, 432–33.

40. "The American Telephone & Telegraph network is the most important communication network we have to service our strategic systems in this country . . . it seems to me essential that we keep together this one communications network we now have, and have to rely on" (*Department of Defense Supplemental Authorization Act: Hearing on S. 694 Before the S. Comm. on Armed Services*, 97th Congress 1 [1981] [Statement of Caspar Weinberger, Sec. of Def.]). "The Department of Commerce also lined up solidly in support of Defense's campaign to have the case dropped. Secretary Baldrige . . . wanted a legislative, not a judicial, solution of the telecommunications problem, and Baldrige felt that the presence of the case inhibited congressional action" (Peter Temin, with Louis Galambos, *The Fall of the Bell System: A Study in Prices and Politics* [New York: Cambridge University Press, 1987], 227).

41. Representative Ed Markey, interview with the author, January 2011.

42. *United States v. AT&T Co.*, 552 F. Supp. 131 (D.D.C. 1982), aff'd mem. sub nom. *Maryland v. United States*, 460 U.S. 1001 (1983). See also Parsons, *Blue Skies*, 433–34.

43. Joseph D. Kearney, "From the Fall of the Bell System to the Telecommunications Act: Regulation of Telecommunications Under Judge Greene," *Hastings Law Journal* 50 (Aug. 1999): 1395–1418.

44. Markey, interview with the author, January 2011; James C. Goodale and Rob Frieden, *All About Cable and Broadband* (New York: Law Journal Press, 2006), 116–17. Judge Greene's opinion was decided in 1991 and affirmed by the Court of Appeals in 1993: *United States v. Western Electric Co.*, 767 F. Supp 308 (D.D.C.), affirmed by *United States v. Western Electric Co.*, 993 F.2d 1572 (D.C. Cir. 1993).

45. Parsons, *Blue Skies* 632; H.R. 3626, 103rd Cong. (1994).

46. Parsons, *Blue Skies* 632–33; Telecommunications Act of 1996, Pub. L. No. 104-104, 110 Stat. 56 (1996).

47. Parsons, *Blue Skies* 633–35.

48. Federal Communications Commission, "Implementation of Sections 11 and 13 of the Cable Television Consumer Protection and Competition Act of 1992," *Second Report and Order*, 8 F.C.C.R. 8565 (Oct. 23, 1993).

49. Parsons, *Blue Skies* 643–47, 687–89.

50. Mark D. Schneider and Marc A. Goldman, "The USTA Decisions and the Rise and Fall of Telephone Competition," *Communications Lawyer* 22 (Summer 2004).

51. Parsons, *Blue Skies*, 688–89; Final Transcript, T-Q1 2006 AT&T Conference Call, Thomson Street Events, April 25, 2006, available at http://seekingalpha.com/article/9502-at-t-inc-q1-2006-earnings-conference-call-transcript-t.

52. Federal Communications Commission, "Chairman Michael K. Powell Launches FCC University," news release, August 15, 2002.

53. Declan McCullagh, "Newsmaker: The Technologist Who Has Michael Powell's Ear," *CNET News*, September 30, 2004, http://news.cnet.com/The-technologist-who-has-Michael-Powells-ear/2008-1033_3-5388746.html.

54. Michael K. Powell, "Digital Broadband Migration, Part II," remarks delivered at Federal Communications Commission Press Conference, October 23, 2001, available at http://transition.fcc.gov/Speeches/Powell/2001/spmkp109.html.

55. Michael K. Powell, "The Great Digital Broadband Migration," remarks delivered before the Progress & Freedom Foundation, Washington, D.C., December 8, 2000; Powell, "Before Cellular," remarks delivered before the Telecommunications Internet Association's CTIA Wireless, 2001, Las Vegas, Nev., March 20, 2001; Powell, "Q & A with Chairman Powell," Forrester Research Telecom Forum, Washington, D.C., May 21, 2001; Powell, Remarks delivered to the National Cable Television Association, Washington, D.C., June 12, 2001. Powell's speeches are available at http://transition.fcc.gov/commissioners/previous/powell/speeches.html.

56. Marguerite Reardon, "With Internet TV, Cable Wins Even if It Loses," *CNET News*, October 29, 2010, http://news.cnet.com/8301-30686_3-20021118-266.html.

57. Parsons, *Blue Skies*, 656.

58. National Cable & Telecommunications Association to Hon. Julius Genachowski, Re: *Preserving the Open Internet*, GN Docket No. 09-191; *Broadband Industry Practices*, WC Docket No. 07-52; *A National Broadband Plan for Our Future*, GN Docket No. 09-51, February 22, 2010.

59. Michael K. Powell, "Addressing Academic and Telecom Industry Leaders at University of California (UCSD)," remarks delivered at the University of California, San Diego, December 9, 2003), available at http://www.fcc.gov/realaudio/ch120903.ram.

60. Parsons, *Blue Skies*, 288; *Final Report and Order*, 21 F.C.C.2d 307, reconsidered in part, 22 F.C.C.2d 746 (1970), aff'd sub nom, *General Telephone Co. S.W. v. United*

States, 449 F.2d 846 (5th Cir. 1971); *Second Computer Inquiry,* 77 F.C.C.2d 384 (1980), aff'd sub nom, *Computer & Communications Industries Association v. FCC,* 693 F.2d 198 (D.C. Cir. 1982).

61. Parsons, *Blue Skies,* 433–34. The telecommunications service/information service dichotomy in the 1996 act largely codifies the preexisting regulatory distinction that the Commission had drawn between "basic" common-carrier communications services and "enhanced services." See Jason Oxman, "The FCC and the Unregulation of the Internet," Federal Communications Commission Office of Plans and Policy, July 1999, and Earl W. Comstock and John W. Butler, "Access Denied: The FCC's Failure to Implement Open Access to Cable as Required by the Communications Act," *CommLaw Conspectus* 8 (Winter, 2000): 10–12.

62. *Brand X Internet Services v. F.C.C.,* 345 F.3d 1120, 1127 (9th Cir. 2003) rev'd and remanded sub nom, *Nat'l Cable & Telecommunications Ass'n v. Brand X Internet Services,* 545 U.S. 967 (2005).

63. *In Re Inquiry Concerning High-Speed Access to Internet over Cable & Other Facilities,* 17 F.C.C.R. 4798, 4800 (2002).

64. *Nat'l Cable & Telecommunications Ass'n v. Brand X Internet Services,* 545 U.S. 967, 979, (2005) (Scalia, J., dissenting).

65. *In the Matters of Appropriate Framework for Broadband Access to the Internet over Wireline Facilities Universal Serv. Obligations of Broadband Providers, et al.,* 20 F.C.C.R. 14853 (2005).

66. Mark Thompson, "Questionable Future Looms for Common Carriage Regulations," *OJR: The Online Journalism Review,* December 2, 2004, http://www.ojr.org/ojr/stories/041202thompson/.

67. Michael K. Powell, "Preserving Internet Freedom: Guiding Principles for the Industry," Silicon Flatirons Symposium, *The Digital Broadband Migration: Toward a Regulatory Regime for the Internet Age,* University of Colorado School of Law, Boulder, February 8, 2004, available at http://hraunfoss.fcc.gov/edocs_public/attachmatch/DOC-243556A1.pdf.

68. Statement of FCC Chairman Kevin J. Martin, "Comments on Commission Policy Statement," FCC news release, August 5, 2005 ("While policy statements do not establish rules nor are they enforceable documents, today's statement does reflect core beliefs that each member of this Commission holds regarding how broadband internet access should function."); Statement of Commissioner Michael J. Copps, August 5, 2005 ("While I would have preferred a rule that we could use to bring enforcement action, this is a critical step.").

69. "We respect the leadership of Commissioner Copps and others in attempting to promote the principle of open networks in the Commission's policy statement today, but we also believe consumers and the market would have benefited if the FCC had included an openness requirement in the order itself," (news release cited in "FCC Allows Telcos to Close DSL," *In the Know, Public Knowledge,* August 24, 2005, http://www.publicknowledge.org/news/intheknow/itk-20050824).

70. Peter Eckersley, Fred von Lohmann, and Seth Schoen, "Packet Forgery by ISPs: A Report on the Comcast Affair," Electronic Frontier Foundation, last modified November 28, 2007, https://www.eff.org/wp/packet-forgery-isps-report-comcast-affair.

71. Peter Svensson, "Comcast Blocks Some Internet Traffic: Tests Confirm Data Discrimination by Number 2 U.S. Service Provider," *MSNBC*, last modified, October 19, 2007, http://www.msnbc.msn.com/id/21376597/ns/technology_and_science-internet/t/comcast-blocks-some-internet-traffic/.

72. Neda Ulaby, "Kevin Martin's Contentious Turn at Helm of FCC," *National Public Radio*, February 5, 2008, available at http://www.npr.org/templates/story/story.php?storyId=18711487; Matthew Lasar, "Comcast, Net Neutrality Advocates Clash at FCC Hearing," *Ars Technica*, February 25, 2008, http://arstechnica.com/old/content/2008/02/comcast-and-net-neutrality-advocates-clash-at-fcc-hearing.ars; Matthew Lasar, "Big ISPs a No Show at Second FCC Net Neutrality Hearing," *Ars Technica*, April 17, 2008.

73. *"Comm'n Orders Comcast to End Discriminatory Network Mgmt. Practices,"* 07-52, 2008 WL 2966428 (F.C.C. Aug. 1, 2008).

74. *Comcast Corp. v. Federal Communications Commission*, 600 F.3d 642 (D.C. Cir. 2010).

75. National Cable & Telecommunications Association (NCTA), "Cable Is Committed to Public/Private Efforts to Increase Broadband Adoption," June 2011 position paper, available at http://www.ncta.com/IssueBriefs/Broadband-Adoption.aspx?view=2; NCTA, "Cable: Availability (December 2011)," available at http://www.ncta.com/StatsGroup/Availability.aspx.

76. *Reply Comments of the National Cable & Telecommunications Association, In the Matter of Framework for Broadband Internet Service*, GN Docket No. 10-127 (August 12, 2010).

77. "The majority of U.S. broadband subscribers do not connect to the Internet via local-access infrastructure owned by an incumbent telephone company. The U.S. cable infrastructure was advanced and ubiquitous enough to allow cable companies to offer broadband access services to large portions of the country, in many cases before the telephone companies" (Federal Communications Commission, *National Broadband Plan Connecting America*, chap. 4, p. 37, available at http://www.broadband.gov/plan/. "Congress should make clear that Tribal, state, regional and local governments can build broadband networks" (ibid., chap. 8, p. 153).

78. As reported in Cecilia Kang, "FCC Chairman Genachowski Expected to Leave Broadband Services Deregulated," *Washington Post*, May 3, 2010: "The chairman of the Federal Communications Commission has indicated he wants to keep broadband services deregulated."

79. Federal Communications Commission, "The Third Way: A Narrowly Tailored Broadband Framework," news release, May 6, 2010.

80. "Reclassification is often referred to as the 'nuclear option,'" notes Ryan Singel, "FCC Prepares to Re-Regulate Broadband Providers," *Wired.com*, last modified

May 5, 2010, http://www.wired.com/epicenter/2010/05/fcc-reclassify-broadband/. "We are concerned with reclassifying broadband service as a Title II service, which could create regulatory uncertainty that could dampen investment and innovation and ultimately, damage the consumer experience" (Time Warner Cable news release, May 6, 2010, available at http://ir.timewarnercable.com/phoenix.zhtml?c=207717&p=irol-newsArticle&ID=1423688&highlight=).

81. AT&T reported spending $5,930,381.11 on lobbying in the first quarter of 2010; see AT&T Services, Inc., "Lobbying Report," available at *Public Knowledge*, http://www.publicknowledge.org/node/3095; Cecilia Kang, "Update: AT&T, Verizon Ramped Up Lobbying in Q1," *Washington Post, Post Tech* (blog), April 21, 2010, http://voices.washingtonpost.com/posttech/2010/04/phone_giants_att_verizon_turn.html.

82. Seventy-four House Democrats signed a letter to the chairman, asking that the proposal be dropped. See John Eggerton, "Democrats Take Aim at Title II," *Multichannel News*, May 24, 2010, http://www.multichannel.com/article/453016-Democrats_Take_Aim_at_Title_II.php. The letter stated, "The uncertainty this proposal creates will jeopardize jobs and deter needed investment for years to come. . . . We urge you not to move forward with a proposal that undermines critically important investment in broadband and the jobs that come with it" (Gene Grene to Hon. Julius Genachowski, May 2010, available at http://www.savetheinternet.com/node/30594). Thirty-seven Senate Republicans sent a letter as well: "There is scant evidence that the broadband market lacks competition or that consumers have been harmed in a manner that would warrant the heavy-handed 19th century regulations that you seek to impose on a highly competitive 21st century communications marketplace" (Senate Republicans to Hon. Julius Genachowski, May 24, 2010, available at http://netcompetition.org/Senate_Republican_Letter.pdf).

83. Ron Chernow, *Titan: The Life of John D. Rockefeller, Sr.* (New York: Random House, 1998), 544.

84. Federal Communications Commission, "FCC to Seek Best Legal Framework for Broadband Internet Access," news release, June 17, 2010.

85. *In the Matter of Preserving the Open Internet Broadband Indus. Practices*, 25 F.C.C.R. 17905 (2010).

Chapter 3. A Family Company

Epigraph. Ken Auletta, interview with John Malone, New York, October 16, 2002, available at http://www.kenauletta.com/2002_10_16_johnmalone.html.

1. Susan P. Crawford, "The New Digital Divide," *New York Times*, December 3, 2011; Shalini Ramachandran, "Behind Claims of 'Fastest' Internet Speeds," *Wall Street Journal*, January 31, 2012; Bob Fernandez, "Hoping for FiOS, Some Cities Now Feel Abandoned by Verizon," *Philadelphia Inquirer*, April 29, 2012, available at http://articles.philly.com/2012-04-29/business/31475013_1_fios-verizon-wireless-wireless-spectrum.

2. Bernstein Research, "Broadband Numbers for Susan Crawford," November 7, 2011, on file with author.

3. "In areas that include 75% of the population, consumers will likely have only one service provider (cable companies with DOCSIS 3.0-enabled infrastructure) that can offer very high peak download speeds" (Federal Communications Commission, *National Broadband Plan Connecting America*, chap. 4, p. 42, available at http://www.broadband.gov/plan/). Where Verizon FiOS service exists, there will be competition with cable Internet access service providers for high-speed Internet access at the speeds necessary to carry out real-time videoconferencing or watch high-definition video. Where there is no Verizon FiOS service, there won't be any competition, and consumers will have just one provider to choose from: their local cable monopoly. Most Americans—perhaps more than 75 percent of them—will fall into this category.

4. Robert C. Atkinson, Ivy E. Schultz, Travis Korte, and Timothy Krompinger, "Broadband in America—2nd Edition: Where It Is and Where It Is Going (According to Broadband Service Providers): An Update of the 2009 Report Originally Prepared for the Staff of the FCC's Omnibus Broadband Initiative, May 2011, 69, available at http://www4.gsb.columbia.edu/null/download?&exclusive=filemgr.download&file_id=738763.

5. "Ownership Chart: Cable," *Free Press*, http://www.freepress.net/ownership/chart/cable; Bob Fernandez, "Comcast Earnings Up, Subscriber Defections Down in 3Q," *Philadelphia Inquirer*, November 2, 2011, http://articles.philly.com/2011-11-02/news/30350594_1_comcast-shares-time-warner-cable-cable-tv-subscribers; Peter Svensson, Associated Press, "Comcast Will Start Charging Data Hogs Extra," May 17, 2012, *USA Today*, available at http://www.usatoday.com/money/industries/technology/story/2012-05-17/comcast-data-hog/55045306/1.

6. Associated Press, "Comcast Wins OK to Buy NBC." *Christian Science Monitor*, January 18, 2011, http://www.csmonitor.com/Business/Latest-News-Wires/2011/0118/Comcast-wins-OK-to-buy-NBC; TechnicallyPhilly, "Comcast Adds Internet Customers, Loses Cable Subscribers, Profits Jump," May 3, 2012, http://technicallyphilly.com/2012/05/03/comcast-adds-internet-customers-loses-cable-subscribers-profits-jump-roundup; Brian Roberts biography, Comcast Web site, accessed May 31, 2012, http://www.comcast.com/nbcutransaction/pdfs/Bios%202.13.10.pdf.

7. John Eggerton, "Kagan: Cable Subs Dip As Multichannel Subs Rise" *Multichannel News*, July 28, 2011, available at http://www.multichannel.com/article/471688-Kagan_Cable_Subs_Dip_As_Multichannel_Subs_Rise.php.

8. Craig Moffett, Nicholas Del Deo, Regina Possavino, and Amelia Chan, "U.S. Pay TV: Death, Taxes and Cable and Satellite Rate Hikes . . . Smaller Increases in Store for 2011," Bernstein Research, January 10, 2011; *United States of America, State of California, State of Florida, State of Missouri, State of Texas and State of Washington v. Comcast Corp., General Electric Co., and NBC Universal, Inc.*, No. 1:11–00106 (2011), available at http://www.justice.gov/atr/cases/f266100/266158.htm.

9. *Reply Comments of Time Warner Cable, Inc., In the Matter of Petition for Rulemaking to Amend the Commission's Rules Governing Retransmission Consent,* MB Docket No. 10–71 (June 3, 2010), 16, available at https://prodnet.www.neca.org/publicationsdocs/wwpdf/6310twc2.pdf; e-mail from telecommunications analyst Mitchell Shapiro to author, May 18, 2012 (summarizing Comcast 1Q ARPU public figures).

10. "Comcast Reports 1st Quarter 2012 Results," *Comcast Investor Relations,* May 1, 2012, http://www.cmcsk.com/releasedetail.cfm?ReleaseID=669493. Comcast's prices for DOCSIS 3.0 high-speed Internet access are much higher than prices for faster, better service elsewhere in the world. See Tim Karr, "Verizon's Broadband Bunk," December 8, 2011, http://www.savetheinternet.com/blog/11/12/08/verizons-broadband-bunk ("Compare our circumstances to those in Japan, for example, where Internet users are accustomed to surfing the Web at speeds of 100 Mbps [or megabits per second] at the same prices Americans pay for dial-up. In Hong Kong, one provider now offers a $20 a month "triple play" package that includes a blistering 1,000 Mbps data service.")

11. Craig Moffett et al., "Weekend Media Blast: A Tragedy of the Commons," Bernstein Research, March 26, 2010.

12. Giovanny Moreano, "The Highest Paid CEOs of 2010," *CNBC,* April 13, 2011, http://www.cnbc.com/id/42573061/The_Highest_Paid_CEOs_of_2010.

13. Peter Key, "Comcast CEO Roberts Sells, Donates Stock," *Philadelphia Business Journal,* August 12, 2010, available at http://www.bizjournals.com/philadelphia/blogs/technology/2010/08/comcast_ceo_roberts_sells_donates_stock.html; Douglas McIntyre, "The Most Powerful CEOs in America," *MSNBC, The Bottom Line* (blog), May 9, 2012, http://bottomline.msnbc.msn.com/_news/2012/05/09/11504828-the-most-powerful-ceos-in-america?lite; Comcast Investor Relations, Frequently Asked Questions, http://www.cmcsk.com/faq.cfm, accessed May 31, 2012 ("Comcast has a Class B common stock, which does not trade publicly and is held entirely by BRCC LLC [a limited liability company controlled by Brian L. Roberts, CEO and President of the Company] and two estate planning trusts of Mr. Roberts. The Class B common stock constitutes an undilutable 33 1/3% of the voting power of the total voting power of all classes of the Company's common stock.").

14. Mark Maremont and Tom McGinty, "Corporate Jet Set: Leisure vs. Business," *Wall Street Journal,* June 16, 2011, available at http://online.wsj.com/article/SB10001424052748703551304576260871791710428.html.

15. *"Competition in the Media and Entertainment Distribution Market": Hearing Before the H. Comm. on the Judiciary,* 111th Cong. 63 (2010); Geraldine Fabrikant and Laura Holson, "Family-Dominated Comcast Good at Pleasing Investors," *New York Times,* February 14, 2004, available at http://www.nytimes.com/2004/02/14/business/family-dominated-comcast-good-at-pleasing-investors.html.

16. *Joint Written Statement by Brian L. Roberts and Jeff Zucker to the Senate Judiciary Committee, Subcommittee on Antitrust, Competition Policy, and Consumer Rights,*

February 4, 2010, 2, http://www.judiciary.senate.gov/pdf/10-02-04%20Roberts-Zucker%20Testimony.pdf

17. George Szalai, "Comcast Feels Strategically Complete," *Hollywood Reporter*, December 7, 2009, available at http://www.hollywoodreporter.com/news/comcast-feels-strategically-complete-92063.

18. "CMCSA: Comcast Corporation at Morgan Stanley Technology, Media & Telecom Conference," conference call, March 2, 2011, transcript, 4, available at http://files.shareholder.com/downloads/CMCSA/0x0x447538/c20eba7d-049c-4dc7-a5cd-873f880b42bb/Comcast_MS_Transcript_3.3.11.pdf.

19. Ibid.

20. Geraldine Fabrikant, "The Heir Is Clearly Apparent at Comcast," *New York Times*, June 22, 1997, available at http://www.nytimes.com/1997/06/22/business/the-heir-is-clearly-apparent-at-comcast.html?pagewanted=all&src=pm; Geraldine Fabrikant, "AT&T's Cable Deal: The Family; Philadelphians Take a Giant Step Toward Leading the U.S. Cable Industry," *New York Times*, December 20, 2001, available at http://www.nytimes.com/2001/12/20/business/t-s-cable-deal-family-philadelphians-take-giant-step-toward-leading-us-cable.html.

21. Tom Southwick, interview with Ralph J. Roberts, July 27, 2000, the Cable Center, Barco Library, Hauser Oral and Video History Collection, available at http://www.cablecenter.org/content.cfm?id=641.

22. Joseph diStefano, *Comcasted* (New York: Camino Books, 2005), 35.

23. Jim Keller, interview with Julian Brodsky, June 16, 1998, the Cable Center, Barco Library, Hauser Oral History Collection, available at http://www.cablecenter.org/content.cfm?id=439.

24. "Cable Guy," Wharton Entrepreneurial Programs, University of Pennsylvania, Philadelphia, September 2009, available at http://wep.wharton.upenn.edu/gis/article.aspx?gisID=140.

25. Keller, interview with Julian Brodsky.

26. Ibid.

27. David Lieberman, "Father-Son Odd Couple Make Bid to Rule Cable. One's Calm. One's Wary. Together They're Comcast, *USA Today*, July 23, 2001.

28. "Cable Guy"; "WEP Alumni Impact: Julian Brodsky on the Genesis of Comcast," YouTube video, 0:19–21, posted by "wepvideo" September 21, 2009, http://www.youtube.com/watch?v=2e4xeps9B3w.

29. Keller, interview with Julian Brodsky.

30. Ibid.; "Comcast Is King of Its Empire," *Courier-Post* (Cherry Hill, N.J.), May 14, 2011.

31. Keller, interview with Julian Brodsky.

32. Southwick, interview with Ralph Roberts; "Comcast Corporation," *Funding Universe*, accessed May 31, 2012, http://www.fundinguniverse.com/company-histories/Comcast-Corporation-company-History.html.

33. Federal Communications Commission, "General Cable Television Industry and Regulation Information Fact Sheet," June 2000, available at http://transition.fcc.gov/mb/facts/csgen.html; Keller, interview with Julian Brodsky.

34. Media Commentary Council, *Channels of Communications* 5 (1985): 44; Keller, interview with Julian Brodsky.

35. Keller, interview with Julian Brodsky.

36. K. C. Neel, "The Life of Brian: Roberts Helped Shape the Industry He Grew Up In," *Multichannel News*, December 21, 2009.

37. Southwick, interview with Ralph Roberts.

38. Neel, "Life of Brian"; Lisa Furlong, "CEO List 2006," *Golf Digest*, http://www.golfdigest.com/golf-tours-news/2006-12/CEOrankings_gd2006.

39. Patrick R. Parsons, *Blue Skies: A History of Cable Television* (Philadelphia: Temple University Press, 2008), 481.

40. Betty Liu, "Liberty Media's John Malone Talks Communications," *Bloomberg Television*, July 14, 2010, available as YouTube video, "Malone Says Telecoms Lack 'Firepower' Versus Cable," posted by "Bloomberg," July 14, 2010, http://www.youtube.com/watch?v=QUbQRwKXeCU.

41. Parsons, *Blue Skies*, 481.

42. *Behrend v. Comcast Corp.*, 264 F.R.D. 150, 156 n.8 (E.D. Pa. 2010) (describing the acquisitions and including specific subscriber counts).

43. Reuters, "Comcast to Buy Scripps Cable Television Unit: Media: $1.6 Billion Acquisition Would Make the Firm the Third-Largest U.S. Cable Operator," *Los Angeles Times*, October 30, 1995, available at http://articles.latimes.com/1995-10-30/business/fi-62858_1_cable-operator; "Comcast to Buy MacLean's Cable," *Los Angeles Times*, June 20, 1994, available at http://articles.latimes.com/1994-06-20/business/fi-6190_1_cable-operator.

44. Neel, "Life of Brian."

45. Keller, interview with Julian Brodsky.

46. Leo Hindery, *The Biggest Game of All* (New York: Free Press, 2003), 73–74.

47. Parsons, *Blue Skies*, 670, 675; Matt Carolan, "AT&T Broadband and Comcast to Merge," *PCMag.com*, December 20, 2001, http://www.pcmag.com/article2/0,2817,58020,00.asp; "Comcast, AT&T Broadband in $52 Billion Deal," *ABC News*, December 20, 2001, http://abcnews.go.com/Business/story?id=87476&page=1#.ToPuVFHRfdk.

48. Parsons, *Blue Skies*, 675, quoting Rebecca Blumenstein, "Sweet Revenge: Bid for AT&T Cable," *Wall Street Journal*, July 10, 2001.

49. Jeremy Feiler, "RCN Out to Block Comcast," *Philadelphia Business Review*, August 19, 2002, available at http://www.bizjournals.com/philadelphia/stories/2002/08/19/story7.html?page=2.

50. Federal Communications Commission, "Memorandum Opinion and Order," MB Docket No. 05-192, July 21, 2006.

51. In June 2006, there were 65.3 million basic cable subscribers. Comcast had 21.7 million (33 percent) and Time Warner 11.1 million (17 percent). *In Re Annual Assessment of the Status of Competition in the Market for the Delivery of Video Programming, Thirteenth Ann. Rep.*, 24 F.C.C.R. 542, 555 (2009).

52. As this book went to press, the case continued: *Behrend et al. v. Comcast et al.*, "Memorandum Opinion and Order," CV. No. 03-6604 (E.D. Pa., April 12, 2012),

35, 58, 68 ("We find that the Class has produced evidence from which a jury could find in its favor on the [Sherman Act's] section 1 claim's requirement that Comcast conspired with competitors to allocate markets"; "We find that the Class has succeeded in creating a genuine issue of material fact that Comcast acted with predatory intent regarding RCN's access to cable infrastructure installation contractors"; "The Class has created a genuine issue of material fact that Comcast, a firm possessing market power, was able to lock up 70% to 77% of the potential customer base available to the new entrant. Because it possessed market power, its decision to target promotional discounts to deter a new entrant may be deemed predatory and an exercise of market power to maintain its monopoly.")

53. Todd Wallack, "A Father-Son Team That Usually Wins: Comcast Leaders Set Sights on Disney Co.," *San Francisco Chronicle*, February 15, 2004, available at http://www.sfgate.com/cgi-bin/article.cgi?f=/c/a/2004/02/15/BUGEN50OL71. DTL&ao=all.

54. David Murphy, "Verizon Axes FiOS Expansion," *PCMag.com*, March 27, 2010, http://www.pcmag.com/article2/0,2817,2361919,00.asp.

55. Bernstein Research, "U.S. Telecommunications and U.S. Cable & Satellite: Nature Versus Nurture," May 2012, 133, 132; Verizon Wireless Allies with Cable in $3.6 Billion Deal," *Bloomberg News*, December 2, 2011, http://www.bloomberg. com/news/2011-12-02/verizon-wireless-allies-with-cable-carriers-in-3-6-billion-spectrum-deal.html.

56. Liberty Media Corporation, "Q1 2011 Earnings Call," transcript, May 6, 2011, http://www.morningstar.com/earnings/PrintTranscript.aspx?id=27506514.

57. "A Decade of Innovation: The History of CableLabs, 1988–1998," CableLabs, June 4, 1998, available at http://www.cablelabs.com/downloads/pubs/history. pdf.

58. "Brian L. Roberts, Chairman & CEO, Comcast Corporation," accessed March 9, 2012, http://www.comcast.com/nbcutransaction/pdfs/Bios%202.13.10.pdf.

59. Rob Rowello, "Capturing Major Growth in Commercial Services: An Untapped Opportunity for Cable MSOs," Cisco Internet Business Solutions Group, August 2011, 2, http://www.cisco.com/web/about/ac79/docs/sp/Next-Generation-Access-Networks_Cable-MSOs_and_SMB_Market.pdf. Comcast offers a broad array of promotions and bundles, and it is very difficult to discover its standard pricing for standalone high-speed Internet access. It appears that this product was about $115/ month as of May 2012 for 50Mbps download service (http://www.comcast.com/ internet-service.html, accessed May 31, 2012). This price is far higher than the prices charged for speeds that are twice as fast (or more) in other OECD countries such as the Netherlands, Sweden, Japan, Korea, and France. See OECD, *Communications Outlook 2011*, 274 (esp. fig. 7.28), accessed May 31, 2012, available at http://www.mediatelecom.com.mx/doc_pdf/OCDE%20communications%20 outlook.pdf.

60. Keller, interview with Julian Brodsky.

61. Ibid.

62. Mark Robichaux, *Cable Cowboy: John Malone and the Rise of the Modern Cable Business* (Hoboken, N.J.: Wiley, 2005), 13.

63. Keller, interview with Julian Brodsky.

64. Parsons, *Blue Skies*, 620–21.

65. *In the Matter of Request for Comments on Deployment of Broadband Networks and Advanced Telecommunications*, National Telecommunications and Information Administration, U.S. Department of Commerce, Docket No. 011109273-1273-01 (Comments of Seren Innovations, Inc.), accessed March 9, 2012, http://www. ntia.doc.gov/legacy/ntiahome/broadband/comments4/Seren.htm.

66. Paul R. La Monica, "Comcast Bids for Disney," *CNN Money*, February 18, 2004, http://money.cnn.com/2004/02/11/news/companies/comcast_disney/.

67. Scott W. Fitzgerald, *Corporations and Cultural Industries: Time Warner, Bertelsmann, and News Corporation* (New York: Lexington, 2011).

68. Reinhardt Krause, "Upbeat Mood for Big Cable Show Unlike Gloom of 2009," *Investor's Business Daily*, May 10, 2010.

69. Bob Fernandez, "On Eve of His Departing, Comcast's Brodsky Looks Back at the Many Wins," *Philadelphia Inquirer*, May 1, 2011, available at http://articles.philly. com/2011-05-01/business/29493381_1_comcast-s-brodsky-comcast-board-julian-brodsky; *Testimony of Dr. Mark Cooper on Behalf of Consumer Federation of America, Free Press, Consumers Union Before the Senate Judiciary Committee Subcommittee on Antitrust, Competition Policy and Consumer Rights Regarding "The Comcast/NBC Universal Merger: What Does the Future Hold for Competition and Consumers?"* February 4, 2010, 1, available at http://www.freepress.net/files/Comcast_NBC_ Testimony_of_Mark_Cooper_Senate_Judiciary.pdf.

70. Ron Chernow, *Titan: The Life of John D. Rockefeller, Sr.* (New York: Vintage, 2004), 223.

71. Liu, "Liberty Media's John Malone Talks Communications."

72. Liberty Media Corporation, "Q1 2011 Earnings Call."

Chapter 4. Going Vertical

1. "*The Comcast/NBC Universal Merger: What Does the Future Hold for Competition and Consumers*": Hearing Before the Subcommittee on Antitrust, Competition Policy and Consumer Rights of the Committee on the Judiciary, 111th Cong. 12 (2010) (statement of Colleen Abdoulah, President and CEO of WOW!).

2. WOW! was the fifteenth-largest multichannel video programming distributor in America as of September 2011 with 432,000 video subscribers. "Top 25 Multichannel Video Programming Distributors as of Sept. 2011," National Cable & Telecommunications Association, accessed February 28, 2012, http://www.ncta. com/Stats/TopMSOs.aspx. WOW! has received wide recognition for its customer service, not only from *Consumer Reports* but in the J.D. Power and Associates Internet Service Provider Residential Customer Satisfaction Study. "Save a Bundle: How To Piece Together a Great Deal for TV, Phone, and Internet Service," *Consumer Reports*, February 2010, available at http://www.consumerreports.org/ cro/magazine-archive/2010/february/electronics-and-computers/bundling/

overview/bundling-ov.htm; J.D. Power and Associates Reports, "Press Release: Internet Service Provider Residential Customer Satisfaction Study: Customer Satisfaction with Residential High-Speed Internet Service Declines Slightly from 2009," October 28, 2010, http://www.jdpower.com/content/press-release/ CiPf4Zw/internet-service-provider-residential-customer-satisfaction-study.htm. Colleen Abdoulah made clear in her written testimony that smaller cable systems pay more for programming than large systems; programming entities justify this discrimination by claiming it is based on volume-rated cost differentials, and arbitration proceedings concerning this discrimination are prohibitively expensive (*"Comcast/NBC Universal Merger,"* 8).

3. *"Comcast/NBC Universal Merger,"* 12, 18.

4. Ibid., 34.

5. Tamber Christian, "The Financial Interest and Syndication Rules—Take Two," *Commlaw Conspectus* 3 (1995): 107.

6. *"Comcast/NBC Universal Merger,"* 6.

7. Ibid., 20.

8. Michael Riordan and Steven Salop, "Evaluating Vertical Mergers: A Post-Chicago Approach," *Antitrust Law Journal* 63 (1995): 522.

9. Gregory Rosston, *Benefits Report: An Economic Analysis of Competitive Benefits from the Comcast-NBCU Transaction*, Comcast Corp., General Electric and NBC Universal, Inc., May 24, 2010, 44.

10. Mike Farrell, "Agencies Approves [*sic*] Time Warner Cable Split," *Multichannel News*, February 16, 2009, http://www.multichannel.com/article/174237-Agencies _Approves_Time_Warner_Cable_Split.php.

11. David Lieberman, "Deal Would Give Liberty Reins of DirecTV," *USA Today*, December 7, 2006.

12. James Quinn, "AOL Officially Splits from Time Warner After 10 Years," *The Telegraph*, December 9, 2009.

13. Richard A. Epstein, "The Dogmatic Posture of a Consumer Advocate: A Second Response to Mark Cooper," *The Free State Foundation: Perspectives from FSF Scholars* 5, no. 6 (March 10, 2010): 1–6, 5–6, on file in *"Comcast/NBC Universal Merger*, available at http://www.gpo.gov/fdsys/pkg/CHRG-111shrg66290/pdf/CHRG-111shrg66290.pdf.

14. Holly Becker, *America Online*, Lehman Brothers, June 29, 2000.

15. Andy Kessler, "The Sinking Case of AOL Time Warner," *Wall Street Journal*, October 8, 2002.

16. "AOL-Time Warner Merger: 10 Years Later," *CNBC* video, January 4, 2010. http:// video.cnbc.com/gallery/?video=1376488035.

17. *Amendments of Part 69 of the Commission's Rules Relating to Enhanced Service Providers: Notice of Proposed Rulemaking*, 2 F.C.C.R. 4305 (July 17, 1987).

18. Karyl Scott, "Foes of FCC Plan Cry Foul," *Network World*, October 5, 1987.

19. Mary Sit, "Data Industry Threatened by Phone Fees, Hearing Told," *Boston Globe*, October 3, 1987.

20. Deborah Mesce, "Computer Users Criticize Plan to Hike Phone Fees," Associated Press, October 3, 1987.

21. "FCC Chief Defends Data Plans," Associated Press, October 3, 1987.

22. Representative Ed Markey, interview with the author, January 2011.

23. *Amendments of Part 69 of the Commission's Rules Relating to Enhanced Service Providers: Order,* 3 F.C.C.R. 2631 (April 27, 1988).

24. Markey, interview with the author, January 2011.

25. Ibid.

26. Kara Swisher, *There Must Be a Pony in Here Somewhere: The AOL-Time Warner Debacle and the Quest for a Digital Future* (New York: Random House Digital, 2003), 41.

27. "AOL: The Internet Company That Grew Up," *BBC News,* October 11, 2000, http://news.bbc.co.uk/2/hi/business/597479.stm.

28. Greg Sandoval, "AOL, Here's How You Screwed Up," *CNET News,* August 5, 2010, http://news.cnet.com/8301-31001_3-20012730-261.html.

29. "Thriving Netscape Could Set Standard for All Commercial On-Line Businesses," *San Francisco Chronicle,* April 3, 1995.

30. "The growth of the Web was supposed to kill proprietary online services. That was why the New Media committee at Time Warner had recommended against buying AOL in 1994" (David Streitfeld, "AOL Rode a Wave, Time Missed the Boat; How Steve Case's Crew Beat the Odds," *Washington Post,* January 16, 2000); Stacy Cowley, "Red Hat Picks up Pieces of Netscape," *InfoWorld Daily,* September 30, 2004. Kara Swisher (*There Must Be a Pony,* 58) quotes Steven Levy's crack of 1996: "Every day the Net gets closer to filling its ambitious promise, [the Big Three's—CompuServe, Prodigy, and AOL] clock ticks closer to midnight. They look a lot like dead men walking." Steven Levy, "Dead Men Walking?" *Newsweek,* January 21, 1996, http://www.thedailybeast.com/newsweek/1996/01/21/dead-men-walking.html.

31. "Historic Dates for AOL," *San Jose Mercury News,* January 11, 2000.

32. *In the Matter of Applications for Consent to the Transfer of Control of Licenses and Section 214 Authorizations by Time Warner Inc. and America Online, Inc., to AOL Time Warner Inc.,* 16 F.C.C.R. 6547 (January 22, 2001).

33. This statistic was set out in a staff report to FCC chairman William Kennard: Deborah Lathen, *Broadband Today* (Washington, D.C.: Federal Communications Commission, 1999).

34. Ibid., 11–12.

35. "Management's goal is to make AOL services available from any electronic device short of a blow dryer (and maybe even a blow dryer) within a handful of years" (Jeff Fischer, "AOL Anywhere," *The Motley Fool,* May 12, 1999, http://www.fool.com/portfolios/RuleBreaker/1999/RuleBreaker990512.htm).

36. Swisher, *There Must Be a Pony,* 156.

37. *In the Matter of Applications for Consent to the Transfer,* 16 F.C.C.R. at 6561.

38. Ibid., 6566.

39. Swisher, *There Must Be a Pony*, 80–81.
40. "AOL-Time Warner Merger," *PBS Online NewsHour*, January 10, 2000, http://www.pbs.org/newshour/bb/business/jan-june00/aol_01-10.html.
41. Nina Munk, "Power Failure," *Vanity Fair*, July 2002.
42. "Reliable Sources," *CNN*, January 15, 2000, http://transcripts.cnn.com/TRANSCRIPTS/0001/15/rs.00.html.
43. "NBC Warns on Merger Plans," *Financial Times*, July 26, 2000.
44. Allan Sloan, "3 Worst Deals of 2009," *Fortune*, November 17, 2009, available at http://money.cnn.com/2009/11/16/news/economy/bad_business.fortune/index.htm.
45. Content industry executive, interview with the author, June 24, 2010.
46. Andrew Jay Schwartzman, Counsel for Consumers Union, et. al., to Deborah Lathen, Chief, Cable Services Bureau, Federal Communications Commission, November 14, 2000, cited in *In the Matter of Applications for Consent to the Transfer*, 16 F.C.C.R. at 6658, n. 687.
47. "AOL-Time Warner Merger."
48. Tom Rosenstiel and Bill Kovach, "The Bad Business of Media Mergers," *New York Times*, January 14, 2000, available at http://www.nytimes.com/2000/01/14/opinion/the-bad-business-of-media-mergers.html?scp=2&sq=aol+time+warner+merger+press&st=nyt.
49. Richard Cotton, Executive Vice President and General Counsel, and Diane Zipursky, Vice President, Washington Law and Policy, National Broadcasting Company, Inc., to Magalie Roman Salas, Secretary of the Federal Communications Commission, July 24, 2000, cited in *In the Matter of Applications for Consent to the Transfer*, 16 F.C.C.R. at 6591, n. 298; David Hatch, "NBC on Record Opposing Consolidation," *National Journal*, December 7, 2009, available at http://techdailydose.nationaljournal.com/2009/12/nbc-on-record-opposing-consoli.php; Mike Masnick, "A Look Back: NBC's Words Against AOL/Time Warner Merger May Come Back to Haunt," *TechDirt*, December 8, 2009, http://www.techdirt.com/articles/20091207/1559557238.shtml.
50. *In the Matter of Applications for Consent to the Transfer*, 16 F.C.C.R. at 6644.
51. "AOL/Time Warner: Open Up," *The Economist*, November 23, 2000, available at http://www.economist.com/node/434130; *Bloomberg News*, "AOL, Time Warner Grant Access to 2nd Web Firm," *Baltimore Sun*, November 21, 2000, available at http://articles.baltimoresun.com/2000-11-21/business/0011210008_1_time-warner-aol-america-online.
52. Federal Trade Commission, "FTC Approves AOL/Time Warner Merger with Conditions," news release, December 14, 2000, http://www.ftc.gov/opa/2000/12/aol.shtm; Jim Hu, "FTC Approves AOL-Time Warner Merger," *CNET News*, December 14, 2000, http://news.cnet.com/2100-1023-249897.html; Federal Communications Commission, "Subject to Conditions Commission Approves Merger Between America Online, Inc. and Time Warner, Inc.," news release, January 11, 2001, http://transition.fcc.gov/Bureaus/Cable/Public_Notices/2001/fcc01011.txt.

53. In 2003, the AOL Time Warner Inc. board voted to drop "AOL" from its name. See Chris Isidore, "Time Warner Drops AOL Name," *CNN Money*, September 18, 2003, http://money.cnn.com/2003/09/18/technology/aol_name/. "Employees from the Time Warner side blame [Steve Case] for crippling their company (and destroying their retirement accounts)" (see Nina Munk, "Steve Case's Last Stand," *Vanity Fair*, January 2003, available at http://www.ninamunk.com/documents/SteveCasesLastStand.htm). In 2005, six former executives of Time Warner Inc.'s America Online unit and former business partner PurchasePro.com were indicted on charges of conspiracy to inflate revenues through back-dated contracts and revenue swaps. See Andy Sullivan, "Former AOL, PurchasePro Execs Indicted," *Reuters*, January 10, 2005, available at http://www.eweek.com/c/a/IT-Management/Former-AOL-PurchasePro-Execs-Indicted/.

54. As John Malone said in November 2009, "I think it [TW's inability to make vertical integration work] really speaks to the kind of silo mentality that Time Warner had. They were never really able to get the synergies out of the AOL deal, they were never able to get the synergies out of owning content and cable" ("John Malone and David Faber," video of interview, 40:00–40:45, *CNBC*, November 23, 2009, http://video.cnbc.com/gallery/?video=1340949341); Nina Munk, *Fools Rush In: Steve Case, Jerry Levin, and the Unmaking of AOL Time Warner* (New York: Harper Collins, 2004).

55. "Time Warner Chairman and CEO Jeff Bewkes Addresses the AOL Time Warner Merger," YouTube video, 1:01 from a TVWeek.com Innovation360 recording on October 13, 2009, posted by "trukdivad," October 16, 2009, http://www.youtube.com/watch?v=nxUz3zzfWJk.

56. John Borland, "Comcast, AT&T Cable Deal to Create Net Giant," *CNET News*, December 20, 2001, http://news.cnet.com/2100-1033-277261.html; David Lieberman, "Comcast to Buy AT&T Broadband," *USA Today*, December 20, 2001, available at http://www.usatoday.com/tech/techinvestor/2001/12/20/att-comcast.htm.

57. "AOL-Time Warner Merger: 10 Years Later"; "Levin Is Sorry for Creating AOL Time Warner," *New York Times, DealBook* (blog), January 4, 2010, http://dealbook.nytimes.com/2010/01/04/levin-apologizes-for-aol-time-warner-a-decade-later/.

58. The current combined values of the now-separated companies is about 14 percent of their worth on the day of the merger. Tim Arango, "How the AOL-Time Warner Merger Went So Wrong," *New York Times*, January 10, 2010, available at http://www.nytimes.com/2010/01/11/business/media/11merger.html?pagewanted=all. As Allan Sloan reported, "The day the deal was announced, Jan. 10, 2000, Time Warner closed at the equivalent of $184.50 a share. After almost 10 years of travail, the $184.50 has shrunk to about $42.25, consisting of one Time Warner share and a quarter of a Time Warner Cable share. The 77 percent decline is triple the decline in the Standard & Poor's 500-stock index over the same period" ("Deals: The Financial World's Turkeys of the Year," *Washington Post*, November 17, 2009, available at http://www.washingtonpost.com/wp-dyn/content/article/2009/11/16/AR2009111603775.html).

59. "AOL-Time Warner Merger: 10 Years Later."

60. Federal Trade Commission, "FTC Appoints Monitor Trustee in AOL/Time Warner Matter," news release, February 26, 2001, http://www.ftc.gov/opa/2001/02/montrust.shtm.

61. *In the Matter of Applications for Consent to the Transfer*, 16 F.C.C.R. at 6603-04.

62. David D. Kirkpatrick, "F.C.C. Lifts Ban on Video for AOL Instant Messaging," *New York Times*, August 21, 2003, available at http://www.nytimes.com/2003/08/21/technology/21AOL.html; Declan McCullagh and Jim Hu, "FCC Lifts AOL Messaging Limits," *CNET News*, August 20, 2003, http://news.cnet.com/2100-1032_3-5065650.html; Jim Hu, "AOL Asks FCC to Lift IM Restriction," *CNET News*, April 4, 2003, http://news.cnet.com/2100-1032-995595.html.

63. Ledbetter made this statement in an interview with Ray Suarez. See "AOL-Time Warner Merger," *PBS Online NewsHour*.

64. *Behrend v. Comcast Corp.*, 655 F.3d 182, 187 (3d Cir., August 23, 2011) (describing clustering as a strategy used by cable operators to concentrate their operations in regional geographic areas in regions where the operator already has a significant presence); *In the Matter of Review of the Commissioner's Program Access Rules and Examination of Program Tying Arrangements*, 25 F.C.C.R. 746, 764 (January 20, 2010) (describing incumbent clustering of cable systems). The acquisition of Adelphia Communications enabled Time Warner to cluster cable holdings in geographic areas. See Geraldine Fabrikant, "Time Warner and Comcast Seal Adelphia Purchase," *New York Times*, April 22, 2005, available at http://www.nytimes.com/2005/04/22/business/media/22cable.html.

65. "*Comcast/NBC Universal Merger*," at 14 (statement of Mark Cooper, Director of Research, Consumer Federation of America).

66. Charles B. Goldfarb, "The Proposed Comcast-NBC Universal Combination: How It Might Affect the Video Market," *Congressional Research Service*, February 2, 2010, http://assets.opencrs.com/rpts/R41063_20100202.pdf.

67. Comment by "Rick," in response to Karl Bode, "Will Cable's 'TV Everywhere' Be a Big Pile of Fail?" *Broadband Reports*, March 24, 2010, http://www.broadbandreports.com/forum/r24000094-Sorry-Karl-but. Two-dot ellipses were silently changed to three-dot ellipses.

68. Ken Auletta, "A Conversation with John Malone," October 16, 2002 (transcript), http://www.kenauletta.com/2002_10_16_johnmalone.html.

69. Ibid.

70. Steven Levy, "Dead Men Walking?"

71. "What makes this issue particularly touchy: Xfinity is only available to people who subscribe to cable video in addition to broadband. So Comcast's policy effectively could be a deterrent against its customers cutting the cable cord to rely on online video" (Shalini Ramachandran, "Netflix CEO's Comcast Complaints Draw in FCC," *Wall Street Journal, Digits* (blog), April 16, 2012, http://blogs.wsj.com/digits/2012/04/16/netflix-ceos-comcast-complaints-draw-in-fcc/.

72. "Time Warner Chief Invokes Past in Criticizing NBC Talks," *New York Times, DealBook* (blog), October 13, 2009, http://dealbook.nytimes.com/2009/10/13/ time-warner-chief-invokes-past-in-assessing-nbc-talks/.

73. Margaret Kane, "Time Warner to Split Off Cable Service," *CNET News*, April 30, 2008, http://news.cnet.com/8301-10784_3-9932113-7.html. News Corp. made a deal to swap DirecTV, along with additional assets and cash, for Liberty Media's stake in News Corp. See "News Corp. Reaches Deal with Liberty Media," *New York Times, DealBook* (blog), December 22, 2006, http://dealbook.nytimes. com/2006/12/22/news-corp-reaches-deal-with-liberty-media/.

74. Oliver E. Williamson, "Antitrust Enforcement and the Modern Corporation," *Economic Research: Retrospect and Prospect* 3 (1972): 22, available at *The National Bureau of Economic Research* Web site, http://www.nber.org/books/fuch72-2.

75. *United States v. Paramount Pictures, Inc.*, 334 U.S. 131 (1948).

76. Ibid., 154. Modern economists have suggested that vertical integration should be implemented as a solution to the vulnerabilities of complex, global companies. See "Moving on Up: Is the Recession Heralding a Return to Henry Ford's Model?" *The Economist*, March 27, 2009, available at http://www.economist.com/ node/13173671. Commentators have reported on a "return" of vertical integration in business. See Daniel Gross, "Dis-Integration? Why Michael Dell Needs to Act More Like John D. Rockefeller," *Slate*, August 17, 2006, http://www.slate.com/ articles/business/moneybox/2006/08/disintegration.html.

77. As a witness at the July 2010 FCC forum in Chicago about the deal, I expressed concern that the addition of the NBC Universal content to Comcast's current dominant distribution operations would enable and incentivize Comcast to constrain nascent competitive online pay-TV distributors and competition for high-speed Internet access provision to Americans. See Susan Crawford, "Comcast-NBCU Forum Today in Chicago," *Susan Crawford* (blog), July 13, 2010, http://scrawford. net/blog/comcast-nbcu-forum-today-in-chicago/1372/. Other critics suggested that a vertically integrated company could foreclose competitors from the market, stifling competition. See Charles B. Goldfarb, *The Proposed Comcast-NBC Universal Combination: How It Might Affect the Video Market* (Washington, D.C.: Congressional Research Service, 2010), 19; Emily Bell, "NBC Universal and Comcast's Merger Is No Joke," *The Guardian*, January 21, 2011, available at http://www.guardian.co.uk/media/2011/jan/21/nbc-universal-comcast.

78. *United States v. Microsoft Corp.*, 253 F.3d 34, 55, 60 (D.C. Cir. 2001).

Chapter 5. Netflix, Dead or Alive

1. *"The Comcast/NBC Universal Merger: What Does the Future Hold for Competition and Consumers?": Hearing Before the Subcomm. on Antitrust, Competition Policy and Consumer Rights of the Committee of the Judiciary*, 111th Cong. 24 (2010).

2. Ibid., 23.

3. "Only 8% of U.S. households with a television rely on antenna reception," according to the Consumer Electronics Association, "CEA Study: Consumers Are Tuning

Out Over-the-Air TV," survey, May 31, 2011, available at http://www.ce.org/Press/CurrentNews/press_release_detail.asp?id=12105.

4. See Nigel Hollis, "Why Good Advertising Works (Even When You Think It Doesn't)," *Atlantic*, August 31, 2011: "I often respond by pointing out that U.S. companies would not invest $70 billion (yes, that's the size of TV's ad market) in something they thought didn't work."

5. Shahid Kahn, "Time Warner Cable's iPad App," *Mediamorph* (blog), March 28, 2011, http://www.mediamorph.com/blog/?p=153.

6. Lauren A. E. Schuker, "Customers Say to Cable Firms, 'Let's Make a Deal,'" *Wall Street Journal*, December 29, 2011.

7. "From the richest to the poorest, inflation-adjusted incomes were lower in 2010 than they were a decade ago" ("Cutting the Cake: The Real Incomes of America's Richest and Poorest Households," *Economist Online* [blog], September 14, 2011, http://www.economist.com/blogs/dailychart/2011/09/us-household-income).

8. Liberty Media Corporation, "Q1 2011 Earnings Call," transcript, May 6, 2011, http://www.morningstar.com/earnings/PrintTranscript.aspx?id=27506514.

9. "For the moment it looks like satellite, telcos are continuing to gain video share, but the cable guys are driving to some incredible high penetration rates on broadband. I'm very impressed to hear that Comcast have 17 million broadband customers, out of what was it 22 million?" (ibid.).

10. Jessica E. Vascellaro, "At Comcast, No Fear of Web Video," *Wall Street Journal*, February 28, 2011.

11. "Comcast's CEO Discusses Q1 2012 Results—Earnings Call Transcript," *Seeking Alpha*, May 2, 2012, available at http://finance.yahoo.com/news/comcasts-ceo-discusses-q1-2012-163011159.html (the average revenue per user was up 4 percent from the previous quarter).

12. "Comcast, Time Warner, Bright to Sell Spectrum Worth $3.6 Bln to Verizon Wireless," *RTT News*, December 2, 2011, http://www.rttnews.com/1773694/comcast-time-warner-bright-to-sell-spectrum-worth-3-6-bln-to-verizon-wireless.aspx; Cecilia King, "Verizon Wireless Makes Marketing, Airwave Deal with Three Cable Companies," *Washington Post*, December 2, 2011.

13. Jessica E. Vascellaro, "Malone Is Fired Up by Cable and Ready to Buy," *Wall Street Journal*, July 12, 2010.

14. "Starz will bring 2,500 movies and TV shows to Netflix.com, through its Starz Play broadband movie service. Netflix subscribers will pay nothing extra—and may for the first time find that online streaming is a satisfying alternative to waiting for the mailman," wrote Brad Stone, "Starz Gives Netflix Fans a Reason to Stream," *New York Times*, October 1, 2008. "The original deal from 2008, in which Netflix paid an estimated $25 million annually—a paltry sum, executives say, compared with the hundreds of millions of dollars cable and satellite companies pay Starz for the same movies—is now seen as a major coup for Netflix, and a major mistake by Starz. Michael Nathanson, a media analyst at Nomura, called it 'probably one of the dumbest deals ever. Starz gave up valuable content for tens

of millions of dollars,'" noted Tim Arango, "Time Warner Views Netflix as a Fading Star," *New York Times*, December 12, 2010.

15. Stone, "Starz Gives Netflix Fans a Reason to Stream."

16. Sue Zeidler and Jennifer Saba, "Netflix, Epix Strike Programming Deal," *Reuters*, August 10, 2010.

17. Dean Takahashi, "Netflix Confirms Deal to Launch Kevin Spacey Series via Video Streaming," *Reuters*, March 21, 2011.

18. "Netflix Now Represents 29.7% of North American Peak Downstream Traffic," Spring 2011 Global Internet Phenomena Report, Sandvine, Intelligent Broadband Networks, May 17, 2011, available at http://www.sandvine.com/news/pr_detail. asp?ID=312.

19. "Netflix estimates it will spend about $600 million on postage this year, with the annual cost rising to $800 million within the next few years," reported Michael Liedtke, "Netflix Adds 1.1M Customers, 4Q Profit up 36%," Associated Press, January 28, 2010.

20. An article in *Forbes* described Netflix's open, collaborative approach to developing new algorithmic software designed to tailor individual customer video recommendations based on the customer's viewing history. See Lee Gomes, "Netflix's Law: The Future of Software," *Forbes*, November 12, 2009.

21. Janko Roettgers, "Netflix Streaming Users Now Outnumber DVD Subscribers 2:1," *GigaOM* video, January 25, 2012, http://gigaom.com/video/netflix-streaming-vs-dvds/.

22. As Don Davis reported, "Netflix is besieged with requests from manufacturers of consumer electronics devices to embed its software into their Internet-enabled machines so consumers can access videos from Netflix. 'It's possible that within a few years nearly all Internet-connected CE devices sold will include a Netflix streaming client,' Hastings said" ("Netflix Will Mail DVDs on Saturday, but Also Invest More in Streaming Video," *Internet Retailer*, April 24, 2009, http://www.internetretailer.com/2009/04/24/netflix-will-mail-dvds-on-saturday-but-also-invest-more-in-stre.

23. "Netflix said today that it 'hates' upsetting customers by raising prices as much as 60 percent and acknowledged that the customer backlash to the rate hike would likely stifle growth and hurt earnings in the short term," reported Greg Sandoval, "Netflix 'Hates' Upsetting Customers, but Most Won't Cancel," *CNET News*, July 25, 2011, http://news.cnet.com/8301-31001_3-20083201-261/netflix-hates-upsetting-customers-but-most-wont-cancel/?tag—ncol;txt. "Netflix lost 800,000 U.S. subscribers in the quarter that just ended, which was littered with PR nightmares including a price hike and the Qwikster debacle," noted Julianne Pepitone, "Netflix Loses 800,000 Subscribers," *CNN Money*, October 24, 2011, http://money.cnn.com/2011/10/24/technology/netflix_earnings/index.htm. While the loss of 800,000 subscribers is significant, the overwhelming majority of Netflix's 25 million subscribers elected to swallow the price hike and continue with the service.

24. Tim Arango, "Netflix as a Fading Star.".

25. Ibid.

26. Ben Fritz, Joe Flint, and Dawn C. Chmielewski, "Starz to End Streaming Deal with Netflix," *Los Angeles Times*, September 2, 2011.

27. Paul Bond, "Starz Not 'Reveling' in Netflix's Pain After Severing Ties with the Company, Says Top Exec," *Los Angeles Times*, December 5, 2011.

28. Ben Fritz, "Netflix Stock Drops 9% on News That Starz Deal Will End," *Los Angeles Times, Company Town* (blog), September 2, 2011, http://latimesblogs.latimes.com/entertainmentnewsbuzz/2011/09/netflix-stock-drops-9-on-news-starz-deal-will-end.html. Moreover, from the announcement of the price hike in July 2011 through the Starz's abrupt walkout on negotiations in September, and to the end of the fourth quarter, Netflix's stock tumbled from a high of three hundred dollars to below fifty dollars per share.

29. Elliot Van Buskirk, "Cable Departs from Hulu Model with 'TV Everywhere,'" *CNN Asia*, June 26, 2009, http://asia.cnn.com/2009/TECH/biztech/06/26/wired.tv.everywhere/index.html.

30. "Broadband gross margin dollars per subscriber were up even more at 5.4%, where margins expanded by 130 bps from the already stratospheric level of 93.2% a year ago (yes, ladies and gentlemen)," reported Craig Moffett, "Quick Take—Comcast—Designated Driver at the Buyback Party," Alliance Bernstein Research, February 16, 2011.

31. Yinka Adegoke, "In Switch, Cable Operators Want to Go 'a la Carte,'" *Reuters*, September 27, 2011, http://www.reuters.com/article/2011/09/27/cable-idUSSiE78K05L20110927.

32. "When retrans fever first erupted several years ago, broadcasters targeted small cable operators, satellite TV and new entrants such as Verizon FiOS with the first wave of deals. These newer companies lacked clout, either nationally or with heft of concentration in any one local market, so they pay the highest per capita fees," (Robert Marich, "Broadcast's $1 Billion Pot of Gold," *Broadcasting and Cable*, July 6, 2008, http://www.broadcastingcable.com/article/114424-Broadcast_s_1_Billion_Pot_of_Gold.php).

33. For example, in the latest deal between Comcast and ESPN/Disney, Comcast agreed in January 2012 to pay an undisclosed amount to Disney Corporation in order to strike a ten-year deal to carry all of Disney's stations and programming—including in an on-demand format—thereby cementing the distribution and reach of all of Disney's content. See Meg James, "Disney Partners with Comcast to Provide ABC, ESPN On-demand," *Los Angeles Times, Company Town* (blog), January 4, 2012, http://latimesblogs.latimes.com/entertainmentnewsbuzz/2012/01/walt-disney-co-partners-with-comcast-to-provide-abc-and-espn-on-demand.html.

34. Dawn C. Chmielewski and Ben Fritz, "Fox Restricts Free Online Access to Its Shows," *Los Angeles Times*, July 27, 2011.

35. Sam Schechner and Jessica E. Vascellaro, "Hulu Reworks Its Script as Digital Change Hits TV," *Wall Street Journal*, January 27, 2011.

36. King, "Verizon Wireless Makes Marketing, Airwave Deal with Three Cable Companies."

Chapter 6. The Peacock Disappears

Epigraph. "Don Geiss, America and Hope," *30 Rock*, Season 4, Episode 15, NBC Universal, March 18, 2010.

1. *"The Comcast/NBC Universal Merger: What Does the Future Hold for Competition and Consumers"*: *Hearing Before the Subcommittee on Antitrust, Competition Policy and Consumer Rights of the Committee on the Judiciary,"* 111th Cong. 12 (2010) (Statement of Senator Herb Kohl).

2. Robert Edelstein, "Jeff Zucker, President and CEO, NBC Universal," *Broadcasting and Cable*, October 20, 2009, http://www.broadcastingcable.com/hof/1603-Jeff_ Zucker.php.

3. Staci D. Kramer, "Zucker Will Leave NBCU Following Comcast Merger; All About Burke Now," *PaidContent.org*, September 24, 2010, http://paidcontent.org/ article/419-zucker-will-leave-nbcu-following-comcast-merger/.

4. Claire Atkinson, "NBC Boss Eyes $30M+ Exit Deal from Comcast," *New York Post*, June 2, 2010, available at http://www.nypost.com/p/news/business/see_ya_ zuckers_50BszoRLEkIzFgg7px5IFN.

5. Frazier Moore, "Two Media Companies, Two Bosses Exiting," Associated Press, September 24, 2010, available at http://www.boston.com/ae/tv/articles/2010/ 09/24/2_media_companies_2_bosses_exiting/.

6. Andrew Wallenstein, "Was Jeff Zucker Really So Bad for NBC Universal?" *Paid-Content.org*, January 28, 2011, http://paidcontent.org/article/419-was-jeff-zucker-really-so-bad-for-nbc-universal/.

7. *"The Comcast/NBC Universal Merger,"* 11 (2010) (Statement of Jeff Zucker, President and Chief Executive Officer, NBC Universal).

8. Amy Chozick and Brian Stelter, "Comcast Rises on Cable; Film Helps Time Warner," *New York Times*, November 2, 2011, available at http://www.nytimes. com/2011/11/03/business/media/internet-customers-and-advertising-sales-bolster-comcasts-profits.html.

9. Jon Lafayette, "An Amazing Story of Cable Network Margins," *Broadcasting and Cable*, November 22, 2011, http://www.navigationpartnersllc.com/an-amazing-story-of-cable-network-margins/.

10. "Corporate Info," *NBC.com*, accessed March 9, 2012, http://www.nbc.com/nbc/ header/Corporate_Info.shtml.

11. Jeff Gerth and Brady Dennis, "Loophole Helps GE Benefit from Bank Rescue Program," *Washington Post*, June 29, 2009 available at http://www.washingtonpost .com/wp-dyn/content/article/2009/06/28/AR2009062802955. html?sid=ST2009062803183; Rachel Layne and Rebecca Christie, "GE Wins FDIC Insurance for up to $139 Billion in Debt," *Bloomberg*, November 12, 2008, http://www.bloomberg.com/apps/news?pid=newsarchive&sid=a3I211f0pz9s&d bk; Cambridge Winter Center for Financial Institutions Policy, "The Killer G's:

Resolution Authority, Financial Stabilization, and Taxpayer Bailouts; Research Note," April 23, 2010, available at http://www.cambridgewinter.org/Cambridge_Winter/Welcome_files/killer%20g′s%20042310.pdf.

12. Rachel Layne, "GE Exiting NBC Universal Brings Immelt Cash," *Bloomberg*, December 3, 2009, http://www.bloomberg.com/apps/news?pid=newsarchive&sid=aMzZBVMqKcHc.

13. "Chief Executive Says GE Won't Sell NBC Universal," *Los Angeles Times*, March 12, 2008, available at http://articles.latimes.com/2008/mar/12/business/fi-ge12.

14. Ibid.

15. "NBC Universal History," NBC Universal, accessed March 9, 2012, http://www.nbcuni.com/corporate/about-us/history/; Moore, "Two Media Companies."

16. Layne, "GE Exiting NBC Universal."

17. Glenn Greenwald, "The Scope—and Dangers—of GE's Control of NBC and MS-NBC," *Salon*, August 3, 2009; Brian Stelter, "Voices from Above Silence a Cable TV Feud," *New York Times*, July 31, 2009, available at http://www.nytimes.com/2009/08/01/business/media/01feud.html?_r=2&src=twt&twt=nytimes,

18. Jonathan Blakely, "Connecting Dots: Obama Seeks Big Picture to Frame an Agenda," *ABC News*, January 25, 2010, http://abcnews.go.com/blogs/politics/2010/01/connecting-dots/.

19. Julianna Goldman and Rachel Layne, "Obama Asks GE's Immelt to Head Economic Advisory Panel, Replacing Volcker," *Bloomberg*, January 21, 2001, http://www.bloomberg.com/news/2011-01-21/obama-taps-ge-s-immelt-for-economy-panel-replace-volcker.html.

20. Tim Arango, "Vivendi's Stake in NBC Universal May Be Sold," *New York Times*, September 18, 2009, available at http://www.nytimes.com/2009/09/19/business/media/19electric.html; banking industry employee, interview with the author, July 2010.

21. Bob O'Brien, "GE Shares Pitch to 14-Year Low," *Barron's*, February 20, 2009, http://blogs.barrons.com/stockstowatchtoday/2009/02/20/ge-shares-pitch-to-14-year-low/.

22. Andrew Ross Sorkin and Tim Arango, "In Secret Meetings, Comcast Wooed G.E. and Won NBC," *New York Times*, December 2, 2009, available at http://www.nytimes.com/2009/12/03/business/media/03nbc.html.

23. Ibid.

24. "Mrs. Donaghy," *30 Rock*, Season 5, Episode 11, NBC Universal, January 20, 2011.

25. Sorkin and Arango, "In Secret Meetings."

26. Sharon Waxman, "Exclusive: Comcast in Talks to Buy NBC-Universal," *The Wrap*, September 30, 2009, http://www.thewrap.com/deal-central/article/exclusive-comcast-buy-nbc-universal-general-electric-8002.

27. Banking industry employee, interview with the author, July 2010.

28. Mitchell Stephens, "History of Television," *Groiler Multimedia Encyclopedia*, 2000 ed., accessed March 9, 2012, http://www.nyu.edu/classes/stephens/History%20of%20Television%20page.htm.

29. *Television History—The First 75 Years*, accessed March 9, 2012, http://www.tvhistory.tv.

30. Edmund Lindop and Margaret J. Goldstein, *America in the 1940s* (Minneapolis: Twenty-First Century Books, 2010), 106.

31. *Television History—The First 75 Years*.

32. Radio Corporation of America, "RCA-NBC Firsts in Color Television, a Chronological List of Significant Firsts by the Radio Corporation of America and the National Broadcasting Company in Color Television," news release, March 27, 1955, available at http://www.novia.net/~ereitan/rca-nbc_firsts.html.

33. Stephens, "History of Television."

34. Robert Abelman and David J. Atkin, *The Televiewing Audience: The Art and Science of Watching TV* (New York: Peter Lang, 2010), 81.

35. Senator Al Franken, "Franken Statement from Hearing on NBC/Comcast Merger" news release, February 4, 2010, http://www.franken.senate.gov/?p=press_release&id=483.

36. Ibid.

37. William T. Bielby and Denise D. Bielby, "Controlling Prime-Time: Organizational Concentration and Network Television Programming Strategies," *Journal of Broadcasting and Electronic Media* 47 (2003): 583.

38. William M. Kunz, *Culture Conglomerates: Consolidation in the Motion Picture and Television Industries* (Lanham, Md.: Rowman and Littlefield, 2007), 159.

39. Senator Al Franken, interview with the author, September 30, 2010.

40. Bielby and Bielby, "Controlling Prime-Time"; Franken, "Franken Statement."

41. "*Competition in the Media and Entertainment Distribution Market*": Hearing Before the H. Comm. on the Judiciary, 111th Cong. 137 (2010).

42. "Corporate Info," *NBC.com*.

43. David B. Wilkerson, "NBC Universal's Quarterly Profit Plunges 30%," *Wall Street Journal*, January 22, 2010, available at http://articles.marketwatch.com/2010-01-22/industries/30771774_1_nbc-universal-financial-officer-keith-sherin-operating-profit; Marc Graser, "GE Earnings Drop 19% in Fourth Quarter," *Variety*, January 22, 2010, available at http://www.variety.com/article/VR1118014177?refCatId=3765; "*Competition in the Media and Entertainment Distribution Market*," 111th Cong. 13 (Joint Written Testimony of Brian L. Roberts, Chairman and Chief Executive Officer, Comcast Corporation and Jeff Zucker, President and Chief Executive Officer, NBC Universal).

44. Robert Seidman, "The Reason Why NBC Universal Is Losing So Much on the Olympics: It Paid Too Much for Them!" *tvbythenumbers.com*, February 14, 2010, http://tvbythenumbers.zap2it.com/2010/02/14/the-reason-why-nbc-universal-is-losing-so-much-money-on-the-olympics-it-paid-too-much-for-them/.

45. "Is Free TV Coming to an End?" *CBSnews*, December 29, 2009, http://www.cbsnews.com/stories/2009/12/29/entertainment/main6032487.shtml.

46. Suzanne M. Kirchhoff, "Advertising Industry in the Digital Age" (Washington, D.C.: Congressional Research Service, November 9, 2009), available at http://www.fas.org/sgp/crs/misc/R40908.pdf.

47. Todd Spangler, "Cable Network Advertising up 16% in 2009: Nielsen," *Multichannel News*, April 28, 2010, http://www.multichannel.com/article/451991-Cable_Network_Advertising_Up_16_In_2009_Nielsen.php.

48. Diane Mermigas, "5 Strategies Comcast Needs to Pursue," *Mediapost.com*, May 14, 2010, http://www.mediapost.com/publications/article/128278/.

49. Nellie Andreeva, "2011 Basic Cable Ratings: USA Still on Top, History & FX Up, Nick at Nite & TBS Down," *Deadline.com*, December 28, 2011, http://www.deadline.com/2011/12/2011-basic-cable-ratings-usa-still-on-top-history-fx-up-nick-at-nite-tbs-down/.

50. Nikki Finke, "Jeff Zucker Fired by Steve Burke: Comcast 'Wanted to Move on' After Merge; NBCU Chief Emails Staff About Forced Exit," *Deadline.com*, September 24, 2010, http://www.deadline.com/2010/09/cnbc-zucker-wont-make-comcast-merger/.

51. NBC Universal, "NBC Universal Cable Networks." *NBC.com*, accessed March 9, 2012, http://www.nbc.com/nbc/NBC_Universal_Cable_Networks/; "About Bravo," *Bravotv.com*, accessed March 9, 2012, http://www.bravotv.com/about-bravo; "About CNBC U.S.," *CNBC.com*, accessed March 9, 2012, http://www.cnbc.com/id/15907487/.

52. "General Electric Company Q4 2009 Earnings Call Transcript," *Seeking Alpha*, January 22, 2010, available at http://seekingalpha.com/article/183965-general-electric-company-q4-2009-earnings-call-transcript.

53. Mermigas, "5 Strategies Comcast Needs to Pursue."

54. Brian Stelter, "NBC-Comcast Deal Puts Broadcast TV in Doubt," *New York Times*, December 7, 2009, available at http://www.nytimes.com/2009/12/07/business/media/07nbc.html.

55. Federal Communications Commission, "General Cable Television Industry and Regulation Information Fact Sheet," June 2000, available at http://transition.fcc.gov/mb/facts/csgen.html.

56. Kunz, *Culture Conglomerates*, 175.

57. Seth Schiesel, "In Cable TV, Programmers Provide a Power Balance," *New York Times*, July 16, 2001, available at http://www.nytimes.com/2001/07/16/business/in-cable-tv-programmers-provide-a-power-balance.html?pagewanted=all.

58. *"Television Viewers, Retransmission Consent and the Public Interest": Hearing Before the Subcomm. on Communications, Technology and the Internet of the S. Comm. on Commerce, Science and Transportation.* 111th Cong. 23–45 (2010).

59. Jesse Ward, "Fox vs. Cablevision," *National Telecommunications Cooperative Association: New Edge*, October 18, 2010, http://www.ntca.org/new-edge/video/fox-vs-cablevision.

60. Joe Flint, "Washington Weighs in on Disney-Cablevision Fight," *Los Angeles Times*, March 3, 2010, available at http://latimesblogs.latimes.com/entertainmentnewsbuzz/2010/03/washington-weighs-in-on-disney-cablevision-fight.html.

61. Bruce Edward Walker, "Proposed Retransmission Rules May Ease Broadcast Blackouts," *Heartlander*, May 31, 2011, http://news.heartland.org/newspaper-article/2011/05/31/proposed-retransmission-rules-may-ease-broadcast-blackouts.

62. Wayne Friedman, "Kagan: Retrans Revs Are Future Goldmine," *MediaPost Publications*, January 5, 2009, http://www.mediapost.com/publications/article/97766/ kagan-retrans-revs-are-future-goldmine.html?print; Sergio Ibarra, "Analyst Sees Stations' Retrans Revenue Tripling," *TV Week*, January 5, 2009; "SNL Kagan Releases Broadcast Retransmission Fee Projections through 2017," *PRWeb*, May 25, 2011, http://www.prweb.com/releases/2011/5/prweb8483711.htm.

63. Ryan Nakashima, "CBS Sales of Shows Partially Offset Drop in 3rd-Qtr Ad Revenue; Moonves in Talks with Oprah," Associated Press, *StarTribune.com*, November 5, 2009, http://www.startribune.com/templates/Print_This_Story?sid=69314097; Scott Canon, "In a Tangled TV Market, It's Hard for Rivals to Uproot Established Cable Providers," *Kansas City Star*, July 18, 2010.

64. Ron Chernow, *Titan: The Life of John D. Rockefeller, Sr.* (New York: Vintage, 2004), 140.

65. CBS Corporation, "CBS and Comcast Sign Ten-Year Content Carriage Agreement," news release, August 2, 2010, http://www.cbscorporation.com/news-article.php?id=666.

66. *Applications and Public Interest Statement of Comcast Corporation, General Electric Company, and NBC Universal, Inc., In the Matter of Applications for Consent to the Transfer of Control of Licenses*, Federal Communications Commission, May 4, 2010, 121; *Competition in the Media and Entertainment Distribution Market": Hearing Before the H. Comm. on the Judiciary*, 111th Cong. 137 (2010), 147.

67. "Cable: E!" *NBC Universal*, accessed March 9, 2012, http://www.nbcuni.com/ cable/e.

68. In November 2009, John Malone characterized the deal as "heavily engineered" to fit the needs of GE and Comcast. See "John Malone and David Faber," video of interview, 37:54–38:28 *CNBC*, November 23, 2009, http://video.cnbc.com/ gallery/?video=1340949341 ("It's a heavily engineered deal; [it] obviously was custom-tailored for both sides' needs. The way I see it, it de-leverages GE, and allows them to get their basis out of the whole thing, and then to the degree they want to sell down in the future, it's going to be nicely profitable. For Brian, it's a way to get into content, and get some market power in content, without betting the farm. He can easily afford the cash that's going in. He's getting a mark-up on the programming assets he's putting in. And Vivendi is probably going to walk away with a little more money than they could expect. So they're probably pretty happy. So I think it's custom-tailored for the needs of the participants.").

69. Kelly Riddell and Rachel Layne, "Comcast, GE Value Cable Channels at Up to $7 Billion" (Washington, D.C.: Benton Foundation, December 1, 2009), http:// benton.org/node/30166; David Goldman and Julianne Pepitone, "GE, Comcast Announce Joint NBC Deal," *CNNMoney*, December 3, 2009, http://money.cnn. com/2009/12/03/news/companies/comcast_nbc/index.htm.

70. David Carr, "A Big Deal, but Not a Good One," *New York Times*, October 25, 2009, available at http://www.nytimes.com/2009/10/26/business/media/26carr.html.

71. Liberty Media Corporation, "Q1 2011 Earnings Call," transcript, May 6, 2011, http://www.morningstar.com/earnings/PrintTranscript.aspx?id=27506514.

72. *"Examination of Cable Rates": Hearing Before the S. Commerce, Transportation and Science Committee*, 105th Cong. 6 (1998) (Testimony of Rep. Billy Tauzin); Jeremy Feiler, "RCN out to Block Comcast," *Philadelphia Business Journal*, August 19, 2002, available at http://www.bizjournals.com/philadelphia/stories/2002/08/19/story7.html?page=3.

73. *Applications and Public Interest Statement of Comcast Corporation, General Electric Company, and NBC Universal, Inc., In the Matter of Applications for Consent to the Transfer of Control of Licenses*, Federal Communications Commission, January 28, 2010, 83.

74. Chernow, *Titan*, 553.

Chapter 7. The Programming Battering Ram

Epigraph. Dan Shanoff, "Comcast-NBC: Online Sports Juggernaut?" *DanShanoff. com*, December 3, 2009, reposted January 18, 2011, http://www.danshanoff.com/2009/12/comcast-nbc-online-sports-juggernaut.html.

1. "InterMedia's Hindery Interview on Social Media," *Bloomberg*, video, May 27, 2011, http://www.bloomberg.com/video/70253338/; "John Malone and David Faber," video of interview, 39:00–40:00, *CNBC*, November 23, 2009, http://video.cnbc.com/gallery/?video=1340949341.

2. Associated Press, "Comcast-NBC Merger Without Question 'Biggest Thing' in Last 40 Years of Broadcasting," *National Sports Journalism Center*, December 28, 2009, http://sportsjournalism.org/sports-media-news/comcast-nbc-merger-without-question-biggest-thing-in-last-40-years-of-broadcasting/.

3. "'We intend to use sport as a battering-ram in all our pay-television operations,' said Mr Murdoch a couple of years ago," "Murdoch United," *The Economist*, September 10, 1998, available at http://www.economist.com/node/164106.

4. *In the Matter of General Motors Corporation and Hughes Electronics Corporation and The News Corporation Limited for Authority to Transfer Control*, 19 F.C.C.R. 473, 535 (January 14, 2004).

5. Charles B. Goldfarb, *The Proposed Comcast-NBC Universal Combination: How It Might Affect the Video Market* (Washington, D.C.: Congressional Research Service, February 2, 2010), 13.

6. *In the Matter of General Motors Corporation*, 19 F.C.C.R. 473, 537.

7. *In the Matter of Applications for Consent to the Assignment and/or Transfer of Control of Licenses*, 21 F.C.C.R. 8203, 8259 (July 21, 2006).

8. In 1997, SportsNet launched as "a continuous seven-day-a-week, 12-month-a-year potpourri of area sports with the focus on the 76ers, Flyers, Eagles and Phillies," reported Mike Bruton, "Comcast's Sportsnet Premieres," *Philadelphia Inquirer*, October 2, 1997, available at http://articles.philly.com/1997-10-02/sports/25540320_1_sportsrise-comcast-sportsnet-leslie-gudel. In 2010, CSN Houston became Comcast's ninth regional sports network. See "CSN Houston Marks Comcast's Latest Regional Sports Network," *Sports Business Daily*, November 9, 2010, http://www.sportsbusinessdaily.com/Daily/Issues/2010/11/Issue-42/Sports-Media/CSN-Houston-Marks-Comcasts-Latest-Regional-Sports-Network.

aspx. "Comcast SportsNet (CSN) includes CSN Bay Area, CSN California, CSN Chicago, CSN Philadelphia, CSN New England, CSN Mid-Atlantic, CSN Northwest, CSN Southeast, CSN Southwest, SportNet New York (partial), MountainWest Sports Network (partial), CSS (partial)" ("Who Owns the Media: Media Ownership Charts: Cable and Telecommunications," *FreePress.net*, last modified January 18, 2011, http://www.freepress.net/ownership/chart/cable).

9. Dish Network complained that Comcast refused to deliver SportsNet Philadelphia to its customers. See Marguerite Reardon, "Telcos and Satellite Get Closer to Local TV Sports," *CNET News*, August 2, 2010, http://news.cnet.com/8301-30686_3-20012274-266.html. For the 1992 act, see Cable Television Consumer Protection and Competition Act of 1992, Pub. L. No. 102-385, 106 Stat. 1460 (1992).

10. "Up until recently the regulations only required them to do this for video feeds that are distributed via satellite. Channels that are transmitted locally on terrestrial cable infrastructure, such as local sports, have been exempt. Many people in the industry have referred to this as a loophole in regulation that has allowed cable companies to deny access to these sports channels to TV competitors. In January, the FCC voted to close this loophole. And as of June 21, cable operators are required to offer local sports feeds at fair rates to competitors. Dish argues that Comcast is violating this regulation" (Reardon, "Telcos and Satellite Get Closer to Local TV Sports").

Section 628 of the Cable Television Consumer Protection and Competition Act of 1992 was enacted to "increase the availability of satellite cable programming and satellite broadcast programming" (Cable Television Consumer Protection and Competition Act of 1992 § 628[a]). The FCC enacted rules to further the goals set out by Congress in the act. See Federal Communications Commission, "General Cable Television Industry and Regulation Information Fact Sheet," June 2000, available at http://transition.fcc.gov/mb/facts/csgen.html.

11. *In the Matter of Applications of Comcast Corporation, General Electric Company and NBC Universal, Inc. for Consent to Assign Licenses and Transfer Control of Licenses*, 26 F.C.C.R. 4238, 4255 (January 20, 2011).

12. *"The Comcast/NBC Universal Merger: What Does the Future Hold for Competition and Consumers?": Hearing Before the Subcomm. on Antitrust, Competition Policy and Consumer Rights of the S. Comm. on the Judiciary*, 111th Cong. 12 (2010) (statement of Colleen Abdoulah, President and CEO of WOW!).

13. Keith Klovers, "Americans' Addiction to Sports Programming," memo to the author, April 15, 2010.

14. National Basketball Association, "Comcast SportsNet, Portland Trail Blazers Announce a New Regional Sports Network," news release, May 21, 2007, http://www.nba.com/blazers/news/Comcast_Sports_Net_Portland_T-225869-1218.html; Brian Frederick, "Blazer TV Access: Stop Hogging the Ball, Comcast," *OregonLive.com*, October 15, 2010, http://www.oregonlive.com/opinion/index.ssf/2010/10/blazer_tv_access_stop_hogging.html; Mike Rogoway, "FCC's Ruling on Comcast-NBC Won't Unlock Blazers on Satellite TV," *OregonLive.com*,

January 19, 2011, http://blog.oregonlive.com/siliconforest/2011/01/fccs_ruling_
on_comcast-nbc_cou.html; Brian Frederick, "Comcast Is Holding Trail Blazers
Fans Hostage, You Could Be Next," *Huffington Post*, August 16, 2010, http://www.
huffingtonpost.com/brian-frederick/comcast-is-holding-trail_b_681627.html.

15. *In the Matter of Herring Broadcasting, Inc. v. Time Warner Cable Inc., et al.*, 23
    F.C.C.R. 14787, 14817 (October 10, 2008) (testimony of Paul Tagliabue, available at
    http://ecfsdocs.fcc.gov/filings/2009/04/22/5515359636.html; testimony of Frank
    Hawkins, available at http://ecfsdocs.fcc.gov/filings/2009/04/22/5515359633.
    html; John Eggerton, "Comcast Would Move NFL Network off Tier If Service Drops
    Price: Roberts," *Multichannel News*, last modified April 18, 2009, http://www.
    multichannel.com/article/209442-Updated_Comcast_Would_Move_NFL_
    Network_Off_Tier_If_Service_Drops_Price_Roberts.php.

16. *In the Matter of Herring Broadcasting, Inc. v. Time Warner Cable Inc., et al.*, 23
    F.C.C.R. 14787, 14825.

17. "Critical to the settlement was the [NFL's] decision to reduce the price it charged
    for the network, from a monthly subscriber fee of 70 cents to an average of a little
    over 50 cents through the life of the contract. . . . [T]he league will presumably
    offer Time Warner, Cablevision and Charter terms similar to those given to Com-
    cast to gain footholds in those systems" (Richard Sandomir, "Comcast and NFL
    Network Agree to 9-Year Deal," *New York Times*, May 19, 2009, http://www.
    nytimes.com/2009/05/20/sports/football/19nflnetwork.html?_r=1).

18. "*The Comcast/NBC Universal Merger*" (Written Testimony of Andrew Jay Schwartz-
    man, President and Chief Executive Officer of Media Access Project).

19. "Major League Baseball learned from the NFL's experience, and took a different
    tack. When it created the MLB Network it did what the NFL has refused to do, and
    offered significant ownership interests to the major cable operators, including
    Comcast. Not surprisingly, from the moment of its launch, the MLB Network has
    been carried on the basic cable tier" (ibid.).

20. Matt Egan, "Comcast Skates Away with 10-Year TV Deal for NHL," *Fox Business*,
    April 19, 2011, available at http://www.foxbusiness.com/industries/2011/04/19/
    comcast-skates-away-10-year-tv-deal-nhl/. On Murdoch see Stanley J. Baran, "The
    Industrial Benefits of Televised Sports," *The Museum of Broadcast Communica-
    tions*, accessed March 3, 2012, http://www.museum.tv/eotvsection.php?entrycode
    =sportsandte. On ESPN see Richard Sandomir, "With Armstrong out, N.H.L. May
    Be in at OLN," *New York Times*, July 28, 2005, available at http://www.nytimes.
    com/2005/07/28/sports/hockey/28sandomir.html. The Comcast deal "calls for
    the networks to televise 100 regular-season games each season and air a national
    NBC broadcast on the day after the U.S. Thanksgiving holiday in late November.
    It also includes national distribution of all NHL playoff games" (Mason Levinson
    and Michele Steele, "Comcast Extends U.S. NHL Rights; 10-Year Deal Said
    to Reach $2 Billion," *Bloomberg*, April 19, 2011, http://www.bloomberg.com/
    news/2011-04-19/comcast-said-to-agree-to-10-year-2-billion-television-contract-
    with-nhl.html). The two-billion-dollar Comcast deal "will put up to 90 regular

season games on the NBC Sports Network every year for the next ten years" (Barry Petchesky, "At the Winter Classic, a New Year Belongs to Gary Bettman," *DeadSpin*, January 3, 2012, http://deadspin.com/5872548/at-the-winter-classic-a-new-year-belongs-to-gary-bettman/).

21. "The 50 Most Influential List, 1–10," *Sports Business Journal*, December 14, 2009, http://www.sportsbusinessdaily.com/Journal/Issues/2009/12/20091214/Special-Report/The-50-Most-Influential-List-1-10.aspx.

22. Alex Sherman, "Comcast CEO's Bet on Profitable Olympics Met with Skepticism," *Bloomberg*, June 9, 2011, http://www.bloomberg.com/news/2011-06-09/comcast-s-bet-on-a-profitable-olympics-greeted-with-skepticism-by-analysts.html; Patrick Rishe, "Comcast/NBC Overpays for Olympic Rights: Strategically Savvy or Slightly Stupid?" *Forbes*, June 8, 2011, available at http://www.forbes.com/sites/sportsmoney/2011/06/08/comcastnbc-overpays-for-olympic-rights-strategically-savvy-or-slightly-stupid/; Richard Sandomir, "NBC Wins U.S. Television Rights to Four More Olympics," *New York Times*, June 7, 2011, available at http://www.nytimes.com/2011/06/08/sports/nbc-wins-tv-rights-to-next-four-olympics.html?pagewanted=all.

23. Comcast's acquisition of AT&T Broadband took it from having 8.5 million cable subscribers to placing it "in the forefront of every emerging digital media technology of the cable industry," reported Erin Joyce, "Comcast, AT&T Broadband Close Merger," *InternetNews.com*, November 18, 2002, http://www.internetnews.com/xSP/article.php/1503051/Comcast+ATT+Broadband+Close+Merger.htm. Comcast's bid was three times more than the previous rights holder, FSN Northwest, was willing to pay. See Mike Rogoway, "Comcast's Sports Channel Fuels Bidding War," *OregonLive.com*, May 29, 2007, http://blog.oregonlive.com/siliconforest/2007/05/comcasts_sports_channels_fuel.html; "Comcast SportsNet, Blazers Create Network," *Portland Business Journal*, May 21, 2007, http://www.bizjournals.com/portland/stories/2007/05/21/daily12.html?page=all. Once Comcast acquired the broadcast rights to the Trail Blazers, it "jacked up the fees for other cable and satellite carriers in the region to show Blazers games" (Frederick, "Comcast Is Holding Trail Blazers Fans Hostage").

24. *Reply Comments of Verizon, In the Matter of The Regional Sports Network Marketplace*, Federal Communications Commission, MB Docket No. 11-128 (September 26, 2011).

25. "Comcast plans to mitigate costs by charging higher adverting rates and higher distribution fees for access to its affiliated TV stations and TV networks that carry the games," reported Diane Mermigas, "Innovative Delivery Could Make Olympics Pay," *MediaPost* (blog), June 17, 2011, http://www.mediapost.com/publications/article/152654/innovative-delivery-could-make-olympics-pay.html. For a corroborating report, see Sherman, "Comcast CEO's Bet on Profitable Olympics Met with Skepticism."

26. "50 Most Influential People in Sports Business 2008," *Sports Business Journal*, December 15, 2008, http://www.sportsbusinessdaily.com/Journal/Issues/2008/

12/20081215/Special-Report/50-Most-Influential-People-In-Sports-Business-2008.aspx; "The 50 Most Influential List, 1–10"; "The 50 Most Influential People in Sports Business," *Sports Business Journal*, December 12, 2011, http://www.sportsbusinessdaily.com/Journal/Issues/2011/12/12/Most-Influential/1.aspx.

27. Stanley J. Baran, "Sports and Television," in *The Business of Sports*, ed. Scott Rosner and Kenneth L. Shropshire (Burlington, Mass.: Jones and Bartlett Learning, 2004), 143; Baran, "Industrial Benefits of Televised Sports."

28. "Bill Rasmussen, ESPN Founder; CEO/Founder of College Fanz Sports Network," *Sports Business Journal*, May 31, 2010, http://www.sportsbusinessdaily.com/Journal/Issues/2010/05/20100531/What-I-Like/Bill-Rasmussen-ESPN-Founder-Ceofounder-Of-College-Fanz-Sports-Network.aspx. In the 1980s, Roger Werner joined ESPN and implemented the policy of "charging cable operators, who had been receiving ESPN programming for free, small monthly fees, starting at six cents per subscriber and gradually increasing to 10 cents by 1985" ("Company Histories & Profiles: ESPN, Inc.," *FundingUniverse.com*, accessed March 3, 2012, http://www.fundinguniverse.com/company-histories/ESPN-Inc-company-History.html. It has been suggested that ESPN's success is due to its ability to command high fees where other companies cannot, because of its aggregation of sports programming. See Jessica Shambora, "Why ESPN Thrives Where Most Cable Networks Fail," *CNN Money*, July 22, 2011, http://tech.fortune.cnn.com/2011/07/22/why-espn-thrives-where-most-cable-networks-fail/. "ESPN charges the highest per-household subscription fee of any cable channel" (Sam Schechner and Martin Peers, "Cable-TV Honchos Cry Foul over Soaring Cost of ESPN," *Wall Street Journal*, December 6, 2011, available at http://online.wsj.com/article/SB10001424052970204083204577080793289112260.html. In 2011, ESPN charged cable operators $4.89 per subscriber, and was moving to increase that fee to $7. See Joseph Barracato, "Audible Groans: ESPN's $15B NFL Deal May Snap Budgets," *New York Post*, last updated September 18, 2011, http://www.nypost.com/p/news/business/audible_groans_agEjp5JOGPSLOVhRkFZL3I.

29. "Looking Back, Back, Back . . . ," *ESPN.com*, accessed March 3, 2012, http://espn.go.com/espninc/pressreleases/chronology.html; Stuart Elliott, "The Media Business: Advertising; In a Campaign to Build Its 'Brand Character,' ESPN Is Playing a Provocative New Game," *New York Times*, January 7, 1994, available at http://www.nytimes.com/1994/01/07/business/media-business-advertising-campaign-build-its-brand-character-espn-playing.html?src=pm; "ABC Unit to Buy Stake in ESPN," *New York Times*, January 4, 1984, available at http://www.nytimes.com/1984/01/04/business/abc-unit-buy-stake-espn-abc-video-enterprises-plans-acquire-15-percent-espn.html. In 1982, ESPN signed a two-year deal to broadcast National Basketball Association games, and in 1985 ESPN signed a three-year deal with the National Hockey Association. See "Looking Back, Back, Back . . ." In 1987, ESPN began broadcasting National Football League games, and in 1989 ESPN began broadcasting Major League Baseball games. See "Company Histories

& Profiles: ESPN, Inc." "ESPN's combination of Sunday night football and the Major League Baseball playoffs pushed the sports network to the number one ranking in prime time among cable networks in October 1999" (ibid.). In 2011, ESPN's annual affiliate revenue was $5.57 billion. See Anthony Crupi, "Bowling Them Over: BCS Has ESPN Seeing Green; Sales, Ratings Through the Roof as Bowl Season Kicks Off," AdWeek.com, December 20, 2011, http://www.adweek.com/news/television/bowling-them-over-bcs-has-espn-seeing-green-137202. On ESPN's growth in revenue over the past decade, see Associated Press, "Free Broadcast TV May Go Way of VHS Tape," MSNBC.com, December 29, 2009, http://www.msnbc.msn.com/id/34619571/#.T1J85czTOjE. In 2008, "ESPN used its assets to outbid Fox by $100 million for the rights to carry college football's Bowl Championship Series from 2011 to 2014" and had $4.3 billion in revenue (Richard Sandomir, "Assets and Subscriber Revenue Give ESPN an Edge in Rights Bidding," New York Times, November 24, 2008, available at http://www.nytimes.com/2008/11/25/sports/ncaafootball/25sandomir.html).

30. Karen Hogan, "From San Fran to Philly, Comcast Sports Group RSNs Step Up to the Plate," Sports Video Group, March 27, 2012, http://sportsvideo.org/main/blog/2012/03/27/from-san-fran-to-philly-comcast-sports-group-rsns-step-up-to-the-plate/; "This Is NBCUniversal," NBCUni.com. accessed May 25, 2012, http://www.nbcuni.com/corporate/about-us/.

31. Richard Sandomir, "Regional Sports Networks Show the Money," New York Times, August 19, 2011, available at http://www.nytimes.com/2011/08/20/sports/regional-sports-networks-show-teams-the-money.html?pagewanted=all.

32. "Comcast serves approximately 70 percent of MVPD subscribers in the Philadelphia DMA [Designated Market Areas], and it serves approximately 60 percent of MVPD subscribers in the Chicago, Miami, and San Francisco [DMA]." In the Matter of Applications of Comcast Corporation, 26 F.C.C.R. 4238 (CWA Petition, Attachment B, Declaration of Hal Singer, June 21, 2010, at 11).

33. John Borland and Jim Hu, "Comcast Offers $66 Billion for Disney," CNET News, February 11, 2004, http://news.cnet.com/2100-01026_3-5157087.html.

34. Sean Gregory, "Sports Television: Why ESPN Is the Crown Jewel," Time, February 23, 2004, available at http://www.time.com/time/magazine/article/0,9171,993416,00.html.

35. Jessica E. Vascellaro and Matthew Futterman, "Comcast Moves Goal Posts for NBC Sports," Wall Street Journal, April 15, 2011, available at http://online.wsj.com/article/SB10001424052748704547604576263033267695112.html.

36. Sam Schechner, "Comcast-NBC Is a Challenger," Wall Street Journal, October 12, 2009, available at http://online.wsj.com/article/SB20001424052748704882404574463712075917016.html.

37. Sandomir, "NBC Wins U.S. Television Rights to Four More Olympics." The Comcast-NBCU merger will give Roberts "half a leg up" in negotiations with ESPN, according to Jeffrey L. Bewkes in an interview with the author, June 24, 2010.

38. Shanoff, "Comcast-NBC: Online Sports Juggernaut?"

39. Viewers of the Vancouver Winter Olympics "could only access the certain live and pre-recorded coverage of Olympic events on [NBC's] web site if they already subscribed to MVPD service from one of NBC's MVPD partners. Those without MVPD subscriptions could not access this coverage because it was locked behind a 'pay wall,' despite the fact that, as of February 2010, NBC was wholly independent of any MVPD company" (Senator Herb Kohl to Hon. Christine Varney and Hon. Julius Genachowski, May 26, 2010, n. 4), available at http://www.kohl. senate.gov/newsroom/comcast-nbc-letter.cfm?.

40. Eric Benderoff, "TV in View on Web," *Chicago Tribune*, July 5, 2008, available at http://articles.chicagotribune.com/2008-07-05/business/0807031277_1_ internet-service-provider-espn-web.

41. Fox News "is on track to achieve $700 million in operating profit this year, according to analyst estimates that [head of Fox News, Roger] Ailes does not dispute." (David Carr and Tim Arango, "A Fox Chief at the Pinnacle of Media and Politics," *New York Times*, January 9, 2010, available at http://www.nytimes.com/2010/01/10/ business/media/10ailes.html?pagewanted=all). In 2010, Fox News was set to make more than CNN, MSNBC, and the evening newscasts of NBC, ABC and CBS combined. See Henry Blodget, "Fox News Makes More Money Than CNN, MSNBC, and NBC-ABC-and-CBC News Combined," *Business Insider*, January 9, 2010, http:// articles.businessinsider.com/2010-01-09/tech/30010761_1_ailes-fox-news-fox-news. A full list of News Corp.'s holdings can be found at http://www.newscorp.com/.

42. News Corporation, "Chairman's Address to the 2009 Annual Meeting of Stockholders," news release, available at October 16, 2009, http://www.newscorp. com/news/news_432.html.

43. As John Malone put it in 2009: "It's a very powerful interlock between [sports] programming that not everybody's interested in but those who are are intensely interested in it. And distribution" ("David Faber and John Malone," video of interview, 38:42–39:19).

Chapter 8. When Cable Met Wireless

1. Apple, "Apple's App Store Downloads Top 10 Billion," news release, January 22, 2011, http://www.apple.com/se/pr/library/2011/01/22Apples-App-Store-Downloads-Top-10-Billion.html; Josh Lowensohn, "Despite Growth, Google Trails Apple in App Dollars Spent," *CNET News*, November 21, 2011, http://news.cnet.com/8301-27076_3-57328804-248/despite-growth-google-trails-apple-in-app-dollars-spent/#ixzz1nRaZmFsS ("Apple continu[es] to mop up about 85–90 percent of money spent on mobile apps"); Steven Mostyn, "Apple to Ship 30 million iPads in 2011," *Tech Herald*, June 30, 2011, http://www.thetechherald.com/articles/Analyst-Apple-to-ship-30-million-iPads-in-2011; Bianca Bosker, "Apple Announces Plans for $100 Billion Cash Hoard," *Huffington Post*, March 19, 2012, http://www. huffingtonpost.com/2012/03/19/apple-announces-plans-for-cash_n_1362212. html; Sam Gustin, "How Many iPads Can Apple Sell?" *Time*, March 16, 2012, http://business.time.com/2012/03/16/how-many-ipads-can-apple-sell/.

2. Cisco, *Cisco Visual Networking Index: Global Mobile Data Traffic Forecast Update, 2011–2016*, February 14, 2012, http://www.cisco.com/en/US/solutions/collateral/ns341/ns525/ns537/ns705/ns827/white_paper_c11-520862.html.

3. Neil Smit, "Comcast, Time Warner Cable, Bright House Networks and Verizon Wireless Enter into New Agreements," *Comcast Voices* (blog), December 2, 2011, http://blog.comcast.com/2011/12/comcast-time-warner-cable-bright-house-networks-and-verizon-wireless-enter-into-new-agreements.html.

4. Mike Robuck, "Comcast's Smit, TWC's Britt Saddle Up on Verizon Wireless Deal," *CED Magazine*, December 5, 2011, http://www.cedmagazine.com/blogs/2011/12/comcasts-smit-twcs-britt-saddle-up-on-verizon-wireless-deal.

5. Alex Sherman, "Verizon Wireless Allies with Cable in $3.6 Billion Deal," *Bloomberg*, December 2, 2011, http://www.bloomberg.com/news/2011-12-02/verizon-wireless-allies-with-cable-carriers-in-3-6-billion-spectrum-deal.html; Deborah Yao, "Comcast CFO: Not Interested in Acquiring Wireless Network," *SNL Insurance Daily*, September 21, 2011.

6. Sherman, "Verizon Wireless Allies with Cable in $3.6 Billion Deal"; *U.S. Telecommunications, U.S. Cable & Satellite Broadcasting, U.S. Internet: Where to Invest in 2012?* (New York: Bernstein Research, January 5, 2012), 7; Alex Sherman, "Cablevision Falls After Discounting Leads to Cash Flow Drop," *Bloomberg*, May 3, 2012, http://www.bloomberg.com/news/2012-05-03/cablevision-profit-tops-estimates-as-tv-service-gains-customers.html.

7. Shares of U.S. wireless subscribers at the end of 2010: Verizon (33.6 percent), AT&T (31.4 percent), SprintNextel (16.4 percent), T-MobileUSA (11.1 percent). All other regional and pre-paid carriers accounted for the remaining 7.5 percent of the more than 304 million subscriptions. SNLKagan data, cited in Free Press, "Why the AT&T-T-Mobile Deal Is Bad for America," available at http://www.freepress.net/files/ATT-TMobile.pdf, at 5. In 2010, Verizon's average EBITDA (Earnings Before Interest, Taxes, Depreciation, and Amortization) wireless margin was 47 percent while AT&T's was 41 percent. By contrast, Sprint's average wireless margin was 18 percent; U.S. Cellular's was 20 percent; Leap Wireless's was 21 percent; and T-Mobile's was 29 percent. See John Fletcher, "Verizon Wireless: The Best Spectrum, Wireless EBITDA," *SNL Kagan*, March 16, 2011, cited in Free Press Petition, 27, available at http://www.freepress.net/files/FreePress_PetitiontoDeny_ATT_TMobile.pdf.

8. Marguerite Reardon, "AT&T Verizon Price War Debunked (FAQ)," CNETNEWS, January 20, 2010, http://news.cnet.com/8301-30686_3-10437595-266.html. Also in 2010, Verizon eliminated its unlimited data plan for smartphones, migrating new customers into capped plans with overage charges. See Karl Bode, "Verizon Announces Wireless Pricing Changes," *DSLReports.com*, January 15, 2010, http://www.dslreports.com/shownews/Verizon-Announces-Wireless-Pricing-Changes-106425).

9. Edward C. Baig, "New iPad's Speedy 4G Can Use Up Data Allotment in a Flash," *USA Today*, March 21, 2012, http://www.usatoday.com/tech/columnist/

edwardbaig/story/2012-03-21/ipad-data-4g/53692024/1;   Anton   Troianovski, "Video Speed Trap Lurks in New iPad," *Wall Street Journal*, March 22, 2012, http:// online.wsj.com/article/SB10001424052702303812904577293882009811556. html?mod=wsj_share_tweet#articleTabs%3Darticle.

10. Nielsen, "Smartphones Account for Half of All Mobile Phones, Dominate New Phone Purchases in the U.S.," March 29, 2012, *NielsenWire* (blog), http://blog. nielsen.com/nielsenwire/online_mobile/smartphones-account-for-half-of-all-mobile-phones-dominate-new-phone-purchases-in-the-us.

11. Patrick R. Parsons, *The Creation of the Media: Political Origins of Modern Communications* (New York: Basic Books, 2004), 288; Final Report and Order, 21 F.C.C.2d 307, reconsidered in part, 22 F.C.C.2d 746 (1970), aff'd sub nom, *General Telephone Co. S.W. v. United States*, 449 F.2d 846 (5th Cir. 1971); Chapter 2, text at note 60.

12. *In the Matter of Use of the Carterfone Device in Message Toll Tel. Serv.*, 13 F.C.C.2d 420 (1968).

13. "Appropriate Regulatory Treatment for Broadband Access to the Internet over Wireless Networks," WT Docket No. 07-53, Declaratory Ruling, 22 F.C.C. Rcd 5901, 19–26, 29–33 (2007).

14. Handsets are often tied to both a network type and a particular carrier. AT&T uses a different information scheme (Global System for Mobile Communications, or GSM) from Verizon's (Code Division Multiple Access, or CDMA); this means that most handsets, which support just one of these schemes, cannot be used on the other network.

15. Kevin Fitchard, "How Verizon Might Kill Any Hope for LTE Interoperability," *GigaOM*, April 18, 2012, http://gigaom.com/mobile/how-verizon-might-kill-any-hope-for-lte-interoperability/; Kevin Fitchard, "IPad vs. iPad: Which 4G Tablet Should You Choose?" *GigaOM*, March 15, 2012, http://gigaom.com/apple/ipad-vs-ipad-which-4g-tablet-should-you-choose/.

16. Ryan Whitwam, "What Is a Bootloader, and Why Does Verizon Want Them Locked?" *ExtremeTech*,   March   20,   2012,   http://www.extremetech.com/ computing/120771-what-is-a-bootloader-and-why-does-verizon-want-them-locked; comment by Antonio Damian Garrison, March 2012, http://www.extremetech. com/computing/120771-what-is-a-bootloader-and-why-does-verizon-want-them-locked/2#comment-454704316.

17. *"The 700 MHz Auction: Public Safety and Competition": Hearing Before the S. Comm. on Commerce, Science, and Transportation*, 110th Cong. (2007) (Statement of Amol R. Sarva on behalf of the Wireless Founders Coalition for Innovation); Simon Wilkie, *Open Access for the 700 MHz Auction: Wholesale Access Licensing Promotes Competition and Could Increase Auction Revenue, Issue Brief #21* (Washington, D.C.: New America Foundation, Wireless Future Program, July 2007).

18. David B. Wilkerson, "Wireless 'Not Enough' to Support Video Future," *Market-Watch*, June 16, 2011, http://articles.marketwatch.com/2011-06-16/industries /30869054_1_4g-wireless-platform-panel-discussion.

19. Eli Noam, "Let Them Eat Cellphones: Why Mobile Wireless Is No Solution for Broadband," *Journal of Information Policy* 1 (2011): 470–85.

20. Stacey Higginbotham, "Oh No He Didn't: AT&T's CEO Calls DSL Obsolete," *GigaOM*, July 19, 2011, http://gigaom.com/broadband/oh-no-he-didnt-atts-ceo-calls-dsl-obsolete/.

21. Stacey Higginbotham, "Why Verizon Is Killing DSL & Cheap Broadband," *GigaOM*, March 6, 2012, http://gigaom.com/broadband/why-verizon-is-killing-dsl-cheap-broadband/.

22. Richard Morgan, "Verizon Wireless, Cable Companies: What's the Fuss?" *The Deal*, December 9, 2011, http://www.thedeal.com/magazine/ID/043301/commentary/verizon-wireless-cable-companies-whats-the-fuss.php; author's correspondence with telecommunications analyst Mitchell Shapiro, May 20, 2012.

23. Anton Troianovski, "Verizon Pitches Mobile Video," *Wall Street Journal*, March 30, 2012, available at http://online.wsj.com/article/SB10001424052702304177104577312062215910998.html?mod=ITP_marketplace_1.

24. "When the chairman of the Federal Communications Commission (FCC) earlier this month revealed he had circulated among his fellow commissioners a draft proposal to ensure continued Internet openness, the criticism started rolling in. . . . AT&T, Comcast, Verizon and Time Warner Cable have collectively employed more than 60 [lobbying] firms for net neutrality-related work" (Amanda Becker, "Draft Internet Rules Draw Lobbying Crowd," *Washington Post*, December 20, 2010).

25. "Google and Verizon outlined a joint set of proposed rules for the Internet on Monday . . . intended to allow for flexibility for the future. The 'non-discrimination' rule would not apply to wireless services, as well as to what the companies called 'additional, differentiated online services' of the future" (Ted Johnson, "Net True, Rivals Propose Road Rules," *Variety*, August 10, 2010).

26. "You [as the developer of the app] get 70% sales revenue" ("Apple iOS Developer Program: Distribute Your App," Apple Corporation, accessed February 27, 2012, https://developer.apple.com/programs/ios/distribute.html).

27. For example, Apple rejected an app from Google in 2009 that would allow use of Google Voice on the iPhone. The fury that erupted prompted the FCC to demand an explanation. While in response Apple denied rejecting the proposed Google app and insisted that the app was still under review, the company also said that "the application has not been approved because, as submitted for review, it appears to alter the iPhone's distinctive user experience by replacing the iPhone's core mobile telephone functionality and Apple user interface with its own user interface for telephone calls, text messaging and voicemail. Apple spent a lot of time and effort developing this distinct and innovative way to seamlessly deliver core functionality of the iPhone ("Apple Answers the FCC's Questions," Apple Corporation, August 21, 2009, http://www.apple.com/hotnews/apple-answers-fcc-questions/).

28. "We have the nation's fastest mobile broadband network and serve 100.7 million wireless subscribers" ("AT&T Company Information, U.S. Presence," AT&T, accessed February 27, 2012, http://www.att.com/gen/investor-relations?pid=5711);

Peter Svensson, "AT&T Q4 2011: Massive $6.68 Billion Loss on T-Mobile Deal Collapse, iPhone Subsidies, Pension Adjustments," *Huffington Post*, January 26, 2012, http://www.huffingtonpost.com/2012/01/26/att-q4-2011_n_1233533.html.

29. David Lieberman, "'The Daily' Launches on iPad for 99 Cents a Week," *USA Today*, February 3, 2011, available at http://www.usatoday.com/money/media/2011-02-02-the-daily-ipad_N.htm.

30. Staci D. Kramer, "Murdoch Hopes Apple Will Lower Its Share Of 'The Daily' Take," *PaidContent*, February 3, 2011, http://paidcontent.org/article/419-murdoch-hopes-apple-will-lower-its-share-of-the-daily-take/.

31. *Internet Trends*, Morgan Stanley, April 12, 2010, 8, available at http://www.google.com/url?sa=t&rct=j&q=&esrc=s&source=web&cd=1&ved=0CD0QFjAA&url=http%3A%2F%2Fwww.morganstanley.com%2Finstitutional%2Ftechresearch%2Fpdfs%2FInternet_Trends_041210.pdf&ei=V7NLT4elK4TooQHf5ZmdDg&usg=AFQjCNGv_ShtPcQ8l9iw-BIcxhjen3CAzA&sig2=vmr7Z5MuMTe4QkYzF5rEcg.

32. Stephanie Baghdassarian and Carolina Milanesi, *Forecast: Mobile Application Stores, Worldwide, 2008–2014* (Stamford, Conn.: Gartner, December 17, 2010).

33. Walt Mossberg, "Show Me the Money," *Wall Street Journal*, June 2, 2009 (brackets in the original).

34. David Pogue, "Cable TV in Pursuit of Mobility," *New York Times*, March 2, 2011.

35. "Time Warner Cable has been wrestling with programmers for months over this issue. In March, the company released an app that allowed its paying subscribers to watch dozens of cable channels on the iPad at home. The app was challenged by some programmers, led by Viacom, which owns channels like MTV and Nickelodeon and which accused Time Warner Cable in a lawsuit of 'unlicensed distribution' of its content" (Brian Stelter, "Time Warner to Subsidize Subscribers' TV Device," *New York Times*, August 23, 2011).

36. "Comcast's CEO Discusses Q1 2012 Results—Earnings Call Transcript," May 2, 2012, *Seeking Alpha*, http://seekingalpha.com/article/551371-comcast-s-ceo-discusses-q1-2012-results-earnings-call-transcript.

37. Nathan Becker, "Comcast Bringing Live TV to Tablets," *Wall Street Journal, Digits* (blog), January 5, 2011, http://blogs.wsj.com/digits/2011/01/05/comcast-bringing-live-tv-to-tablets/.

38. "Microsoft has sold 50 million Xbox 360s since the console's release in 2005 and it has sold 10 million Kinect sensors, its own motion-control device" (Matt Richtel, "Game Systems Upgraded at a Cost-Conscious Pace," *New York Times*, May 2, 2011).

39. Charlie Rose, "Charlie Rose Talks to Jeffrey Bewkes," *Bloomberg Business Week*, April 28, 2011, http://www.businessweek.com/magazine/content/11_19/b4227021650715.htm.

Chapter 9. The Biggest Squeeze of All

Epigraph. Kelly Riddell, "Malone Sees Pay-TV Industry Consolidation as Fee Disputes Mount," *Bloomberg*, March 19, 2010, http://www.bloomberg.com/apps/news?pid=newsarchive&sid=aWetzLpEbhUo.

1. *"The Comcast/NBC Universal Merger: What Does the Future Hold for Competition and Consumers":* Hearing Before the Subcommittee on Antitrust, Competition Policy and Consumer Rights of the Committee on the Judiciary," 111th Cong. 12 (2010) (Statement of Senator Herb Kohl).

2. Ibid., 24 (Testimony of Andrew Jay Schwartzman, President and Chief Executive Officer of Media Access Project) [hypen added to "over-the-top"].

3. Jason Kilar, "Doing Hard Things," *Hulu* (blog), February 18, 2009, http://blog. hulu.com/2009/02/18/doing-hard-things/.

4. Jason Kilar, "Q2," *Hulu* (blog). July 6, 2011, http://blog.hulu.com/2011/07/06/ q2/; Adam McCrimmon, "2011 Digital Review," *hyconnect*, January 8, 2012, http://www.hyc.com/blog/2011-digital-review/.

5. *"The Comcast/NBC Universal Merger,"* 23 (Testimony of Brian L. Roberts, Chairman and Chief Executive Officer, Comcast Corporation).

6. Meg James, "Comcast Will Retain NBC's Stake in Hulu, but Is Stripped of Control," *Los Angeles Times*, January 18, 2011, available at http://latimesblogs.latimes. com/entertainmentnewsbuzz/2011/01/comcast-will-retain-nbcs-stake-in-hulu-but-is-stripped-of-control.html; Tony Greenberg, "Jumping Through Hoops with Hulu: Will Hollywood Studios Kill Their Offspring Again?" *Jack Myers Media Business Report*, September 26, 2011, http://www.jackmyers.com/jackmyers-think-tank/Jumping-Through-Hoops-with-Hulu-Will-Hollywood-Studios-Kill-Their-Offspring-Again—-Tony-Greenberg.html.

7. Ibid., 8–10, 28 (Statement and testimony of Brian L. Roberts), and 10–12 (Statement of Jeff Zucker, President and Chief Executive Officer, NBC Universal).

8. Stefan Anninger, Jonathan Chaplin, and Tom Champion, "Broadband Wars" (New York, NY: Credit Suisse, October 19, 2010), 8.

9. "Report on Cable Industry Prices" (Washington, D.C.: Federal Communications Commission, February 14, 2011).

10. Dorothy Pomerantz, "12 Million Households Expected to Cut the Cord by 2015," *Forbes*, July 20, 2011, available at http://www.forbes.com/sites/dorothypomerantz /2011/07/20/12-million-households-expected-to-cut-the-cord-by-2015/.

11. "CMCSA: Comcast Corporation at Morgan Stanley Technology, Media & Telecom Conference," conference call, March 2, 2011, transcript, 4, available at http://files. shareholder.com/downloads/CMCSA/0x0x447538/c20eba7d-049c-4dc7-a5cd-873f880b42bb/Comcast_MS_Transcript_3.3.11.pdf.

12. *United States, State of California, State of Florida, State of Missouri, State of Texas, and State of Washington v. Comcast Corp., General Electric Co., and NBC Universal, Inc.,* No. 1:11-00106 (D.C.C., January 18, 2011), 1 (Competitive Impact Statement).

13. Deborah Yao, "Comcast CFO: Not Interested in Acquiring Wireless Network," *SNL Insurance Daily*, September 21, 2011.

14. Alan Quayle, "70% rise in NFL fee to ESPN will Herald a New Round of Cord Cutting," *Insights on the Telecom Industry* (blog), December 7, 2011, http://www. alanquayle.com/blog/2011/12/70-rise-in-espn-fee-to-the-nfl.html.

15. Steve Adams, "Cable, Satellite TV Prices Continue to Rise," *Patriot Ledger*, April 18, 2011, available at http://www.wickedlocal.com/bourne/news/business/x4328 85704/Cable-satellite-TV-prices-continue-to-rise#axzz1ntkjm2Fd.

16. Mike Farrell, "Analyst: Comcast Could Own 100% of NBCU by 2014," *Multichannel News*, December 17, 2009, http://benton.org/node/30689.

17. "Comcast's CEO Discusses Q4 2011 Results—Earnings Call Transcript," question and answer session, *Seeking Alpha*, February 15, 2012, available at http:// seekingalpha.com/article/368451-comcast-s-ceo-discusses-q4-2011-results-earnings-call-transcript?part=qanda.

18. "CMCSA," 4.

19. Martin Peers, "Heard on the Street: Comcast Could Suffer from Universal Access," *Wall Street Journal*, September 30, 2010, available at http://online.wsj. com/article/SB10001424052748704116004575522141414844222.html.

20. Grant Gross, "What's in the FCC's New Net Neutrality Rules?" *Computer World*, December 27, 2010, http://www.computerworld.com/s/article/9202519/What_ s_in_the_FCC_s_new_Net_neutrality_rules_.

21. Yinka Degoke and Lisa Richwine, "Exclusive: Netflix in Talks for Cable Partnership," *Reuters*, March 6, 2012.

22. Don Reisinger, "Time Warner Cable Tries to Cap Broadband Data Usage—Again," *CNET News*, February 29, 2012, http://news.cnet.com/8301-13506_3-57387445-17/time-warner-cable-tries-to-cap-broadband-data-usage-again/.

23. Adam Wajnberg, "Why Is My Internet Connection So Slow?" *Broadband News*, February 20, 2012, http://www.comparebroadband.com.au/article_1300_Why-is-my-internet-connection-so-slow.htm.

24. Tillman L. Lay, "Taking Another Look at Federal/State Jurisdictional Relationships in the New Broadband World," National Regulatory Research Institute, September 11–15, 2011, 16, available at http://www.spiegelmcd.com/files/20111003_NRRI_ Broadband_2011_10_14_02_00_32.pdf.

25. "Netflix Letter to Shareholders," January 26, 2011, available at http://files.shareholder.com/downloads/NFLX/1144945482x0x437075/925e81c4-3d5d-44b6-ae5e-a70c91251131/Q410%20Letter%20to%20shareholders.pdf.

26. Karl Bode, "Shaw 'Listens,' Proceeds with Usage-Billing Anyway," *DSLReports.com*, April 21, 2011, http://www.dslreports.com/shownews/Shaw-Listens-Proceeds-With-UsageBilling-Anyway-113858.

27. *Broadband Performance*, OBI Technical Paper no. 4. (Washington, D.C.: Federal Communications Commission, August, 2010), 11–15.

28. Jared Moya, "Canada Approves Consumption-Based Billing," *ZeroPaid.com*, May 7, 2010, http://www.zeropaid.com/news/89044/canada-approves-consumption-based-billing/.

29. Josh Sanburn, "Why Verizon Dropped Its Unlimited Data Plan (And What You Can Do About It)," *Time.com*, June 23, 2011, http://moneyland.time.com/2011/06/23/ why-verizon-dropped-its-unlimited-data-plan/.

30. Jamie Sturgeon, "Taking Fire, Bell Insists Internet Caps Suitable for 'Vast Majority,'" *Financial Post*, January 31, 2011, available at http://business.financialpost.com/2011/01/31/taking-fire-bell-insists-internet-caps-suitable-for-vast-majority/.

31. Etan Viessing, "Bell Canada to End Internet Traffic Throttling," *Hollywood Reporter*, December 20, 2011, available at http://www.hollywoodreporter.com/news/bell-canada-end-internet-traffic-275721.

32. Michael Geist, "Unpacking the Policy Issues Behind Bandwidth Caps & Usage Based Billing," *MichaelGeist* (blog), February 1, 2011, http://www.michaelgeist.ca/content/view/5611/125/.

33. Cory Doctorow, "Canadian ISPs Admit That Their Pricing Is Structured to Discourage Internet Use," *Boingboing.net*, March 29, 2011, http://www.boingboing.net/2011/03/29/canadian-isps-admit.html.

34. "CRTC Rejects Plan for Wholesale Internet Billing," *CTV.ca*, November 15, 2011, http://www.ctv.ca/CTVNews/SciTech/20111115/crtc-decision-independent-internet-providers-111115/.

35. Michael Lewis, "Bell Backs off on Internet Billing," *Moneyville.ca*, March 28, 2011, http://www.moneyville.ca/article/963044—bell-backs-off-on-internet-billing?bn=1.

36. Neil Hunt, "Netflix Lowers Data Usage by 2/3 for Members in Canada," *Netflix, US & Canada* (blog), March 28, 2011, http://blog.netflix.com/2011/03/netflix-lowers-data-usage-by-23-for.html.

37. Geist, "Unpacking the Policy Issues."

38. Jesse Brown, "Bell Toots an Extinguisher on UBB, Netflix Pours Gasoline," *Macleans.ca*, March 29, 2011, http://www2.macleans.ca/2011/03/29/bell-toots-an-extinguisher-on-ubb-netflix-pours-gasoline/.

39. Devendra T. Kumar, counsel for Netflix, Inc., to Federal Communications Commission, WC Docket No. 07-52, May 10, 2011, 6.

40. Michael Geist, "Door Opens for Internet Providers to Truly Compete," *Toronto Star*, November 19, 2011, available at http://www.thestar.com/article/1089576—door-opens-for-internet-providers-to-truly-compete.

41. Todd Spangler, "Time Warner Cable Postpones Internet-Billing Trials," *Multichannel News*, April 16, 2009, http://www.multichannel.com/article/196377-Time_Warner_Cable_Postpones_Internet_Billing_Trials.php.

42. Julius Genachowski, "Remarks on Preserving Internet Freedom and Openness," Federal Communications Commission, December 1, 2010, available at http://hraunfoss.fcc.gov/edocs_public/attachmatch/DOC-303136A1.pdf.

43. Todd Shields, "AT&T Gains FCC's Ear as Regulators Near Decision on Net Neutrality Rules," *Bloomberg*, November 30, 2010, http://www.bloomberg.com/news/2010-11-30/at-t-gains-fcc-s-ear-as-regulators-near-decision-on-net-neutrality-rules.html.

44. *Applications of Comcast Corporation, General Electric Company and NBC Universal, Inc. for Consent to Assign Licenses and Transfer Control of Licensees*, Federal Communications Commission, MB Docket No. 10-56, January 18, 2011, 38.

45. Karl Bode, "Exclusive: AT&T To Impose Caps, Overages," *DSLReports.com*, March 13, 2011, http://www.dslreports.com/shownews/Exclusive-ATT-Will-Soon-Impose-150GB-DSL-Cap-Overages-113149.

46. Xfinity Network Management Policy, "Announcement Regarding an Amendment to Our Acceptable Use Policy," *Xfinity.comcast.net*, http://xfinity.comcast.net/terms/network/amendment/.

47. Karl Bode, "AT&T to Kill Grandfathered Unlimited if You Tether Unofficially," *DSLReports.com*, August 4, 2011, http://www.dslreports.com/shownews/ATT-to-Kill-Grandfathered-Unlimited-If-You-Tether-Unofficially-115528.

48. Federal Communications Commission, "Public Notice: FCC Enforcement Bureau and Office of General Counsel Issue Advisory Guidance for Compliance with Open Internet Transparency Rule," news release, June 30, 2011, available at http://transition.fcc.gov/Daily_Releases/Daily_Business/2011/db0630/DA-11-1148A1.pdf.

49. John Eggerton, "Top Op's Top Washington Exec Has 'High Hopes' for Commission Under Genachowski," *Multichannel News*, July 30, 2009.

50. Cisco's John Chapman presented a paper at the National Cable & Telecommunications Association Cable Show in Boston in May 2012, written jointly by CISCO, ARRIS, and MOTO, claiming that the next-generation DOCSIS cable platforms could achieve a capacity of ten gigabits per second (download) and two gigabits per second (upload). See Jeff Baumgartner, "Does Docsis have a 10-Gig Future?" *Light Reading Cable*, May 23, 2012, http://www.lightreading.com/document.asp?doc_id=221264&site=lr_cable.

51. Ken Florence, "Netflix Performance on Top ISP Networks." *Netflix, Tech* (blog), January 27, 2011, http://techblog.netflix.com/2011/01/netflix-performance-on-top-isp-networks.html.

52. "Comcast's CEO Discusses Q1 2012 Results—Earnings Call Transcript," *Seeking Alpha*, May 2, 2012, available at http://finance.yahoo.com/news/comcasts-ceo-discusses-q1-2012-163011159.html ("High-Speed Internet revenue was a large contributor to Cable revenue growth in the first quarter [of 2012]. HSI revenue increased 10.3%, reflecting rate adjustments, continued growth in our customer base and an increasing number of our customers taking higher-speed services. Today, 26% of our Residential HSI customers take a higher-speed tier above our primary service.").

53. Stacey Higginbotham, "FCC Opens the Door for Metered Broadband," *GigaOM*, December 1, 2010, http://gigaom.com/2010/12/01/fcc-opens-the-door-for-metered-web-access/.

54. Martin A. Brown, Alin Popescu and Earl Zmijewski, *Peering Wars: Lessons Learned from the Cogen-Telia De-peering*, Renesys Corporation, June 2008, 13, available at http://www.renesys.com/tech/presentations/pdf/nanog43-peeringwars.pdf.

55. Bradley D. Bopp, NationalNet; Adam Davenport, Choopa, LLC; Randy Epstein, BroadbandONE; Anton Kapela, Five Nines Data, et al., to Hon. Julius Genachowski et al., Re: *Peering Representations by Comcast (NASDAQ: CMCSA); Comcast*

and NBC Universal Merger, MB Docket No. 10-56; Open Internet Broadband Industry Practices (GN Docket No. 09–191), December 20, 2010.

56. TR Daily, "Comcast-Level 3 Dispute over Content Delivery Fees Cited in Net Neutrality, NBCU Venture Policy Debates," *Telecommunications Reports International,* December 15, 2010; Earl Zmijewski, "A Baker's Dozen, 2011 Edition," *Renesys* (blog), February 8, 2012, http://www.renesys.com/blog/2012/02/a-bakers-dozen-2011-edition.shtml.

57. Evelyn M. Rusli, "Level 3's Bid for Global Crossing Could Lead to More Deals," *New York Times,* April 11, 2011, available at http://dealbook.nytimes.com/2011/04/11/in-level-3-takeover-an-opportunity-for-more-deals/.

58. Stacey Higginbotham, "Google's Fiber Network Could Foil ISPs and Fuel Innovation." *GigaOM,* February 10, 2010, http://gigaom.com/2010/02/10/google-fiber/.

59. Cathy Avgiris, "Extreme 105: Powering Digital Families," *Comcast Voices* (blog), April 14, 2011, http://blog.comcast.com/2011/04/extreme-105-powering-digital-families.html; Dwight Silverman, "The Woodlands Gets Comcast's Extreme 105 First," *Houston Chronicle, Tech* (blog), April 19, 2011, http://blog.chron.com/techblog/2011/04/the-woodlands-gets-comcasts-extreme-105-first/.

60. Tim Beyers, "Give It Up, Comcast," *Motley Fool,* April 15, 2011, http://www.fool.com/investing/general/2011/04/15/give-it-up-comcast.aspx?source=isesitlnkoo00001&mrr=1.00.

61. Avgiris, "Extreme 105"; Susan P. Crawford, "The New Digital Divide," *New York Times,* December 3, 2011, available at http://www.nytimes.com/2011/12/04/opinion/sunday/internet-access-and-the-new-divide.html?pagewanted=all.

62. *In the Matter of Inquiry Concerning the Deployment of Advanced Telecommunications Capability to All Americans in a Reasonable and Timely Fashion,* 26 F.C.C.R. 8008, 8009, 8099 (Seventh Broadband Progress Report and Order on Reconsideration).

63. Federal Communications Commission, "FCC & 'Connect to Compete' Tackle Barriers to Broadband Adoption" news release, March 8, 2012, available at http://hraunfoss.fcc.gov/edocs_public/attachmatch/DOC-310924A1.pdf.

64. *In the Matter of Inquiry Concerning the Deployment of Advanced Telecommunications Capability,* 26 F.C.C.R. 8008, 8042–43.

65. Mark McDonald, "Home Internet May Get Even Faster in South Korea," *New York Times,* February 21, 2011, available at http://www.nytimes.com/2011/02/22/technology/22iht-broadband22.html.

66. Cecilia Kang, "FCC Chairman Supports Broadband Data Caps amid Netflix Protests," *Washington Post, Post Tech* (blog), May 22, 2012, http://www.washingtonpost.com/blogs/post-tech/post/fcc-chairman-supports-broadband-data-caps-amid-netflix-protests/2012/05/22/gIQAfdN9hU_blog.html?wprss=rss_technology.

67. Representative Ed Markey, interview with the author, January 1, 2011.

Chapter 10. Comcast's Marathon

1. *"The Comcast/NBC Universal Merger: What Does the Future Hold for Competition and Consumers?":* Hearing Before the Subcomm. on Antitrust, Competition Policy and

Consumer Rights of the S. Comm. on the Judiciary, 111th Cong. 12 (2010) (Opening Statement of Senator Herb Kohl).

2. *Applications and Public Interest Statement of Comcast Corporation, General Electric Company, and NBC Universal, Inc., In the Matter of Applications for Consent to the Transfer of Control of Licenses*, Federal Communications Commission, May 4, 2010, 134.

3. Ibid., 39.

4. Ibid., 46, 47; Common Sense Media, "Common Sense Media Honors Innovators in Media, Public Policy and Technology–PHOTO," news release, February 26, 2010, http://www.reuters.com/article/2010/02/26/idUS219181+26-Feb-2010+BW 20100226.

5. "I want to thank my friends, Gary Knell and Jim Steyer," Julius Genachowski, remarks presented at the National Museum of American History, Washington, D.C., March 12, 2010.

6. "Commitment # 12. To enhance localism and strengthen educational and governmental access programming, Comcast will also develop a platform to host PEG content On Demand and On Demand Online within three years of closing" (*Applications and Public Interest Statement*). "Commitment # 16. The combined entity will continue the policy of journalistic independence with respect to the news programming organizations of all NBCU networks and stations, and will extend these policies to the potential influence of each of the owners. To ensure such independence, the combined entity will continue in effect the position and authority of the NBC News ombudsman to address any issues that may arise" (ibid.).

Copps, widely identified publicly as a Democrat, was a longtime outspoken critic of consolidation. See Joe Flint, "Michael Copps Frets over Media Landscape as He Prepares to Leave FCC," *Los Angeles Times*, December 13, 2011, available at http://articles.latimes.com/2011/dec/13/business/la-fi-ct-copps-20111213. David Cohen of Comcast also publicly praised both Genachowski and Copps on CSPAN in August 2009. See "The Communicators: David Cohen, Comcast Corp.," You-Tube video, 1:10, from an interview televised by CSPAN, July 24, 2009, posted by "CSPAN," August 2, 2009, http://www.youtube.com/watch?v=sI0zcgvdehs.

7. TR Daily, "Comcast Expects to Make FCC Public Interest Filing in 30–45 Days," *Telecommunications Reports International*, December 4, 2009, available via Westlaw (www.westlaw.com) at 2009 WLNR 24519526.

8. Commitment 1 addressed the continuing provision of free over-the-air television through owned and operated broadcast stations and local broadcast; commitment 16 addressed journalistic independence; commitment 6 promised expansion of "the availability of over-the-air programming to the Hispanic community utilizing a portion of the digital broadcast spectrum of Telemundo's O&Os (as well as offering it to Telemundo affiliates) to enhance the current programming of Telemundo and mun2"; Comcast "represented that it will honor all of NBCU's collective bargaining agreements" *Applications and Public Interest Statement*, 40, 133, 48, 38 n. 69.

9. Consumer Federation of America, Consumers Union and Free Press, *Comcast's Hollow "Public Interest" Commitments*, 2, accessed March 4, 2012, http://www.freepress.net/node/76419.

10. Hill staffer, interview with the author, August 23, 2010. Cohen's compensation was valued at $9,839,379 in 2009, and $12,696,578 in 2010. See "David L. Cohen," *Forbes*, accessed March 4, 2012, http://people.forbes.com/profile/david-l-cohen/21325; "David L. Cohen," *Bloomberg Businessweek*, accessed March 4, 2012, http://investing.businessweek.com/research/stocks/people/person.asp?pe rsonId=1997632&ticker=CMCSA:US; Meg James, "NBCUniversal CEO Steve Burke Is Comcast's Most Highly Compensated Executive," *Los Angeles Times*, April 2, 2011, available at http://articles.latimes.com/2011/apr/02/business/la-fi-ct-burke-20110402.

11. Gail Shister, "Another Chair for a Man Who Just Can't Sit Still, For David Cohen, Penn a Passion Among Many," *Philadelphia Inquirer*, December 5, 2008, available at http://articles.philly.com/2008-12-05/news/25244395_1_penn-greater-philadelphia-chamber-law-school.

12. Robert Huber, "David L., Explained," *Philadelphia Magazine*, November 2006, available at http://www.phillymag.com/health/articles/david_l_cohen_profile_david_l_explained/page1; Hill staffer, interview with the author, September 3, 2010.

13. Huber, "David L., Explained."

14. Buzz Bissinger, *A Prayer for the City* (New York: Random House, 1999), xxiii.

15. *The Pennsylvania Report* 18, Iss. 03-02 (Harrisburg: Capital Growth, 2003), 4.

16. Thomas Fitzgerald, "Hoeffel, Castor Casting Shadows," *Philadelphia Inquirer*, October 22, 2007, available at http://articles.philly.com/2007-10-22/news/25232443_1_marcel-groen-democrat-joe-hoeffel-damsker.

17. Huber, "David L., Explained"; Bissinger, *Prayer for the City.*

18. Peter Nicholas, "For Rendell, GOP Convention Work Is Done: As Mayor, He Lobbied Hard to Bring the Gathering Here. As Head of the DNC, He Will Be Keeping His Distance," *Philadelphia Inquirer*, July 7, 2000, available at http://articles.philly.com/2000-07-07/news/25609716_1_biggest-convention-ed-rendell-edward-g-rendell.

19. Patricia Horn, "Cashing in On the GOP Convention Comcast Branded the Gathering in Every Way It Could," *Philadelphia Inquirer*, August 6, 2000, available at http://articles.philly.com/2000-08-06/business/25594260_1_philadelphia-s-comcast-corp-comcast-executive-vice-president-comcast-country.

20. David Cohen's affiliations are detailed in his biography on the Comcast Web site: "Biography: David L. Cohen," Comcast, accessed March 4, 2012, http://www.comcast.com/corporate/about/pressroom/corporateoverview/corporateexecutives/davidcohen.html?SCRedirect=true. PolitickerPA.com was shuttered in 2009, but the *Pittsburgh Tribune-Review* reported on PolitickerPA's ranking of David Cohen in "Manzo's Alleged Squeeze Is a Multitasker," *Pittsburgh Tribune-Review*, July 20, 2008, http://www.pittsburghlive.com/x/pittsburghtrib/s_578353.html.

21. Edmund Sanders, "Comcast Country Tough on Intruders," *Los Angeles Times*, July 16, 2001, available at http://articles.latimes.com/2001/jul/16/business/fi-22884; Ken Dilanian and Wendy Tanaka, "RCN Pulls Cable TV Proposal: A Senior Company Official Blamed City Council Delays. Phila. Says the Company Left Because of Finances," *Philadelphia Inquirer*, February 15, 2001, http://articles.philly.com/2001-02-15/news/25316899_1_rcn-city-council-delays-cable-tv-proposal; Patricia Horn and Ken Dilanian, "Where Connections Are Key to Connecting: RCN's Effort to Compete with Comcast Illustrates the City's Barriers to Business," *Philadelphia Inquirer*, January 28, 2001, available at http://articles.philly.com/2001-01-28/news/25311516_1_rcn-corp-telephone-and-internet-services-cable. RCN discussed the episode in its 2002 filing with the FCC in opposition to Comcast Corporation's proposed acquisition of AT&T Comcast. See *Petition of RCN Telecom Services, Inc., to Deny Applications or Condition Consent, In the Matter of Applications for Consent to the Transfer of Control of Licenses*, Federal Communications Commission, April 29, 2002.

22. "Cohen said the firm did not expect Rendell to do too much legal work during his first year on the job because he will be busy raising money for the Democratic Party and trying to help the Democrats hold onto the White House" (Cynthia Burton, "Rendell to Become Partner at Law Firm When He Leaves Office In January, He Will Join Ballard Spahr. He Has Strong Ties to the Firm," *Philadelphia Inquirer*, December 23, 1999, available at http://articles.philly.com/1999-12-23/news/25479149_1_ed-rendell-ballard-spahr-firm.

23. "Scrutiny Ahead for Comcast," *Pittsburgh Tribune-Review*, December 4, 2009, available at http://www.pittsburghlive.com/x/pittsburghtrib/business/s_656133.html; Dan Gelston, "Pennsylvania Governor Trades Politics for Pigskin," *Spartanburg Herald-Journal*, November 7, 2004, available at http://news.google.com/newspapers?nid=1876&dat=20041107&id=a-YoAAAAIBAJ&sjid=TNAEAAAAIBAJ&pg=5805,1649963.

24. Kim Hart, "Comcast-NBC Deal Finds Campaign Cash Converging with Obama's Principles," *The Hill, Hillicon Valley* (blog), December 5, 2009, http://thehill.com/blogs/hillicon-valley/technology/70767-comcast-nbc-deal-finds-campaign-cash-converging-with-obamas-principles; the White House, "Remarks by the President at Fundraising Event for Arlen Specter," news release, September 15, 2009, available at http://www.whitehouse.gov/the-press-office/remarks-president-fundraising-event-senator-arlen-specter-philadelphia; Dan Gross, "Jon Bon Jovi to Perform at Private Obama Fundraiser," *Philadelphia Inquirer*, September 29, 2008, available at http://www.philly.com/philly/blogs/phillygossip/Jon_Bon_Jovi_to_perform_at_private_Obama_fundraiser.html?jCount=2. David Cohen is a "member" of President Obama's "$500,000 bundling club," according to Eric Lichtblau, "Obama Backers Tied to Lobbies Raise Millions," *New York Times*, October 27, 2011, available at http://www.nytimes.com/2011/10/28/us/politics/obama-bundlers-have-ties-to-lobbying.html?pagewanted=all.

25. "Phila. Fundraiser Set for Hillary Clinton Bailout [Compliments of Comcast CEO]," *Philadelphia Daily News*, December 31, 2008, available at http://www.freerepublic.

com/focus/f-news/2156877/posts. Cohen gave $2,300 to Clinton's campaign in 2007, according to *CampaignMoney.com*, accessed March 4, 2012, http://www. campaignmoney.com/political/contributions/david-cohen.asp?cycle=08. "Rendell claims now that if Hillary Clinton had been elected president, he would have called her up the next day and told her, 'I know you don't know David as well as you'd like to know a chief of staff—you should bring him on as a deputy.' Chiefs of staff, Rendell says, always leave after a few months, and then Cohen could have stepped right on up" (Huber, "David L., Explained").

26. Peter Nicholas and Josh Drobnyk, "Obama Supporting Specter in Primary Battle," *Los Angeles Times*, September 15, 2009, available at http://articles.latimes. com/2009/sep/15/nation/na-obama-specter15; "Fundraisers Mobilize for Specter; Obama to Come," *Philadelphia Inquirer*, June 8, 2009, available at http:// www.philly.com/philly/blogs/harrisburg_politics/Fundraisers_Mobilize_for_ Specter_Obama_to_come.html.

27. Before leaving office, Specter set up meetings between senators and Comcast's Brian Roberts, according to a Hill staffer I interviewed on August 23, 2010; *Hearing Before the Subcommittee on Antitrust, Competition Policy and Consumer Rights*, 5 (Statement of Senator Arlen Specter).

28. Charles B. Goldfarb, *Public, Educational, and Governmental (PEG) Access Cable Television Channels: Issues for Congress* (Washington, D.C.: Congressional Research Service, September 5, 2008), 11–12 (citing Herb Kirchhoff, "U.S., Michigan Courts Block Comcast Plan to Move Public Access Channels," *Communications Daily*, January 16, 2008); *"Public, Educational, and Governmental (PEG) Services in the Digital TV Age": Hearing Before the Subcommittee on Telecommunications and the Internet*, 110th Cong., 2d sess., January 29, 2008, transcript available at https:// house.resource.org/110/org.c-span.203829-1.raw.txt.

29. *"Public, Educational, and Governmental Services in the Digital TV Age": Hearing Before the Subcomm. on Telecommunications and the Internet of the H. Comm. on Energy and Commerce*, 110th Cong. (2008), 30 (Statement of Congressman John D. Dingell) and 2 (Testimony of David L. Cohen).

30. *Digital Television Transition: Implementation of the Converter Box Subsidy Program Is Under Way, but Preparedness to Manage an Increase in Subsidy Demand Is Unclear* (Washington, D.C.: United States Government Accountability Office, September 2008), 7.

31. Cynthia Littleton, "Big Agenda for FCC Chief," *Variety*, April 14, 2010, available at http://www.variety.com/article/VR1118017701?refcatid=14.

32. Hill staffer, interview with the author, August 23, 2010.

33. Huber, "David L., Explained."

34. *"Competition in the Media and Entertainment Distribution Market": Hearing Before the S. Comm. on the Judiciary*, 111th Cong. 144 (February 25, 2010). The Waters-Zucker colloquy is at 111–14, Lee at 107, Gutierrez at 142–43, Roberts at 145.

35. Maxine Waters to Julius Genachowski, April 12, 2010, available at http://www. freepress.net/files/Rep.Waters_Letter_to_FCC_on_Extending_Comment_

Period_in_Comcast-NBC_Merger.pdf; Waters and other members of Congress to Genachowski, May 7, 2010, available at http://waters.house.gov/UploadedFiles/ FCC_Letter_on_Hearings_and_Questions.pdf; Waters to Mignon Clyburn, May 23, 2010, available at http://apps.fcc.gov/ecfs//document/view.action?id=7020550283.

36. *"Proposed Combination of Comcast and NBC-Universal": Field Hearing Before the H. Comm. on the Judiciary*, 111th Cong. 189 (June 7, 2010) (Statement of Rep. Maxine Waters).

37. Ibid., 101 (Testimony of Stanley E. Washington, Chairman and CEO, National Coalition of African American Owned Media).

38. Ibid., 102, 101.

39. Ibid., 184.

40. Ibid., 5 (Statement of Rep. Maxine Waters).

41. "Queen Latifah Tackles NBC's Lack of Diversity on '30 Rock,'" *Huffington Post*, October 8, 2010, http://www.huffingtonpost.com/2010/10/08/queen-latifah-tackles-nbc_n_755666.html.

42. *"Proposed Combination of Comcast and NBC-Universal,"* 189.

43. Joe Flint, "Comcast-Universal Merger Attacked," *Los Angeles Times*, June 8, 2010, available at http://articles.latimes.com/2010/jun/08/business/la-fi-ct-comcast-20100608; *"Proposed Combination of Comcast and NBC-Universal,"* 3.

44. *"Comcast and NBC Universal: Who Benefits?": Field Hearing Before the Subcomm. on Communications, Technology, and the Internet of the H. Comm. on Energy and Commerce*, 111th Cong. 49 (July 8, 2010) (Testimony of Joseph Waz, Jr., Senior Vice President, External Affairs and Public Policy Counsel, Comcast Corporation) (preliminary transcript).

45. Ibid., 23 (Testimony of Jonathan Jackson, Rainbow PUSH Coalition, on behalf of Rev. Jesse Jackson).

46. Joe Flint, "Comcast Promises to Add Latino to Board of Directors as Part of Outreach Effort," *Los Angeles Times*, June 30, 2010, available at http://latimesblogs. latimes.com/entertainmentnewsbuzz/2010/06/comcast-promies-to-add-latino-to-board-of-directors-as-part-of-outreach-effort.html; *"Comcast and NBC Universal: Who Benefits?"* 11 (Testimony of Joseph Waz, Jr.); Bob Fernandez, "Comcast Adding Networks Owned by African Americans and Asian Americans," *Philadelphia Inquirer*, December 17, 2010, available at http://articles.philly.com/2010-12-17/ business/25293404_1_comcast-nbc-universal-comcast-lineup-comcast-corp; William Crowder, "Minority Entrepreneur Accelerator Program Kicks Off in Philadelphia," *Comcast Voices* (blog), September 21, 2011, http://blog.comcast.com/2011/09/ minority-entrepreneur-accelerator-program-kicks-off-in-philadelphia.html.

47. Bill Allison, "Net Neutrality: Do Campaign Contributions Tell the Whole Story?" *Sunlight Foundation Reporting Group* (blog), June 2, 2010, http://reporting. sunlightfoundation.com/2010/Net-neutrality-contribs/; Hon. Bobby L. Rush to Hon. Julius Genachowski et al., October 21, 2010 ("For the reasons set forth below, I would urge the Commission to approve this proposed joint venture"); "Comcast has the best Infrastructure of Inclusion to build upon in the media

industry"("*Proposed Combination of Comcast and NBC-Universal,*" 114 (Testimony of Will Griffin, Chairman and Chief Executive Officer, Hip Hop on Demand).

48. "*Comcast and NBC Universal: Who Benefits?*" 55, 56.

49. Ibid., 69.

50. Maxine Waters to Julius Genachowski, October 22, 2010, available at http://apps.fcc.gov/ecfs//document/view.action?id=7020918846.

51. Eric Lipton, "House Inquiry Tied to Bank," *New York Times*, July 31, 2010, available at http://www.nytimes.com/2010/08/01/us/politics/01ethics.html; Ashley Parker, "New E-Mails Delay Ethics Trial of Lawmaker," *New York Times*, November 19, 2010, available at http://www.nytimes.com/2010/11/20/us/politics/20waters.html?_r=1&ref—axinewaters; Larry Margasak, "Maxine Waters Ethics Probe: Six out of Ten Committee Members Recuse Themselves," *Huffington Post*, February 17 2012, http://www.huffingtonpost.com/2012/02/17/maxine-waters-ethics-investigation-recusal_n_1285286.html.

52. Hill staffer, interview with the author, August 23, 2010.

53. "*Competition in the Media and Entertainment Distribution Market,*" 1, 6 (Testimony of Jean Prewitt, President and CEO, Independent Film & Television Alliance).

54. Independent Film & Television Alliance, "Independent Film & Television Alliance Reaches Television, New Media Agreement with Comcast and NBC Universal," news release, July 12, 2010, http://www.ifta-online.org/independent-film-television-alliance-reaches-television-new-media-agreement-comcast-and-nbc-universa.

55. "I have heard that network affiliates have some concerns about the merger, including the fear that NBC will move its most popular programming from broadcast television to cable, which would decrease viewers and revenues and thus could severely impact the ability of these local stations to deliver local news and information" ("*Competition in the Media and Entertainment Distribution Market,*" 101 [Questioning of Jeff Zucker, President and Chief Executive Officer, NBC Universal, by Rep. Bob Goodlatte]). "Some observers, noting that broadcast networks traditionally have had only a single revenue source—advertising—that currently is facing serious cyclical and structural challenges, have predicted that Comcast might convert NBC to a cable network, abandoning its local affiliated broadcast stations and their local programming," reported Charles B. Goldfarb, *The Proposed Comcast-NBC Universal Combination: How It Might Affect the Video Market*, Congressional Research Service, February 2, 2010, 24 (citing Andrew Vanacore, "Broadcasters' Woes Could Spell Trouble for Free TV," *Yahoo! News*, December 29, 2009, http://www.lubbockonline.com/stories/122909/bus_540670417.shtml).

56. Appendix F of the FCC's approval of the merger set out the "Agreements Between Applicants and Network Affiliate Organizations." See *In the Matter of Applications of Comcast Corporation, General Electric Company and NBC Universal, Inc. for Consent to Assign Licenses and Transfer Control of Licenses*, 26 F.C.C.R. 4238, 4430 (2011), Appendix F.

57. Sen. Bernie Sanders, "NBC-Comcast Merger Not in the Public Interest," *Huffington Post*, December 6, 2010, http://www.huffingtonpost.com/rep-bernie-sanders/

nbc-comcast-merger-not-in_b_792858.html; "Comcast-NBC Merger: Read the FCC Approval Letter," *Wall Street Journal, Deal Journal* (blog), January 18, 2011, http://blogs.wsj.com/deals/2011/01/18/comcast-nbc-merger-read-the-fcc-approval-letter/. Numerous form letters from individuals were filed with the FCC, which can be found through the FCC's Electronic Comment Filing System, available at http://apps.fcc.gov/ecfs//fulltext/form.jsp.

58. The numerous letters filed in favor of the merger can also be found through the FCC's Electronic Comment Filing System.

59. John Eggerton, "Waters: Commissioner-Lite Chicago Forum 'Unacceptable,'" *Broadcasting & Cable,* July 11, 2010, http://www.broadcastingcable.com/article/454666-Waters_Commissioner_Lite_Chicago_Forum_Unacceptable_.php; "An open-mic session at a Chicago field hearing on the merger, held by the FCC's Media Bureau, was almost completely dominated by nonprofit organizations for everything from companion animals to the elderly testifying as to Comcast's goodwill and constant support" (Susan Crawford, "Comcast-NBC Merger Is All About Money, Politics," *Sacramento Bee,* September 15, 2010, available at http://gfem.org/node/1051).

60. Comcast Corporation, *Corporate Responsibility Report,* accessed March 4, 2012, available at http://www.cmcsk.com/documentdisplay.cfm?documentid=6024 #top.

61. "Money Politics; Rep. Bachmann in Overdrive; Predicting a GOP Wave; Craigslist 'Censored,'" transcript of *Anderson Cooper 360,* aired on CNN on September 6, 2010, http://transcripts.cnn.com/TRANSCRIPTS/1009/06/acd.02.html.

62. Gov. Arnold Schwarzenegger, Gov. David Paterson, Gov. Ed Rendell to Hon. Julius Genachowski et al., May 25, 2010, available at http://transition.fcc.gov/transaction/comcast-nbcu-cgo.html.

63. *"Confirmation of Elena Kagan to Be a Supreme Court Justice": Hearing Before the Senate Judiciary Committee,* 111th Cong., 2d sess. (2010) (Statement of Senator Al Franken).

64. Ron Chernow, *Titan: The Life of John D. Rockefeller, Sr.* (New York: Random House, 2008), 207.

65. "Herb Kohl for Senate 1988—'Nobody's Senator but Yours,'" YouTube video, 0:27, posted by "AlmostOnTheLake," November 5, 2010, http://www.youtube.com/watch?v=cZQgY7Plobc. On industry consolidation and antitrust exemptions for the airline industry, see Senator Herb Kohl, "Kohl Announces Antitrust Subcommittee Agenda for the 112th Congress," news release, March 10, 2011, available at http://www.kohl.senate.gov/newsroom/pressrelease.cfm?customel_dataPageID_1464=4332. On antitrust exemptions for the railroad industry, see Senator Herb Kohl, "Kohl Discusses Railroad Antitrust Amendment on the Senate Floor," news release, February 29, 2012, available at http://www.kohl.senate.gov/newsroom/pressrelease.cfm?customel_dataPageID_1464=4928. On the Sirius–XM satellite radio merger, see "Kohl Says 'No' to Sirius-XM Merger," *Wall Street Journal, Washington Wire* (blog), May 23, 2007, http://blogs.wsj.com/

washwire/2007/05/23/kohl-says-%E2%80%98no%E2%80%99-to-sirius-
xm-merger/. On the Comcast/NBCU merger, see "Kohl Wants Conditions on
Comcast/NBC Deal, Weighs in With DOJ & FCC," news release, May 26, 2010,
available at http://www.kohl.senate.gov/newsroom/comcast-nbc-letter.cfm.

66. Kohl, "Kohl Wants Conditions on Comcast/NBC Deal"; Senator Bernie Sanders,
"Sanders Statement on FCC and Comcast," news release, December 23, 2010,
available at http://www.sanders.senate.gov/newsroom/news/?id=a9d88ea4-4c3c-
45f2-ac70-016493cc40ef.

67. "Oversight of the U.S. Department of Justice": Hearing Before the S. Comm. on the Judiciary, 111th Cong., 36–37 (2010) available at http://www.gpo.gov/fdsys/pkg/CHRG-
111shrg63323/pdf/CHRG-111shrg63323.pdf; Senator Al Franken, "Sen. Franken's
Speech to Free Press Group in Minneapolis," news release, August 19, 2010, available at http://www.franken.senate.gov/?p=news&id=1044 [brackets in the original].

68. "Bottom Line," *TheHill,* available at October 4, 2010, http://thehill.com/business-
a-lobbying/lobbying-hires/122495-bottom-line.

69. Sen. Al Franken, interview with the author, September 30, 2010.

Chapter 11. The FCC Approves

1. Media executive, interview with the author, August 6, 2010.

2. *In the Matter of Application of EchoStar Communications Corporation, General Mo-
tors Corporation, and Hughes Electronics Corporation and EchoStar Communications
Corporation,* 17 F.C.C.R. 20559 (October 18, 2002); *In the Matter of Applications of
AT&T Inc. and Deutsche Telekom AG for Consent to Assign or Transfer Control of
Licenses and Authorizations,* Federal Communications Commission, WT Docket
No. 11-65 (November 29, 2011).

3. *In the Matter of Applications for Consent to the Transfer of Control of Licenses XM
Satellite Radio Holdings Inc. to Sirius Satellite Radio, Inc.,* 23 F.C.C.R. 12348
(August 5, 2008).

4. Ibid., 12375 ("the price cap condition ameliorates possible harm to consumers,
and the new programming packages offer consumers more pricing choices").

5. Media executive, interview with the author, August 6, 2010.

6. *In the Matter of SBC Communications Inc. and AT&T Corp. Applications for
Approval of Transfer of Control,* 20 F.C.C.R. 18290, 18392 (November 17, 2005); *In
the Matter of Verizon Communications Inc. and MCI, Inc. Applications for Approval
of Transfer of Control,* 20 F.C.C.R. 18433, 18537 (November 17, 2005); "Consumers
are entitled to access the lawful Internet content of their choice . . . to run applications and use services of their choice . . . to connect their choice of legal devices
. . . [and] consumers are entitled to competition among network providers, application and service providers, and content providers" (*In the Matters of Appropriate
Framework for Broadband Access to the Internet over Wireline Facilities, et al.,* 20
F.C.C.R. 14853, 14988 [September 23, 2005]).

7. *In the Matter of Verizon Communications,* 20 F.C.C.R. at 18573 (Statement of
Comm. Kathleen Q. Abernathy).

8. Thomas M. Koutsky and Lawrence J. Spiwak, "Separating Politics from Policy in FCC Merger Reviews: A Basic Legal Primer of the 'Public Interest' Standard," *Phoenix Center Policy Bulletin* no. 18 (May 2007): 14.

9. "[W]e refer to 'intermodal competition' as the competing provision of services over alternative technological platforms" (*In the Matter of Review of the Section 251 Unbundling Obligations of Incumbent Local Exchange Carriers, Implementation of the Local Competition Provisions of the Telecommunications Act of 1996, Deployment of Wireline Services Offering Advanced Telecommunications Capability*, 16 F.C.C.R. 22794 note 73 [December 20, 2001]).

10. Stuart M. Chemtob, "The Role of Competition Agencies in Regulated Sectors," Fifth International Symposium on Competition Policy and Law, Chinese Academy of Social Sciences, Beijing, May 11–12, 2007, 5, available at http://www.justice.gov/atr/public/speeches/225219.htm#N_1_.

11. *In Re Applications of Ameritech Corp. and SBC Communications Inc., for Consent to Transfer Control of Corporations Holding Licenses and Lines Pursuant to Section 251 and 310(d) of the Communications Act and Parts 5, 22, 24, 25, 63, 90, 95 and 101 of the Commission's Rules*, 14 F.C.C.R. 14712, 14887 (October 8, 1999). "While the SBC-Ameritech merger was consummated in October 1999, SBC has yet to compete in those markets outside of its region. Under the merger conditions placed on SBC by the FCC, it is liable for voluntary penalties for failure to enter the 30 out of region markets" (*ALTS [Association for Local Telecommunications Service] Response to NTIA [National Telecommunications and Information Administration] Request for Comment on Deployment of Broadband Networks and Advanced Telecommunications Services*, December 19, 2001, available at http://www.ntia.doc.gov/legacy/ntiahome/broadband/comments3/ALTS.htm).

12. "Most importantly, all of the commitments we have made, and conditions that we have agreed to, are wholly consistent with the manner in which we have always intended to conduct the Comcast and NBC Universal businesses. None of them will prevent us from executing on our business plans or will impair the competitiveness of any of our businesses." (David L. Cohen, "Regulatory Approval Received for Comcast/GE Joint Venture for NBC Universal," *Comcast Voices* (blog), January 18, 2011, http://blog.comcast.com/2011/01/regulatory-approval-received-for-comcastge-joint-venture-for-nbc-universal.html).

13. In May 2011, Meredith Attwell Baker announced that she would leave the FCC, when her term ended in June, for a position as senior vice president for government affairs for NBC Universal. See Marguerite Reardon, "FCC Commissioner Leaves for Comcast," *CNET News*, May 11, 2011, http://news.cnet.com/8301-30686_3-20062054-266.html; Edward Wyatt, "F.C.C. Commissioner Leaving to Join Comcast," *New York Times, Media Decoder* (blog), May 11, 2011, http://mediadecoder.blogs.nytimes.com/2011/05/11/f-c-c-commissioner-to-join-comcast/.

14. John Dunbar, "Ex-Reps. to Aid Comcast Takeover Bid," *Politico*, May 26, 2010, http://www.politico.com/news/stories/0510/37772.html.

15. "Comcast has become one of the bigger meal tickets in Washington, on its way to spending more $12.5 million [in 2010] in lobbying, more than six times the amount it spent around the time of its last major merger, the 2002 acquisition of AT&T's broadband Internet business" (Cecilia Kang, "Comcast's Fast-Growing Washington Presence," *Washington Post*, February 4, 2010, available at http://voices.washingtonpost.com/posttech/2010/02/comcasts_mighty_washington_prc.html); Hill staffer, interview with the author, August 23, 2010.

16. Federal Communications Commission, "John Flynn Named Senior Counsel to the Chairman for Transactions," news release, May 19, 2010.

17. Government official, interview with the author, January 20, 2011.

18. Ibid. Several other people also mentioned this.

19. Content-industry employee, interview with the author, August 6, 2010.

20. Washington, D.C., bloggers such as Marvin Ammori have noted Chairman Genachowski's reputedly "thin skin." See Marvin Ammori, "The FCC Chairman's D.C. Reputation: Or the Wimpy Kid Who Could Preserve an Open Internet, *Marvin Ammori* blog, December 1, 2010, http://ammori.org/2010/12/01/the-fcc-chairmans-d-c-reputation-or-the-wimpy-kid-who-could-preserve-an-open-internet/.

21. Josh Silver, "Comcastrophe: Obama's FCC Approves Enormous Corporate Media Merger for Comcast/NBC," *Alternet*, January 18, 2011, http://www.alternet.org/media/149579/comcastrophe%3A_obama%27s_fcc_approves_enormous_corporate_media_merger_for_comcast_nbc/?page=entire.

22. "*The Comcast/NBC Universal Merger: What Does the Future Hold for Competition and Consumers*": Hearing Before the Subcomm. on Antitrust, Competition Policy and Consumer Rights of the S. Comm. on the Judiciary, 111th Cong., 15–17 (February 4, 2010) (Statement of Andrew Jay Schwartzman, President and Chief Executive Officer of Media Access Project).

23. Harold Feld, "Where Does Comcast/NBC Rate on the 'Trade Association Scale'?" *Huffington Post*, December 3, 2009, http://www.huffingtonpost.com/harold-feld/where-does-comcastnbc-rat_b_379574.html. See also Harold Feld, "Public Knowledge Comment on Comcast-NBCU Merger," Public Knowledge, January 18, 2011, http://www.publicknowledge.org/public-knowledge-comment-comcast-nbcu-merger.

24. John Eggerton, "Public Interest Groups, Cable Ops, Unions Slam Comcast/NBCU Merger," *Broadcast Union News* (blog), February 4, 2010, http://broadcastunionnews.blogspot.com/2010/02/public-interest-groups-cable-ops-unions.html.

25. Letters opposing and in support of the merger can all be found through the FCC's Electronic Comment Filing System, available at http://apps.fcc.gov/ecfs//fulltext/form.jsp.

26. A Hill staffer told me in an interview on September 3, 2010, that blocking the merger was always considered unrealistic. "[T]he elimination of double marginalization of NBCU programming costs likely will result in some benefits for consumers" (*In the Matter of Applications of Comcast Corporation, General Electric Company and NBC Universal, Inc. for Consent to Assign Licenses and Transfer*

Control of Licenses, 26 F.C.C.R. 4238, 4335 ([January 20, 2011]). Jonathan B. Baker, "Comcast/NBCU: The FCC Provides a Roadmap for Vertical Merger Analysis," *Antitrust* 25, no. 2 (spring 2011): 36–42, available at http://transition.fcc.gov/osp/projects/baker_vertical_mergers.pdf ("When analyzing vertical mergers, the antitrust enforcement agencies employ a contemporary economic analysis of exclusionary conduct, but they have not litigated any vertical merger challenges to a decision in the modern era. All such mergers have been permitted to proceed without a challenge, or challenges were settled by consent.").

27. "Malone Says Telecoms Lack 'Firepower' Versus Cable," YouTube video, 06:04, posted by "*Bloomberg,*" July 14, 2010, http://www.youtube.com/watch?v=QUbQRwKXeCU; "John Malone and David Faber," video of interview, 41:07–41:22, *CNBC,* November 23, 2009, http://video.cnbc.com/gallery/?video=1340949341.

28. "AT&T Chief Executive Randall Stephenson . . . told Dow Jones Newswires . . . that he wasn't nervous about the deal, and expects to get the same access to programming" (Robert Cheng, "Update: Comcast Makes Switch to Content Partner from Rival," *Dow Jones Newswires,* March 12, 2009). Companies including DirecTV, Dish Network, News Corporation, and Viacom filed letters with the FCC expressing concerns about possible anticompetitive results of the merger. See William M. Wiltshire, Counsel for DirecTV, to Marlene H. Dortch, Secretary of the Federal Communications Commission, January 12, 2011; Pantelis Michaelopoulos and Christopher Bjornson, Counsel for Dish Network, to Marlene H. Dortch, January 14, 2011; Maureen A. O'Connell, Senior Vice President, Regulatory & Government Affairs, News Corporation, to Marlene H. Dortch, January 13, 2011; Keith R. Murphy, Vice President, Government Relations and Regulatory Counsel, Viacom Inc., to Marlene H. Dortch, January 13, 2011.

29. According to the Independent Film & Television Alliance, "since the mid-1990s—when ownership of major studios, broadcast networks and cable companies 'have become almost fully intertwined'—the volume of independent produced programming available to the public 'has dropped precipitously'" (*Comments of the Independent Film & Television Alliance, In the Matter of Applications of Comcast Corporation, General Electric, and NBC Universal, Inc., For Consent to Assign and Transfer Control of FCC Licenses,* Federal Communications Commission, August 17, 2010). Al Jazeera has been unable to reach a deal with Comcast since at least 2006. See Michael Matza, "Protesters Seek to Get Al Jazeera on Comcast," *Philadelphia Inquirer,* February 14, 2012, available at http://articles.philly.com/2012-02-14/news/31059023_1_al-jazeera-english-comcast-demonstrators; Sam Gustin, "Al Jazeera in Talks with Comcast over U.S. Distribution," *Wired Magazine,* February 22, 2011, http://www.wired.com/epicenter/2011/02/al-jazeera-comcast/; "Al Jazeera Meets American Resistance," *Bloomberg Businessweek,* April 23, 2006, http://www.businessweek.com/magazine/content/06_14/b3978036.htm.

30. Stephen Díaz Gavin, Counsel for Bloomberg, LP, to Marlene H. Dortch, Secretary of the Federal Communications Commission, November 16, 2010, available at http://apps.fcc.gov/ecfs//document/view.action?id=7020920769.

31. In its order approving the Comcast-NBCU merger, the FCC "Recogniz[ed] the danger this transaction could present to the development of innovative online video distribution" (*In the Matter of Applications of Comcast Corporation*, 26 F.C.C.R. at 4241). Jeffrey Silva, telecommunications and media analyst with Medley Global Advisors, said, while the merger was still being considered, "Online video is an emerging market and if someone gained power really early, it could stifle it" (Joe Flint, "Internet Issues Bog Down Comcast-NBC Merger," *Los Angeles Times*, December 10, 2010, available at http://articles.latimes.com/2010/dec/10/business/la-fi-ct-comcast-20101210).

32. The FCC noted, in its approval order, "EarthLink and DISH also express concern that Comcast will have an increased incentive post-transaction to raise the price of its standalone broadband service, thereby effectively tying its cable and broadband services by making the bundled option the consumer's only reasonable economic choice" (*In the Matter of Applications of Comcast Corporation*, 26 F.C.C.R. at 4278).

33. Consumer Federation of America, Consumers Union and Free Press, *Comcast's Hollow "Public Interest" Commitments*, 2, accessed March 4, 2012, http://www.freepress.net/node/76419; Michael Hiltzik, "Comcast-NBC Merger Does Nothing to Enhance the Public Interest," *Los Angeles Times*, January 1, 2011, available at http://articles.latimes.com/2011/jan/01/business/la-fi-hiltzik-20110101.

34. Content-industry executive, interview with the author, October 11, 2010.

35. "And when Comcast wanted to merge with NBC Universal, Clyburn withheld her support until she got assurances from Comcast that it would launch—and regularly make improvements to—a program to provide cheap broadband service and digital equipment to low-income families" (Kim Hart, "Mignon Clyburn: When a Daughter Votes Her Mind," *Politico*, February 13, 2012, http://www.politico.com/news/stories/0212/72822.html).

36. Government staffer, interview with the author, January 20, 2011.

37. By January 13, 2011, Commissioner Genachowski was circulating a draft order approving the merger, among his colleagues. See Zachary Hunchar, "NBC Universal/Comcast Merger Closer to Approval by FCC," *Technorati* (blog), January 13, 2011, http://technorati.com/entertainment/tv/article/nbc-universalcomcast-merger-closer-to-approval/. Kim Hart, "Mignon Clyburn." Author interviews with government staffers, January 20, 2011.

38. "FCC Approves Comcast NBC Merger," *NASDAQ* blog, January 19, 2011, http://community.nasdaq.com/News/2011-01/fcc-approves-comcast-nbc-merger.aspx?storyid=53900. The information that Comcast could still bundle at will came up in my interview with a government official, February 4, 2011.

39. "For any Qualified OVD that meets the Benchmark Condition, C-NBCU Programmers shall provide Online Video Programming sought by the OVD that constitutes Comparable Programming" (*In the Matter of Applications of Comcast Corporation*, 26 F.C.C.R. at 4360); Ben Fritz, "Comcast Tries Tiered Data Pricing, Continues Fight with Netflix," *Los Angeles Times*, May 17, 2012, available at http://

www.latimes.com/entertainment/envelope/cotown/la-et-ct-comcast-netflix-20120517,0,4027578.story.

40. "At a minimum, Comcast shall offer a service of at least 6 Mbps down at a price no greater than $49.95 for three years (provided that the price can be increased by no more than any increase in the CPI-U for Communications after two years)" (*In the Matter of Applications of Comcast Corporation*, 26 F.C.C.R. at 4362). "Within nine months of the Closing of the Transaction, Comcast shall commence a program, the Comcast Broadband Opportunity Program ('CBOP'), to substantially increase broadband adoption in low income homes throughout Comcast's service area . . . each eligible participating household shall . . . receive the Economy version of Comcast's Broadband Internet Access Service for $9.95 per month" (ibid., 4379).

41. Content-industry executive, interview with the author, February 13, 2011.

42. Joe Flint, "Bloomberg and Comcast Fighting Again," *Los Angeles Times, Company Town* (blog), May 27, 2011, available at http://latimesblogs.latimes.com/entertainmentnewsbuzz/2011/05/bloomberg-and-comcast-fighting-again.html?dlvrit=52115. Fitzmaurice said (correctly), "The FCC clearly stated that 'we decline to adopt a requirement that Comcast affirmatively undertake neighborhooding.'" However, the FCC did explicitly "adopt a narrowly tailored condition related to channel placement for independent news channels," noted Joe Flint, "Bloomberg Files FCC Complaint over Comcast Channel Lineups," *Los Angeles Times*, June 14, 2011, available at http://articles.latimes.com/2011/jun/14/business/la-fi-ct-bloomberg-comcast-20110614; see *In the Matter of Applications of Comcast Corporation*, 26 F.C.C.R. at 4287–88. Greg Babyak, *Bloomberg's* head of government affairs, called it a "test case," as reported in Brooks Boliek, "Bloomberg: Comcast Is Cheating," *Politico*, May 26, 2011, http://www.politico.com/news/stories/0511/55810.html.

43. Thomson StreetEvents, "Comcast Corporation Conference Call to Discuss It's [sic] Joint Venture with General Electric," January 18, 2011, available at http://www.comcast.com/nbcutransaction/pdfs/CMCSATranscript-1.18.2011.pdf.

44. Marguerite Reardon, "FCC Commissioner Leaves for Comcast"; Edward Wyatt, "F.C.C. Commissioner Leaving to Join Comcast."

45. Cecilia Kang, "Tweet About FCC Member's New Job at Comcast Sets off Firestorm," *Washington Post*, May 19, 2011, available at http://www.washingtonpost.com/business/economy/tweet-about-fcc-members-new-job-at-comcast-sets-off-firestorm/2011/05/19/AFZNiP7G_story.html; Cecilia Kang, "Reel Grrls Turns Down Comcast Funds, Cites Free Expression," *Washington Post, Post Tech* (blog), May 20, 2011, http://www.washingtonpost.com/blogs/post-tech/post/reel-grrls-turns-down-comcast-funds-cites-free-expression/2011/05/20/AFYAJx7G_blog.html.

46. Kim Hart and Eliza Krigman, "Comcast Eyes Future, Hires Big Guns," *Politico*, September 12, 2011, http://www.politico.com/news/stories/0911/63313.html.

Chapter 12. Aftermath

1. Joelle Tessler, "Conditions on Comcast, NBC Deal Sought: FCC Wants Guarantees that Cable Giant Will Not Stifle Video Competition," Associated Press, December 24, 2010.

2. Sam Thielman, "Comcast-NBC U Execs Tout Synergy, Muscle," *Daily Variety*, January 27, 2011, available at http://www.variety.com/article/VR1118031020?refc atid=4076&printerfriendly=true.

3. Brian L. Roberts, "The President's Council on Jobs and Competitiveness," *Comcast Voices* (blog), February 23, 2011, http://blog.comcast.com/2011/02/the-presidents-council-on-jobs-and-competitiveness.html.

4. "In 2010, we added 1.3 million net new customers to end the year with 22.8 million video customers, 17.0 million high-speed internet customers" (Comcast, *Comcast 2010 Annual Review*, available at http://www.comcast.com/2010annualre view/?SCRedirect=true#/highlights). "Combined Video, High-Speed Internet and Voice customers increased by 414,000" (Comcast, *Comcast Reports 4th Quarter and Year End 2010 Results*, December 31, 2010, available at http://www.cmcsk.com/releasedetail.cfm?ReleaseID=550450).

5. Jennifer Saba, "Time Warner Raises Outlook; Ad Revenue up 9 Pct," *Reuters*, May 5, 2010; "Cable Networks Weather Economic Storm, Positioned to Remain Strong," SNL Kagan, August 2011; Tom Lowry, "Poverty a Problem for Pay TV," *Variety*, May 31, 2011, available at http://www.variety.com/article/VR1118037755?refcatid=14; Henry A. Jessell, "Uncovering the Truth About Retrans Value," *TVNewsCheck*, December 2, 2011, http://www.tvnewscheck.com/article/55785/uncovering-the-truth-about-retrans-value.

6. Michael Powell, "Let's Be True to Our Principles," *Cable Tech Talk*, September 28, 2011, http://www.cabletechtalk.com/fcc/2011/09/28/let%E2%80%99s-be-true-to-our-principles/.

7. "I think [Brian Roberts will] get the deal through. The question is really what kind of restraints he'll have to agree to. And that will then be a clue to other distributors as to whether they need to go vertical, and have something to fight back with" ("John Malone and David Faber," video of interview, 41:07–41:22, *CNBC*, November 23, 2009, http://video.cnbc.com/gallery/?video=1340949341).

8. Mike Flacy, "Comcast Rolling Out Test of $60 First-Run, Theatrical Movies over VoD," *Digital Trends*, October 6, 2011, http://www.digitaltrends.com/home-theater/comcast-rolling-out-test-of-60-first-run-theatrical-movies-over-vod/; Mike Masnick, "No One Wanted to Pay $30 For In-Home Movie Rentals . . . So Now Universal Will Try $60?" *Tech Dirt*, October 7, 2011, http://www.techdirt.com/articles/20111007/02570316246/no-one-wanted-to-pay-30-in-home-movie-rentals-so-now-universal-will-try-60.shtml.

9. Swanni, "Universal Comes to Senses; Drops $60 VOD," *TVPredictions*, October 13, 2011, http://www.tvpredictions.com/universal101311.htm.

10. Deborah Yao, "Comcast CFO: Not Interested in Acquiring Wireless Network," *SNL Insurance Daily*, September 21, 2011.

11. "Wireline Costs and Caps: A Few Facts," *FNN: DSL Prime*, March 6, 2011, http://dslprime.com/dslprime/42-d/4148-costs-and-caps.

12. Comcast Corporation, "Q4 2010 Earnings Call," transcript, February 16, 2011, available at http://www.google.com/url?sa=t&rct=j&q=&esrc=s&source=web&cd=3&cts=1330567895551&ved=0CDYQFjAC&url=http%3A%2F%2Ffiles.shareholder.com%2Fdownloads%2FCMCSA%2Foxox442204%2Fdc126a85-c48e-4f65-85ce-750ed50a1fdd%2FCMCSA_Transcript_2.16.11.pdf&ei=C9pOT8fGJ6LgoQHQ56i_DQ&usg=AFQjCNGJAWH3Ql6oyAojg_BCvriu1YEa9g&sig2=6yEI8oJEKQ_iygHx7Xyasg.

13. Bob Fernandez, "Comcast Fourth Quarter Profit Jumps," *Philadelphia Inquirer*, February 17, 2011.

14. "Q1 '11 Cable, DBS, Telco Video Subscribers by DMA," *OSP Mag*, July 4, 2011, http://www.ospmag.com/osp-central/ospcentralresearchreport/q111-cable-dbs-telco-video-subscribers-dma.

15. Comcast Corporation, "Q4 2010 Earnings Call."

16. "Comcast Is King of Its Empire," *Courier-Post* (Cherry Hill, N.J.), May 14, 2011, available via Westlaw (www.westlaw.com) at 2011 WLNR 9636907.

17. Jessica E. Vascellaro and Lauren A.E. Schuker, "Comcast Plays Up 'Symphony,'" *Wall Street Journal*, April 30, 2011.

18. Ken Auletta, "A Conversation with John Malone," New York, October 16, 2002, available at http://www.kenauletta.com/2002_10_16_johnmalone.html.

19. Betty Liu, interview with John Malone, *Bloomberg News*, July 14, 2010, Voxant Business Transcripts, available via Westlaw (www.westlaw.com), 2010 WLNR 14208095.

20. Jonathan Baker, "Continuing a Conversation About the FCC's Merger Review Process," *Reboot FCC* blog, March 17, 2011, http://reboot.fcc.gov/blog?entryId=1340463.

21. *In the Matter of Media Bureau Seeks Comment on the Regional Sports Network Marketplace*, Federal Communications Commission, MB Docket No. 11-128, September 9, 2011, 2 (Comments of Comcast Corporation).

22. The Commission established these terms as preconditions to approval of the NBCU-Comcast merger in the hope that they would protect nascent Online Video Distributors like Netflix. See Thomson StreetEvents, "Comcast Corporation Conference Call to Discuss It's [sic] Joint Venture with General Electric Related to Regulatory Clearance of NBCU Transaction," January 18, 2011, available at http://www.comcast.com/nbcutransaction/pdfs/CMCSATranscript-1.18.2011.pdf. *In the Matter of Media Bureau Seeks Comment*, 3.

23. "We call [this] the full freight door. . . . Under this door, an OVD that does not have a deal with anyone else can come to NBC Universal and ask for the full linear NBC Universal lineup that is typically made available to other multichannel video distributors. So this is not—you can't ask for one network. You can't cherry pick networks. You can't cherry pick programs. You have to go and ask for the whole linear lineup from NBC Universal. And the OVD in that case has to agree to pay the economic equivalent of what NBC Universal would receive for giving the same set of content to an MVPD. So that would include MVPD affiliate fees,

retransmission consent fees. But it would also include revenue that we might lose because this content was being delivered in an online video format instead of in the multichannel video distributor format. For example, advertising revenues" ("Comcast Corporation Conference Call").

24. David Faber, "Interview with John Malone," *CNBC*, April 4, 2011, transcript at http://msnbcmedia.msn.com/i/CNBC/Sections/News_And_Analysis/_ News/__EDIT%20Englewood%20Cliffs/john_malone_interview.pdf.

25. Karl Bode, "Earthlink Wants Wholesale Access as NBC/U Condition," *DSLReports.com*, October 7, 2010, http://www.dslreports.com/shownews/Earthlink-Wants-Wholesale-Access-As-NBCU-Condition-110777. EarthLink supported its contention with studies by Professor Simon J. Wilkie that were filed with the FCC. See Simon J. Wilkie, "Consumer Sovereignty, Disintermediation, and the Economic Impact of the Proposed Comcast/NBCU Transaction" (June 21, 2010) ("Wilkie Report"), available at http://www.competitioneconomics.com/wp-content/uploads/2010/08/Report-of-Professor-Simon-J-Wilkie-on-Behalf-of-EarthLink-06-21-2010-MB-Docket-No-10-56-2.pdf; Simon J. Wilkie, "Economic Analysis of the Proposed Comcast-NBCU-GE Transaction" (August 19, 2010) ("Wilkie Reply Report"), available at http://www.competitioneconomics.com/wp-content/uploads/2010/08/Reply-Report-of-Professor-Simon-J.-Wilkie-on-Behalf-of-EarthLink-08-19-2010-MB-Docket-No.-10-56.pdf. "Next Generation Connectivity: A Review of Broadband Internet Transitions and Policy from Around the World, Final Report," Yochai Benkler, Principal Investigator (Cambridge, Mass.: Berkman Center for Internet and Society at Harvard University, February 2010), 15, available at http://cyber.law.harvard.edu/sites/cyber.law.harvard.edu/files/Berkman_Center_Broadband_Final_Report_15Feb2010.pdf.

26. "The Communicators: David Cohen, Comcast Corp.," YouTube video, 14:59–15:15, posted by "C-SPAN," August 2, 2009, http://www.youtube.com/watch?v=sIozcgvdehs; Ron Chernow, *Titan: The Life of John D. Rockefeller, Sr.* (New York: Random House, 1998), 547.

27. The FCC report covers EarthLink's request for wholesale access in note 224 ("While we agree with EarthLink that stimulating development, innovation and investment in the OVD market, and in the broadband market as a whole, are critical public policy goals, we find that the open Internet and standalone broadband conditions that we are imposing on this transaction are sufficient to protect the broadband industry and the interests of consumers"): *Memorandum Opinion and Order, "In the Matter of Applications of Comcast Corporation, General Electric Company and NBC Universal, Inc. For Consent to Assign Licenses and Transfer Control of Licensees,"* FCC, January 18, 2011, 41.

28. TR Daily, "FCC Official: Managed Network Issues Likely to Be Decided Case-by-Case," September 26, 2011, *Telecommunications Reports*, available via Westlaw (www.westlaw.com) at 2011 WLNR 19546357. (FCC officials participated in a Federal Communications Bar Association event on the condition that their remarks not be attributed to any individual.)

29. David Hyman, "Why Bandwidth Pricing Is Anti-Competitive," *Wall Street Journal*, July 7, 2011.
30. "The Communicators: David Cohen, Comcast Corp.," YouTube video, 5:37–6:15.
31. Sen. Al Franken, interview with the author, September 30, 2010.
32. "Per capita, fewer of us have broadband than in South Korea, Japan, or just about anywhere in Europe," according to Nick Judd, "Gig.U Asks Universities and Telcos to Work Together for the Internet of the Future, Starting Today," *Tech President*, September 15, 2011, http://techpresident.com/blog-entry/gigu-asks-universites-and-telcos-work-together-internet-future. "Other countries, such as Korea, Japan, and France, offer speeds 20 to 100 times faster in both directions, and for the price of the inferior copper-based DSL offered in the U.S. The American public is the big loser," noted David Rosen, "The Comcast-NBC Merger & the Future of Internet Video," *Z Magazine*, March 2010. And the *Economist* pointed out: "Having led the world in internet access, America has slipped over the past decade to 22nd (behind Latvia and the Czech Republic) with an average download speed of a mere 3.8 megabits per second (Mbps) compared with South Korea's average of 14.6Mbps. Worse, Americans pay through the nose for their high-speed access. According to the New America Foundation, a 100Mbps internet connection costs $16 a month in Sweden and $24 a month in South Korea. In Hong Kong, 160Mbps can be had for $65 a month. Thanks to the lack of competition, Americans have to stump up $145 a month for 50Mbps—less than a third the Japanese internet speed for over twice the price. By any measure, that is a terrible deal" ("The Difference Engine: Politics and the Web," December 24, 2010). "Approximately 100 million Americans do not have broadband at home," according to the National Broadband Plan Executive Summary, accessed March 1, 2012, http://www.broadband.gov/plan/executive-summary/.

Chapter 13. The AT&T–T-Mobile Deal

Epigraph. Ian Shapira, "James Cicconi, Head of AT&T Lobbying Effort, Confident in Approval of T-Mobile Deal," *Washington Post*, March 23, 2011.
1. Tom Schoenberg, Sara Forden, and Jeff Bliss, "T-Mobile Antitrust Challenge Leaves AT&T with Little Recourse On Takeover," *Bloomberg*, September 1, 2011, http://www.bloomberg.com/news/2011-08-31/u-s-files-antitrust-complaint-to-block-proposed-at-t-t-mobile-merger.html.
2. Craig Moffett, *The Rationing Impulse . . . [For Straws] in the Wind* (Washington, D.C.: Bernstein Research, June 10, 2011).
3. Eli Noam, "Let Them Eat Cellphones: Why Mobile Wireless Is No Solution for Broadband," *Journal of Information Policy* 1 (2011): 470–85.
4. The cost of installing a wireless network is consistently less than that for a wired network. In some parts of the country, the wireless cost advantage exceeds $7,500 per customer. See Coleman Bazelon, "The Benefits of Wireless Broadband for Rural Deployments" (Cambridge, Mass: The Brattle Group, March 16, 2010), available at http://www.brattle.com/_documents/uploadlibrary/upload837.pdf.

5. Greg Besinger, "For Sprint, Free Pays Off," *Wall Street Journal*, November 10, 2011; Craig Moffett, *U.S. & European Telecommunications: Stuck in the Middle . . . Will T-Mobile USA Be the Next Sprint?* (Washington, D.C.: Bernstein Research, February 5, 2009).

6. "During a recent Citibank investor's [*sic*] conference, John Stankey, AT&T's President, said that the service provider is confident it can pass 55–60 percent of the homes in their service region," reported Sean Buckley, "AT&T Nears End of Its U-Verse Service Buildout," *Fierce Telecom*, May 20, 2011, http://www.fiercetelecom.com/story/att-nears-end-its-u-verse-service-buildout/2011-05-20.

7. Karl Bode, "AT&T: The U-Verse Build Is Over," *DSLReports.com*, February 9, 2012, http://www.dslreports.com/shownews/ATT-The-UVerse-Build-is-Over-118297.

8. Noam, "Let Them Eat Cellphones," 481.

9. John Horrigan, "Wireless Internet Use" (Washington, D.C.: Pew Internet, July 2009); *In the Matter of Lifeline and Link Up Reform and Modernization*, Federal Communications Commission, WC Docket No. 11-42, April 21, 2011 (Comments of Media Action Grassroots Network).

10. Kai Jakobs, *Information Technology Standards and Standardization: A Global Perspective* (Hershey, Pa.: Idea Group, 2000), 206-08

11. Ibid., 214.

12. *Enhanced Data Collection Could Help FCC Better Monitor Competition in the Wireless Industry* (Washington, D.C.: Government Accountability Office, July 2010), 8.

13. Charles Edquist, *The Internet and Mobile Telecommunications System of Innovation* (Northampton, Mass.: Edward Elgar Publishing, 2003), 83–85.

14. Ibid., 73.

15. As part of the Omnibus Budget Reconciliation Act of 1993, Pub. L. No. 103-66, § 6002, 107 Stat. 312, 387-392 (the "1993 Budget Act"), Congress added Section 309(j) to the Communications Act of 1934, as amended (the "Communications Act"), authorizing the Federal Communications Commission to award licenses for rights to use the radio spectrum through competitive bidding.

16. "Broadband Personal Communications Service (PCS)," Federal Communications Commission Encyclopedia, accessed March 3, 2012, http://www.fcc.gov/encyclopedia/broadband-personal-communications-service-pcs; *Where Do We Go from Here? The FCC Auctions and the Future of Radio Spectrum Management* (Washington, D.C.: Congressional Budget Office, April 1997), 12–17.

17. Guy Klemens, *The Cellphone: The History and Technology of the Gadget That Changed the World* (Jefferson, Ill.: McFarland, 2010), 134.

18. Ibid., 134–35.

19. Ibid., 135–36.

20. "Cingular Nabs AT&T Wireless for $41B," *CNN Money*, February 17, 2004, http://money.cnn.com/2004/02/17/technology/cingular_att/?cnn=yes.

21. Saul Hansell, "Verizon and AT&T Win Big in Auction of Spectrum," *New York Times*, March 21, 2008; "AT&T Talks Up LTE," *Daily Wireless*, accessed March 3, 2012, http://www.dailywireless.org/2011/05/25/att-talks-up-lte/.

22. Sinead Carew and Diane Bartz, "Sprint Files to Block AT&T purchase of T-Mobile USA," *Reuters*, May 31, 2011, available at http://www.reuters.com/article/2011/05/31/us-att-tomobile-sprint-idUSTRE74U5Y320110531.

23. Gigi Wang, *AT&T/T-Mobile Merger: More Market Concentration, Less Choice, Higher Prices* (Boston: Yankee Group, August 2011).

24. U.S. Department of Commerce, National Telecommunications and Information Administration, "Digital Nation: Expanding Internet Usage," NTIA Research Preview, February 2011, available at http://www.ntia.doc.gov/files/ntia/publications/ntia_internet_use_report_february_2011.pdf.

25. *Report and Order and Further Notice of Proposed Rulemaking, In the Matter of Connect America Fund, a National Broadband Plan for Our Future, Establishing Just and Reasonable Rates for Local Exchange Carriers, et al.*, Federal Communications Commission, WC Docket No. 10-90, GN Docket No. 09-51, WC Docket No. 07-135, et al., November 18, 2011, p. 4, n. 3.

26. *Description of Transaction, Public Interest Showing, and Related Demonstrations, In the Matter of Applications of AT&T Inc. and Deutsche Telekom AG for Consent to Assign or Transfer Control of License and Authorizations*, Federal Communications Commission, WT Docket No. 11-65, April 21, 2011.

27. Allen Tsai, "Obama to Double Available Wireless Spectrum," *Mobiledia*, June 28, 2010, http://www.mobiledia.com/news/71990.html.

28. Federal Communications Commission, "National Broadband Plan," (2010), chaps. 5–6, available at http://www.broadband.gov/plan/.

29. *Ex Parte Submission of the United States Department of Justice, In the Matter of Economic Issues in Broadband Competition: A National Broadband Plan for Our Future*, Federal Communications Commission, GN Docket No. 09-51, January 4, 2010.

30. *Description of Transaction, Public Interest Showing, and Related Demonstrations, In the Matter of Applications of AT&T Inc.*

31. Ben Protess and Michael J. De La Marced, "JPMorgan, the Lender Behind the T-Mobile Deal," *New York Times*, March 21, 2011, available at http://dealbook.nytimes.com/2011/03/21/jpmorgan-the-lender-behind-the-t-mobile-deal/.

32. *Description of Transaction, Public Interest Showing, and Related Demonstrations, In the Matter of Applications of AT&T Inc.*

33. *Why the AT&T-T-Mobile Deal Is Bad for America* (Washington, D.C.: Free Press, March 21, 2011), available at http://www.freepress.net/files/ATT-TMobile.pdf.

34. "T-Mobile Coverage Map," T-Mobile, accessed March 10, 2012, http://www.t-mobile.com/coverage/pcc.aspx; "AT&T Wireless Coverage Map," AT&T, accessed March 10, 2012, http://www.wireless.att.com/coverageviewer/#?type=voice.

35. *Description of Transaction, Public Interest Showing, and Related Demonstrations, In the Matter of Applications of AT&T Inc.*

36. "[The] transaction would reduce competition and harm consumers" (Matthew Spankey, "Sprint Releases Official Statement in Opposition of AT&T/T-Mobile Merger," Sprint Nextel, news release, March 28, 2011 http://www.sprintusers.com/sprint-releases-official-statement-in-opposition-of-att-t-mobile-merger/).

37. "As recently as last October, Mr. Hesse said the wireless industry is 'hyper competitive.' The month prior, his CFO talked about how 'tough' retail competition is in the wireless market, citing at least six major competitors. In February of last year, Mr. Hesse said, 'M&A is absolutely a way to get the growth in the industry, if a particular transaction makes sense for anybody.' He went on to say, 'I think consolidation will be healthy for the industry, some consolidation. It is, needless to say, very competitive'" (Jim Cicconi, "AT&T Response to Hesse Remarks," *AT&T Public Policy* (blog), April 15, 2011, http://attpublicpolicy.com/government-policy/att-response-to-hesse-remarks/.

38. Shayndi Rice and Thomas Catan, "AT&T's Critics On Deal Growing," *Wall Street Journal*, May 31, 2011.

39. Communications Workers of America, "T-Mobile USA and AT&T Merger Means Faster and More Widespread Broadband," news release, March 20, 2011, available at http://www.cwa-union.org/news/entry/t-_mobile_usa_and_att_merger_means_faster_and_more_widespread_broadband.

40. "As represented in the FCC docket, the proposed merger of AT&T and T-Mobile has received substantive support from national Hispanic organizations including Hispanic Federation" ("NAACP Endorses AT&T Deal," *Los Angeles Sentinel*, June 3, 2011, available at http://www.lasentinel.net/NAACP-endorses-ATT-deal.html); Jason A. Lorenz, "AT&T, T-Mobile Merger Can Benefit Latinos, *LatinoLA*, June 14, 2011, http://latinola.com/story.php?story=9591.

41. Edward Wyatt, "AT&T Plans to Woo U.S. and Fight It," *New York Times*, September 2, 2011.

42. "We begin by describing the strong competitors that the combined company will continue to face after this transaction is complete. These include not only providers that market service to customers living in most U.S. markets, but also 'regional' providers that market only where they operate networks. Again, providers in both categories offer their customers nationwide service plans" (*Description of Transaction, Public Interest Showing, and Related Demonstrations, In the Matter of Applications of AT&T Inc.*).

43. T-Mobile, investor conference call, transcript, January 20, 2011) available at http://www.google.com/url?sa=t&rct=j&q=&esrc=s&source=web&cd=1&cts=13310406 73578&sqi=2&ved=0CDEQFjAA&url=http%3A%2F%2Fwww.telekom.com%2Fstatic%2F-%2F18868%2F1%2F110126-transcription-inday-si&ei=nhF WT9OyFaH1ogGnvf28Cg&usg=AFQjCNGk8RXAWEnaBP9Fab1v8bfjScZRLA &sig2=QS_CDMMarvKtp6_LR-g1jQ.

44. John Delaney, "Analysis: AT&T Acquires T-Mobile US," *Comms Dealer*, March 21, 2011, http://www.comms-dealer.com/market-analysis/analysis-att-acquires-t-mobile-us.

45. *Description of Transaction, Public Interest Showing, and Related Demonstrations, In the Matter of Applications of AT&T Inc.*, 2.

46. Casey Johnston, "Obama Pitches Plan to Free 500MHz, Raise $28B, and Bring 4G to Everyone," *Ars Technica*, February 10, 2011, http://arstechnica.com/

tech-policy/news/2011/02/us-government-announces-plan-to-free-up-500-mhz-of-spectrum-implement-4g.ars.

47. "The process of revisiting or revising spectrum allocations has historically taken 6–13 years" (Federal Communications Commission, "National Broadband Plan," 79).

48. Ibid., 269.

49. "AT&T is today sitting on more spectrum than any other wireless operator in the top 21 markets in the U.S., and about a third of that spectrum is still being unused," reported Marguerite Reardon, "Is AT&T a Wireless Spectrum Hog?" *CNET News*, April 29, 2011, http://news.cnet.com/8301-30686_3-20058494-266.html.

50. Wayne Watts, "AT&T Statement on Department of Justice Action," news release, August 31, 2011.

51. Stacy Cowley, "AT&T CEO Pay Docked $2 Million for T-Mobile Debacle," *CNN Money*, February 22, 2012, http://money.cnn.com/2012/02/22/technology/att_ceo_pay/index.htm.

52. Karl Bode, "The AT&T T-Mobile Deal Is Officially Dead After Historic Consumer, Industry and Regulatory Opposition," *DSLReports.com*, December 19, 2011, http://www.dslreports.com/shownews/The-ATT-TMobile-Deal-Is-Officially-Dead-117504.

53. Mike Isaac, "T-Mobile Users Rejoice at Justice Dept. Blocking AT&T Merger," *Wired, CNN Tech*, September 1, 2011, http://www.cnn.com/2011/09/01/tech/mobile/t-mobile-users-rejoice/index.html.

54. Anton Troianovski, "AT&T May Try Billing App Makers," *Wall Street Journal*, February 28, 2012, available at http://online.wsj.com/article/SB10001424052970204653604577249080966030276.html?mod=googlenews_wsj.

55. Colin Weir, "AT&T Mulls Third-Party Billing for Data," *ETI Views and News*, March, 2012, http://www.econtech.com/newsletter/march2012/march2012a2.php.

56. "U.S. Telecommunications and U.S. Cable and Satellite: Nature vs. Nurture" (Bernstein Research, May 2012), 27.

Chapter 14. The Costly Gift

1. "Terry Huval F2C Interview," YouTube video, 00:36, posted by "Fiberevolution," April 3, 2009, http://www.youtube.com/watch?v=_bponvXxsks.

2. Ibid., at 02:22.

3. Ibid., at 07:38.

4. Phillip Dampier, "Lafayette Municipal Fiber Provider Filing Complaint Against Cable Co-Op over Access," *stopthecap.com*, June 14, 2010, http://stopthecap.com/2010/06/14/lafayette-municipal-fiber-provider-filing-complaint-against-cable-co-op-over-access/.

5. Rick Jervis, "Louisiana City Blazes High-Speed Web Trail," *USA Today*, February 5, 2012, http://www.usatoday.com/news/nation/story/2012-02-01/broadband-telecom-lafayette/52920278/1; John, "LUS Fiber Financials Covered in Local

Media (and More)," *Lafayette Pro-Fiber* (blog), August 10, 2011, http://blog. lafayetteprofiber.com/2011/08/lus-fiber-financials-covered-in-local.html.

6. Christopher Mitchell and David Morris, "The Battle Is Raging for Control of the Internet—And Big Corporations May Come Out on the Losing Side," *AlterNet*, June 21, 2010, http://www.alternet.org/media/147267/the_battle_is_raging_for_ control_of_the_internet_—_and_big_corporations_may_come_out_on_the_ losing_side/?page=entire.

7. "FTTH Economics," *Institute for Local Self-Reliance: Community Broadband Networks*. http://www.muninetworks.org/content/successes-and-failures.

8. FTTH Council, "Municipal Fiber to the Home Deployments: Next Generation Broadband as a Municipal Utility," *Institute for Local Self-Reliance: Community Broadband Networks*, April 9, 2008, http://www.muninetworks.org/reports/municipal-fiber-home-deployments-next-generation-broadband-municipal-utility.

9. Mitchell and Morris, "Battle Is Raging for Control of the Internet."

10. "Chattanooga Community Fiber Network Profiled on the Southern Way," *Institute for Local Self-Reliance: Community Broadband Networks*, 03:35, posted by "christopher," November 29, 2011, http://www.muninetworks.org/content/chattanooga-community-fiber-network-profiled-southern-way.

11. "Knoxville News Station Envious of Chattanooga Fiber Network," *Institute for Local Self-Reliance: Community Broadband Networks*, 01:30, posted by "christopher," January 4, 2012, http://www.muninetworks.org/content/knoxville-news-station-envious-chattanooga-fiber-network.

12. Christopher Mitchell, "Tennessee Bill to Encourage Economic Development Killed by Telco Lobbyists," *Institute for Local Self-Reliance: Community Broadband Networks*, May 3, 2011, http://www.muninetworks.org/content/tennessee-bill-encourage-economic-development-killed-telco-lobbyists.

13. Jonathan Feldman, "Global CIO: What North Carolina's Broadband Battlefield Means to You," *InformationWeek*, June 2, 2011, http://www.informationweek. com/news/global-cio/interviews/229900048.

14. Joey Mornin, "How Time Warner Cable Is Spending Millions to Fight Municipal Broadband in North Carolina," *Morninj* (blog), May 10, 2011, http://www.morninj. com/2011/05/how-time-warner-is-spending-millions-to-fight-municipal-broadband-in-north-carolina/.

15. "Community Broadband Preemption Map," *Institute for Local Self-Reliance: Community Broadband Networks*, http://www.muninetworks.org/content/community-broadband-preemption-map.

16. FTTH Council, "Award Recipients," http://www.ftthcouncil.org/en/content/ award-recipients.

17. Glenn Fleishman, "The Killer App of 1900," *Publicola*, December 11, 2009, http://publicola.com/2009/12/11/the-killer-app-of-1900-2/.

18. James Baller, "The Essential Role of Consumer-Owned Electric Utilities in Developing the National Information Infrastructure: A Historical Perspective," paper presented at the American Public Power Association Annual Telecommunications

Conference, Nashville, Tennessee, October 31–November 1, 1994, available at http://www.baller.com/library-art-history.html.

19. *Moody's Magazine*, October and November 1906, available at http://www.baller.com/pdfs/Moody´s.pdf.

20. *Comments of the American Public Power Association, Proposed Rule Registration of Municipal Advisors*, Securities and Exchange Commission, February 22, 2011, available at http://www.publicpower.org/files/PDFs/SECCommentsS74510Municipal Advisors02222011.pdf.

21. Craig Moffett, Nicholas Del Deo, Regina Possavino, and Patricia Pan, *U.S. Telecommunications, Cable & Satellite: The Dumb Pipe Paradox, Revisited* (Washington, D.C.: Bernstein Research, June 11, 2009), 19.

22. Bernstein Research, "U.S. Telecommunications and U.S. Cable & Satellite: Nature Versus Nurture," May 2012, 105.

23. FTTH Council, "The Growth of Fiber to the Home," available at http://www.ftthcouncil.org/en/content/the-growth-of-fiber-to-the-home; "Media Solutions Strategies," *Thrive*, accessed March 10, 2012, http://www.thrivemovement.com/media-solutions-strategies-1.

24. John B. Horrigan, *Broadband Adoption and Use in America*, OBI Working Paper Series no. 1 (Federal Communications Commission, February 2010), available at http://hraunfoss.fcc.gov/edocs_public/attachmatch/DOC-296442A1.pdf.

25. Federal Communications Commission, "National Broadband Plan," 9, 135.

26. Om Malik, "Finally, 100 Mbps Everywhere (If You Have Comcast)," *GigaOM*, April 14, 2011, http://gigaom.com/broadband/finally-100-mbps-everywhere-if-you-have-comcast/.

27. Mark McDonald, "Home Internet May Get Even Faster in South Korea," *New York Times*, February 21, 2011, available at http://www.nytimes.com/2011/02/22/technology/22iht-broadband22.html; Vaiva Lazauskaite, *Developments of Next Generation Networks (NGN): Country Case Studies* (Geneva: International Telecommunication Union, 2009), 36–7, 66–68; Karl Bode, "Australia's Labor Party Win, FTTH Build Greenlighted," *DSLReports.com*, September 8, 2010, http://www.dslreports.com/shownews/Australias-Labor-Party-Wins-FTTH-Build-Greenlighted-110255; Stacey Higginbotham, "BT Openreach Building a 300 Mbps Open Network," *GigaOM*, October 5, 2011, http://gigaom.com/broadband/bt-openreach-building-a-300-mbps-open-network/.

28. If you subtract capital expenditure (investments in expanding networks) from operating cash flow, you get "free cash flow." Comcast is spending more than 30 percent of its free cash flow on "return of capital to shareholders," that is, dividends and buybacks. The telephone companies, AT&T and Verizon, spend 40 percent of free cash flow on dividends and buybacks. Meanwhile, capital expenditures for all of these companies are steadily decreasing as a yearly percentage of revenue. See Bernstein Research, "U.S. Telecommunications and U.S. Cable & Satellite: Nature Versus Nurture," May 2012.

29. *Comments of the Fiber-to-the-Home Council, In the Matters of International Comparison and Survey Requirements in the Broadband Data Improvement Act, et al.*, Federal Communications Commission, GN Docket No. 09–47 et al., November 6, 2009, 3.

30. Sharon K. Black, *Telecommunications Law in the Internet Age* (Waltham, Mass.: Morgan Kaufman, 2002), 25.

31. Ron Chernow, *Titan: The Life of John D. Rockefeller Sr.* (New York: Vintage, 2004), 553.

32. Marguerite Reardon, "FCC Unveils National Broadband Plan," *CNET News*, March 15, 2010, http://news.cnet.com/8301-30686_3-20000453-266.html; Jil Nishi, Deputy Director, U.S. Libraries, Bill and Melinda Gates Foundation, to Marlene H. Dortch, Secretary to the Federal Communications Commission, October 5, 2009, http://apps.fcc.gov/ecfs/document/view?id=7020040706; *FTTH Deployment Assessment* (Boston: CSMG, October 13, 2009), available at http://s.ftthcouncil.org/files/ftth_deployment_assessment_-_corning_10_12_09_final.pdf.

33. Committee for a Responsible Federal Budget, "Increases and Decreases to Discretionary Spending in the President's Budget," *The Bottom Line* (blog), February 15, 2011, http://crfb.org/blogs/increases-and-decreases-discretionary-spending-presidents-budget; *The Budget for the Fiscal Year of 2012: Department of Defense* (Washington, D.C.: Office of Management and Budget), 64, accessed March 10, 2012, available at http://m.whitehouse.gov/sites/default/files/omb/budget/fy2012/assets/defense.pdf; "Simplified FTTH Installation Brings Increased Job Possibilities at Reduced Costs," paper presented at the FTTH Conference and Expo, Orlando, Florida, September 26–30, 2011, 3, available at http://www.m2fx.com/wordpress_m2fx/wp-content/uploads/2011/11/m2fx_FTTH_Council_Whitepaper_2011.pdf.

34. Sen. Al Franken, interview with the author, September 30, 2010.

ACKNOWLEDGMENTS

Thanks to several generations of students from several different schools, including Keith Klovers, Olivia Greer, Michael Steffen, Anjali Dalal, Eric Null, Shane Wagman, Hanna Siegel, and Daniel Goldmintz. Special thanks to Clay Risen, Representative Ed Markey, Senator Al Franken, Colin Crowell, and the dozens of people from across the media and telecommunications landscape in America who talked to me but did not want their names used in this book.

INDEX

Aaron, Dan, 70, 81
Abbott, Ernest Hamlin, 29
ABC, 84, 88, 120, 129, 132, 134, 150
Abdoulah, Colleen, 6, 86–87, 107, 145
Abernathy, Kathleen, 209
Adelphia, 76, 77
Advertising revenues, 132, 136, 150, 202
Aggregators in online video, 118–22
Al Jazeera, 217, 227
Amalgamated Copper, 26
Amazon, 116, 264
American Cable Systems (early name of Comcast), 69–71
America Online. *See* AOL
Ameritech, 50, 210, 239
Anderson, Henry, 257
Angelakis, Michael, 127, 157, 172, 225
Antitrust: Microsoft litigation, 108; railroad industry, 24–25. *See also* AOL–Time Warner; Justice Department; Sherman Antitrust Act; Vertical mergers and integration; *specific headings starting with "Merger"*
AOL: as dial-up service, 93–94; early success of, 89–93; separated from Time Warner, 100; vulnerability of, 95, 106

AOL–Time Warner: benefits of, 95; Comcast and NBCU merger compared to, 105–6, 226; in failed vertical merger, 89, 96–103; hailed as symbol of new era, 95; losses recorded by, 98; mismatch of corporate styles, 98–100, 226; negative predictions about merger, 96–97; and online video, 102–3; pricing to allow open access, 101
Apple, 156, 158, 159, 163–65, 168, 224. *See also* iPads
Arango, Tim, 115–16
Arbitration, 219
AT&T: acquiring and divesting Western Union, 32–33; and Apple devices, 163–64; attempt to get into local phone markets, 50; and auctions of low-frequency spectrum, 240; Broadband Internet Access Policy Statement, agreement to, 209; cable and Internet divisions bought by Comcast, 76, 82; in cellphone market, 16; cooperation with Comcast not to compete head to head, 9–10, 44, 160–61, 168; Digital One flat rate, 240; divestiture (1984), 16, 47–48, 55,